contents

introduction

There has always been a fascination in Western countries with the mysteries of the East—and in recent decades that interest has extended to the spiritual realm. As people begin to define themselves as "spiritual" rather than "religious"—dropping out of organized religions in search of a more open and individual approach to the sacred—the Eastern wisdom traditions have held a special appeal.

Unlike the religions that were born in the Middle East—Judaism, Christianity, and Islam—most Eastern approaches to spirituality place little or no emphasis on a supreme being as a source of divine guidance and dispenser of blessings. Rather, the emphasis is to develop one's own inner sense of the sacred—or, in the words of Buddha, to "be a light unto yourself."

This volume explores four major streams of Eastern wisdom as seen through the understanding of a contemporary mystic, Osho. In the course of his own search, Osho has deeply explored both the differences and the common concerns of East and West, psychology and philosophy, the religions of prayer, and the paths of meditation. The depth and breadth of that understanding is apparent in these pages. Originally published separately as books on Buddha, Zen, Tantra, and Tao, this combined volume offers the reader a window into a broad spectrum of new possibilities, from the relaxed acceptance of Tao and Tantra to the disciplined awareness of Buddha and Zen. Each has something to offer the Western reader with an open mind and a taste for the challenge of breaking old patterns and exploring new possibilities.

Osho says: The Western mind can succeed as far as science is concerned, but it cannot succeed in religious consciousness. Whenever a religious mind is born, even in the West, it is Eastern. In Eckhart, in Boehme, the very quality of the mind is Eastern. And whenever a scientific mind is born in the East, it is bound to be Western.

East and West are not geographical. West means the Aristotelian, and East means the non-Aristotelian. West means equilibrium, and East means no equilibrium. West means the rational and East means the irrational.

Tertullian was one of the most Eastern minds in the West. He said, "I believe in God because it is impossible to believe. I believe in God because it is absurd." This is the basic Eastern attitude: because it is absurd. No one can say this in the West. In the West they say that you should believe something only when it is rational; otherwise it is just a superstition.

Eckhart, too, is an Eastern mind. He says, "If you believe in the possible, it is of no consequence. If you believe in the argument, it is not religious. This approach belongs to science. Only if you believe in the absurd does something come to you that is beyond the mind." This concept is not Western. It belongs to the East.

Confucius, on the other hand, is a Western mind. People in the West can understand Confucius, but they find it difficult understand Lao Tzu. Lao Tzu says, "You are a fool if you are only rational. To be rational, reasonable, is not enough. The irrational must have its own corner to exist. Only if a person is both rational and irrational is he reasonable."

A totally rational person can never be reasonable. Reason has its own dark corner of irrationality. A child is born in a dark womb. A flower is born in the dark, in the underground roots. The dark must not be denied; it is the base. It is the most significant, the most life-giving thing.

The Western mind has something to contribute to the world—it is science, not spirituality. The Eastern mind can contribute spirituality, but not technology or science. Science and spirituality are complementary. If we can realize both their differences and their complementariness, then a better world culture can be born out of it.

BUDDHA
his life and teachings

Gautam Buddha's given name was Siddhartha. Gautama is his family name so his full name was Gautama Siddhartha. Buddha is not his name, it is his awakening. Buddha simply means "one who is awakened." Gautam Buddha is the most famous awakened person but that does not mean that he is the only awakened person. There have been many buddhas before him and there have been many buddhas after him—and as long as every human being can become a buddha, new buddhas will go on springing up in the future. Everyone has the potentiality... it is only a matter of waiting for the right time. Some day, tortured by the outside reality, in despair of having seen everything and found nothing, you are bound to turn inward.

The very word *buddha* means "awakened intelligence." The word *buddhi*, "intellect," also comes from the same root. The root word *budh* has many dimensions to it. There is no single English word that can translate it. It has many implications; it is fluid and poetic. In no other language does any word like budh exist, with so many meanings. There are at least five meanings to the word *budh*.

The first is to awake, to wake oneself up, to awaken others, to be awake. As such, it is opposed to being asleep, in the slumber of delusion from which the enlightened awakens as from a dream. That is the first meaning of intelligence, budh: to create an awakening in you.

Ordinarily people are asleep. Even while you think you are awake, you are not. Walking on the road, you are fully awake—in your mind. But from the perspective of a buddha, you are fast asleep, because a thousand and one dreams and thoughts are clamoring inside you.

Your inner light is clouded in a kind of sleep. Yes, your eyes are open, obviously, but people can walk in a dream, in sleep, with open eyes. Buddha says you are also walking in sleep with open eyes.

But your inner eye is not open. You don't know yet who you are. You have not looked into your own reality. You are not awake. A mind full of thoughts is not awake, cannot be awake.

Only a mind that has dropped thoughts and thinking—which has dispersed the clouds so the sun is burning bright in a sky utterly empty of clouds—is the mind that is intelligent, that is awake.

Intelligence is the capacity to be in the present. The more you are in the past or in the future, the less intelligent you are. Intelligence is the capacity to be here now, to be in this moment and nowhere else. Then you are awake.

For example, you are sitting in a house and the house suddenly catches fire; your life is in danger. Then for a moment you will be awake. In that moment you will not think many thoughts. In that moment you forget your past. In that moment you will not be clamored at by your psychological memories: that you had loved a woman thirty years before, and boy, it was fantastic! Or that the other day you had been to the Chinese restaurant, and still the taste lingers with the aroma of the freshly cooked food. You will not be in those thoughts. No, when your house is on fire you cannot afford this kind of thinking. Suddenly you will rush to this moment: the house is on fire and your life is at stake. You will not dream about the future or about what you are going to do tomorrow. Tomorrow is no longer relevant, yesterday is no longer relevant—even today is no longer relevant! Only this moment, this split second.

That is the first meaning of budh, intelligence. And then there are great insights. A man who wants to be awake, wants to be a buddha, has to live each moment in such intensity as you live only rarely—rarely, in some danger. The first meaning is the opposite of sleep. Naturally, you can see reality only when you are not asleep. You can face it, you can look into the eyes of truth—or call it "God"— only when you are awake. Do you understand the point of intensity, the point of being on fire? Utterly awake, there is insight. That insight brings freedom; that insight brings truth.

The second meaning of budh is to recognize, to become aware of, acquainted with, to notice, give heed to. A buddha is one who has recognized the false as the false, and has opened his eyes to the true as the true. To see the false as false is the beginning of understanding what truth is. Only when you see the false as false can you see what truth is. You cannot go on living in illusions; you cannot go on living in your beliefs; you cannot go on living in your prejudices if you want to know truth. The false has to be recognized as false. That is the second meaning of budh—recognition of the false as false, of the untrue as untrue.

For example, you have believed in God; you were born a Christian or a Hindu or a Mohammedan. You have been taught that God exists, you have been made afraid of God—if you don't believe in him you will suffer, you will be punished. God is ferocious; he will never forgive you. The Jewish God says, "I am a jealous God. Worship only me and nobody else!" The Mohammedan God says the same thing: "There is only one God, and no other God; and there is only one prophet of God, Mohammed, and no other prophet."

This conditioning can go so deep in you that it can linger even if you start disbelieving in God.

You have been brought up to believe in God, and you have believed. This is a belief. Whether God actually exists or not has nothing to do with your belief. Truth has nothing to do with your belief! Whether you believe or not makes no difference to truth. But if you believe in God you will go on seeing—at least thinking that you see—God. If you don't believe in God, that disbelief in God will prevent you from knowing. All beliefs prevent you because they become prejudices around you, they become "thought-coverings"—what Buddha calls *avarnas*.

The man of intelligence does not believe in anything and does not *dis*believe in anything. The man of intelligence is open to recognizing whatsoever is the case. If God is there he will recognize—but not according to his belief. He has no belief.

Only in a nonbelieving intelligence can truth appear. When you already believe, you don't allow truth any space to come to you. Your prejudice is already enthroned. You cannot see something that goes against your belief; you will become afraid, you will become shaky, you will start trembling. You have put so much into your belief— so much life, so much time, so many prayers, five prayers every day. For fifty years a man has been devoted to his belief—now, suddenly, how can he recognize the fact that there is no God? A man has put his whole life into communism, believing that there is no God; how can he come to see if God is there? He will go on avoiding.

I'm not saying anything about whether God exists or is not. What I am saying is something concerned with you, not with God. A clear mind is needed, an intelligence is needed that does not cling to any belief. Then you are like a mirror: you reflect that which is; you don't distort it.

That is the second meaning of *budh*. An intelligent person is neither a communist nor a Catholic. An intelligent person does not believe, does not disbelieve. That is not his way. He looks into life and whatsoever is there he is ready to see it. He has no barriers to his vision; his vision is transparent. Only those few people attain to truth.

The third meaning of the root *budh*, intelligence, is to know, to understand. Buddha knows that which is; he understands that which is, and in that very understanding he is free from all bondage. Budh means to know in the sense of to *understand*, not in the sense of knowledgeability. Buddha is not knowledgeable.

An intelligent person does not care much about information and knowledge. An intelligent person cares much more for the capacity to know. His authentic interest is in knowing, not in knowledge.

Knowing gives you understanding; knowledge only gives you a feeling of understanding without giving you *real* understanding. Knowledge is a false coin; it is deceptive. It only gives you the feeling that you know, yet you don't know at all. You can accumulate knowledge as much as you want, you can go on hoarding, you can become extremely knowledgeable. You can write books, you can have degrees, you can have PhDs and LittDs, and still you remain the same ignorant, stupid person you have always been. Those degrees don't change you; they *can't* change you. In fact, your stupidity becomes stronger; it has degrees now! It can prove itself through certificates. It cannot prove itself through life, but it can prove itself through the certificates. It cannot prove anything in any other way, but it will carry degrees, certificates, recognitions from society. People think you know, and you also think you know.

Have you not seen this? The people who are thought to be very knowledgeable are as ignorant as anybody, sometimes more ignorant. It is rare to find intelligent people in the academic world, very rare. I have been in the academic world and I say it through my own experience. I have seen intelligent farmers, but I have not seen intelligent professors. I have seen intelligent woodcutters, but I have not seen intelligent professors. Why? What has gone wrong with these people?

One thing has gone wrong: they can depend on knowledge. They need not become knowers, they can depend on knowledge. They have found a secondhand way. The firsthand needs courage. The firsthand, knowing, only a few people can afford—the adventurers, people who go beyond the ordinary path where crowds move, people who take small footpaths into the jungle of the unknowable. The danger is that they may get lost. The risk is high. When you can get secondhand knowledge, why bother? You can just sit in your chair. You can go to the library or to the university, you can collect information. You can make a big pile of information and sit on top of it.

Through knowledge your memory becomes bigger and bigger, but your intelligence does not become bigger. Sometimes it happens when you don't know much, when you are not very knowledgeable, that you will have to be intelligent.

I have heard...

A woman bought a tin of fruit but she could not open the tin. She did not know how to open it, so she rushed to her study to look in a cookbook. By the time she looked in the book and found the page and reference, and came rushing back ready to open the tin, the servant had already opened it.

She asked, "But how did you do it?"

The servant said, "Madam, when you can't read, you have to use your mind."

Yes, that's how it happens! That's why illiterate farmers, gardeners, woodcutters, are more intelligent, have a kind of freshness around them. They can't read, so they have to use their minds. One has to live and one has to use one's mind.

The third meaning of budh is to know, in the sense of understanding. The Buddha has seen that which is. He understands that which is, and in that very understanding he is free from all bondage.

What does it mean? If you want to get rid of fear you will have to understand fear. But if you want to avoid the fact that fear is there, that the fear of death is there…if you are afraid inside, you will have to create something strong around you like a hard shell, so nobody comes to know that you are afraid. And that is not the only point—you also will not know that you are afraid because of that hard shell. It will protect you from others and it will protect you from your own understanding.

An intelligent person does not escape from any fact. If it is fear he will go into it, because the way out is through. If he feels fear and trembling arising in him, he will leave everything else aside: first this fear has to be gone through. He will go into it; he will try to understand. He will not try to figure out how not to be afraid; he will not ask that question. He will simply ask one question: "What is this fear? It is there, it is part

of me, it is my reality. I have to go into it, I have to understand it. If I don't understand it then a part of me will always remain unknown to me. And how am I going to know who I am if I go on avoiding parts of myself? I will not understand fear, I will not understand death, I will not understand anger. I will not understand my hatred, I will not understand my jealousy, I will not understand this and that...."

Then how are you going to know yourself? All these things are you! This is your being. You have to go into everything that is there, every nook and corner. You have to explore fear. Even if you are trembling it is nothing to be worried about: tremble, but go in. It is far better to tremble than to escape, because once you escape, that part will remain unknown to you. And you will become more and more afraid to look at it, because that fear will go on accumulating. It will become bigger and bigger if you don't go into it right now, this moment. Tomorrow it will have lived twenty-four hours more. Beware!—it will have grown more roots in you, it will have bigger foliage, it will have become stronger, and then it will be more difficult to tackle. It is better to go right now. It is already late.

Go into it and see it.... And seeing means without prejudice. Seeing means that you don't condemn fear as bad from the very beginning. Who knows?—it is not bad—who knows that it is? The explorer has to remain open to all the possibilities; he cannot afford a closed mind. A closed mind and exploration don't go together. He will go into it. If it brings suffering and pain, he will suffer the pain but he will go into it.

Trembling, hesitant, but he will go into it: "It is my territory, I have to know what it is. Maybe it is carrying some treasure for me? Maybe the fear is only there to protect the treasure."

That's my experience; that's my understanding: If you go deep into your fear you will find love. That's why it happens that when you are in love, fear disappears. And when you are afraid, you cannot be in love. What does this mean? A simple arithmetic—fear and love don't exist together. That means it must be the same energy that becomes fear; then there is nothing left to become love. It becomes love; then there is nothing left to become fear.

Go into each negative thing and you will find the positive. And knowing the negative and the positive, the third, the ultimate happens—the transcendental. That is the meaning of understanding, *budh*, intelligence.

The fourth meaning is to be enlightened and to enlighten. The Buddha is the light; he has become the light. And since he's the light and he has become the light, he shows the light to others, too—naturally, obviously. He is illumination. His darkness has disappeared; his inner flame is burning bright. Smokeless is his flame. This meaning is opposed to darkness and the corresponding blindness and ignorance. This is the fourth meaning: to become light, to become enlightened.

Ordinarily you are a darkness, a continent of darkness, a dark continent, unexplored. People are a little strange: they go on exploring the Himalayas, they go on exploring the Pacific, they go on reaching for the moon and Mars; there is just one thing they never try—exploring the inner being. Humankind has landed on the moon, but people have not landed yet in their own beings. This is strange. Maybe landing on the moon is just an escape, going to Everest is just an escape. Maybe he does not want to go inside because he's very much afraid. He substitutes with some other explorations to feel good; otherwise, he will have to feel guilty. You start climbing a mountain and you feel good— but the greatest mountain is within you and is yet unclimbed! You start diving deep into the Pacific, but the greatest Pacific is within you and uncharted, unmapped. And you start going to the moon—what foolishness! You are wasting your energy in going to the moon, when the real moon is within you—because the real light is within you.

The intelligent person will go inward first. Before going anywhere else, you will go into your own being. That is the first thing, and it should have the first preference. Only when you have known yourself can you go anywhere else. Then wherever you go you will carry a blissfulness around you, a peace, a silence, a celebration.

The fourth meaning is to be enlightened. Intelligence is the spark. Helped, cooperated with, it can become the fire and the light and the warmth. It can become light, it can become life, it can become love—those are all included in the word *enlightenment*. An enlightened person has no dark corners in his being. All is like the morning—the sun is on the horizon, the darkness and the dismalness of the night have disappeared, and the shadows of the night have disappeared. The earth is again awake. To be a buddha is to attain to a morning, a dawn within you. That is the function of intelligence, the ultimate function.

The fifth meaning of budh is to fathom. A depth is there in you, a bottomless depth, which has to be fathomed. The fifth meaning can also be to penetrate, to drop all that obstructs and penetrate to the core of your being.

People try to penetrate many things in life. Your urge, your desire for sex is nothing but a kind of penetration. But that is a penetration into the other. The same penetration has to happen into your own being—you have to penetrate yourself. If you penetrate somebody else it can give you a momentary glimpse, but if you penetrate yourself you can attain to the universal, cosmic orgasm that remains and remains and remains.

A man meets an outer woman, and a woman meets an outer man: this is a very superficial meeting—yet meaningful, yet it brings moments of joy. But when the inner woman meets the inner man.... And you are carrying both inside you: a part of you is feminine, a part of you is masculine. Whether you are man or woman does not matter; everybody is bisexual. The fifth meaning of the root budh is penetration. When your inner man penetrates your inner woman there is a meeting; you become whole, you become one. All desires for the outer disappear. In that desirelessness is freedom, nirvana.

The path of Buddha is the path of budh. Remember that "Buddha" is not the name of Gautama the Buddha; Buddha is the state that he has attained. His name was Gautama Siddhartha. Then one day he became Buddha, one day his *bodhi*, his intelligence, bloomed. "Buddha" means exactly what "Christ" means. Jesus' name is not Christ; that is the ultimate flowering that happened to him. So it is with Buddha. There have been many buddhas other than Gautama Siddhartha.

Everybody has the capacity for budh. But budh, that capacity to see, is just like a seed in you—if it sprouts, becomes a big tree, blooms, starts dancing in the sky, starts whispering to the stars, you are a buddha.

The path of Buddha is the path of intelligence. It is not an emotional path, no, not at all. Not that emotional people cannot reach; there are other paths for them—the path of devotion, *Bhakti Yoga*. Buddha's path is pure *Gyan Yoga*, the path of knowing. Buddha's path is the path of meditation, not of love.

The intellect has to be used, not discarded; it has to be transcended, not discarded. It can be transcended only when you have reached the uppermost rung of the ladder. You have to go on growing in intelligence. Then a moment will come when intelligence has done all that it can do. In that moment, say goodbye to intelligence. It has helped you a long way, it has brought you far enough, it has been a good vehicle. It has been a boat you crossed with; you have reached the other shore, then you leave the boat. You don't carry the boat on your head; that would be foolish.

Buddha's path goes through intelligence and goes beyond it. A moment comes when intelligence has given you all that it can give, then it is no longer needed. Then finally you drop it, too; its work is finished. The disease is gone, now the medicine has to go, too. When you are free of the disease and the medicine, too, only then are you free. Sometimes it happens that the disease is gone, but you have become addicted to the medicine. This is not freedom. A thorn is in your foot and is hurting. You take another thorn so that the thorn in your foot can be taken out with the help of the other. When you have taken the thorn out, you throw away both; you don't save the one that has been helpful. It is now meaningless.

The work of intelligence is to help you to become aware of your being. Once that work has happened and your being is there, there is no need for this instrument. You can say goodbye, you can say thank you. Buddha's path is the path of intelligence, pure intelligence, although it goes beyond it.

the birth of an

emperor

These beautiful metaphors have to be understood with great sympathy, with great intuitiveness, with love, poetry. Not with logic; otherwise you will destroy them.

buddha's arrival

Every human being is born to be a Buddha; every person has the seed of buddhahood within. If you look at the masses, it doesn't seem to be true. If it were true, there would be many buddhas— but one rarely hears about a buddha. We only know that somewhere, twenty-five centuries ago, a certain Siddhartha Gautama became Buddha. Who knows whether it is true or not? It may be a myth, a beautiful story, a consolation, an opiate for the masses to keep them hoping that one day they will also become buddhas. Who knows whether Buddha is an historic reality?

SO MANY STORIES have been woven around Buddha that he looks more like a mythological figure than a reality. When he becomes enlightened, gods come from heaven, play beautiful music, and dance around him. Now, how can this be historical? Flowers shower on him from the sky—flowers of gold and silver, flowers of diamonds and emeralds. Who can belie've that this is historical?

This is not history, true—I agree. This is poetry. But it symbolizes something historical, because something so unique has happened in Buddha that there is no other way to describe it than to bring poetry in. Real flowers have not showered on Buddha, but whenever somebody becomes enlightened the whole existence rejoices—because we are not separate from it. When you have a headache your whole body suffers, and when the headache goes away, your whole body feels good, feels a sense of well being. We are not separate from existence. Until you are a buddha you are a headache—a headache to yourself, a headache

to others, a headache to existence. You are a thorn in the flesh of existence. When the headache disappears, when the thorn becomes a flower, when one person becomes a buddha, a great pain that he was creating for himself and others disappears. Certainly—I vouch for it, I am a witness to it—certainly the whole of existence rejoices, dances, sings. But how to describe it? It is nothing visible; photographs cannot be taken of it. Hence the poetry; hence these metaphors, symbols, similes.

It is said that when Buddha was born his mother immediately died. It may not be a historical fact or it may be. But my feeling is that it is not a historical fact, because it is said that whenever a buddha is born, the mother immediately dies, and that is not true. There have been many buddhas—Jesus' mother did not die, Mahavira's mother did not die, Krishna's mother did not die. Maybe Siddhartha Gautama's mother died, but it cannot be said that whenever a buddha is born the mother dies, not historically.

But I know it has some significance of its own that is not historical. By the "mother" is not really meant the mother; by the "mother" is meant your past. You are reborn when you become a buddha; your past functions as a womb, as the mother. The moment a buddha is born, the moment you become enlightened, your past dies. That death is necessary. This is absolutely true. It happened with Mahavira, with Krishna, with Jesus; it has always happened. To communicate it, it is said that whenever a buddha is born the mother dies. You will have to be sympathetic to understand these things.

I can understand that it is difficult, looking at the greater part of humanity, to see that there is any possibility of every human being becoming a Christ or a Buddha. Looking at a seed, can you believe that one day it can become a lotus? Just looking at the seed, dissecting the seed, can you conclude that this seed is going to become a lotus? There seems to be no relationship at all. The seed looks like nothing, and when you dissect it you find nothing in it, only emptiness. Still, each seed carries a lotus within it—and each human being carries the buddha within.

When Buddha was born, it is said that a great sage, one hundred and twenty years old, immediately rushed from the Himalayas. His disciples asked, "Where are you going?" He ran! They had rarely even seen him walk, because he was so old. And he didn't answer them because there was no time; he just said, "No time to answer."

ENLIGHTENED INNOCENCE

The story is that Gautam Buddha was born while his mother was standing under a saal tree. And not only that, he was born standing. The first thing he did was to take seven steps in front of his mother and declare to the universe, "I am the most enlightened person ever."

In fact, every newborn child, if he could, would say the same thing, "I am enlightened." If every newborn child could walk, he would take seven steps and declare to the whole world, "I am the most enlightened person, unique."

Perhaps the story is a symbolic way of recognizing each child's innocence as his enlightenment, as his ultimate experience.

The disciples followed the old sage down into the plains. Buddha was born close to the Himalayas, on the border of Nepal and India. The old man immediately went to the king's palace. The king could not believe his eyes, because this man was not known to go anywhere. For at least fifty years he had lived in a single cave. Buddha's father could not believe it. He touched the old man's feet and said, "Why have you come? What has happened?"

The old man said, "I don't have much time, because my death is approaching. That's why I had to run. Where is your child? I have come to see him."

Buddha was just one day old. The moment he was born this old man had started running; it took twenty-four hours for him to reach the plains. The king could not believe it, because this old man was famous, a Master of Masters—why should he be interested in his child?

The child was brought immediately, and the old man, one hundred and twenty years old, touched Buddha's feet and started crying. The father was puzzled, the mother was shocked. "Why is he crying? Is there something wrong?" They asked him, "Why are you crying? Isn't the child going to survive? Is there going to be some calamity? Say it clearly—why are you crying?"

He said, "No, I am not crying because of any calamity. I am crying for joy because I have seen, and I am crying also because I will not live to see the full flowering of this man. I have seen him only in the bud, but even that is too much, to see a buddha in the bud. I am crying for joy, because a god is born! I am also crying in sadness because I will not be able to see him grow; my days are numbered. Soon I will be leaving my body; I will not be able to see what flowering he brings to the world, what fragrance he brings to the world. Millions and millions of people will become enlightened because of him. He has brought a light; he has brought a revolution into the world…. But don't be worried; be happy, rejoice!"

These are parables. These events may not have happened historically, but history is not our concern at all. Our concern is something more important, more essential, more eternal. History is a procession of events in time. Even if it did not happen historically, it doesn't matter; the parable is beautiful: a one-hundred-twenty-year-old saint bowing down to one-day-old Buddha. Age does not matter; awareness has no age. Ordinary formalities have to be dropped. The old man touching the feet of a child, a one-day-old child, crying for joy—those who understand will always cry for joy whenever they see something of immense value happening in the world.

But few will be able to see—even the father had not seen, the mother had not seen. Only those who have eyes will be able to see. The three wise men from the East had to travel thousands of miles to see, but the people of Jesus' own country could not see. Jesus' parents had to escape from Jerusalem; they had to escape to Egypt. And Jesus could not appear back in Jerusalem. After thirty years we hear of him again, and then he could survive only three years. The people of his own country killed him. Blind people killed the man who had eyes; mad people killed one of the sanest men.

Even the parents... Jesus' parents were not aware of what had happened. Three men from the East were needed to recognize him. Only those who have learned something of meditation will be able to recognize a buddha. When you come across a buddha it is not easy to recognize him. It is easy to be antagonized, it is easy to be angered; it is easy to be offended by his presence because his presence makes you feel so small that it offends you. His presence makes you feel so empty that it humiliates you—not that he means any humiliation, but because of your ego you start

feeling humiliated. Your mind wants to take revenge. That's why Socrates was poisoned, Mansoor was killed, Jesus was crucified—and it has always been so. Whenever there has been a buddha, the society has been very inimical toward him.

Even in India, even in the East, the same thing happened. Buddha lived in India, preached there, transformed thousands of people into a world of light, but Buddhism

> *When you come across a buddha it is not easy to recognize him*

disappeared from India. It was destroyed. After Buddha died, within five hundred years the religion was uprooted from there. The Brahmins did not like the idea; the pundits, the scholars did not like the idea—it was dangerous to their profession. If Buddha is right, then all the priests are wrong.

But, remember, these beautiful metaphors have to be understood with great sympathy, with great intuitiveness, with love, poetry. Not with logic; otherwise, you will destroy them; you will kill them. Sometimes beautiful metaphors have been used…and the religions, the so-called religions, the followers, have killed these metaphors themselves.

It is said that whenever Mohammed moved in the desert, a cloud would move just over his head to shelter him. Now, to be in the Arabian deserts is to be in fire! It is not a historical fact. No cloud will do this. Even human beings don't understand Mohammed—how will the poor cloud understand Mohammed? People were after Mohammed; his whole life he was escaping from one town to another town. His whole life he was always in danger, his survival was always in question. When men were not able to understand him, how could a poor cloud understand him? So it can't be historical.

But still I love it—the metaphor is beautiful. The metaphor simply says that clouds are far more intelligent than humans; it says that even clouds understood the beauty of the man and protected him, even against the laws of nature. Wherever Mohammed was going they would go; even if the wind was not going there, the cloud would go on sheltering him. It shows that the ignorance of humanity is so great that even clouds are far more intelligent.

It is said that whenever Buddha came and wherever he moved, trees would bloom out of season, trees that had been long dead would again start sprouting green leaves. Beautiful poetry, significant poetry, lovely poetry to be meditated upon—I don't think it is historical, but it is still significant. It may not be a fact, but it is a truth.

Facts belong to ordinary events. The fact is that Buddha's own cousin, Devadatta, tried to kill him in many ways. Once when Buddha was meditating, Devadatta threw a rock at him from the top of a hill; a great rock started rolling downward. This is a fact—Devadatta tried to kill Buddha because he could not believe it: "How can Buddha become enlightened? We have played together; we have always been together in our childhood; we were educated together. If I am not enlightened, how is he enlightened?"

Devadatta declared himself enlightened, although he was not. And he would have been accepted as enlightened if Buddha had not been there. But how can you declare your unenlightened being to be enlightened in the presence of a Buddha? It was impossible.

The only problem was how to destroy Buddha. He released a rock. The story goes that the rock came close to Buddha and then changed its course. That cannot be a fact, but it is a truth. Truth is a much higher phenomenon.

Devadatta released a mad elephant to kill Buddha. The mad elephant came ferociously, but when he reached Buddha, he looked at him and he bowed down and touched his feet. That Devadatta released a mad elephant is a fact; that it bowed to Buddha is not a fact. That is poetry, sheer poetry—but of immense truth.

Remember, scriptures talk about truth; they are not history books. History books talk about facts. That's why in history books you will find Alexander the Great, Ivan the Terrible, Adolf Hitler, and all kinds of neurotics. But Buddha, Mahavira, Jesus...they are not part of the history books. For them we need a totally different approach. It is good they are not part of history books, for they are not part of history; they come from the beyond; they belong to the beyond. They are only for those who are ready to rise and soar to the beyond.

The day Buddha was born—he was the son of a great king, the only son, and he was born when the king was getting old, very old—there was great rejoicing in the kingdom. The people had waited long. The king was much loved by the people; he had served them, he had been kind and compassionate, he had been loving and sharing. He had made his kingdom one of the richest, loveliest kingdoms of those days.

People were praying that their king should have a son because there was nobody to inherit. Then Buddha was born in the king's very old age—unexpected was his birth. There was great celebration, great rejoicing! All the astrologers of the kingdom gathered to make predictions about Buddha. He was given the name Siddhartha, because it means fulfillment. The king was fulfilled, his desire was fulfilled, his deepest longing was fulfilled. He had wanted a son his whole life; hence the name Siddhartha. It simply means "fulfillment of the deepest desire."

This son made the king's life meaningful, significant. The great astrologers made predictions—and they were all in agreement except for one young astrologer. His name was Kodanna. The king had asked, "What is going to happen in the life of my son?" And all the astrologers raised two fingers, except Kodanna, who raised only one finger.

The king said, "Please don't talk in symbols—I am a simple man, I don't know anything about astrology. Tell me, what do you mean by two fingers?"

And they all said, "Either he is going to become a *chakravartin*—a world ruler—or he will renounce the world and will become a buddha, an enlightened person. These two alternatives are there; hence, we raise two fingers."

The king was worried about the second alternative, that his son would renounce the world, so again the problem would arise. "Who will inherit my kingdom if he renounces the world?" He asked Kodanna, "Why do you raise only one finger?"

Kodanna said, "I am absolutely certain that he will renounce the world—he will become a buddha, an enlightened one, an awakened one."

The king was not happy with Kodanna. Truth is very difficult to accept. He ignored Kodanna and did not reward him at all—truth is not rewarded in this world. On the contrary, truth is punished in a thousand and one ways. In fact, Kodanna's prestige fell after that day. Because the king did not reward him, the rumor spread that he was a fool. When all the other astrologers were in agreement, he was the only one who was not.

The king asked the other astrologers, "What do you suggest? What should I do so that he does not renounce the world? I would not want him to be a beggar, I would not like to see him a monk, a *sannyasin*. I would like him to become a *chakravartin*—a ruler of all six continents." This is the ambition of all parents. Who would like their son or daughter to renounce the world and to move into the mountains, to go into their own inner world to seek and search for the self? Our desires are for external things. The king was an ordinary man, just like everybody else, with the same desires and the same ambitions.

The astrologers said, "It can be arranged. Give him as much pleasure as possible, keep him in as much comfort and luxury as is humanly possible. Don't allow him to know about illness, old age, and particularly death. Don't let him come to know about death and he will never renounce."

They were right in a way, because death is the central question. Once it arises in your heart, your lifestyle is bound to change. You cannot go on living in the old foolish way. If this life is going to end in death, then this life cannot be the real life; this life must be an illusion. Truth has to be eternal if it is true—only lies are momentary. If life is momentary, then it must be an illusion, a lie, a misconception, a misunderstanding; then our conception of life must be rooted somewhere in ignorance. We must be living it in such a way that it comes to an end. We can live in a different way so that we can become part of the eternal flow of existence.... Only death can give you that radical shift. So the astrologers said, "Please don't let him know anything about death."

The king made all the arrangements. He made three palaces for Siddhartha for different seasons, in different places, so that he would ever come to know the discomforts of the seasons. When it was hot he had a palace in the hills where it was always cool. When it was cold he had another palace by the side of a river where it was always warm. The king made all the arrangements so Siddhartha never felt any discomfort.

No old man or woman was allowed to enter the palaces where he lived—only young people. He gathered all the beautiful young women of the kingdom around so that Siddhartha would remain allured, fascinated, so he would remain in dreams, desires. A sweet dream world was created for him. The gardeners were told that dead leaves had to be removed in the night; fading, withering flowers had to be removed in the night—because who knows? Seeing a dead leaf, the boy might start asking about what happened to this leaf, and the question of death could arise. Seeing a withering rose, petals falling, he might ask, "What has happened to this rose?" and he might start brooding, meditating, about death.

He was kept absolutely unaware of death for twenty-nine years. But how long can you avoid it? Death is such an important phenomenon. How long can you deceive a person? Sooner or later he had to enter into the world. Now the king was getting older and the son had to know the ways of the world. Gradually he was allowed out, but whenever he would pass through any street of the capital, the old men and women would be removed. Beggars would be removed. No *sannyasin* was allowed to appear while he was passing by, because seeing a *sannyasin* he might ask, "What type of man is this? Why is he in ochre robes? What has happened to him? Why does he look different, detached, distant? His eyes are different, his flavor is different, his

presence has a different quality to it. What has happened to this man?" And then the question of renunciation would arise, and fundamentally the question of death....

But one day, it had to happen. It couldn't be avoided. One day Siddhartha had to become aware, and he became aware. The prince, of course, was supposed to inaugurate the yearly youth festival. It was a beautiful evening; the youth of the kingdom had gathered to dance and sing and rejoice the whole night. The first day of the year—a nightlong celebration and Siddhartha was going to open it.

On the way he met what his father had been afraid of him ever seeing—he came across those things....

coming of age

THE STORY is beautiful. From here it becomes mythological, but still it is significant.

The story goes that Indra, who was the chief of all the gods, became worried that a man who was capable of becoming enlightened was being distracted. Something had to be done; existence should not be allowed to miss an enlightened being. So it is said that Indra took a few gods with him to earth.

The street was always cleared when Siddhartha passed, so it was impossible for any person to enter there. Only gods could enter—that's why they had to create the mythology—because gods are invisible yet they can become visible any moment.

First a god, sick and feverish, passed by the chariot. If the street had been full of traffic, perhaps Siddhartha would have missed seeing him. But the street was empty, the houses were empty; there were no other vehicles, only his golden chariot. Siddhartha saw this man trembling, and he asked his charioteer, "What has happened to this man?"

Now, the man who was driving the chariot was in a dilemma because the orders of the king were that this young man should not know that anybody ever gets sick. This man was so sick that it seemed as if he was going to fall down right there and die. But Indra was determined.

He forced the charioteer to tell the truth—"because ultimately your commitment is not toward that old king, your commitment is toward truth. Don't miss this point, because this man is going to become an enlightened one, and you will be immensely blessed because you will be the cause of triggering the process. Don't miss it—you may not find it again in millions of lives."

Of course it was clear. The charioteer said, "I am not supposed to say this, but how can I lie to you? The truth is that before this, all people have been removed from the streets where you travel. I wonder where this man has come from, because everywhere there are guards and the army. Nobody is allowed to enter the path where the chariot is moving. This man is sick."

Siddhartha asked, "What is sickness?"

The charioteer explained, "Sickness is something we are born with, we are carrying all kinds of sickness in the body. Sometimes, in a certain situation, a weakness that you are carrying within you gets support from the outside and you get an infection, you become sick."

Then an old man appeared, another god, almost a hunchback, so old that Siddhartha could not believe his eyes: "What has happened to this man?" The charioteer said, "This is what happens after many sicknesses... this man has become old."

OBSERVE THE SETTING SUN

Buddha chose for his *sannyasins* the yellow robe. Yellow represents death, the yellow leaf. Yellow represents the setting sun, the evening. Buddha emphasized death, and it helps in a way. People become more and more aware of life in contrast to death. When you emphasize death again and again and again, you help people to awaken; they have to be awake because death is coming. Whenever Buddha would initiate a new sannyasin, he would tell him, "Go to the cemetery: just be there and watch funeral pyres, dead bodies being carried and burned...go on watching. And remember that this is going to happen to you, too." Three months' meditation on death, then coming back—that was the beginning of *sannyas*.

And then, a dead body—another god posing as a dead body—came by, with four gods carrying him on a stretcher. Siddhartha asked, "What is happening?"

The charioteer said, "This man is at the last stage. After that old man, this is what happens."

Siddhartha said, "Stop the chariot here and answer me truthfully: Is all this going to happen to me too?"

At that moment he saw a monk, another god pretending to be a monk. Siddhartha said,

"And what stage is this? With a shaven head, a staff in his hand, a begging bowl..."

The charioteer said, "This is not a stage like the others; this is a type of person who has become aware of life's misery, suffering, anguish, sickness, old age, death. He has dropped out of life and is in search of truth, in search of finding something that is immortal— the deathless, the truth."

Siddhartha said, "Return to the house. I have become sick, sick unto death. I have

become old, old even though to all appearances I am young. What does it matter if old age is a few years ahead of me, soon it is going to be walking by my side! I don't want to be like that dead man. Although I am alive for all ordinary purposes, I died with that dead man. Death is going to come; it is only a question of time, a question of sooner or later. It can come tomorrow or years from tomorrow; anyway, some day it is going to happen."

He said, "Tonight keep the chariot ready. I am going to be the last type of man. I am renouncing all that I have. I have not found happiness here. I will seek it, I will pursue it, I will do everything that is needed to find happiness."

What the astrologers had suggested to Buddha's father had looked like common

sense...but common sense is superficial. They could not figure out one simple thing: that you cannot keep a man for his whole life unaware of reality. It is better to let him know from the beginning; otherwise, it will come as a big explosion in his life.

And that's what happened.

All the commentaries have said that Buddha renounced the world. It is not true. The world simply fell away; it ceased to have any meaning for him.

The night he moved away from his palace to the mountains, when he was crossing the boundary of his kingdom, his charioteer tried to convince him to go back to the palace. The charioteer was an old man. He had known Buddha from his childhood; he was almost the same age as Buddha's father. He said, "What are you doing? This is sheer madness. Have you gone insane or what? Look back!"

It was a full-moon night and his marble palace looked so beautiful. In the light of the full moon, the white marble of his palace was a joy to see. People used to come from faraway places just to have a glimpse of Buddha's palace in the full moon, just as people go to see the Taj Mahal. White marble has a tremendous beauty when the moon is full. There is synchronicity between the full moon and white marble, a certain harmony, a rhythm, a communion. The charioteer said, "Look back at least once to your beautiful palace. Nobody else has such a beautiful palace."

Buddha looked back and told the old man, "I don't see any palace there but only a great fire. The palace is on fire, only flames. Simply leave me here and go back; if you see the palace, go back to the palace. I don't see any palace there, because death is coming closer every moment. And I don't see any palace there because all palaces disappear sooner or later. In this world, everything is momentary and I am in search of the eternal.

Seeing the momentariness of this world, I can no longer fool myself."

These are his exact words, "I cannot fool myself anymore."

Not that he is renouncing the world! What can he do? If you see something as rubbish, if you see that the stones that you have carried all this time are not real diamonds, what are you going to do with them? It will not need great courage to drop them, to throw them away. It will not need great intelligence to get rid of them—they will immediately fall from your hands. You were not clinging to those stones, but to the idea that they were diamonds. You were clinging to your fallacy, your illusion.

Buddha has not renounced the world, he has renounced his illusions about it. And that, too, was a *happening*, not an act. When renunciation comes as a happening it has a tremendous beauty, because there is no motive in it. It is not a means to gain something else. It is total. You are finished with desiring, you are finished with the future, you are finished with power, money, and prestige, because you have seen the futility of it all.

awakening at bodhgaya

F OR SIX YEARS Buddha did everything that anybody could do. He went to all kinds of teachers, masters, scholars, wise men, sages, saints. And India is so full of these people that you need not seek or search; you simply move anywhere and you meet them. They are all over the place; if you don't seek them, they will seek you! And particularly in Buddha's time it was at a peak. The country was agog with only one thing: how to find something that transcends death.

But after six years' tremendous effort—austerities, fasting, and yoga postures—nothing had happened. Then one day... Even Buddhists have not been able to understand the significance of this story. This is the most important story in Gautam Buddha's life. Nothing else is comparable to it.

Just think of Gautam Buddha. He was his original self—that is his beauty and that is his greatness. He was not a Buddhist; he was simply himself. He had tried for six years continuously with different masters to find the truth, but nothing happened except frustration and failure. He was in great despair because he had been with all the great teachers that were available. Those teachers themselves had to say to him—because of his sincerity, his honesty—

"Whatever we knew we have taught to you. If you want more, then you will have to find it for yourself. This is all that we know. And we understand perfectly that you are not satisfied; neither are we satisfied, but we are not so courageous to go on trying to find. Even if it takes lives, go on trying to find it."

Finally, Buddha had to drop all the teachers and all the masters and start on his own. He worked tremendously hard. One of the most significant things happened that has to be remembered by all seekers, wherever they are in the world; it will always remain a significant milestone for future humanity.

One day he was staying by the side of Niranjana River. I have been to the place. The river is a small river; perhaps in the rainy season it becomes bigger, but when I went there in summer, it was just a small current of water.

He went down into the river to take a bath, but he had been fasting too long. He was so weak, and the current was so fast and strong that he was almost swept down the river. Somehow he caught hold of the roots of a tree, and in that moment an idea came to him: "I have become so weak by fasting because all the teachers, all the scriptures, constantly insist that unless you purify yourself by fasting, you cannot

attain enlightenment. I have weakened myself so much, but enlightenment has not happened. I cannot even get out of this small Niranjana River. How am I supposed to get out of the ocean of the whole world?"

In the Indian mythologies the world is compared to the ocean—*bhavsagar*. "How am I going to cross bhavsagar, the ocean of the world, if I cannot even cross the Niranjana River?"

It was a great moment of insight: "I have been unnecessarily torturing my body. It was not purification, it was weakening myself. It has not made me spiritual; it has made me sick."

Meantime, a woman in the town had made a promise to the tree under which Gautam Buddha was staying. Her promise was that if her son got well from a sickness, then she would come on the full-moon night and bring a bowl of sweets in gratitude to the deity of the tree.

It was a full-moon night, and just by coincidence Buddha was sitting under the tree. The woman thought, "My God, the deity himself is sitting under the tree waiting for me!" She was overjoyed. She placed the sweets at his feet, and she said, "I have never heard of the deity himself coming out of the tree and accepting the offering of us poor people, but you are great and you have helped me tremendously. Please forgive me for giving you so much trouble, but accept this small offering."

Buddha ate for the first time in years without any guilt.

All the religions have created guilt about everything. If you are eating something good—guilty. If you are wearing something beautiful—guilty. If you are happy, something must be wrong. You should be serious, you should be sad—only then can you be thought to be religious. A religious person is not supposed to laugh.

Buddha, for the first time, was out of the grip of tradition. Nobody has analyzed the state of his mind in that moment, which is significant to the psychology of spiritual enlightenment. Buddha dropped out of the whole tradition, orthodoxy, all that he had been told, all that he had been conditioned for. He simply dropped everything.

He did not even ask the woman, "To what caste do you belong?" As far as I understand she must have belonged to the *Sudras*. It is written nowhere, but my conclusion has some reason because her name was Sujata. *Sujata* means "born into a high-caste family." Only somebody who is *not* born into a high-caste family can have such a name. One who is born in a high-caste family need not have such a name. You can find the poorest man in the town, and his name will be Dhanidas, "the rich man"... the ugliest woman in the town, and her name will be Sunderbai, "beautiful woman." People substitute names to add height to their reality. The name of the girl was Sujata.

Buddha dropped the structure that had surrounded him that evening. He did not ask the caste, the creed. He accepted the offering, he ate the sweets, and after many days he slept for the first time without any guilt about sleeping. Your so-called spiritual people are afraid of sleep. Even sleep is a sin—it has to be cut. The less you sleep, the greater a spiritual person you are.

That night Buddha slept just like a child, with no conception of what is right and what is wrong: innocent, unburdened from conditioning, tradition, orthodoxy, religion. He was not even worried that night about truth or enlightenment. He slept a deep, dreamless sleep, because dreams come to you only when you have desires. That night was absolutely desireless. He had no desire; hence, there was no question of any dream. In the morning when he opened his eyes, he was utterly silent. Outside it was absolutely silent. Soon the sun started to rise, and as the sun was rising, something inside him also started rising.

He was not searching for it; he was not looking for it. For the first time he was not desiring it and it happened—he was full of light.

The man Siddhartha became Gautam Buddha.

In that illumination, in that moment of enlightenment, *nirvana*, he did not find any God. The whole of existence is divine; there is no separate creator. The whole of existence is full of light and full of consciousness; hence, there is no God, but there is godliness.

It is a revolution in the world of religions. Buddha created a religion without God. For the first time God was no longer at the center of a religion. The human being becomes the center of religion, his innermost being becomes godliness, for which you do not have to go anywhere, you simply have to stop going outside. You have to remain within, slowly, slowly settling at your center. The day you are settled at the center, the explosion happens.

THE SMALLEST GESTURE

One day Buddha was walking with a disciple—it must have been just before he was enlightened. He had gathered a few disciples even before he became enlightened, because a light had started spreading—just like early in the morning, when the sun has not yet risen but the sky becomes red and the earth becomes full of light; the sun is just about to rise above the horizon. Before Buddha became enlightened, he had five disciples. He was walking with those five disciples; a fly sat on his head. He was talking to the disciples and without paying much attention, mechanically, he moved his hand and the fly went away. Then he stopped, closed his eyes. The disciples could not understand what was happening, but they all became silent—something precious was happening.

His face became luminous, and he raised his hand slowly, and again moved it near his forehead as if the fly were still sitting there—it was not there anymore. The disciples asked, "What are you doing? The fly is no longer there."

He said, "But now I am moving my hand consciously—that time I did it unconsciously. I missed an opportunity of being conscious. I was too much engaged in talking with you and the hand simply moved mechanically. It should have moved consciously. Now I am moving it as it should have moved."

This is what Buddha means when he talks about the path of virtue: to become so alert that even small acts, even small gestures, movements, all become full of awareness.

the life of

buddha

Buddha, Mahavira, Jesus... they are not part of the history

books. For them we need a totally different approach.

They are not part of history; they come from the beyond.

in search of enlightenment

The day before Gautam Buddha left the palace in the middle of the night, a child had been born to his wife. It is such a human story, so beautiful... Before leaving the palace, he wanted to see at least once the face of the child, his child, the symbol of his love with his wife. So he went into his wife's bedchamber. She was asleep, and the child was lying next to her, covered by a blanket. He wanted to remove the blanket and to see the face of the child, because perhaps he would never come back again.

H E WAS GOING ON AN unknown pilgrimage. Nothing could be known of what would happen in his life. He risked everything—his kingdom, his wife, his child, himself—in search of enlightenment, something he had only heard of as a possibility, something that had happened before to a few people who looked for it.

He was as full of doubts as anyone, but the moment of decision had come.... That very day he had seen death, he had seen old age, he had seen sickness, and he had also seen a sannyasin for the first time. It had become an ultimate question in him: "If there is death, then wasting time in the palace is dangerous. Before death comes I have to find something that is beyond death." He was determined to leave. But the human mind, human nature... He wanted to see the child's face—he had not even seen the face of his own child. But he was afraid that if he removed the blanket, if Yashodhara, his wife, woke up—there was

every possibility she would wake up—she would ask, "What are you doing in the middle of the night in my room? And you seem to be ready to go somewhere..."

The chariot was standing outside the gate, everything was ready; he was just about to leave, and he had said to his charioteer, "Just wait a minute. Let me go and see the child's face. I may never come back again."

But he could not look because of the fear that Yashodhara might wake up, start crying, weeping, "Where are you going? What are you doing? What is this renunciation? What is this enlightenment?" One never knew—she might wake up the whole palace! The old father would come, and the whole thing would be spoiled. So he simply escaped.

After twelve years, when he was enlightened, the first thing he wanted to do was to come back to his palace to apologize to his father, to his wife, to his son who must be now twelve years of age. He was aware

that they would be angry. The father was very angry—he was the first one to meet him, and for half an hour he continued abusing Buddha. But then suddenly the father became aware that he was saying so many things and his son was just standing there like a marble statue, as if nothing was affecting him.

The father looked at him, and Gautam Buddha said, "That's what I wanted. Please dry your tears. Look at me: I am not the same boy who left the palace. Your son died long ago. I look similar to your son, but my whole consciousness is different. You just look."

The father said, "I am seeing it. For half an hour I have been abusing you, and that is enough proof that you have changed. Otherwise I know how temperamental you were; you could not stand so silently. What has happened to you?"

Buddha said, "I will tell you. Just let me first see my wife and my child. They must be waiting—they must have heard that I have come."

The first thing his wife said to him was, "I can see that you are transformed. These twelve years were a great suffering, but not because you had gone; I suffered because you did not tell me. If you had simply told me that you were going to seek the truth, do you think I would have prevented you? You have insulted me very badly. This is the wound that I have been carrying for twelve years.

"It was not that you had gone in search of truth—that is something to rejoice in. Not that you had gone to become enlightened—I would not have prevented you. Like you, I also belong to the warrior caste; do you think I am so weak that I would have cried and screamed and stopped you?

"All these twelve years my only suffering was that you did not trust me. I would have allowed you, I would have given you a send-off, I would have come up to the chariot to say goodbye. So first I want to ask the only question that has been in my mind for these

twelve years, which is that whatever you have attained... and it certainly seems you have attained something. You are no longer the same person who left this palace; you radiate a different light, your presence is totally new and fresh, your eyes are as pure and clear as a cloudless sky. You have become so beautiful... you were always beautiful, but this beauty seems to be not of this world. Some grace from the beyond has descended on you. My question is: Whatever you have attained, was it not possible to attain it here in this palace? Can the palace prevent the truth?"

It was a tremendously intelligent question, and Gautam Buddha had to agree: "I could have attained it here, but I had no idea at that moment. Now I can say that I could have attained it here in this palace; there was no need to go to the mountains, there was no need to go anywhere. I had to go inside, and that could have happened anywhere. This palace

was as good as any other place, but only now I can say it. At that moment I had no idea.

"So you have to forgive me, because it is not that I did not trust you or your courage. In fact, I was doubtful of myself. If I had seen you wake up, and if I had seen the child, I may have started wondering, 'What am I doing, leaving my beautiful wife, whose total love, whose total devotion is for me. And leaving my day-old child... if I am to leave him then why did you give birth to him? I am escaping from my responsibilities.' If my old father had awakened, it would have become impossible for me.

"It was not that I did not trust you; it was that I did not trust myself. I knew that there was a wavering; I was not total in renouncing. A part of me was saying, 'What are you doing?' and a part of me was saying, 'This is the time to do it. If you don't do it now it will become more and more difficult. Your father is preparing to crown you. Once you are crowned as king, it will be more difficult.'"

Yashodhara said to him, "This is the only question that I wanted to ask, and I am immensely happy that you have been absolutely truthful in saying that it can be attained here, that it can be attained anywhere. Now your son, who is standing there, a little boy of twelve years, has been continually asking about you, and I have been telling him, 'Just wait. He will come back; he cannot be so cruel, he cannot be so unkind, he cannot be so inhuman. One day he will come. Perhaps whatever he has gone to realize is taking time; once he has realized it, the first thing he will do is to come back.'

"So your son is here, and I want you to tell me, what heritage are you leaving for him? What have you got to give to your son? You have given him life—now what else?"

Buddha had nothing except his begging bowl, so he called his son, whose name was Rahul, the name Gautam Buddha had given him. He called Rahul close to him and gave him the begging bowl. He said, "I don't have anything. This is my only possession; from now onward I will have to use my hands as a begging bowl to take my food, to beg my food. By giving you this begging bowl, I am initiating you into *sannyas*. That is the only treasure that I have found, and I would like you to find it too."

He said to Yashodhara, "You have to be ready to become a part of my commune of sannyasins," and he initiated his wife. The old man had come and was watching the whole scene. He said to Gautam Buddha, "Why are you leaving me out? Don't you want to share what you have found with your old father? My death is very close… initiate me also."

Buddha said, "I had come, in fact, to take you all with me, because what I have found is a far greater kingdom—a kingdom that is going to last forever, a kingdom that cannot be conquered. I came here so that you could feel my presence, so that you could feel my realization and I could persuade you to become my fellow-travelers." So he initiated all three of them.

He had given his son the name Rahul from the Indian mythology about a moon eclipse. In the mythology, the moon is a person, a god, and he has two enemies: one is Rahu and the other is Ketu. When the moon eclipse happens,

> *If you are courageous enough to risk everything for being alert and aware, enlightenment is going to happen*

it happens because Rahu and Ketu catch hold of the moon. They try to kill it, but each time the moon escapes from their grip.

Gautam Buddha had given the name Rahul to his son because he thought, "This son of mine is going to be my greatest hindrance; he is going to be my greatest enemy. He will prevent me from going to the Himalayas. Love for him, attachment to him, will be my chains." That's why he had given him the name Rahul.

They all moved into the forest outside the city, where all of Buddha's disciples were staying. In the first sermon to the disciples that evening he told them, "My wife Yashodhara has asked me a question that is of tremendous importance. She has asked me, 'Was it not possible to become enlightened in the palace as a king?' And I have told her the truth: There is no question of any place, any time. One can become enlightened anywhere, but at that time nobody was there to say it to me. I had no idea of where it was to be found, whom I had to ask, where I had to go. I just jumped into the unknown. But now I can say that wherever you are, if you are courageous enough to risk everything for being alert and aware, enlightenment is going to happen."

sermons in silence

THERE IS NO language that can express the experience of enlightenment. There cannot be, by the very nature of the phenomenon. Enlightenment happens beyond mind, and language is part of the mind. Enlightenment is experienced in utter silence.

If you want to call silence a language, then of course enlightenment has a language—which consists of silence, which consists of blissfulness, which consists of ecstasy, which consists of innocence. But this is not the ordinary meaning of language. The ordinary meaning is that words have to be used as a vehicle to convey something. Silence cannot be conveyed by words; nor can ecstasy nor love nor blissfulness. In fact, enlightenment can be seen, can be understood, can be felt—but cannot be heard and cannot be spoken.

When Gautam Buddha became enlightened, he remained silent for seven days. All of existence waited breathlessly to hear him, to hear his music, to hear his soundless song, his words coming from the land of the beyond—words of truth. All of existence was waiting and those seven days seemed like seven centuries.

The story is tremendously beautiful. Up to a certain point it is factual and beyond that it becomes mythological, but by mythological I do not mean it becomes a lie. There are a few truths that can be expressed only through myths. He attained enlightenment—that is a truth. He remained silent for seven days—that is a truth. That the whole of existence waited to hear him is a truth—but only for those who had experienced something of enlightenment and who had experienced the waiting existence, not for everybody.

But still it can be understood that existence rejoices whenever somebody becomes enlightened because it is a part of existence itself that is coming to its highest expression, a part of existence that is becoming an Everest, the highest peak. Naturally, it is existence's crowning glory. It is the very longing of the whole to one day become enlightened, one day to dispel all unconsciousness and flood the whole of existence with consciousness and light, to destroy all misery and bring as many flowers of joy as possible.

Beyond this point it becomes pure mythology, but still it has its own significance and its own truth.

The gods in heaven became worried. One thing has to be understood: Buddhism does not believe in a God, nor does Jainism believe in a God, but they believe in *gods*. They are far more democratic in their concepts than

Mohammedanism, Judaism, or Christianity. Those religions are more elitist. One God, one religion, one holy scripture, one prophet—they are very monopolistic. But Buddhism has a different approach, far more democratic, far more human. It conceives millions of gods.

In fact, every being in existence has to become a god one day. When he becomes enlightened, he will be a god. According to Buddhism there is no God as a creator, and that brings dignity to every being. You are not puppets, you have an individuality and a freedom and a pride. Nobody can create you, nobody can destroy you. Hence, another concept has come out of this: Nobody can save you except yourself. In Christianity there is the idea of the savior; in Judaism there is the idea of the savior. If there is a God, he can send his messengers, prophets, messiahs to save you. Even liberating yourself is not within your hands. Even your liberation is going to be a sort of slavery—somebody else liberates you, and a liberation that is in somebody else's hands is not much of a liberation.

Freedom has to be achieved, not to be begged for. Freedom has to be snatched, not to be prayed for. A freedom that is given to you as a gift out of compassion is not of much value. Hence, in Buddhism there is no savior either. But there are gods—those who have become enlightened before. Since eternity, millions of people must have become enlightened; they are all gods.

These gods became disturbed when seven days of silence passed after Gautam Buddha's enlightenment, because it rarely happens that a human being becomes enlightened. It is such a rare and unique phenomenon that the very soul of existence waits for it, longs for it. Thousands of years pass, and then somebody becomes enlightened. What if Gautam Buddha is not going to speak, what if he chooses to remain silent? This is a natural possibility because silence is the only right language for enlightenment. The moment you try to bring it into language it becomes distorted. And the distortion happens on many levels.

First, it becomes distorted when you drag it down from its height, from the peaks to the dark valleys of the mind. The first distortion happens there. Almost ninety percent of its reality is lost.

Then you speak. The second distortion happens because what you can conceive in the deepest core of your heart is one thing; the moment you bring it into expression as words, that is another thing. You feel great love, but when you say to someone, "I love you," suddenly you realize the word *love* is too small to express what you are feeling. It seems embarrassing to use it.

The third distortion happens when it is heard by somebody else, because he has his own ideas, his own conditionings, his own thoughts, opinions, philosophies, ideologies, prejudices. He will immediately interpret it according to himself. By the time it reaches the person, it is no longer the same thing that had started from the highest peak of your consciousness. It has gone through so many changes that it is altogether something else. So it has happened many times that enlightened people have not spoken. Out of a hundred enlightened people, perhaps one may have chosen to speak.

Gautam Buddha was such a rare human being, so cultured, so articulate that if he had chosen to remain silent the world would have missed a great opportunity.

The gods came down, touched the feet of Gautam Buddha and asked him to speak: "Existence is waiting. The trees are waiting, the mountains are waiting, the valleys are waiting. The clouds are waiting, the stars are waiting. Don't frustrate everyone. Don't be so unkind, have some mercy and speak."

But Gautam Buddha had his own argument. He said, "I can understand your compassion, and I would like to speak. For seven days I have been wavering between the two, whether to speak or not to speak, and every argument goes for not speaking. I have not been able to find a single argument in favor of speaking. I am going to be misunderstood, so what is the point when you are going to be misunderstood— which is absolutely certain. I am going to be condemned; nobody is going to listen to me in the way that the words of an enlightened man have to be listened to. Listening needs a certain training, a discipline; it is not just hearing.

"And even if somebody understands me, he is not going to take a single step, because every step is dangerous; it is walking on a razor's edge. I am not against speaking, I just cannot see that there is any use, and I have found every argument against it."

The gods looked at each other. What Gautam Buddha was saying was right. They went aside to discuss what to do next. "We cannot say that what he is saying is wrong, but still we would like him to speak. Some way has to be found to convince him." They discussed for a long time and finally they came to a conclusion.

They came back to Gautam Buddha and they said, "We have found one single, small argument. It is very small in comparison to all the arguments that go against it, but still we would like you to consider. Our argument is that you may be misunderstood by ninety-nine percent of the people, but you cannot say that you will be misunderstood by a hundred percent of the people. You have to give at least a little margin—just one percent. That one

percent is not small in this vast universe; that one percent is a big enough portion. Perhaps out of that one percent, few will be able to follow the path.

"But even if one person in the whole universe becomes enlightened because of your speaking, it is worth it. Enlightenment is such a great experience that even if your whole life's effort can make one person enlightened you have done well. To ask for more is not right; this is more than enough. There are a few people—you must be aware, as we are aware—who are just on the borderline. A little push, a little encouragement, a little hope and perhaps they will cross the boundary of ignorance, they will cross the boundary of bondage, they will come out of their prisons. You have to speak."

Gautam Buddha closed his eyes and he thought for a few moments, and he said, "I cannot deny that much possibility. It is not much, but I do understand that all my arguments, howsoever great, are small in comparison to the compassion. I will live for at least forty-two years, and if I can make a single individual enlightened I will feel immensely rewarded. I will speak. You can go back unburdened of your worry and concern."

He spoke for forty-two years, and certainly not just one, but about two dozen people became enlightened. These two dozen people were the people who learned the art of listening, who learned the art of being silent. They did not become enlightened because of what Buddha was saying, they became enlightened because they could feel what Buddha *was*—his presence, his vibe, his silence, his depth, his height.

These two dozen people were not becoming enlightened just by listening to the words of Gautam Buddha. The words helped—they helped them to be in the presence of Gautam Buddha, they helped them to understand the beauty that ordinary words take on when they are used by an enlightened person.

Ordinary gestures become so graceful, ordinary eyes become so beautiful, with such depth and meaning. The way Buddha walks has a different quality to it; the way he sleeps has a different significance to it. These were the people who tried to understand not what Gautam Buddha was *saying*, but what he was *being*. His being is the only authentic language.

Millions heard him and became knowledgeable. The day he died, the same day, thirty-two schools sprang up, thirty-two divisions amongst the disciples, because they differed in their interpretations of what Gautam Buddha had said. Every effort was made that they should gather together and compile whatever they had heard from Gautam Buddha, but all their efforts were failures. There are thirty-two versions, so different that one cannot believe how people can hear one person in so many ways.

Even today those thirty-two schools go on quarreling. For twenty-five centuries they have not been reconciled with each other. In fact, they have gone farther and farther away from each other. Now they have become independent philosophies, each proposing that "This is what Gautam Buddha has said and everybody else is wrong. This is the holy scripture; others are just collections by people who don't understand."

It is one of the great puzzles: What is the language of enlightenment? The *being* of the enlightened person is his language. To be in contact with him, to drop all defenses, to open all the doors of your heart, to allow his love to reach to you, to allow his vibe to become your vibe.... Slowly, slowly, if one is ready, unafraid, then something transpires which nobody can see. Something has happened; something that has not been said has been heard. Something

that is not possible to bring into words has been conveyed through silence.

Buddha was speaking against Brahmans, against Hindus, but all his great disciples were Brahmans. It seems sensible because he was appealing to the best in the society. Although he was against Brahmans, the Brahmans were at the top of the ladder and out of the Brahmans came the greater part of the intelligentsia.

Sariputta was a Brahman, Moggalayan was a Brahman, Mahakashyapa was a Brahman. They all had come to Buddha not because they were illiterate idiots, the rejected— gamblers, prostitutes, tax collectors, thieves— no, but because they were great scholars and they could understand that what Buddha was saying was right.

When Sariputta came to Buddha, he himself had five hundred disciples of his own coming with him—all great scholars. He had come first to have a discussion, and Buddha was very happy: what could be more welcome? But Buddha asked, "Have you experienced the truth, or are you only a great scholar? I have heard your name...."

Looking at Buddha for a moment in silence, as if looking in a mirror, utterly naked, Sariputta said, "I am a great scholar, but as far as knowing the truth is concerned, I have not known it."

Buddha said, "Then it will be very difficult to argue. Argument is possible between two people who don't know truth. They can argue till eternity because neither knows. Both are ignorant, so they can go on playing with words and logic and quotations and scriptures. But because neither knows, there is no possibility of

their coming to a conclusion. At the most what can happen is that whoever is more clever and cunning and tricky may defeat the other, and the other will become the follower of the more cunning or more sophisticated. But is this any decision about truth?

"Or there is a possibility of a meeting of two people who both have realized the truth, but then there is no way to argue. What is there to argue about? They will sit silently; perhaps they may smile, or hold each other's hands, but what is there to say? Looking into each other's eyes they will see that there is nothing to say— we both know the same things, we are in the same space—so there will be only silence.

"The third possibility is that one knows and one does not know. Then it is going to be very troublesome because the one who knows cannot translate what he knows into the language of the ignorant one. And the one who does not know will be unnecessarily wasting his time, his mind, because he cannot convince the one who knows. The whole world cannot convince the person who knows, because he knows and you don't know. You may be all together...."

Buddha said, "You have come with your five hundred disciples. You don't know, and it is absolutely certain that among these five hundred disciples no one knows; otherwise he would not be your disciple, he would be your master. You are more scholarly, they are less scholarly. You are older, they are younger. They are your disciples. But how are we going to discuss anything? I am ready... but I *know*. One thing is certain, you cannot convert me. The only possibility is that you will be converted, so think twice."

But Sariputta was already converted and he was intelligent enough; he had defeated many great scholars. It was a tradition in India in those days that scholars would move all over the country defeating other scholars.

Unless a person had defeated all the scholars, he would not be recognized by the scholarly mob as a wise man. But to stand before a buddha, before one who knows, it is not a question of your scholarship and how many scholars you have defeated.

Buddha said, "I am ready. If you want to argue I am ready, but what argument is possible? I have eyes; you don't have eyes.

I cannot explain to you what light is. You cannot have any idea what light is. You will hear only the word *light* but the word will not have any meaning for you. It will be without content—heard, but not understood.

"So if you are really interested in truth, and not in getting defeated or being victorious… because that is not my interest. I have arrived. Who cares to defeat anybody? For what? If you are interested in truth then be here and do what I say. You can argue later on when you have come to know something substantial, existential. Then you can argue."

But Sariputta was a tremendously intelligent man. He said, "I know that neither can I argue

now, nor will I be able to argue then. You have finished my argumentation. Now I cannot argue because I don't have eyes; then I will not be able to argue because I will have eyes. But I am going to stay."

He stayed with his five hundred disciples. He said to the disciples, "Now I am no longer your master. Here is the man; I will be sitting by his side as his disciple. Please forget me as your master. If you want to be here, he is your master now."

One day a man came up to Gautam Buddha in the morning, and asked him, "Does God exist?" Buddha looked at the man for a moment, and then he said, "Yes." The man could not believe it because he had heard that Buddha does not believe in God. Now, what to make of his answer?

One of Buddha's closest disciples, Ananda, was with him. He was shocked. Buddha had never said with such certainty, without any ifs and buts, a simple yes—to God! He had his whole life been fighting against the idea of God.

But there was an agreement between Buddha and Ananda. Ananda was Buddha's elder cousin. When he was ready to become a disciple of Buddha, Ananda had asked beforehand, "You have to promise me a few things. Right now I am your elder cousin. After the initiation I will be your disciple; then whatever you say I will have to do. But right now I can ask you for something and you will have to do it."

Buddha said, "I know you. You cannot ask anything that will put your younger cousin in any difficulty. You can ask."

Ananda said, "They are not big things, just simple things. One is that every night before going to sleep, if I want to ask something, you will have to answer. You can't say, 'I am tired from the day's journey, and so many people and so many meetings...' You will have to answer me. I will never ask in the day, I will not disturb you the whole day. But I am a human being and I am not enlightened; certain questions may arise."

Buddha said, "That is accepted."

In the same way Ananda asked two more things: "One is that you will never tell me to go anywhere else; I will always be with you, to serve you till my last breath. You will not tell me, 'Now you go and spread my message,' the way you send others. You cannot send me."

Buddha said, "Okay, that's not a problem."

And third, Ananda said, "If I ask you to give some time to somebody, at any hour—it may be an odd hour, in the middle of the night—you will have to meet the person. That much privilege you have to give me."

Buddha said, "That, too, is okay because I know you. You will not take advantage of these conditions...."

Ananda was puzzled by Buddha's answer that God exists. But as he could not ask in the day, he had to wait for the night. In the afternoon, another man came and asked the same question: "Is there a God?" And Buddha said, "No, not at all."

Now, things became more complicated! Ananda was almost in a state of falling apart. But this was nothing. In the evening, a third man came, and he sat in front of Buddha and asked,

> *Belief as such is the barrier; it does not matter what belief it is, true or false*

"Will you say something about God?"

Buddha looked at him, closed his eyes, and remained silent. The man also closed his eyes. They sat in silence for half an hour; then the man touched Buddha's feet and said, "Thank you for your answer," and went away.

Now, it was too much. The time was passing so slowly and Ananda was boiling within; when everybody was gone, he jumped up. He said, "This is too much! You should take care, at least, of us poor disciples. Those three persons don't know all the three answers, they only know one answer. But we are with you, we have heard all the answers. You should think of us too, we have been going crazy. If this is going to continue, what will happen to us?"

Buddha said, "You should remember one thing. First, those questions were not your questions; those answers were not given to you. Why should you jump into it? It is none of your business. It was something between me and those three people."

Ananda said, "That I can understand. It is not my question, and you have not answered me. But I have ears and I can hear; I heard the question, I heard the answer. And all three answers are contradiction upon contradiction.

First you say yes, then you say no, and then you remain silent, you don't say anything and that man touched your feet and said, 'Thank you for your answer.' And we are sitting here… there has been no answer at all!"

Buddha said, "You think about life in terms of absolutes; that's your trouble. Life is relative. To the first man, the answer was yes; it was relative to him, related to the implications of his questions, his being, his life. That man to whom I said yes was an atheist; he does not believe in God and I do not want to support his stupid atheism. He goes on proclaiming there is no God. Even if a small space is left unexplored, perhaps in that space God exists. You can say with absolute certainty that there is no God when you have explored all of existence. That is possible only at the very end, and that man was simply believing that there was no God—he had no existential experience of there being no God. I had to shatter him, I had to bring him down to earth. I had to hit him hard on the head. My yes was relative to that person, to his whole personality. His question was not just words. The same question from somebody else may have received another answer.

"And that's what happened when I said to the other person, 'No.' The question was the same, the words were the same, but the man behind those words was different, so the relationship between the words and the implications had changed. It is relative. The second man was as much an idiot as was the first, but on the opposite pole. He believed there is a God, and he had come to get my support for his belief. I don't support anybody's belief because belief as such is the barrier. It does not matter what belief it is, true or false. No belief is true, no belief is false; all beliefs are simply idiotic. I had to say to that man, 'No.'

"The third man had come with no belief. He had not asked me, 'Is there a God?' No, he had come with an open heart, with no mind, no belief, no ideology. He was a sane man, intelligent. He asked me, 'Would you say something about God?' He was not in search of somebody's support for his belief system, he was not in search of a faith, he was not asking with a prejudiced mind. He was asking about my experience: 'Would you say something about God?'

"I could see that this man has no belief, this way or that; he is innocent. With such an innocent person, language is meaningless. I cannot say yes, I cannot say no; only silence is the answer. So I closed my eyes and remained silent. And my feeling about the man proved to be true. He closed his eyes—seeing me close my eyes, he closed his eyes. He understood my answer: Be silent, go in. He remained in silence for half an hour with me and received the answer that God is not a theory, a belief you have to be for or against. That's why he thanked me for the answer.

"And you are puzzled about what answer he thanked me for? He received the answer that silence is divine, and to be silent is to be godly; there is no other god than silence. And he went tremendously fulfilled, contented. He has found the answer. I have not given him the answer; *he* has found the answer. I simply allowed him to have a taste of my presence."

the peaceful warrior

GAUTAM BUDDHA was surrounded by a crowd that was abusing him, using ugly words, obscene words, because he was against the organized religion of the Hindus and against the Hindu holy scriptures, the *Vedas*. He had condemned the priesthood, saying that these were exploiters, parasites. Naturally, the Brahmans were enraged.

This was a Brahman village through which he was passing and the Brahmans surrounded him and said every kind of bad thing that they could manage. He listened silently. His disciples became angry, but because Buddha was present it was not courteous to say anything. The master was standing so silent, and listening as if these people were saying sweet things.

Finally Buddha said to them, "If the things that you wanted to say to me are finished, I would like to go on to the next village where

> " ...you cannot make me angry unless I accept your humiliation, your insult "

people are waiting for me. But if you are not finished, after a few days I will be returning and I will inform you. Then I will have enough time to listen to all that you want to say."

One man said, "Do you think that we are saying something? We are condemning you! Do you understand or not? Because anybody else would become angry, and you are standing silently...."

The statement that Buddha made to these village people is immensely significant. He said, "You have come a little too late. If you had come ten years ago when I was as insane as you are, not a single person would have left here alive."

Ten years ago he was a prince, a warrior, one of the best archers of his time, a great swordsman, and those Brahmans...he could have removed their heads with a single blow, without any difficulty, because those Brahmans know nothing about swords or arrows or being a warrior. He would have cut them almost like vegetables.

He said, "You have come late. Ten years ago if you had come...but now I am no longer insane; I cannot react. But I would like to ask you one question. In the last village people came with sweets and fruits and flowers to receive me; however, we take food only once a day and we had already taken our food. And we don't carry things. So we had to tell them, 'You please forgive us, we cannot accept sweets, flowers. We accept your love, but these things you will have to keep.' I want to ask you," he said to this angry crowd, "what must they have done with the sweets and flowers they had brought as presents for us?"

One man said, "What is the mystery in it? They must have distributed the sweets in the village."

Buddha said, "That makes me very sad. What will you do?—because I don't accept what you have brought, in the same way I did not accept the sweets and the flowers and other things that the people brought to me in the other village. If I don't accept your obscenity, your ugly words, your dirty words—if I don't accept them, what can you do? What are you going to do with all this garbage that you have come with? You will have to take it back to your homes and give it to your wives, to your children, to your neighbors. You will have to distribute it, because I refuse to take it. And you cannot make me angry unless I accept your humiliation, your insult.

"Ten years ago I was not conscious; if somebody had insulted me he would have lost his life immediately. I had no idea that insulting me is his problem, and that I have nothing to do with it. I can simply listen and go on my way."

There was one man who was a mad murderer. He had taken a vow that he would kill one thousand people, not fewer than that, because the society had not treated him well. He would take his revenge by killing one thousand people. And from every person killed he would take one finger and make a rosary around his neck—one thousand fingers. Because of this, his name became Angulimala, the man with a rosary of fingers.

He killed nine hundred and ninety-nine people. Nobody would move in those parts; wherever people came to know that Angulimala was, the traffic would stop. And then it became very difficult for him to find one man, and only one more man was needed.

Buddha was moving toward a forest; people came to him from the villages and they said,

STILLNESS

Buddha always slept in the same posture. He would remain the whole night in the same posture; he would not change his position at all. That posture has become famous—there are many statues with Buddha in that posture in Ceylon, China, Japan, and India. If you go to Ajanta, there is a statue of Buddha lying down. That posture was reported by his disciple Ananda: Buddha slept in the same posture the whole night, never even changing sides.

One day Ananda asked, "One thing puzzles me. You remain in the same posture the whole night. Are you asleep or not? If someone is asleep, he will change his posture. Even while you are asleep—or appear to be asleep—it looks as if you are alert. It seems you know what the body is doing; you will not even change your posture unconsciously."

Buddha said, "Yes, when the mind is silent, not dreaming, only the body sleeps. The consciousness remains alert."

"Don't go! Angulimala is there, that mad murderer! He doesn't think twice, he simply murders; and he will not think about the fact that you are a buddha. Don't go that way; there is another path, you can move on that one, but don't go through this forest!"

Buddha said, "If I don't go, then who will go? And he is waiting for one more, so I have to go."

Angulimala had almost completed his vow. And he was a man of energy because he was fighting the whole society. Only one man, and he had killed a thousand people. Kings were afraid of him, generals were afraid, and the government and the law and the police—nobody could do anything. But Buddha said, "He is a man, he needs me. I must take the risk. Either he will kill me or I will kill him."

This is what buddhas do: they stake their lives. Buddha went. Even the closest disciples who had said that they would remain with him up to the very end started lagging behind because this was dangerous! So when Buddha reached the hill where Angulimala was sitting on a rock, there was no one behind him, he was alone. All the disciples had disappeared. Angulimala looked at this innocent man: childlike, so beautiful, he thought, that even a murderer felt compassion for him. He thought, "This man seems to be absolutely unaware that I am here, otherwise nobody goes along this path." And the man looked so innocent, so beautiful, that even Angulimala thought, "It is not good to kill this man. I'll leave him, I can find somebody else."

Then he said to Buddha, "Go back! Stop there now and go back! Don't move a step forward! I am Angulimala, and these are nine hundred and ninety-nine fingers here, and I need one finger more—even if my mother comes I will kill her and fulfill my vow! So don't come near, I'm dangerous! And I am not a believer in religion, I'm not bothered who you are. You may be a very good monk, a great saint maybe, but I don't care! I only care about the finger, and your finger is as good as anybody else's so don't come a single step further, otherwise I will kill you. Stop!" But Buddha continued moving.

Then Angulimala thought, "Either this man is deaf or mad!" He again shouted, "Stop! Don't move!"

Buddha said, "I stopped long ago; I am not moving, Angulimala, you are moving. I stopped long ago. All movement has stopped because all motivation has stopped. When there is no motivation, how can movement happen? There is no goal for me, I have achieved the goal, so why should I move? You are moving—and I say to you: you stop!"

Angulimala was sitting on the rock and he started laughing. He said, "You are really mad! I am sitting and you say to me that I am moving. And you are moving and you say that you have stopped. You are really a fool or mad—or I don't know what type, what manner of man you are!"

Buddha came near and he said, "I have heard that you need one more finger. As far as this body is concerned, my goal is achieved; this body is useless. When I die people will burn it, it will be of no use to anyone. You can use it, your vow can be fulfilled: cut off my finger and cut off my head. I have come on purpose because

SEEDS OF SALVATION

A young child died; the father of the child had already died and the woman was living only for this child. That child was her whole life and her only hope; otherwise, there was nothing for her to live for. And the child died—she was almost on the verge of going crazy. She wouldn't allow anyone to take the child to the crematorium. She was hugging the child in the hope that perhaps he might start breathing again. She was ready to give her own life if the child could live.

The people said, "This is not possible, it is against the law of nature." But she was in such misery that she could not listen to anybody. Then somebody said, "The best way is, let us take this woman to Gautam Buddha who, just by chance, is in the village."

This appealed to the woman. A man like Gautam Buddha can do anything, and this is a small miracle—nothing much—to make the child start breathing again. She went, crying and weeping, put the child's dead body at the feet of Buddha, and said to him, "You are a great master, you know the secrets of life and death, and I have come with great hope. Make my child alive again."

Buddha said, "That I will do, but you have to fulfill a condition before I do it."

She said, "I am ready to fulfill any condition. I am ready to give my life, but let my child live."

Buddha said, "No, the condition you have to fulfill is very simple. You just go around the village and find a few mustard seeds from a house where death has never happened."

She was in such despair, she went from one house to another. And all those people said, "We can give you as many mustard seeds as you want, but those mustard seeds will not help you. Not only one, but many have died in our family; perhaps thousands have died over the generations."

By the evening, a great awakening had happened to the woman. She had gone through the whole village and got the same reply.... They were all ready to help her but they said, "These mustard seeds won't help. Buddha has made it clear to you, 'Bring the mustard seeds from a family where nobody has ever died.'"

By the evening, when she returned, she was a totally different woman. She was not the same woman who had come in the morning. She had become absolutely aware that death is a reality of life—it cannot be changed.

And what is the point? "Even if my child lives for a few years, he will have to die again. In the first place it is not possible; in the second place, even if it were possible, it is pointless."

Now there were no more tears in her eyes; she was very quiet, serene. A tremendous understanding had come to her: she had been asking for the impossible. She dropped that desire. She came and fell at Buddha's feet.

Buddha said, "Where are the mustard seeds? I have been waiting the whole day."

The woman, instead of crying, laughed. She said, "You played a good joke! Forget all about the child, what is gone is gone.

"Now I have come to be initiated and to become a *sannyasin*. The way you have found the truth that never dies, I also want to find. I am no longer concerned with the child or anybody else.

My concern is now, how to find the truth the never dies, the truth that is life itself."

Buddha said, "Forgive me that I had to ask you for something I knew was impossible. But it was a simple device to bring you to your senses, and it worked."

this is the last chance for my body to be used in some way; otherwise people will burn it."

Angulimala said, "What are you saying? I thought that I was the only madman around here. And don't try to be clever because I am dangerous, I can still kill you!"

Buddha said, "Before you kill me, do one thing. Just the wish of a dying man—cut off a branch of this tree." Angulimala hit his sword against the tree and a big branch fell down. Buddha said, "Just one thing more: join it again to the tree!"

Angulimala said, "Now I know perfectly that you are mad—I can cut, but I cannot join."

Then Buddha started laughing and he said, "When you can only destroy and cannot create, you should not destroy. Destruction can be done by children; there is no bravery in it. This branch can be cut by a child, but to join it a master is needed. And if you cannot even join back a branch to the tree, how can you cut off human heads? Have you ever thought about it?"

Angulimala closed his eyes, fell down at Buddha's feet, and he said, "You lead me on that path!" And it is said that in a single moment he became enlightened.

Next day he was a *bhikkhu*, a beggar, Buddha's monk, and begging in the city. The whole city was closed up. People were so afraid, they said, "Even if he has become a beggar he cannot be believed. That man is so dangerous!" People were not out on the roads. When Angulimala came to beg, nobody was there to give him food, because who would take the risk? People were standing on their terraces looking down. And then they started throwing stones at him because he had killed nine hundred and ninety-nine men of that town. Almost every family had been a victim, so they started throwing stones.

Angulimala fell down on the street, blood was flowing from all over his body, he had many wounds. And Buddha came with his disciples and he said, "Look! Angulimala, how are you feeling?"

Angulimala opened his eyes and said, "I am so grateful to you. They can kill the body but they cannot touch me. And that is what I was doing my whole life and never realized the fact."

Buddha said, "Angulimala has become enlightened; he has become a Brahman, a knower of Brahma."

physician of the soul

GAUTAM BUDDHA came into a town. That town had a blind man who was a great logician, very rational, and the whole town had tried to tell him that light exists, but nobody could prove it.

There is no way to prove light. Either you can see it or you cannot see it, but there is no other proof.

The blind man said, "I am ready. I can touch things and I can feel them with my hands. You bring your light and I would like to touch it and feel it."

But light is not something tangible. They said, "No, it cannot be touched or felt."

He said, "I have other ways. I can smell it, I can taste it. I can beat on it and hear the sound. But these are my only instruments—my ears, my nose, my tongue, my hands—I am making available to you all my faculties. Should I listen to my own common sense, or should I listen to you? I say there is no light; it is simply an invention, an invention of cunning people to deceive simple people like me so that you can prove that I am blind and you have eyes. The whole strategy is that you are not interested in light, you are interested in proving that you have eyes and I don't have eyes. You want to be higher, superior. Because you cannot be logically, rationally superior to me you have brought in something absurd. Forget all about it, you are all blind. Nobody has seen light because light does not exist."

When they heard that Buddha had come to the town, the people said, "It is a good opportunity. We should take our logician the blind man to Gautam Buddha; perhaps he can convince him—we cannot find a better man to do it."

They brought the blind man to Gautam Buddha. They told the story that was going on. One blind man was proving them all blind, was proving that there is no light, and they were absolutely incapable of proving the existence of light.

The words of Gautam Buddha are worth remembering. He said, "You have brought him to the wrong person. He does not need a

> *The bee never gathers for tomorrow; today is enough unto itself*

LIKE A HONEYBEE

The *bhikkhu*, the Buddhist sannyasin, goes from house to house; he never asks from just one house because that may be too much of a burden. So he asks from many houses—just a little bit from one house, a little bit from another, so he is not a burden on anybody. And he never goes to the same house again. This is called madhukari—like a honeybee. The bee goes from one flower to another, and goes on moving from flower to flower—it is nonpossessive. It takes so little from one flower that the beauty is not marred, the perfume is not destroyed. The flower never becomes aware of the bee; it comes so silently and goes so silently.

Buddha says: The man of awareness lives in this world like a bee. He never mars the beauty of this world, he never destroys the perfume of this world. He lives silently, moves silently. He asks only as much as is needed. His life is simple, it is not complex. He does not gather for tomorrow. The bee never gathers for tomorrow; today is enough unto itself.

PORTRAIT

For five hundred years after Buddha's
death his statue was not created,
his picture was not painted. For five
hundred years, whenever a Buddhist
temple was created, only the picture
of the bodhi tree was there. That was
beautiful—because in that moment
when Gautam Siddhartha became
Buddha, he was not there, only the tree
was there. He had disappeared for a
moment and only the tree remained.

philosopher, he needs a physician. It is not a
question of convincing him, it is a question of
curing his eyes. But don't be worried, I have
my personal physician with me." One of the
emperors of those days had given his own
personal physician to Gautam Buddha to take
care of him twenty-four hours a day, to be with
him like a shadow.

He said to the physician, "You take care of
this man's eyes."

The physician looked at the man's eyes
and he said, "It is not a difficult case; a certain
disease is crippling his eyes, which can be
cured. It may take at the most six months."

Buddha left his physician in the village,
and after six months the man opened
his eyes. All his logic, all his rationality
disappeared. He said, "My God, I was telling
those people that they were cheating me,
deceiving me. Light exists—I was blind! Had
I accepted the idea of my blindness before,

there would have been no need for me to
live my whole life in blindness."

Buddha had gone far away in those six
months, but the man came dancing, fell
at Buddha's feet and said to him, "Your
compassion is great that you did not argue
with me, that you did not try to convince me
about the light, but gave me a physician."

Buddha said, "This is my work. There are
spiritually blind people all around. My work
is not to convince them about the beauty, the
blissfulness, the ecstasy of existence; my
work is that of a physician."

One morning a great king, Prasenjita,
came to Gautam Buddha. He had in one of
his hands a beautiful lotus flower, and in the
other hand a most precious diamond. He had
come because his wife was persistent:
"When Gautam Buddha is here, you waste
your time with idiots, talking about
unnecessary things…"

From her childhood she had been going to Gautam Buddha; then she got married. Prasenjita had no inclination of that kind but because she was so insistent he said, "It is worth at least one visit to go and see what kind of man this is."

But he was a man of great ego, so he took out the most precious diamond from his treasure to present to Gautam Buddha. He did not want to go there as an ordinary man. Everybody had to know...in fact, he wanted everybody to know, "Who is greater—Gautam Buddha or Prasenjita?" That diamond was so precious that many fights had happened, wars had happened over it.

His wife laughed and she said, "You are absolutely unaware of the man I'm taking you to. It is better that you take a flower rather than a stone to present to him." He could not understand, but he said, "There is no harm, I can take both. Let us see."

When he reached there, he offered his diamond, which he was carrying in one of his hands, and Buddha said simply, "Drop it!" Naturally, what can you do? He dropped it. He thought that perhaps his wife was right. In the other hand he was carrying the lotus, and as he tried to offer the lotus, Buddha said, "Drop it!"

He dropped that too, and became a little afraid: the man seemed to be insane! But ten thousand disciples were there... And Prasenjita stood there thinking that these people must believe that he was stupid. And Buddha said the third time, "Don't you listen to me? Drop it!" Prasenjita thought, "He is really gone. Now I have dropped the diamond, I have dropped the lotus; now I don't have anything."

And at that very moment, Sariputta, an old disciple of Gautam Buddha, started laughing. His laughter turned Prasenjita towards him, and he asked, "Why are you laughing?"

He said, "You don't understand the language. He is not saying drop the diamond, he is not saying drop the lotus. He is saying drop yourself, drop the ego. You can have the diamond and you can have the lotus, but drop the ego. Don't take it back."

You have heard of Cleopatra, one of the most beautiful women of Egypt. In India, equivalent to Cleopatra, is the beautiful woman contemporary of Gautam Buddha, Amrapali.

Buddha was staying in Vaishali, where Amrapali lived. Amrapali was a prostitute. In Buddha's time in India it was a convention that the most beautiful woman of any city would not be allowed to get married to any one person, because that would create unnecessary jealousy, conflict, fighting. So
the most beautiful woman had to become *nagarvadhu*—the wife of the whole town.

It was not disrespectful at all; on the contrary, just as in the contemporary world we declare a beautiful woman as "the Woman of the Year," she was greatly respected. She was not an ordinary prostitute. Her function was that of a prostitute, but she was visited only by the very rich, by kings or princes and generals—the highest strata of society.

Amrapali was very beautiful. One day she was standing on her terrace and she saw a young Buddhist monk. She had never fallen in love with anybody, although every day she had to pretend to be a great lover to this king, to that king, to this rich man, to that general. But she fell suddenly in love with this Buddhist monk who had nothing except a begging bowl—a young man, but of a tremendous presence, awareness, grace. The way he was walking.... She rushed down and asked the monk, "Please—today accept my food."

Other monks were also coming behind him, because whenever Buddha was moving anywhere, ten thousand monks were always moving with him. The other monks could not believe this. They were jealous and angry and feeling all the human qualities and frailties as they saw the young man enter the palace of Amrapali.

Amrapali told him, "After three days the rainy season is going to start…" Buddhist monks don't move for four months when it is the rainy season. Those are the four months they stay in one place; for eight months they continuously move; they can't stay more than three days in one place.

It is a strange psychology: to become attached to some place it takes you at least four days. You can observe it in your own experience. For example, for the first day in a new house you may not be able to sleep, the second day it will be little easier, the third day it will be even easier, and the fourth day you will be able to sleep perfectly at home. So before that time is up, if you are a Buddhist monk, you have to leave.

Amrapali said, "After just three days the rainy season is to begin, and I invite you to stay in my house for the four months."

The young monk said, "I will ask my master. If he allows me, I will come."

As he went out the crowd of monks asked him what had happened. He said, "I have taken my meal, and the woman has asked me to stay the four months of the rainy season in her palace. I told her that I will ask my master."

The monks were really angry. One day was already too much…but four months! They rushed to find Gautam Buddha. Before the young man could reach the assembly, there were hundreds of monks standing up and telling Gautam Buddha, "This man has to be stopped. That woman is a prostitute, and a monk staying four months in a prostitute's house…."

> *If meditation is deep, if awareness is clear, nothing can disturb it* "

Buddha said, "You keep quiet! Let him come. He has not agreed to stay; he has agreed only if I allow him. Let him come."

The young monk came, touched the feet of Buddha and told the whole story, "The woman is a prostitute, a famous prostitute, Amrapali. She has asked me to stay for four months in her house. Every monk will be staying somewhere, in somebody's house, for the four months. I have told her that I will ask my master, so I am here… whatever you say."

Buddha looked into his eyes and said, "You can stay."

It was a shock. Ten thousand monks. There was great silence…but also great anger, great jealousy. They could not believe that Buddha had allowed a monk to stay in a prostitute's house. After three days the young man left to stay with Amrapali, and the monks every day started bringing gossip: "The whole city is agog. There is only one topic of talk—that a Buddhist monk is staying with Amrapali for four months."

Buddha said, "You should keep silent. Four months will pass, and I trust my monk. I have looked into his eyes—there was no desire. If I had said no, he would not have felt

anything. I said yes… he simply went. And I trust in my monk, in his awareness, in his meditation. "Why are you getting so agitated and worried? If my monk's meditation is deep then he will change Amrapali, and if his meditation is not deep then Amrapali may change him. It is now a question between meditation and a biological attraction. Just wait for four months. I trust this young man. He has been doing perfectly well and I have every certainty he will come out of this fire test absolutely victorious."

Nobody believed Gautam Buddha. His own disciples thought, "He is trusting too much. The man is too young; he is too fresh and Amrapali is much too beautiful. He is taking an unnecessary risk." But there was nothing else to do.

After four months the young man came, touched Buddha's feet—and following him was Amrapali, dressed as a Buddhist nun. She touched Buddha's feet and she said, "I tried my best to seduce your monk, but he seduced me. He convinced me by his presence and awareness that the real life is at your feet. I want to give all my possessions to the commune of your monks."

She had a beautiful garden and a beautiful palace. She said, "You can make it a place where ten thousand monks can stay in any rainy season."

And Buddha said to the assembly, "Now, are you satisfied or not?"

If meditation is deep, if awareness is clear, nothing can disturb it. Then everything is ephemeral. Amrapali became one of the enlightened women among Buddha's disciples.

the last experiment

IT HAPPENED ON the last day of Gautam Buddha's life on earth. A poor man invited him to take his meal at his home. This was the routine: Buddha would open his doors early in the morning and whoever would invite him first, he would accept the invitation for that day. He would go to the house. He used to take only one meal each day.

It was almost impossible for a poor person to invite him; it was accidental. The king was coming to invite him, but on the way an accident happened and the chariot in which he was coming broke down, so he was delayed. He reached there just a few minutes late. By that time Buddha had already accepted the invitation of the poor man.

The king said, "I know this man. He has been trying his whole life to invite you whenever you come to this town."

Buddha loved a few places very well. Vaishali, one of the cities, was one of his favorites. In his forty-two years as a master he visited Vaishali at least forty times, almost every year. He remained in Vaishali for at least twelve rainy seasons, because in the rainy season it was too difficult to walk.

So for three or four months he would remain in one place and for eight months he would move around.

The places where Buddha moved are in Bihar. The name *Bihar* comes from Buddha's movements and means "the place where a buddha travels." The boundary of this area, where for forty-two years he continuously traveled, defines the whole state of Bihar.

The king said, "I know this man, I have seen him many times. He is always trying...yet he has nothing to offer! Please reject this idea of going to his house."

But Buddha said, "That is impossible. I cannot reject the invitation. I have to go." So he went. And his going became fatal to his body, because in Bihar the poor men collect mushrooms, dry them, and keep them for the rainy season. They use them as vegetables. Sometimes mushrooms are poisonous. And he had prepared mushrooms for Buddha—he had nothing else, just rice and mushrooms.

Buddha looked at what he offered him, but saying no to the poor man would hurt him, so he ate the mushrooms. They were very bitter, but to say that would hurt the poor man, so he ate them all without saying anything, thanked the man, and left. He died of food poisoning.

When he was asked at the last moment, "Why did you accept? You knew, the king had warned you, other disciples were warning you that he is so poor, he would not be able to offer you the right food. And you are old, eighty-two years old—you need the right nourishment. But you didn't listen."

Buddha said, "It was impossible. Whenever truth is invited it has to accept. And he invited me with such passion and love as nobody has ever invited me—it was worth risking my life."

This story is beautiful. It is true about the ultimate truth, also: all that is needed on our part is a total invitation, not holding back even a small part of our being. If we are available, open, ready to receive the host, the host comes. It has never been otherwise.

This is the law of existence: truth cannot be conquered but it can be invited. One has to be a host for the ultimate guest. That's what I call meditation; it makes you empty of all rubbish, it empties you completely so you become spacious, receptive, sensitive, vulnerable, available. And all those qualities make you passionately inviting—an invitation for the unknown, an invitation for the unnamable, an invitation for that which will make your life a fulfillment, without which life is just an exercise in utter futility. But one cannot do anything more than that: just offer an invitation and wait.

This is what I call prayer: an invitation and waiting in deep trust that it is going to happen. And it happens, it has always happened! *Aes dhammo sanantano*, says Buddha—this is the ultimate law of existence.

> " *This is the law of existence: truth cannot be conquered but it can be invited* "

The day Buddha died, in the morning he gathered all his disciples, all his sannyasins, and told them, "The last day has come now, my boat has arrived and I have to leave. This has been a beautiful journey, a beautiful togetherness. If you have any questions to ask, you can ask them, because I will not be available to you physically anymore."

A great silence fell on the disciples, a great sadness. And Buddha laughed and said, "Don't be sad, because that's what I have been teaching you again and again—everything that begins, ends. Now let me teach you by my death too. As I have been teaching you through my life, let me teach you through my death, too."

Nobody could gather the courage to ask a question. Their whole life they had asked thousands and thousands of questions, and this was not a moment to ask anything; they were not in the mood, they were crying and weeping.

So Buddha said, "Goodbye. If you don't have any questions then I will depart." He sat under the tree with closed eyes and he disappeared from the body. In the Buddhist

> *He is no longer a person, no longer a form, no longer a wave; he disappears into the ocean*

tradition, this is called "the first meditation"—to disappear from the body. It means to disidentify yourself from the body, to know totally and absolutely, "I am not the body."

A question is bound to arise in your mind: had Buddha not known it before? He had known it before, but a person like Buddha then has to create some device so that just a little bit of him remains connected with the body. Otherwise he would have died long before—forty-two years before he would have died. The day his enlightenment happened, he would have died. Out of compassion he created a desire, the desire to help people. It is a desire, and it keeps you attached to the body. He created a desire to help people. "Whatsoever I have known, I have to share."

If you want to share, you will have to use the mind and the body. That small part remained attached. Now he cuts even that small root in the body; he becomes disidentified from the body. The first meditation complete, the body is left.

Then the second meditation: the mind is dropped. He had dropped the mind long before; it was dropped as a master, but as a servant it was still used. Now it is not even needed as a servant, it is utterly dropped, totally dropped.

And then the third meditation: he dropped his heart. It had been needed up to now, he had been functioning through his heart; otherwise, compassion would not have been possible. He had been the heart; now he disconnects from the heart.

When these three meditations are completed, the fourth happens. He is no longer a person, no longer a form, no longer a wave; he disappears into the ocean. He becomes that which he had always been, he becomes that which he had known forty-two years before but had been somehow managing to delay in order to help people.

His death is a tremendous experiment in meditation. It is said that many who were present first saw that the body was no longer the same; something had happened, the aliveness had disappeared from the body. The body was there, but like a statue. Those who were more perceptive, more meditative, immediately saw that now the mind had been dropped and there was no mind inside. Those who were even more perceptive could see that the heart was finished. And those who were on the verge of buddhahood, seeing Buddha disappear, they also disappeared.

Many disciples became enlightened the day Buddha died, many—just seeing him dying. They had watched him living, they had seen his life, but now came the crescendo, the climax. They saw him dying such a beautiful death with such grace, such meditativeness… seeing it, many were awakened.

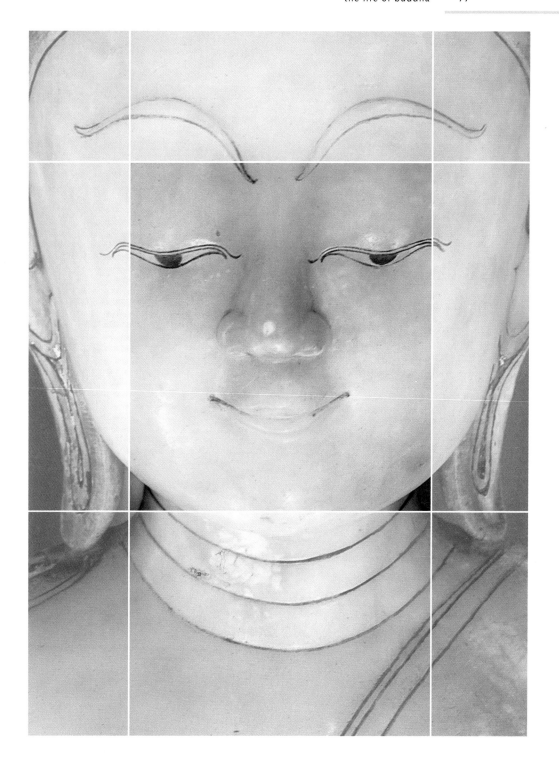

the

teachings

Before enlightenment the master prepares the people who

are going to succeed him, makes them more articulate, makes

them better able to transform the wordless into words, the

absolutely silent into song, the absolutely unmoving into dance.

I have heard

Once Gautam Buddha was passing through a forest and it was the season of autumn. The forest was full of dry leaves, and Ananda, finding him alone, said to him, "I have always wanted to ask, but before the others I could not dare. Just tell me the truth: have you told us everything that you know or are you still holding back a few secrets?"

GAUTAM BUDDHA took a handful of leaves from the ground and said to Ananda, "I have told you only this much—the leaves that you see in my hand—but that which I know is as vast as all the leaves in this great forest. It is not that I want to hold it back, but it is simply impossible! Even to talk about a few leaves is an arduous effort, because it simply goes above your head. You know thoughts, but you have never experienced thoughtlessness. You know emotions, but you have never known a state where all emotions are absent, just as if all the clouds in the sky have disappeared.

"So I am trying my best," he said, "but more than this is not possible to transfer through words. If I can make you understand only this much: that there is much more to life than words can contain; if I can convince you that there is something more than your mind knows, that's enough. Then the seed is sown."

Gautam Buddha, in his whole life, never allowed people to write down what he was saying. His reason was that if you are writing it down, your attention becomes divided. You are no longer total. You have to hear and you have to write, and what he is saying is so subtle that unless you are total, you are going to miss it. So rather than writing it down, try with your totality and intensity to approach your heart, to let it sink within you.

He spoke for forty-two years. After his death, the first task was to write down whatever the disciples remembered; otherwise, it would have been lost to humanity.

They did a great service and also a great disservice. They wrote things down, but they came to see a strange phenomenon—everybody had heard something different. Their memory, their remembrance, was not the same.

Thirty-two schools sprang up, proclaiming, "This is what Buddha has said." Only one man—a man to be remembered forever, his closest disciple, Ananda—who was not even enlightened before Buddha died, out of his humbleness, knew, "I was unenlightened, how can I hear exactly what comes from an enlightened consciousness? I am going to interpret it, I am going to mix it with my own thoughts, I am going to give it my own color, my own nuance. It cannot carry within me the same meaning it has brought, because I don't have yet those eyes that can see and those ears that can hear." Out of this humbleness, the things that he remembered and wrote down became the basic scriptures of Buddhism. They all start with "I have heard Gautam Buddha say..."

All thirty-two philosophical schools—they were led by great scholars, far greater than Ananda, far more capable of interpreting, of bringing meanings to things, of making systems out of words—those thirty-two schools slowly, slowly were rejected. The reason for their rejection was that they had missed a single qualification: "I have heard...." They were saying, "Gautam Buddha said..." and the emphasis was on Gautam Buddha.

Ananda's version is the universally accepted version. Strange...there were enlightened people, but they remained silent because what they had heard was not possible to express. And there were unenlightened, philosophical geniuses, who were articulate and wrote great treatises—but they were not accepted. And the man who was not enlightened, not a great philosopher, just a humble caretaker of Gautam Buddha—his words have been accepted. The reason is his beginning: "I have heard... I don't know whether he was saying it or not. I cannot impose myself on him. All that I can say is what echoed in me. I can talk about my mind—not the silence of Gautam Buddha."

big boat, little boat

BEFORE ENLIGHTENMENT the master prepares the people who are going to succeed him, makes them more articulate, makes them better able to transform the wordless into words, the absolutely silent into song, the absolutely unmoving into dance. Only then will he be able to convey something of help to blind humanity.

Buddha divided his enlightened people into two categories. They both have the same height—there is no quality of lower or higher—they both belong to the same cosmic reality, the fundamental nature. One category is called the *arhatas*—the *arhatas* are the ones who become enlightened and remain silent— and the second category is called *bodhisattvas*. They also become enlightened, but their work is to convey something, some device, some hint about their experience to people.

Arhatas are also called *hinayana*, a little boat in which one man can row and go to the other side. Of course he reaches the other shore. And bodhisattvas are the *mahayana*, a great ship in which thousands of people can move to the other shore. The other shore is the same, but the bodhisattva helps many.

The *arhata* is not articulate; he is a simple, nice, utterly humble person, but will not utter a single word of what he has attained. It is too much for him to say anything. He is completely contented; why should he speak? And anyway, everybody has to find his own way, so why unnecessarily harass people? The *arhata* has his own standpoint.

The *arhata* is someone who makes every effort to become enlightened and once he is enlightened he completely forgets about those who are still groping in the dark. He has no concern with others. It is enough for him to become enlightened. In fact, according to the *arhatas*, even the great idea of compassion is nothing but another kind of attachment.

Compassion is also a relationship; howsoever beautiful and great, it is also a concern with others. It is also a desire. Although it is a good desire, it makes no difference—according to the *arhatas*, desire is a bondage whether it is good or bad. The chains can be made of gold or of steel, it doesn't matter; chains are chains. Compassion is a golden chain.

The *arhata* insists that nobody can help anybody else at all. The very idea of helping others is based on wrong foundations. You can help only yourself.

It may occur to the ordinary mind that the *arhata* is very selfish. But if you look without any prejudice, perhaps he also has something immensely important to declare to the world. Even helping the other is an interference in his life, in his lifestyle, in his destiny, in his future. Hence, *arhatas* don't believe in compassion. Compassion to them is another beautiful desire to keep you tethered to the world of attachments. It is another name—beautiful, but it is still just a name—for a desiring mind.

Why should you be interested in somebody becoming enlightened? It is none of your business. Everybody has absolute freedom to be himself. The *arhata* insists on individuality and its absolute freedom. Even for the sake of good, nobody can be allowed to interfere in anybody else's life.

Hence the moment he becomes enlightened, the *arhata* does not accept disciples, he never preaches, he never helps in any way. He simply lives in his ecstasy. If somebody on his own can drink out of his well, he will not prevent him, but he will not send an invitation. If you come to him on your own accord and sit by his side and drink his presence and get on the path, that is your business. If you go astray, he will not stop you.

In a certain way this is the greatest respect ever paid to individual freedom—to the logical extreme. Even if you are falling into deep darkness, the *arhata* will silently wait. If his presence can help, that is okay, but he is not going to move his hands to help you, give you a hand, pull you out of a ditch. You are free to fall in a ditch and if you can fall in a ditch, you are absolutely capable of getting out of it. The very idea of compassion is foreign to the philosophy of the *arhatas*.

Gautam Buddha accepted that there are a few people who will become *arhatas*, and

their path will be called *hinayana* —"the small vehicle"—the small boat in which only one person can go to the other shore. The *arhata* does not create a big ship or collect a crowd in a Noah's Ark to take them to the further shore. He goes by himself in his small boat, which cannot

even contain two. He is born alone in the world, he has lived and died millions of times alone in the world, and alone he is going to the universal source.

Buddha accepts and respects the way of the *arhata*, but he also knows there are people who have immense compassion and when they become enlightened, their first longing is to share their joy, to share their truth. Compassion is their way. They also have a profound truth. These people are the *bodhisattvas*. They provoke and invite others to the same experience. And they wait on this shore as long as possible to help all seekers who are ready to move on the path, and who just need a guide, a helping hand. The *bodhisattvas* can postpone going to the far shore out of compassion for blind people groping in darkness.

Buddha had such a comprehensive and vast perception that he accepted both—that it is the nature of a few people to be *arhatas*, and it is also the nature of other people to be bodhisattvas. It is the standpoint of Gautam Buddha that such is the case and nothing can be done about it—an *arhata* will be an *arhata*

and a bodhisattva will be a bodhisattva. Their natures have different destinies, although they reach the same goal finally. But after reaching the goal there is a parting of the ways.

The *arhatas* don't stay on this shore even for a single moment. They are tired, they have been long enough in this wheel of *samsara*, moving through birth and death millions of times. It has already been too much. They are bored and don't want to stay even a single minute more. Their boat has arrived, and immediately they start moving toward the further shore. This is their suchness.

Then there are *bodhisattvas* who tell the boatman, "Wait, there is no hurry. I have lingered on this shore long enough—in misery, in suffering, in anguish, in agony. Now all that has disappeared. I am in absolute bliss, silence, and peace, and I don't see that there is anything more on the other shore. So as long as I can manage, I will be here to help people."

Gautam Buddha was certainly one of those people who can see the truth even in contradictions. He accepted both without making anybody feel lower or higher.

suchness

TRY TO UNDERSTAND the word *suchness*. Buddha depends on that word. In Buddha's own language it is *tathata*—suchness. The whole Buddhist meditation consists of living in this word, living with this word, so deeply that the word disappears and you become the suchness.

For example, you are ill. The attitude of suchness is: accept it—and say to yourself, "Such is the way of the body," or, "Things are such." Don't create a fight, don't start struggling. You have a headache—accept it. Such is the nature of things. Suddenly there is a change, because when this attitude comes in, a change follows just like a shadow. If you can accept your headache, the headache disappears.

Try it. If you accept a discomfort, it starts dispersing. Why does this happen? It happens because whenever you are fighting, your energy is divided: half the energy moving into discomfort, the headache, and half the energy fighting the headache—a rift, a gap, and thus the fight. Really, this fight is a deeper headache. Once you accept, once you don't complain, once you don't fight, the energy becomes one within. The rift is bridged, and so much energy is released because now there is no conflict that the release of energy itself becomes a healing force.

Healing doesn't come from outside. All that medicine can do is to help the body bring its own healing force into action. All that a doctor can do is to help you find your own healing power. Health cannot be forced from outside; it is your energy flowering.

This word *suchness* can work so deeply with physical illness, with mental illness, and finally with spiritual illness—this is a secret method—that they all dissolve. Start with the body, because that is the lowest layer. If you succeed there, then higher levels can be tried. If you fail there, then it will be difficult for you to move higher.

Something is wrong in the body: relax and accept it, and simply say inside—not only in words, but also feel it deeply—"such is the nature of things."

A body is a compound with many things combined in it. The body is born, it is prone to death. It is a mechanism, and complex; there is every possibility of something or other going wrong. Accept it, and don't be identified. When you accept you remain above, you remain beyond. When you fight you come down to the same level. Acceptance is transcendence.

When you accept, you are on a hill; the body is left behind. You say, "Yes, such is the nature of it. Things born will have to die. And if things born have to die, they will be ill sometimes. Nothing to be worried about too much"—as if it is not happening to you, just happening in the world of things. This is the beauty: when you are not fighting, you transcend. You are no longer on the same level. This transcendence becomes a healing force. Suddenly the body starts changing.

The same happens to mental worries, tensions, anxieties, anguish. You are worried about a certain thing. What is the worry? You cannot accept the fact; that's the worry. You would like it in some way to be different from how it is happening. You are worried because you have some ideas to enforce on nature.

For example, you are getting old. You are worried. You would like to remain young forever—this is the worry. You love your wife, you depend on her, and she is thinking of leaving, or moving in with another man, and you are worried—worried because what will happen to you? You depend on her so much, you feel so much security with her. When she is gone there will be no security. She has not only been a wife to you, she has been a mother also, a shelter; you can come to her and hide from the world. You can rely on her; she will be there. Even if the whole world is against you, she will not be against

many people are doing—you can force her to stay. The dead body will be there, but the living spirit will have left. Then *that* will be a tension for you.

Against nature, nothing can be done. Love was a flowering, but now the flower has faded. The breeze came into your house, now it has moved into another. Such is the way of things, they go on moving and changing. The world of things is in flux, nothing is permanent there. Don't expect! If you expect permanency in a world where everything is impermanent, you will create worry.

You would like this love to be forever. Nothing can be forever in this world—all that belongs to this world is momentary. This is the nature of things, suchness, *tathata*. So you know now the love has disappeared. It gives you sadness—accept sadness. You feel trembling—accept trembling, don't suppress it. You feel like crying, cry. Accept it! Don't force it, don't put on a face; don't pretend that you are not worried, because that won't help. If you are worried, you are worried. If the wife is leaving, she is leaving. If the love is no more, it is no more. You cannot fight the fact; you have to accept it.

If you accept it grudgingly, then you will be continually in pain and suffering. If you accept it without any complaint—not in helplessness, but in understanding—it becomes suchness. Then you are no longer worried, then there is no problem. The problem arose not because of the fact, but because you couldn't accept it the way it was happening. You wanted it to follow your idea.

you; she is a consolation. Now she is leaving, what will happen to you? Suddenly you are in a panic, worried.

What are you saying? What are you saying with your worry? You are saying that you cannot accept this happening, this should not be so. You expected it otherwise, just the contrary; you wanted this wife to be yours forever and ever, and now she is leaving.

But what can you do? When love disappears what can you do? There is no way; you cannot force love, you cannot force this wife to remain with you. Rather, you can force—that's what

Remember, life is not going to follow you—you have to follow life. Grudgingly or happily, that's your choice. If you follow grudgingly you will be in suffering. If you follow happily you become a buddha, your life becomes an ecstasy.

Buddha also has to die—things won't change specially for him—but he dies in a different way. He dies so happily, as if there is no death. He simply disappears, because he says, "Anything that is born is going to die. Birth implies death, so it is okay, nothing can be done about it."

You can be miserable and die. Then you miss the point, the beauty that death can give to you, the grace that happens in the last moment, the illumination that happens when body and soul part. You will miss that because you are so worried, and you are clinging to the past so much, and to the body, and your eyes are closed. You cannot see what is happening because you cannot accept it. So you close your eyes, you close your whole being and you die—you will die many times, and you will go on missing the point of it.

Death is beautiful if you can accept, if you can open the door with a welcoming heart, a warm reception: "Yes, because if I am born I am going to die. So the day has come, the circle becomes complete." You receive death as a guest, a welcome guest, and the quality of the phenomenon changes immediately. Suddenly you are deathless: the body is dying, you are not dying. You can see it now—only the clothes are dropping, not you. Only the cover, the container, not the content; the consciousness

> *Remember, life is not going to follow you—you have to follow life*

remains in its illumination. More so, because in life, many were the covers on your consciousness. In death it is naked. And when consciousness is totally naked it has a splendor of its own; it is the most beautiful thing in the world.

But for that, an attitude of suchness has to be imbibed. When I say imbibed, I mean imbibed—not just as a mental thought, not the "philosophy of suchness," but your whole way of life becomes suchness. You don't even think about it; it simply becomes natural.

You eat in suchness, you sleep in suchness, you breathe in suchness. You love in suchness, you weep in suchness. It becomes your lifestyle. You need not bother about it, you need not think about it; it is the way you are. That is what I mean by the word *imbibe*. You imbibe it, you digest it. It flows in your blood, it goes deep into your bones; it reaches to the very beat of your heart. You accept.

The word *accept* is not very good. It is loaded—because of you, not because of the word—because you accept only when you feel helpless. You accept grudgingly, you accept halfheartedly. You accept only when you cannot do anything else. But deep down you still wish it were otherwise; you would have been happy if it had been otherwise. You accept like a beggar, not like a king—and the difference is great.

If your wife or husband leaves, finally you come to accept it. What can be done? You weep and cry, and many nights you brood and worry, and many nightmares are around you, and suffering...and then what to do? Time heals, not understanding. Time—and remember, time is needed only because you are not understanding. Otherwise *instant* healing happens. Time is needed because you are not understanding. So, by and by—six months, eight months, a year—things become dim, they are lost in the memory, covered with much dust. And the gap grows over one year; by and by you forget.

Still, sometimes the wound hurts. Sometimes a woman passes on the road and suddenly you remember. Some similarity, the way she walks, and the wife is remembered— and the wound. Then you fall in love with someone. Then more dust gathers, the less you remember. But even with a new woman, sometimes the way she looks...and your wife comes to mind. The way she sings in the bathroom...and the memory surfaces and the wound is there, green.

It hurts because you carry the past. You carry everything; that's why you are so burdened. You carry everything! You were a child; the child is still there, you are carrying it. You were a young man; the young man is still there with all his wounds, experiences, stupidities—he is there. You carry your whole past, layers upon layers—everything is there.

That's why you sometimes regress. If something happens and you feel helpless, you start crying like a child. You have regressed in time, the child has taken over. The child is more efficient in weeping than you, so the child comes in and takes over and you start crying and weeping. You can even start kicking, just like a child in a tantrum. But everything is there.

Why is so much load carried? Because you never really accepted anything. Listen—if you accept something it never becomes a load; the wound is not carried. You accepted the phenomenon; there is nothing to carry from it, you are out of it. Through acceptance you are out of it. Through half-hearted, helpless acceptance, it is carried.

Remember one thing: Anything incomplete is carried by the mind forever and forever. Anything complete is dropped. Mind has a tendency to carry the incomplete things in the hope that some day there may be an opportunity to complete them. You are still waiting for the wife to come back, or for the husband, or for the days that have gone—you are still waiting. You have not transcended the past. And because of such a loaded past, you cannot live in the present. Your present is a mess because of the past, and your future is going to be the same—because the past will become more and more heavy. Every day it is becoming heavier and heavier.

When you really accept, in that attitude of suchness there is no grudge, you are not helpless. Simply you understand that this is the

COMPLETE CONTENTMENT

When you accept everything, your life becomes cheerful. Nobody can make you miserable, no thing can make you miserable.

A man with three hairs on his otherwise bald head came into a hair salon and asked to get his hair shampooed and braided. The hairdresser got on with his job but just as he was about to finish combing it, one of the hairs fell out.

The hairdresser was very embarrassed, but the man only said, "Well, what to do? I guess I will have to part my hair in the middle!"

The hairdresser very carefully put one hair to the right side and was about to put the other to the left side when that one fell out too. The hairdresser could not apologize enough but the man took it calmly.

"Well," he said, "I guess now I will have to run around with my hair all ruffled up."

This is *tathata*, this is total acceptance! You cannot disturb such a man. He is always contented, always finds a way to be contented. It is a great art. And a man who always finds a way to remain contented has the capacity to see things transparently.

Discontent clouds your eyes and your vision; contentment makes your eyes unclouded and your vision clear. You can see through and through; you can understand things as they are.

nature of things.

For example, if I want to go out of the room, I will go out through the door, not through the wall, because to enter the wall will mean hitting my head against it. It is foolish. It is the nature of the wall to hinder, so you don't try to pass through it! It is the nature of the door that you pass through it; because the door is empty, you can pass through it.

When a buddha accepts, he accepts things like the wall and the door. He passes through the door, as that is the only way. First you try to pass through the wall, and you wound yourself in millions of ways. And when you cannot get out—crushed, defeated, depressed, fallen— then you crawl toward the door. You could have gone through the door in the first place! Why did you try to start fighting with the wall?

If you can look at things with clarity, you won't do things like this—trying to make a door out of a wall? If love disappears, it has disappeared! Now there is a wall; don't try to go through it. Now the door is no longer there, the heart is no longer there; the heart has opened to somebody else. You are not alone here; there are others also. The door is no more—for you, it has become a wall. Don't try, and don't knock your head against it. You will be wounded unnecessarily. And wounded, defeated, even the door will not be such a beautiful thing to pass through.

Simply look at things. If something is natural, don't try to force any unnatural thing on it. Choose the door and be out of it. If you are every day trying the foolishness of passing through the wall, then you become

tense and you feel constant confusion. Anguish becomes your very life, the core of it.

Why not look at the facts as they are? Why can't you look at the facts? Because your wishes are too great. You go on hoping against all hope.

Just look: Whenever there is a situation, don't desire anything, because desire will lead you astray. Don't wish and don't imagine. Simply look at the fact with your total consciousness available...and suddenly a door opens. You never move through the wall, you move through the door, unscratched. Then you remain unburdened.

Remember, suchness is an understanding, not a helpless fate. That's the difference. There are people who believe in fate, destiny. They say, "What can you do? God has willed it in such a way. My young child has died, so it is God's will and this is my fate. It was written, it was going to happen."

However, deep down there is rejection. These are just tricks to polish the rejection.

Do you know God? Do you know fate? Do you know that it was written? No, these are all rationalizations—ideas that you use just to console yourself.

The attitude of suchness is not a fatalist attitude. It does not bring in God, or fate, or destiny—nothing. It says, "Simply look at things. Simply look at the facticity of things, understand. And there is a door, there is always a door." You transcend.

Suchness means acceptance with a total, welcoming heart, not in helplessness.

the middle way

GAUTAM BUDDHA was the first man to use the words "to be in the middle," and of course nobody has been able to improve upon the meanings that he gave to the word *middle*.

He called his path the middle path. The first meaning is that if you can avoid both the extremes, the rightist and the leftist—if you can be exactly in the middle of both the extremes, you will not be in the middle, you will have transcended the whole trinity of extremes, *and* the middle. If you drop both the extremes, the middle disappears on its own accord. Middle of what...?

Gautam Buddha's insistence on the middle is not on the middle itself; it is, in fact, a subtle way to persuade you for transformation. But to tell you directly to be transformed may make you apprehensive, afraid. To be in the middle seems to be very simple.

Gautam Buddha played with the word out of sheer compassion. His own term for the middle is *majjhim nikaya*, the middle path. Every extreme has to exclude the other extreme; every extreme has to be in opposition to the other polarity. The negative is against the positive, the minus is against the plus, death is against life. If you take them as extremes, they naturally appear as opposites.

But the man who can stop exactly in the middle immediately transcends all the extremes and the middle together. From the higher standpoint of the transformed being, you can see there is no opposition at all. The extremes are not opposites, not contradictories, but only complementaries.

Life and death are not enemies, they are part of one single process. Death does not end life, it simply renews it. It gives it a new form, a new body, a new plane of consciousness. It is not against life; looked at rightly, it is a process of refreshing life, of rejuvenating life. The day is not against the night....

In existence there is no opposition in anything; all opposites contribute to the whole. Existence is an organic unity. It does not exclude anything; it is all-inclusive.

The man who can stop in the middle comes to know this tremendous experience, that there are no opposites, no contradictories.

> *Existence is an organic unity. It does not exclude anything; it is all-inclusive*

The whole existence is one, and in that oneness all contradictions, all oppositions, all contraries disappear into a single unity. Then life includes death, then day includes night. A man who can experience this organic unity becomes fearless, becomes without any anguish or angst. For the first time he realizes his vastness—he is as vast as the whole of existence. The moment somebody transcends the opposites and comes to know them as complementaries, he is not only part of the whole, he becomes the whole.

Let me tell you the final absurdity. Once in a while—in someone like Gautam Buddha, or Mahavira, or Chuang Tzu, or Lao Tzu—it happens that the part becomes *bigger* than the whole. Absolutely illogical, absolutely unmathematical—but still absolutely right. A Gautam Buddha not only contains the whole, but because of his transformation he is a little bit more than the whole. The whole is not aware of its complementariness. Gautam Buddha is aware of its complementariness, and that's where he transcends and becomes bigger than the whole, although he is still a part of it. To be in the middle is one of the great methods of transforming yourself into the

ultimate. To prepare yourself for being in the middle you will have to drop all extremist ideas. And all your ideas are extremist—either leftist or rightist, either Christian or Mohammedan, either Hindu or Buddhist. You have chosen; you have not allowed a choiceless consciousness, accepting everything that is.

All your prejudices are your choices. I am against all your prejudices, in order to bring you into the middle.

The pope heard that a certain lady in Ireland had produced ten children, so he sent one of his cardinals to grant her his blessings.

When he met the lady, the cardinal was disgusted to learn that she was not a Catholic. "Do you mean to say," he thundered, "that

I have come all this way to meet a sex-mad Protestant?"

This is the way of all prejudices. A *sannyasin* is one who has no prejudices, who has not chosen any ideology to be his own, who is choicelessly aware of all that is. In this choicelessness you will be in the middle. The moment you choose, you choose some extreme. The moment you choose, you choose against something; otherwise there is no question of choice. Being in a choiceless awareness is another meaning of being in the middle.

It happened that a very beautiful young prince—his name was Shrona—listened for the first time to Gautam Buddha. Buddha was visiting the capital of the young man's kingdom, and listening to Gautam Buddha, the prince immediately asked to be initiated. He was well known as a sitar player and he was also well known for luxurious living, utterly luxurious.

It was said that even when he was going upstairs, rather than having a railing on the staircase, naked, beautiful women used to stand all along the staircase so that he could move from one woman's shoulder to another woman's shoulder. That was his way to go upstairs. He used to sleep the whole day because the hangover of the night before was too much; the whole night was a night of celebrations, drinking, eating, music, dance. There was no time for him to sleep in the night.

All these things were well known to the people. Gautam Buddha had never hesitated to give initiation to any man before. Now he hesitated. He said, "Shrona, I know everything about you; I would like you to reconsider; think it over. I am still going to stay in this capital for the four months of the rainy season."

For four months, in the rainy season, Gautam Buddha never used to move around, nor did his *sannyasins*. Eight months of the year they were continuously wandering and sharing their experiences of meditation and higher states of consciousness. But because twenty-five centuries ago there were only mud roads and Buddha had not allowed his disciples to have any possessions—not even an umbrella, no shoes, and just three pieces of cloth. One was for any emergency, and two so that you could change every day after the bath;

more than three were not allowed. In the rainy season when it was pouring it would have been difficult to keep those three cloths dry, and to walk in the mud in the pouring rain might make many people sick.

For that reason he had made it a point that for four months you remain in one place, and those who want to see you can come. Eight months you should go to every thirsty person; for four months let others come to you.

So he said, "There is no hurry, Shrona."

But Shrona said, "Once I have made a decision I never reconsider. You have to give me initiation right now."

Buddha still tried to persuade him: "There is no harm in reconsidering it, because you have lived a life of utter luxury. You have never walked on the road, you have been always in a golden chariot. You have never come out of your luxurious palace and gardens. You have lived continuously with beautiful women, with great musicians, with dancers. All that will not be possible when you become a sannyasin." He told Shrona, "You will not be able. And I don't like anybody to return to the world, because that makes him lose his self-respect. That's why I tell you to consider...."

Shrona said, "I have considered again and again and I still want to be *initiated* right now. The more you tell me to consider the more I become adamant and stubborn."

Gautam Buddha had to relent and give him initiation, and from the second day there was trouble, but trouble that no *sannyasin* of Gautam Buddha had expected. A trouble that perhaps Gautam Buddha had expected started happening.

When all the monks had three pieces of cloth, Shrona started living naked—from one extreme to the other extreme. When all the Buddhist bhikkus were walking on the road, Shrona would always walk by the side of the road in the thorns. When the other monks were resting under the shade of the trees, Shrona would always stand in the hot sun in the middle of the day.

Within six months the beautiful young prince became almost old, a skeleton, black; one could not recognize that this was the man who used to be a great prince and was famous for his luxurious life. His feet were bleeding, his whole body had shrunk, and one night after six months Gautam Buddha went to the tree under which he was sleeping. It is one of the rare occasions when Buddha went in the night to any *sannyasin* for any reason. There is no other incident, at least in the Buddhist scriptures. This is the only incident.

He woke Shrona up and asked him a strange question: "I have heard that when you were a prince you were also the greatest sitarist in the country. Is that right?"

Shrona said, "You could have asked at any time. I don't see the point in the middle of the night."

Gautam Buddha said, "Just wait a little, you will see the point."

Shrona said, "Yes, it is true."

Buddha said, "Now the second question is, if the strings of the sitar are too tight, will there be any music born out of those strings?"

Shrona said, "Of course not. If they are too tight they will be broken."

> *Always find the middle and you have found the path of meditation and the path of liberation*

Buddha said, "If they are too loose, will there be any music?"

Shrona said, "You are asking strange questions in the middle of the night. When the strings are too loose they cannot create any music. A certain tension is needed. In fact to play on a sitar is simple. The real mastery is to keep the strings exactly in the middle, neither too tight nor too loose."

Buddha said, "This is the point I came to make to you. Life is also a musical instrument: too tight and there is no music, too loose and there is no music. The strings of life have to be exactly in the middle, neither too tight nor too loose; only then is there music. And only a master knows how to keep them in the middle. Because you have been a master sitarist I would like you also to become a master of life. Don't move from one extreme to another, from luxury to austerity, from pleasures to self-torture. Try to be exactly in the middle."

Gautam Buddha in a sense is one of the most profound psychologists that the world has produced. To be in the middle in every action of your life—always find the middle and you have found the path of meditation and the path of liberation.

right mindfulness

A HUMAN IS A CROWD, a crowd of many voices—relevant, irrelevant, consistent, inconsistent—each voice pulling in its own way; all the voices pulling the individual apart. Ordinarily, a human is a mess, virtually a kind of madness. You somehow manage to look sane. Deep down, layers and layers of insanity are boiling within you. They can erupt any moment, your control can be lost any moment, because your control is enforced from without. It is not a discipline that has come from your center of being.

For social reasons, economic reasons, political reasons, you have enforced a certain character upon yourself. But many vital forces exist against that character within you. They are continuously sabotaging your character. Hence, every day you commit many mistakes, many errors. Even sometimes you feel that you never wanted to do it. In spite of yourself, you go on committing many mistakes—because you are not one, you are many.

Buddha does not call these mistakes sins, because to call them sin would be condemning. He simply calls them misdemeanors, mistakes, errors. To err is human, not to err is divine, and the way from the human to the divine goes through mindfulness. These many voices within you can stop torturing you, pulling you, pushing you. These many voices can disappear if you become mindful.

In a mindful state mistakes are not committed—not that you control them, but in a mindful state, in an alert, aware state, voices, many voices cease—you become one, and whatsoever you do comes from the core of your being. It is never wrong. This has to be understood.

In the modern Human Potential Movement is a parallel to help you understand it. That's what Transactional Analysis calls the triangle of PAC. P means parent, A means adult, C means child. These are your three layers, as if you are a three-storied building.

The first floor is that of the child, the second floor is that of the parent, the third floor is that of the adult. All three exist together. This is your inner triangle and conflict. Your child says one thing, your parent says something else, and your adult, rational mind says something else.

The child says, "Enjoy." For the child this moment is the only moment; he has no other considerations. The child is spontaneous, but unaware of the consequences—unaware of past, unaware of future. He lives in the moment. He has no values and he has no mindfulness, no awareness. The child consists of felt concepts; he lives through feeling. His whole being is irrational.

Of course he comes into many conflicts with others. He comes into many contradictions within himself, because one feeling helps him to do one thing, then suddenly he starts feeling another emotion. A child never can complete anything. By the time he can complete it, his feeling has changed. He starts many things but never comes to any conclusion. A child remains inconclusive. He enjoys, but his enjoyment is not creative, cannot be creative. He delights, but life cannot be lived only through delight. You cannot remain a child forever. You will have to learn many things, because you are not alone here.

If you were alone then there would be no question—you could have remained a child forever. But the society is there, millions of people are there; you have to follow many rules, you have to hold many values. Otherwise, there would be so much conflict that life would become impossible. The child has to be disciplined, and that's where the parent comes in.

The parental voice in you is the voice of the society, culture, civilization; the voice that makes you capable of living in a world where you are not alone, where there are many individuals with conflicting ambitions, where there is much struggle for survival, where there is much conflict. You have to pave your path, and you have to move cautiously.

The parental voice is that of caution. It makes you civilized. The child is wild; the parental voice helps you to become civilized. The word *civil* is good. It means one who has become capable of living in a city; who has become capable of being a member of a group, of a society.

The child is very dictatorial. The child thinks he is the center of the world. The parents have to teach you that you are not the center of the world—everybody thinks that way. They have to make you more and more alert that there are many people in the world and you are not alone. You have to consider them if you want to be considered by them. Otherwise, you will be crushed. It is a sheer question of survival, of policy, of politics.

The parental voice gives you some commandments—what to do, what not to do. The parent makes you cautious. It is needed.

And then there is the third voice within you, the third layer, when you have become adult and you are no longer controlled by your parents; your own reason has come of age and you can think on your own.

The child consists of felt concepts; the parent consists of taught concepts; and the adult consists of thought concepts. These three layers are continuously in conflict. The child says one thing, the parent says the opposite, and reason may say something totally different.

You see beautiful food. The child says to eat as much as you want. The parental voice says that many things have to be considered—whether you are feeling hungry, whether the smell or the taste of the food is its only appeal. Is this food really nutritious? Is it going to nourish your body or can it become harmful to you? Wait, listen, don't rush. And then there is the rational mind, the adult mind, which may say something entirely different.

There is no need for your adult mind to agree with your parents. Your parents were not omniscient, they were not all-knowing.

They were human beings as fallible as you are, and many times you find loopholes in their thinking. Many times you find them dogmatic, superstitious, believing in foolish things, holding irrational ideologies. Your adult says no. Your parent says do it, your adult says it is not worth doing, and your child is pulling you somewhere else. This is the triangle within you.

If you listen to the child, the parent feels angry. So one part feels good—you can eat as much ice cream as you want—but the parent inside feels angry; a part of you starts condemning. Then you start feeling guilty. The same guilt arises as it used to arise when you were a child. You are no longer a child, but the child has not disappeared. It is there; it is your ground floor, your base, your foundation.

If you follow the child, if you follow the feeling, the parent becomes angry and then you start feeling guilt. If you follow the parent, then your child feels that he is being forced into things which he does not want to do. Then your child feels he is being unnecessarily interfered with, unnecessarily trespassed upon.

> *Buddha says right mindfulness is the only virtue there is*

Freedom is lost when you listen to the parent, and your child starts feeling rebellious.

If you listen to the parent, your adult mind says, "What nonsense! These people never knew anything. You know more, you are more in tune with the modern world, you are more contemporary. These ideologies are just dead ideologies, out of date—why are you bothering?" If you listen to your reason then you also feel as if you are betraying your parents. Again guilt arises. What to do? It is almost impossible to find something on which all these three layers agree.

This is human anxiety. No, never do all these three layers agree on any point. There is no agreement ever.

Now there are teachers who believe in the child. They emphasize the child more. For example, Lao Tzu. He says, "The agreement is not going to come. You drop this parental voice, these commandments, these Old Testaments. Drop all 'shoulds' and become a child again." That's what Jesus says. Lao Tzu and Jesus—their emphasis is to become a child again—because only with the child will you be able to gain your spontaneity, will you again become part of the natural flow, Tao.

Their message is beautiful, but seems to be almost impractical. Sometimes, yes, it has happened—a person has become a child again. But it is so exceptional that it is not possible to think that humanity is ever going to become a child again. It is beautiful like a star... far distant, but out of reach.

Then there are other teachers—Mahavira, Moses, Mohammed, Manu—who say, listen to the parental voice, listen to the moral, what the society says, what you have been taught. Listen and follow it. If you want to be at ease in the world, if you want to be peaceful in the world, listen to the parent. Never go against the parental voice.

That's how the world has followed, more or less. But then one never feels spontaneous, one never feels natural. One always feels confined, caged. And when you don't feel free, you may feel peaceful, but that peacefulness is worthless. Unless peace comes with freedom, you cannot accept it. Unless peace comes with bliss, you cannot accept it. It brings convenience and comfort, but your soul suffers.

Yes, there have been a few people who have achieved through the parental voice, who have attained the truth. But that, too, is very rare. And that world is gone. Maybe in the past, Moses and Manu and Mohammed were useful. They gave commandments to the world: "Do this. Don't do that." They made things simple, very simple. They have not left anything for you to decide; they don't trust that you will be able to decide. They simply give you a ready-made formula—"These are the Ten

Commandments to be followed. You do these and all that you hope, all that you desire, will happen as a consequence. Just be obedient."

All the old religions emphasized obedience too much. Disobedience is the only sin—that's what Christianity says. Adam and Eve were expelled from the garden of God because they disobeyed. God had said not to eat the fruit of the tree of knowledge and they disobeyed. That was their only sin. But every child is committing that sin. The father says, "Don't smoke," but the child tries it. The father says, "Don't go to the movie," but she goes. The story of Adam and Eve is the story of every child. And then condemnation, expulsion....

Obedience is religion for Manu, Mohammed, Moses. But that world has gone, and through it many have not attained. Many became peaceful, good citizens, respectable members of the society, but nothing much.

Then there is the third emphasis on being adult. Confucius, Patanjali, or modern agnostics like Bertrand Russell—the humanists of the world—all emphasize: "Believe only in your own reason." That seems arduous, so much so that one's whole life becomes a conflict. Because you have been brought up by your parents, you have been conditioned by your parents. If you listen only to your reason, you have to deny many things in your being. In fact, your whole mind has to be denied. It is not easy to erase it.

And you were born, as children, without any reason; that, too, is there. Basically you are a feeling being; reason comes very late. It comes when all that has to happen has

happened. Psychologists say a child learns almost seventy-five percent of his whole knowledge by the time he is seven years old. Seventy-five percent of his whole knowledge he has learned by the time he is seven years old, fifty percent by the time he is four years old. This learning happens when you are a child, and reason comes late. It is a late arrival.

It is difficult to live just with reason. People have tried—a Bertrand Russell here and there—but nobody has achieved truth through it, because reason alone is not enough.

All these angles have been chosen and tried, and nothing has worked. Buddha's standpoint is totally different. That's his original contribution to human consciousness. He says not to choose any, he says move in the center of the triangle. Don't choose reason, don't choose the parent, and don't choose the child. Move in the very center of the triangle and remain silent and become mindful. His approach is tremendously meaningful. And then you will be able to have a clear perspective of your being. Out of that perspective and clarity, let the response come.

We can say it in another way. If you function as a child, that is a childish reaction. Many times you function as a child. Somebody says something and you get hurt, and in a tantrum of anger and temper you lose everything. Later on you feel bad about it—that you lost your image. Everybody thinks you are so sober yet you were so childish, and nothing much was at stake.

Or you follow your parental voice, but later on you think that still you are dominated by your parents. You have not yet become an adult, mature enough to take the reins of your life into your own hands.

Sometimes you follow reason, but then you think that reason is not enough, feeling also is needed. And without feeling, a rational being becomes just the head; he loses contact with the body, he loses contact with life, he becomes disconnected. He functions only as a thinking mechanism. But thinking cannot make you alive; in thinking there is no juice of life. It is a dry thing. Then you hanker for something that can again allow your energies to stream, can again allow you to be green and alive and

young. This goes on and you go on chasing your own tail.

Buddha says these are all reactions and any reaction is bound to be partial—only response is total, and whatsoever is partial is a mistake. That's his definition of error: whatsoever is partial is a mistake. Because your other parts will remain unfulfilled and they will take their revenge. Be total. Response is total; reaction is partial.

When you listen to one voice and follow it you are getting into trouble. You will never be satisfied with it. Only one part will be satisfied; the other two parts will be dissatisfied. So two-thirds of your being will be dissatisfied, one-third of your being will be satisfied, and you will always remain in a turmoil. Whatsoever you do, reaction can never satisfy you because reaction is partial.

Respond—response is total. Then you don't function from any point on the triangle, you don't choose; you simply remain in a choiceless awareness. You remain centered. And out of that centering you act, whatsoever it is. It is neither child nor parent nor adult. You have

gone beyond "PAC." It is you now—your being. That PAC is like a cyclone and your center is the center of the cyclone.

Whenever there is a need to respond, the first thing, Buddha says, is to become mindful, become aware. Remember your center. Become grounded in your center. Be there for a few moments before you do anything.

There is no need to think about it because thinking is partial. There is no need to feel about it because feeling is partial. There is no need to find clues from your parents, the Bible, Koran, Gita—these are all "P"—there is no need. Simply remain tranquil, silent, alert—watching the situation as if you are absolutely out of it, aloof, a watcher on the hills.

This is the first requirement—to be centered whenever you want to act. Then out of this centering let the act arise, and whatsoever you do will be virtuous, whatsoever you do will be right.

Buddha says right mindfulness is the only virtue there is. Not to be mindful is to fall into error. To act unconsciously is to fall into error.

WAIT FOR CLARITY

One day Buddha is passing through a forest. It is a hot summer day and he is feeling very thirsty. He says to Ananda, his caretaker, "Ananda, you go back. Just three, four miles back we passed a small stream of water. You bring a little water—take my begging bowl. I am feeling very thirsty and tired."

Ananda goes back, but by the time he reaches the stream, a few bullock carts have just passed through the stream and they have made the whole stream muddy. Dead leaves that had settled into the bed have risen up; it is no longer possible to drink this water—it is too dirty. He comes back empty-handed, and he says, "You will have to wait a little. I will go ahead. I have heard that just two, three miles ahead there is a big river. I will bring water from there."

But Buddha insists. He says, "You go back and bring water from the same stream."

Ananda could not understand the insistence, but if the master says so, the disciple has to follow. Seeing the absurdity of it—that again he will have to walk three, four miles, and he knows that water is not worth drinking—he goes.

When he is going, Buddha says, "And don't come back if the water is still dirty. If it is dirty, simply sit on the bank silently. Don't do anything, don't get into the stream. Sit on the bank silently and watch. Sooner or later the water will be clear again, and then you fill the bowl and come back."

Ananda goes there. Buddha is right: the water is almost clear, the leaves have moved, the dust has settled. But it is not absolutely clear yet, so he sits on the bank just watching the river flow by. Slowly, slowly, it becomes crystal-clear. Then he comes back dancing; he understands why Buddha was so insistent. There was a certain message in it for him, and he has understood the message. He gives the water to Buddha, and he thanks Buddha, touches his feet.

Buddha says, "What are you doing? I should thank *you* because you have brought water for me."

Ananda says, "Now I can understand. First I was angry; I didn't show it, but I was angry because it was absurd to go back. But now I understand the message. This is what I actually needed in this moment. The same is the case with my mind—sitting on the bank of that small stream, I became aware that the same is the case with my mind. If I jump into the stream I will make it dirty again. If I jump into the mind more noise is created, more problems start coming up, surfacing. Sitting by the side of the stream, I learned the technique.

"Now I will be sitting by the side of my mind too, watching it with all its dirtiness and problems and old leaves and hurts and wounds, memories, desires. Unconcerned I will sit on the bank and wait for the moment when everything is clear."

via negativa

THE WAY OF the Buddha is known as *via negativa*—the path of negation. This attitude, this approach has to be understood.

Buddha's approach is unique. All other religions of the world are positive religions, they have a positive goal—call it God, liberation, salvation, self-realization—but there is a goal to be achieved. And positive effort is needed on the part of the seeker. Unless you make hard effort you will not reach the goal.

Buddha's approach is totally different, diametrically opposite. He says you are already that which you want to become, the goal is within you; it is your own nature. You are not to achieve it. It is not in the future, it is not somewhere else. It is you right now, this very moment. But there are a few obstacles and those obstacles have to be removed.

It is not that you have to attain godhood—godhood is your nature—but there are a few obstacles to be removed. Once those obstacles are removed, you are that which you have always been seeking. Even when you were not aware of who you are, you were that. You cannot be otherwise. Obstacles have to be eliminated, dropped. Nothing else has to be added to you.

The positive religion tries to add something to you: virtue, righteousness, meditation, prayer. The positive religion says you are lacking something; you have to be in search of that which you are lacking. You have to accumulate something.

Buddha's negative approach says you are not lacking anything. In fact, you are possessing too many things which are not needed. You have to drop something.

It is like this: You go trekking into the Himalayas. The higher you start reaching, the more you will feel the weight of the things you are carrying with you. Your luggage will become more and more heavy. The higher the altitude, the heavier your luggage will become. You will have to drop things. If you want to reach to the highest peak, you will have to drop all.

Once you have dropped all, once you don't possess anything, once you have become a zero, a nothingness, a nobody, you have reached the peak. Something has to be eliminated, not added to you. Something has to be dropped, not accumulated.

When Buddha attained, somebody asked him, "What have you attained?" He laughed. He said, "I have not attained anything, because whatsoever I have attained was always with me. On the contrary, I have lost many things. I have lost my ego. I have lost my thoughts, my mind. I have lost all that I used to feel I possessed. I have lost my body—I used to think I *was* the body. I have lost all that. Now I exist as pure nothingness. This is my achievement."

Let me explain it to you, because this is central.

According to Buddha's approach, in the beginningless beginning of existence there was absolute sleep; existence was fast asleep, snoring, what Hindus call *sushupti*, a state of dreamless sleep. The whole of existence was asleep in *sushupti*. Nothing was moving, everything was at rest—so tremendously, so utterly at rest, you can say it was not existing at all.

When you move into *sushupti* every night, when dreams stop, you again move into that primordial nothingness. And if in the night there are not a few moments of that primordial nothingness, you don't feel rejuvenated, you don't feel revitalized. If the whole night you dream, and turn and toss in the bed, in the morning you are more tired than you were when you went to bed. You could not dissolve, you could not lose yourself.

If you have been in *sushupti*, in a dreamless state, that means you moved into that beginningless beginning again. From there is energy. From there you come back rested, vitalized, new. Again full of juice, full of life and zest. That, Buddha says, was the beginning; but he calls it the beginningless beginning. It was like *sushupti*, it was tremendously unconscious; there was no consciousness in it. It was just like *samadhi*, enlightenment, with only one difference: in *samadhi* one is fully awake. In that *sushupti*, in that dreamless deep sleep, there was

no consciousness, not even a single flame of consciousness—a dark night. It is also a state of utter blissfulness, but the state is unconscious.

In the morning when you become awake, then you say, "Last night was beautiful, I slept very deeply. It was so beautiful and so full of bliss." But this you say in the morning. When you were really in that sleep, you were not aware; you were absolutely unconscious. When you awake in the morning, then you look retrospectively backward and then you are able to recognize that: "Yes, it was beautiful!"

When a person awakes in *samadhi*, then he recognizes that: "All my lives of the past were all blissful. I have been in a tremendously enchanted, magic world. I have never been miserable." *Then* one recognizes, but right now you cannot recognize—you are unconscious. The primordial state is full of bliss but there is nobody to recognize it. Trees still exist in that primordial state; mountains and the ocean and the clouds and the deserts still exist in that primordial consciousness. It is a state of unconsciousness.

This, Buddha calls nothingness, pure nothingness, because there was no distinction, no demarcation. It was nebulous: no form, no name. It was like a dark night.

Then came the explosion. Scientists also talk about this explosion; they call it the Big Bang. Then everything exploded.

The nothingness disappeared and things appeared. It is still a hypothesis, even for scientists, because nobody can go back. For scientists it is a hypothesis, the most probable hypothesis at most.

There are many theories proposed, propounded, but the Big Bang theory is generally accepted—that out of that nothingness, things exploded like a seed explodes and becomes a tree. And in the tree are millions of seeds, and then they explode. A single seed can fill the earth with greenery. This is what explosion means.

Have you observed the fact? Such mystery! A small seed, barely visible, can explode and fill the whole earth with forests. Not only the whole earth, but all the earths possible in existence. A single seed! And if you break the seed, what will you find inside it? Nothingness, just pure nothing. Out of this nothingness, the whole has evolved.

For scientists it is just a hypothesis, an inference. For a Buddha it is not a hypothesis—it is his experience. He has known this happening within himself.

I will try to explain it to you, how one comes to know this beginningless beginning—because you cannot go back, but there is a way to move ahead. And, just as everything moves in a circle, time also moves in a circle.

In the West, the concept of time is linear; time moves in a line, horizontal; it goes on and on and on. But in the East, we believe in a circular time, and the Eastern concept of time is closer to reality, because every movement is circular. The earth moves in a circle, the moon moves in a circle, the stars move in a circle. The year moves in a circle, life moves in a circle: birth, childhood, youth, old age—again birth! What you call death is again birth. Again childhood, again youth... and the wheel goes on moving. The year goes round and round: summer comes, and the rains, and the winter and again summer. Everything is moving in a circle. Why should there be an exception for time? Time also moves in a circle. One cannot go backward, but if you go on ahead, moving ahead, one day, time starts moving in a circle. You reach the beginningless beginning or, now you can call it, the endless end.

Buddha has known it, experienced it.

What the scientists call the Big Bang, I call cosmic orgasm. That seems to me more meaningful. "Big Bang" looks a little ugly, too technological, inhuman. Cosmic orgasm—the cosmos exploded into orgasm. Millions of forms were born out of it. And it was a tremendously blissful experience, so let us call it cosmic orgasm.

In that orgasm three things developed. First, the universe, what we in the East call *sat*. Out of the universe developed life, what we call *ananda*. And out of life developed mind, what we call *chit*. *Sat* means being; *ananda* means celebrating the being—when a tree comes to bloom, it is celebrating its being. And *chit* means consciousness—when you have become conscious about your bliss, about your celebration. These three states: *satchitananda*.

Humanity has come up to the mind. The rocks are still at the first stage, the universe—they exist but they don't flower, they don't celebrate. They are closed, coiled upon themselves. Some day they will start moving, some day they will open their petals, but right now they are caved within themselves, completely closed.

Trees and animals have come to the next stage, life—so happy, so beautiful, so colorful. The birds go on singing, and the trees go on blooming. This is the second stage, life. The third stage, only humans have reached: the state of mind, the state of *chit*—consciousness.

Buddha says these three are like a dream. The first, the beginningless beginning, the primordial state, is like sleep—*sushupti*. These three are like a drama that is unfolding. If you move beyond mind, if you start moving toward meditation, that is, toward no-mind, again another explosion happens. But now it is no longer an explosion, it is implosion. Just as one day the explosion happened and millions of things were born out of nothingness, so when implosion happens, forms and names disappear—again nothingness is born out of it. The circle is complete.

Scientists talk only about explosion, they don't talk about implosion yet, which is illogical. Because if explosion is possible, then implosion is also possible.

A seed is thrown into the earth. It explodes. A tree is born, then on the tree again seeds are born. What is a seed now? When the seed explodes, it is a tree. When the tree implodes, it is again a seed. The seed was carrying a tree; it opened itself and became a tree. Now the tree again closes itself, caves in, becomes a small seed.

If explosion happened in the world, as scientists now trust, then the Buddhist idea of implosion is also a reality. Explosion cannot exist without implosion. They go together. Implosion means that again mind moves into life, life moves into universe, universe moves into nothingness and the circle is complete. Nothingness moves into universe, universe moves into life, life moves into mind, mind again moves into life, life again into universe, universe again into nothingness... the circle is complete.

After implosion, when it has happened, when everything has again come to nothingness, there is a difference. The first nothingness was unconscious; this second nothingness is conscious. The first was like darkness, the second is like light. The first was like night, the second is like day. The first we called *sushupti*; the second we will call *jagriti*— awareness, fully awake. This is the whole circle.

The first, scientists call the Big Bang theory because there was so much explosion and so much noise. It *was* a big bang. A moment

> *Religion means becoming consciousness of that which you are*

T.S. Eliot has written a few beautiful lines:

We shall not cease from exploration
and the end of all our exploring
will be to arrive where we started
and know the place for the first time.

This is the meaning of Buddha's renunciation, his path of *via negativa*. You have to come to the point from where you started. You have to know that which you already are. You have to achieve that which is already achieved. You have to achieve that which, in the nature of things, cannot be lost; there is no way to lose contact with it. At the most we can become unconscious about it.

Religion means becoming conscious of that which you are. It is not a search for something new; it is an effort to know that which has always been there, is eternal. From the beginningless beginning to the endless end, it is always there.

Because the path is negative, there are a few difficulties about it. It is difficult to be attracted to Buddhism, because ordinarily the mind wants something positive to cling to, the mind wants something to achieve—and Buddha says there is nothing to achieve; rather, on the contrary, you have to lose something.

Just the idea of losing something is unappealing, because our social concept is of having more and more and more. Buddha says *having* is the problem. The more you have, the less you are; because the more you have, the less you can recognize yourself—you are lost.

before, everything was silent, there was no noise, no sound, and after one moment, when existence exploded, there was so much sound and so much noise. All sorts of noises started.

What happens when the explosion disappears into an implosion? The soundless sound. Now there is no longer any noise. Again everything is silent. This is what Zen calls the sound of one hand clapping. This is what Hindus have called *anahatnada, omkar*—the soundless sound.

The first, Hindus have called *nadavisphot*—big bang, the sound exploded. And the second is when the sound again moves into silence; the story is complete. Science is still clinging to the half story; the other half is missing. And one who watches this whole play—from sushupti, the dark night of the soul, to dream, and from dream to awareness—the one who watches it all is the witness. The fourth state we call *turiya*—the one who witnesses all. That one known, you become a buddha; that one known, experienced, you have attained.

But the point to be understood is this: that all the time, when you are asleep or dreaming or awake, you are that. Sometimes not aware, sometimes aware, that is the only difference—your nature remains the same.

Your emptiness, your space is covered too much by things. A rich man is poor—poor because he has no space left, poor because everything is occupied, poor because he does not know any emptiness in his being. Through emptiness you have the glimpses of the primordial and the ultimate—and they are both the same.

It is difficult to be attracted to Buddhism. Only rare people who have a quality of tremendous intelligence can be attracted to it. It cannot become a mass religion. When it became a mass religion it became so only when it lost all its originality, when it compromised with the masses.

In India Buddhism disappeared because the followers of Buddha insisted on its purity. There are people who think that it is because Hindu philosophers and Hindu mystics refuted Buddhism, that's why Buddhism disappeared from India—that is wrong. It cannot be refuted. Nobody has ever refuted it. There is no possibility of refuting it, because in the first place it is not based on logic.

If something is based on logic, you can destroy it by logic. If something is based on logical proof, you can refute it. Buddhism is not based on logic at all. It is based on experience; it is existential. It does not believe in any metaphysics—how can you refute it? It never asserts anything about any concept. It simply describes the innermost experience. It has no philosophy, so philosophers cannot refute it.

But it is true that Buddhism disappeared from India. The basic cause of its disappearance is that Buddha and his followers

insisted on its purity. The very insistence on its purity became an unbridgeable gap. The masses could not understand it—only rare people, a very cultured, intelligent, aristocratic few, a chosen few could understand what Buddha meant. Those who understood it, in their very understanding were transformed. But for the masses it was meaningless. It lost its hold on the masses.

In China it succeeded. In Tibet, in Ceylon, in Burma, in Thailand, in Japan, it succeeded— because the missionaries, the Buddhist missionaries who went out of India, seeing what had happened in India, became very compromising. They compromised. They started talking in the positive language. They started talking about achievement, bliss, heaven—from the back door they brought in everything that Buddha had denied. Again

the masses were happy. The whole of China, the whole of Asia was converted to Buddhism—except India. In India they tried to give only the pure message, without any compromise; that was not possible. In China, Buddhism became a mass religion, but then it lost its truth.

Let me tell you one anecdote:

A junior devil has been sent to earth to look around and see how things are progressing. He quickly returns to hell, horrified, and obtains an interview with Beelzebub, the chief devil himself.

"Sir," he sputters, "something awful has happened! There is a man with a beard walking around on earth, speaking truth, and people are beginning to listen to him. Something has to be done immediately."

Beelzebub smiles pleasantly, puffing on his pipe but making no comment.

"Sir! You don't realize the seriousness of the situation," continues the distraught junior devil. "Pretty soon all will be lost!"

Beelzebub removes his pipe slowly, taps it out on the ashtray, and sits back in his swivel chair, hands behind his head.

"Don't worry, son," he counsels. "We will let it go on a little longer and, when it has progressed far enough, we will step in and help them to organize!"

Once a religion is organized, it is dead—because you can organize a religion only when you compromise with the masses. You can organize a religion only when you follow the desires of the common mass. You can organize a religion only when you are ready to make it politics and you are ready to lose its religiousness.

A religion can be organized only when it is no longer a real religion. That is to say, a religion cannot be organized *as religion*. Organized, it is no longer religion. A real religion basically remains unorganized, remains a little chaotic, remains a little disorderly—because real religion is freedom.

the religionless religion

THE WAY OF THE Buddha is not a religion in the ordinary sense of the term, because it has no belief system, no dogma, no scripture. It does not believe in God, it does not believe in the soul, it does not believe in any paradise. It is a tremendous unbelief—and yet it is a religion. It is unique. Nothing has ever happened like it before in the history of human consciousness, and nothing afterward.

Buddha remains utterly unique, incomparable. He says that God is nothing but a search for security, a search for safety, a search for shelter. You believe in God, not because God is there; you believe in God because you feel helpless without that belief. Even if there is no God, you will invent one. The temptation comes from your weakness. It is a projection.

Humans feel limited, helpless, almost victims of circumstance—not knowing from where they come, not knowing where they are going, not knowing why they are here. If there is no God it is difficult for ordinary people to have any meaning in life. The ordinary mind will go berserk without God. God is a prop—it helps you, it consoles you, it comforts you. It says, "Don't be worried—the Almighty God knows everything about why you are here. He is the Creator, He knows why He has created the world. You may not know but the Father knows, and you can trust in Him." It is a great consolation.

The very idea of God gives you a sense of relief—that you are not alone; that somebody is looking after the affairs; that this cosmos is not just chaos, it is truly a cosmos; that there is a system behind it; that there is logic behind it; it is not an illogical jumble of things; it is not anarchy. Somebody rules the cosmos; the sovereign King is there looking after each small detail—not even a leaf moves without His moving it. Everything is planned. You are part of a great destiny. Maybe the meaning is not known to you, but the meaning is there because God is there.

God brings a tremendous relief. One can believe that life is not accidental; there is a certain undercurrent of significance, meaning, destiny. God brings a sense of destiny.

Buddha says there is no God—it simply shows that we do not know why we are here. It shows our helplessness. It shows that there is no meaning available to us. By creating the idea of God we can believe in meaning, and we can live this futile life with the idea that somebody is looking after it.

Just think: you are in an airplane and somebody says, "There is no pilot." Suddenly there will be a panic. No pilot?! No pilot means you are doomed. Then somebody says, "The pilot is there, but invisible. We may not be able to see the pilot, but he is there; otherwise, how is this beautiful mechanism functioning? Just think of it: everything is going so beautifully, there must be a pilot! Maybe we are not capable of seeing him, maybe we are not yet prayerful enough to see him, maybe our eyes are closed, but the pilot is there. Otherwise,

how is it possible? This airplane has taken off, it is flying perfectly well, the engines are humming. Everything is a proof that there is a pilot."

If somebody proves it, you relax again into your chair. You close your eyes, you start dreaming again, you can fall asleep. The pilot is there; you need not worry.

Buddha says: The pilot exists not; it is a human creation. Humankind has created God in its own image. It is a human invention— God is not a discovery, it is an invention. And God is not the truth, it is the greatest lie there is.

That's why I say Buddhism is not a religion in the ordinary sense of the term. A Godless religion—can you imagine? When for the first time Western scholars became aware of Buddhism, they were shocked. They could not comprehend that a religion can exist and be without God. They had known only Judaism, Christianity, and Islam. All these three religions are in a way very immature compared with Buddhism.

Buddhism is religion come of age. Buddhism is the religion of a mature mind. Buddhism is not childish at all, and it doesn't support any childish desires in you. It is merciless. Let me repeat it: There has never been a man more compassionate than Buddha, but his religion is merciless.

In fact, in that mercilessness he is showing his compassion. He will not allow you to cling to any lie. Howsoever consoling, a lie is a lie. Those who have given you the lie are not friends to you, they are enemies—because under the impact of the lie you will live a life full of lies. The truth has to be brought to you, howsoever hard, howsoever shattering, howsoever shocking. Even if you are annihilated by the impact of the truth, it is good.

Buddha says: The truth is that human religions are human inventions. You are in a dark night surrounded by alien forces. You need someone to hang on to, someone to cling to. And everything that you can see is changing—your father will die one day and you will be left alone, your mother will die one day and you will be left alone, and you will be an orphan. From childhood you have been accustomed to having a father to protect you, a mother to love you. Now that childish desire will again assert itself: you will need a father figure. If you cannot find it in the sky, then you will find it in some politician.

Stalin became the father of Soviet Russia; they had dropped the idea of God. Mao became the father of China; they had dropped the idea of God. But people are such that they cannot live without a father figure. People are childish! There are very few rare people who grow to be mature.

> " Don't hide behind beliefs and masks and theologies. Take hold of your life in your own hands "

My own observation is this: people remain near the age of seven, eight, or nine. Their physical bodies go on growing but their minds remain stuck somewhere below the age of ten. Christianity, Judaism, Islam, Hinduism, are religions below the age of ten. They fulfill whatever are your needs; they are not too concerned with the truth. They are more concerned with you, concerned about how to console you.

The situation is such: the mother has died and the child is crying and weeping, and you have to console the child. So you tell lies. You pretend that the mother has not died: "She has gone for a visit to the neighbors—she will be coming. Don't be worried, she will be coming right back." Or, "She has gone for a long journey. It will take a few days but she will be back." Or, "She has gone to visit God—nothing to be worried about. She is still alive—maybe she has left the body, but the soul lives forever."

Buddha is the most shattering individual in the history of humanity. His whole effort is to drop all props. He does not say to believe in anything. He is an unbeliever and his religion is that of unbelief. He does not say "believe," he says "doubt."

Now, you have heard about religions that say "Believe!" You have never heard about a religion that says "Doubt!" Doubt is the very methodology—doubt to the very core, doubt to the very end, doubt to the very last. When you have doubted everything, and you have dropped everything through doubt, then reality arises in your vision. It has nothing to do with your beliefs about God. It is nothing like your so-called God. Then arises reality, absolutely unfamiliar and unknown.

But that possibility exists only when all beliefs have been dropped and the mind has come to a state of maturity, understanding, and acceptance that "Whatsoever is, is, and we don't desire otherwise. If there is no God, there is no God, and we don't have any desire to project a God. If there is no God, then we accept it." This is what maturity is: to accept the fact and not to create a fiction around it; to accept the reality as it is, without trying to sweeten it, without trying to decorate it, without trying to make it more acceptable to your heart. If it is shattering, it is shattering If it is shocking, it is shocking. If the truth kills, then one is ready to be killed.

Buddha is merciless. And nobody has ever opened the door of reality so deeply, so profoundly as he has done. He does not allow you any childish desires. He says: Become more aware, become more conscious, become more courageous. Don't hide behind beliefs and masks and theologies. Take hold of your life in your own hands. Burn bright your inner light and see whatsoever is. And once you have become courageous enough to accept it, it is a benediction. No belief is needed.

That is Buddha's first step towards reality, to say that all belief systems are poisonous; all belief systems are barriers.

He is not a theist. And remember he is not an atheist, either—because, as he says, a few people believe that there is God and a few people believe that there is no God, but both are believers. His nonbelief is so deep

that even those who say there is no God, and believe in it, are not acceptable to him. He says that just to say there is no God makes no difference. If you remain childish, you will create another source of God.

For example, Karl Marx declared there was no God, but then he created a God out of history. History becomes the God; the same function is being done now by history that was done previously by the concept of God. What was God doing? God was the determining factor; God was the managing factor. It was God who was deciding what should be and what should not be. Marx dropped the idea of God, but then history became the determining factor. Then history became the fate, then history became *kismet*—then history is determining everything. Now, what is history? Marx says communism is an inevitable state. History has determined that it will come, and everything is determined by history. Now history becomes a super-God.

But somebody or something to determine reality is needed. People cannot live with indeterminate reality. People cannot live with reality as it is—chaotic, accidental. People cannot live with reality without finding some idea which makes it meaningful, relevant, continuous, which gives it a shape that reason can understand; which can be dissected, analyzed into cause and effect.

Freud dropped the idea of God, but then the unconscious became the God—then everything is determined by the unconscious, and people are helpless in the hands of the unconscious. These are new names for God; it

is a new mythology. The Freudian psychology is a new mythology about God. The name is changed but the content remains the same. The label has changed, the old label has been dropped and a fresh, newly painted label has been put on it—it can deceive people who are not very alert. But if you go deeper into Freudian analysis you will immediately see that the unconscious is doing the same work that God used to do.

So what is wrong with poor God? If you have to invent something—and one has always to be determined by something...history, economics, the unconscious, this and that—if one cannot be free, then what is the point of changing mythologies, theologies? It makes not much difference. You may be a Hindu, you may be a Mohammedan, you may be a Christian, you may be a Jew—it makes not much difference. Your mind remains childish, you remain immature. You remain in search, you continue to search for a father figure—someone, somewhere, who can explain everything, who can become the ultimate explanation. The mature mind is one who can remain without any search even if there is no ultimate explanation of things.

That's why Buddha says, "I am not a metaphysician." He has no metaphysics. Metaphysics means the ultimate explanation about things, and he has no ultimate explanation. He does not say, "I have solved the mystery." He does not say, "Here, I hand over to you what truth is." He says, "The only thing that I can give to you is an impetus, a thirst, a tremendous passion to become aware,

to become conscious, to become alert; to live your life so consciously, so full of light and awareness, that *your life* is solved."

Not that you come to some ultimate explanation of existence—nobody ever has. Buddha denies metaphysics completely. He says metaphysics is a futile search.

The first thing is that he denies God.

The second thing is that he denies paradise, heaven. He says: Your heaven, your paradise, are nothing but your unfulfilled sexual desires, unfulfilled instincts being projected into the other life, the life beyond, the life after death. And he seems to be absolutely right. If you see the descriptions of heaven and paradise in Islam, in Christianity, in Judaism, you will understand perfectly what he is saying. Whatever remains unfulfilled here, you go on projecting in the hereafter. But the desire seems to be the same!

Hindus say there are trees they call *kalpvraksha*—you sit under them and whatsoever you desire, without any lapse of time, is fulfilled. You desire a beautiful woman, she is there—immediately, instantly. In the West you have invented instant coffee and things like that just recently. India discovered a wish-fulfilling tree, and down the centuries has believed in it. The tree is instantly fulfilling—truly instantly, without any time lapse. Here the idea arises, there it is fulfilled; not a single second passes between the two. The idea *is* its fulfillment—you desire a beautiful woman, she is there. You desire delicious food, it is there. You desire a comfortable bed to rest on, it is there.

Now, this is simple psychological analysis. That man is unfulfilled in life, and he spends his whole life trying to fulfill it—still he finds it cannot be fulfilled, so he has to project his desires into the future. Not that in the future they can be fulfilled—desire as such is unfulfillable.

Buddha has said: The very nature of desire is that it remains unfulfilled. Whatever you do, regardless of what you do about it, it remains unfulfilled—that is the intrinsic nature of desire. *Desire as such* remains unfulfilled.

So you can sit under a wish-fulfilling tree, it won't make any difference. You can feel many times that your desire is being fulfilled, and again it arises. Ad infinitum it will go on arising again and again and again.

The Christian, the Muslim, the Jew, the Hindu—all heavens and paradises are nothing but unfulfilled projected desires, repressed desires, frustrated desires. Of course, they console man very much: "If you have not been able to fulfill them here—there. Sooner or later you will reach God; the only thing you have to do is go on praying to him, go on bowing down before some image or some idea or some ideal, and keep him happy. Keep God happy, and then you will reap a great crop of pleasures and gratifications. That will be God's gift to you for your prayers, for your appreciation, for continuous surrender, for again and again touching his feet, for your obedience—that is going to be the reward."

The reward is, of course, after death, because even cunning priests cannot deceive you in this life—even they cannot deceive. They know that desire remains unfulfilled, so they have to invent an afterlife. Nobody has known the afterlife but people can be deceived very easily. If somebody comes and says to you, "God can fulfill your desire here and now," it will be difficult to prove it—because nobody's desire has ever been fulfilled here and now. Then their God will be at stake. They have invented a very cunning device; they say, "After this life...."

Is your God not potent enough to fulfill your desires here? Is your God not potent enough to create wish-fulfillment trees on the earth? Is your God not powerful enough to do something while people are alive? If he cannot fulfill anything here, what is the proof that he is going to fulfill anything hereafter?

Buddha says: Look into the nature of desire. Watch the movement of desire; it is very subtle. And you will be able to see two things: one, that desire by its very nature is unfulfillable. And second, the moment you understand that desire is unfulfillable, desire disappears and you are left desireless. That is the state of peace, silence, tranquility. That is the state of fulfillment! People never come to fulfillment through desire; they come to fulfillment only by transcending desire.

Desire is a great opportunity to understand the functioning of your own mind—how it functions, what the mechanism of it is. And when you have understood that, in that very understanding is transformation. Desire disappears, leaves no trace behind. And when you are desireless, not desiring anything, you are fulfilled. Not that desire is fulfilled, but when desire is transcended there is fulfillment.

Now see the difference. Other religions say, "Desires can be fulfilled in the other world." The worldly people say, "Desires can be fulfilled here." The communists say, "Desires can be fulfilled here. Just a different social structure is needed, just the capitalists have to be overthrown, the proletariat has to take over, the bourgeoisie has to be destroyed, that's all—and desires can be fulfilled here, heaven can be created on this earth here."

> *Desire cannot be fulfilled because its nature is to remain unfulfilled and projected in the future*

The worldly people say, "You can fulfill your desires—struggle hard." That's what the West is doing: "Struggle, compete, succeed by any means and methods. Acquire more wealth, more power!" That's what politicians all over the world are doing: "Become more powerful and your desires can be fulfilled." That's what scientists say, that only a few more technologies have to be invented and paradise is just around the corner. And what do your religions say? They don't say anything different. They say, "Desires can be fulfilled, but not in this life—after death." That is the only difference between the so-called materialists and so-called religious.

To Buddha, both are materialists; and to me also, both are materialists. Your so-called religious people and your so-called irreligious people are both in the same boat. Not a bit of difference! Their attitudes are the same, their approaches are the same.

Buddha is religious in this way, that he says: *Desire cannot be fulfilled*. You have to look into desire. Neither here nor anywhere else has desire ever been fulfilled—never. It has never happened and never is it going to happen because it is against the nature of desire. What

is desire? Have you ever looked into your desiring mind? Have you encountered it? Have you tried any meditation on it? What is desire?

You desire a certain house; you work for it, you work hard. You destroy your whole life for it—then the house is there. But is fulfillment there? Once the house is there, suddenly you feel empty—you feel more empty than before, because before there was an occupation to achieve this house. Now that it is there, immediately your mind starts looking for something else to occupy it. Now there are bigger houses; your mind starts thinking of those bigger houses. There are bigger palaces.... You desire a partner and you have achieved your desire, then suddenly your hands are again empty. Again you start desiring some other lover. This is the nature of desire. Desire always goes ahead of you. Desire is always in the future.

Desire is a hope. Desire cannot be fulfilled because its nature is to remain unfulfilled and projected in the future. It is always on the horizon. You can rush, you can run toward the horizon, but you will never reach it: wherever you go you will find the horizon has receded and the distance between you and the horizon remains absolutely the same. You have ten thousand dollars, your desire is for twenty thousand dollars; you have twenty thousand dollars, your desire is for forty thousand dollars. The distance is the same; the mathematical proportion is the same.

Whatever you have, desire always stays ahead of it.

Buddha says: *Abandon hope, abandon desire*. In abandoning hope, in abandoning desire, you will be here now. Without desire, you will be fulfilled. It is desire that is deceiving you.

So when Buddha said that these so-called religious people are all materialists, of course the Hindus were angry—very angry; they had never been so angry against anybody. They tried to uproot Buddha's religion from India, and they succeeded. Buddhism was born in India but Buddhism doesn't exist now in India, because the religion of the Hindus is one of the most materialistic religions in the world. Just look in the Vedas: all prayer, all worship is just asking for more, for more, from gods or from God—all sacrifice is for more. All worship is desire oriented. "Give us more! Give us plenty! Better crops, better rain, more money, more health, more life, more longevity—give us more!" The Veda is nothing but desire written large, and sometimes ugly. In the Veda not only do the sages pray "Give us more!"—they also pray: "Don't give to our enemies! Give more milk to my cow, but let the enemy's cow die, or let its milk disappear."

What type of religion is this? Even to call it religion looks absurd. If this is religion, then what is materialism? Buddha himself had gone to many masters while he was searching, but from everywhere he came back empty-handed—because he could not see that anybody had understood the nature of desire. They themselves were desiring; of course, their desire was projected in the faraway future, the other life, but still the object of desire was the

same, the desiring mind was the same. It is only a question of time.

A few people desire things for before their death, a few people desire things for after their death, but what is the difference? There is no difference. They desire the same things—they desire! The desire is the same.

Buddha went to many teachers and was frustrated. He could not see religion flowering anywhere, blossoming—they were all materialistic people. They were great ascetics: somebody was fasting for months, somebody was standing for months, somebody had not slept for years, and they were just skeletons. You could not call them worldly and materialistic if you looked at their bodies... but look at their minds, ask them, "Why are you fasting? Why are you trying so hard? For what?" and there surfaces the desire—to

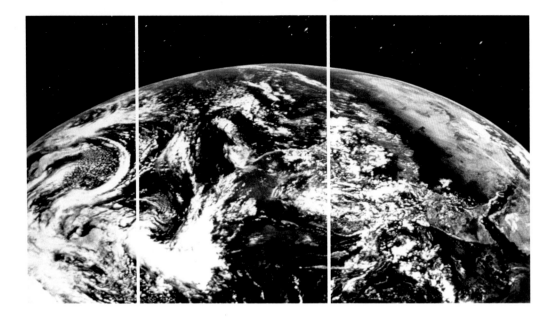

attain to paradise, to heaven, to have eternal gratification in the afterlife.

Listen to their logic and they all will say, "Here, things are fleeting. This life is temporary. Even if you attain, everything is taken away when you die, so what is the point? This life is not going to be forever. We are searching for something that will remain forever—we are after immortality, we are after *absolute* gratification. People who are running after desires here in this life are fools, because death will take everything away. You accumulate wealth and here comes death and all is left behind. We are searching for some treasure that we can take with ourselves, that will never be lost, that cannot be stolen, no government can tax it—nobody can take it away, not even death."

You call these people religious people? They seem to be even worldlier than the so-called worldly; they are more materialistic than the materialists. Of course, their materialism is garbed in a disguise; their materialism has a flavor of spirituality—but it is a deception. It is as if on a dung heap you have thrown some beautiful perfume. The dung heap remains the dung heap; the perfume can deceive only fools.

Buddha was not fooled, he could see through and through. And he could always see that the desire was there. If desire is there you are a materialist and you are worldly.

So he is not preaching any paradise to you, he does not believe in any paradise. Not that he does not believe in blissfulness, no. He believes in blissfulness, but that is not a belief. When all paradises are lost, when all desires drop, suddenly it is your innermost nature to be blissful. For that, nothing is needed—no virtue is needed, no asceticism is needed, no sacrifice is needed. Just understanding is enough.

The way of the Buddha is the way of understanding.

And the third thing: He does not believe in the soul—no God, no paradise, no soul. Now, this seems to be very difficult.

We can accept that there is no God—maybe it is just a projection; who has seen it? We can accept that there is no paradise—maybe it is just our unfulfilled desire, dreaming about it. But no soul? Then you take the whole ground from underneath. No soul? Then what is the point of it all? If there is no soul in man, if there is nothing immortal in man, then why make so much effort? Why meditate? For what?

Buddha says this idea of the self is a misunderstanding. You *are*, but you are not a self. You *are*, but you are not separate from the universe. The separation is the root idea in the concept of self: if I am separate from you then I have a self; if you are separate from me then you have a self.

But Buddha says: *Existence is one*. There are no boundaries. Nobody is separate from anybody else. We live in one ocean of consciousness. We are one consciousness—deluded by the boundaries of the body, deluded by the boundaries of the mind. And because of the body and the mind, and because of the identification with the body and mind, we think we are separate, we think we are "selves." This is how we create the ego.

It is just like on the map you see India, but on the earth itself there is no India—only on the maps of the politicians. On the map you see the American continent and the African continent as separate, but deep down, down under the oceans, the earth is one. All continents are together, they are all one earth.

We are separate only on the surface. The deeper we go, the more the separation disappears. When we come to the very core of our being, suddenly it is universal—there is no selfhood in it, no soul there.

Buddha has no belief in God, in the soul, in paradise. Then what is his teaching? His teaching is a way of life, not a way of belief. His teaching is scientific, empirical, practical. He is not a philosopher, not a metaphysician. He is a down-to-earth man.

Buddha says: You can change your life—these beliefs are not needed. In fact, these beliefs are the barriers for the real change. Start with no belief, start with no metaphysics, start with no dogma. Start absolutely naked and nude, with no theology, no ideology. Start empty! That is the only way to come to truth.

I was reading an anecdote:

The traveling salesman opened the Gideon Bible in his motel room. On the front page he read the inscription: "If you are sick, read Psalm 18; if you are troubled about your family, read Psalm 45; if you are lonely, read Psalm 92."

He was lonely, so he opened to Psalm 92 and read it. When he was through, he noticed on the bottom of the page the handwritten words: "If you are still lonely call 888–3468 and ask for Myrtle."

> *Buddha is down-to-earth. He never flies high into metaphysics*

If you look deep down into your scriptures you will always find a footnote that will be more true. Look for the footnote on every scripture page! Sometimes it may not be written in visible ink, but if you search hard you will always find it there—a footnote which is more real.

Buddha says all your scriptures are nothing but your desires, your instincts, your greed, your lust, your anger. All your scriptures are nothing but creations of your mind, so it is bound to be that they will carry all the seeds of your mind. Scriptures are man-made. That's why religions try so hard to prove that *their* scripture at least is not man-made.

Christians say the Bible is not man-made; the Ten Commandments were delivered to Moses directly from God, directly from the boss himself. The New Testament is a direct message from his own son, the only begotten son, Jesus Christ. It has nothing to do with humanity, it comes from above.

Hindus say that the Vedas are not man-made, they are God-made. And the same story goes on being repeated: Mohammedans say the Koran descended on Mohammed from heaven above.

Why do these religions insist that their scriptures, and especially only *their* scriptures, not anybody else's? Mohammedans are not ready to accept that the Vedas are God-made, neither are Hindus ready to accept that the Koran is God-made—only their Vedas are God-made and everything else is just manufactured. Why this insistence? Because they are aware that whatever people create will have the imprint of human mind and human desires.

Buddha says all the scriptures are man-made, and he is right. He is not a fanatic at all. He does not belong to any country and he does not belong to any race; he does not belong to any religion, to any sect. He is simply a light unto himself. And whatsoever he has said is the purest statement of truth ever made.

A friend sent me this beautiful anecdote:

One of the religious leaders in Ireland was asked by his followers to select a suitable burial place and monument for his mortal remains. A religious war was in progress and his life had been threatened. Three separate plans had been submitted to him, and to the dismay of the committee he chose the least expensive. He was asked why he had made this selection, why he had chosen this humble resting-place when the other two designs were of magnificent tombs.

"Well, my dear friends," he told them, "I appreciate your generosity. But is it worth all this expense when I don't expect to remain in my tomb for more than three days?"

Now, this sort of dogmatic certainty you will never find in Buddha. He is very hesitant. There is only one other name that is also so hesitant and he is Lao Tzu; these two persons are hesitant.

Sometimes, because of their hesitance, they may not impress you—because you are confused, you need somebody to be so confident that you can rely on him. Hence, fanatics impress you.

They may not have anything to say, but they beat the table so much, they make such a fuss about it that their fuss itself gives you the feeling that they must know, otherwise how can they be so certain? Some religious sects are so dogmatic in their assertions that they create a feeling of certainty. And confused people need certainty.

When you come to a buddha, you may not be immediately impressed because he will be so hesitant, he will not assert anything. He knows better than that. He knows that life cannot be confined to any statement, and all statements are partial. No statement can contain the whole truth, so how can you be certain about it? He will remain always relative.

Two great masters of India, Buddha and Mahavira, both were deep into relativity. Einstein discovered it late; Einstein brought relativity to the world of science. Before Einstein, scientists were certain, dogmatically certain, absolutely certain. Einstein brought relativity and humbleness to science; he brought truth to science.

The same was done by Buddha and Mahavira in India: they brought relativity, the

concept that truth cannot be asserted totally, that we can never be certain about it, that at the most we can hint at it. The hint has to be indirect; we cannot pinpoint it directly—it is so big, so vast. And it is natural that we fragile human beings should hesitate. This hesitation shows alertness.

You will always find ignorant people to be dogmatic. The more ignorant a person is, the more dogmatic. This is one of the greatest misfortunes in the world, that the foolish are absolutely certain and the wise are hesitant. Buddha is hesitant.

So if you want to understand him, you will have to be alert and open in your listening. He is not delivering truth to you wholesale. He is simply hinting at it...giving indications at the most, and they, too, are subtle.

As I told you, Buddha is down-to-earth. He never flies high into metaphysics. He never introduces; in fact, he has no preface to his statements. He says them directly, immediately, as simply as possible.

Sometimes his statements do not appear to be of any profound depth—they are. But he does not beat around the bush, he does not make any fuss about it.

I have heard:

She was a sweet young thing; he was a fast-rising account executive with a well-known advertising agency. Everyone thought it wasan ideal marriage. But alas, there was a problem... with sex. The honeymoon hadn't even begun. "Being an advertising man," she sobbed to a friend, "all he does every night is sit on the edge of the bed and tell me how wonderful it's going to be!"

But it never happens!

Buddha has no preface. He never advertises what he is going to say. He simply says it and moves on. He says:

Moved by their selfish desires, people seek after fame and glory. But when they have acquired it, they are already stricken in years. If you hanker after worldly fame and practice not the way, your labors are wrongfully applied and your energy is wasted. It is like burning an incense stick. However much its pleasing odor be admired, the fire that consumes is steadily burning up the stick.

A simple and matter-of-fact statement: *Moved by their selfish desires, people seek after fame and glory.*

What is a selfish desire? In the Buddhist way of expression, a selfish desire is one that is based in the self. Ordinarily, in ordinary language we call a desire selfish if it is against somebody else and you don't care about others. Even if it harms others, you go ahead and fulfill your desire. People call you selfish because you don't care for others, you have no consideration for others.

But when Buddha says a desire is selfish, his meaning is different. He says: If a desire is based in the idea of *self* then it is selfish. For example, you donate money—a million dollars for some good cause, for hospitals to be constructed or schools to be opened, or food to be distributed to the poor, or medicine to be sent to poor parts of the country. Nobody will call it a selfish desire.

Buddha will say it is—if there is any motivation of self. If you think that by donating a million dollars you are going to earn some virtue and be rewarded in heaven, it is a selfish desire. It may not be harmful to others—it is not; in fact, everybody will appreciate it. People will call you great, religious, virtuous; a person of charity, love, compassion, sympathy. But Buddha will say the only thing that determines whether a desire is selfish or not is its motivation.

If you have donated without any motivation, then it is not selfish. If there is any motivation hidden somewhere—conscious, unconscious—that you are going to gain something out of it, here or hereafter, then it is a selfish desire.

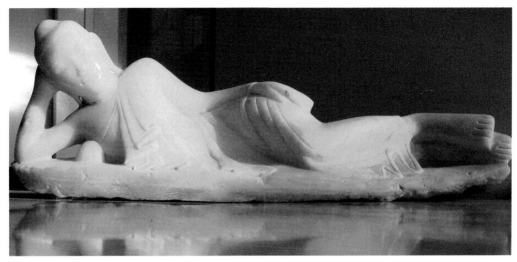

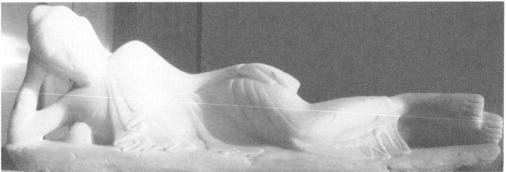

That which comes out of the self is a selfish desire; that which comes as part of the ego is a selfish desire. If you meditate just to attain to your selfhood, then it is a selfish desire.

Buddha has said to his disciples: Whenever you meditate, after each meditation, surrender all that you have earned out of meditation, surrender it to the universe. If you are blissful, pour it back into the universe—don't carry it as a treasure. If you are feeling very happy, share it immediately. Don't become attached to it, otherwise your meditation itself will become a new process of the self. And the ultimate meditation is not a process of the self. The ultimate meditation is a process of getting more and more into un-self, into non-self—it is a disappearance of the self.

Buddha says, *Moved by their selfish desires, people seek after fame and glory. But when they have acquired it, they are already stricken in years.* Look—you can attain fame, glory, power, prestige, respectability in the world. But what are you doing? Are you aware? You are wasting a great opportunity, and for something absolutely meaningless. You are collecting rubbish and destroying your own time, your own life energy.

He says, *If you hanker after worldly fame and practice not the way...* Buddha always calls his religion "the way"—*dhamma*, just "the way." He says, Don't be bothered about the goal; the goal will take care of itself. You simply follow the way, not even with the motivation to reach any goal but out of the sheer delight of meditating, of praying, of loving, of being compassionate, of sharing. Out of sheer delight you practice the way. Not that you are going to gain any profit out of it; don't make it a business.

Life is slipping by; each moment a precious moment is gone and it cannot be reclaimed. Buddha says: Don't waste it in foolish things.

Fame is foolish, it is pointless, meaningless. Even if the whole world knows you, how does it make you richer? How does it make your life more blissful? How does it help you to be more understanding, to be more aware, to be more alert, to be more alive?

If you are not practicing the way, he says, *Your labors are wrongfully applied and your energy is wasted. It is like burning an incense stick. However much its pleasing odor be admired, the fire that consumes is steadily burning up the stick.*

That's how life is—each moment burning. You are always on the funeral pyre because each moment death is coming closer, each moment you are less alive, more dead. So before this opportunity is lost, Buddha says, attain to a state of no-self. Then there will be no death. Then there will be no misery. And then there will be no constant hankering for fame, power, prestige.

In fact, the more empty you are within, the more you seek fame. It is a sort of substitute. The poorer you are within, the more you seek riches; it is a substitute to fill yourself with something.

I observe it every day: whenever people have a problem with love, they immediately start eating too much. Whenever they feel that their love is in a crisis, they are not being loved, or they are not able to love, something has blocked their love energy, they immediately start stuffing themselves with things. They start eating. Why? What are they doing with the food? They feel empty and that emptiness makes them afraid. They have to somehow stuff it with food.

If you are feeling happy inside, you don't bother about fame; only unhappy people bother about fame. Who bothers whether anybody knows you or not, if you know yourself? If you know yourself, who you are, then there is no need. But when you don't know who you are you would like everybody to know—you want everybody to know who you are. You will collect opinions, you will collect people's ideas, and out of that collection you will try to arrange some identity: "Yes, I am this person. People say to me that I am intelligent, so I must be intelligent." You are not certain. If you were certain, why bother with what people say or don't say?

You look into people's eyes to see your face—you don't know your own face. You beg: "Say something about me. Say I am beautiful. Say I am lovable. Say I am charismatic. Say something about me!" Have you watched yourself begging? "Say something about my body, about my mind, about my understanding—say something!"

You immediately grab onto it if somebody says something. But if it is shocking and shattering, you become angry. The person is destroying your image if he says something against you. If he says something in favor of you, he helps your image to be a little more decorated, it becomes a little more ornamental, and you come home happy. If people applaud you, you feel happy. Why?

You don't know who you are. That's why you are seeking. You ask people "Who am I? Tell me!" Then you have to depend on them. The irony of it is that those same people don't know who *they* are! Beggars begging from other beggars. They have come to beg from you, so there is a mutual deception.

A man meets a woman and says, "How beautiful! How divine!" And she says, "Yes,and I have never come across such a beautiful man as you." This is a mutual deception. They may call it love, but this is a mutual deception. Both are hankering for a certain identity around themselves. Both fulfill each other's desires. Things will go well until one of the two decides that enough is enough and starts dropping the deception. Then the honeymoon is over...and marriage starts.Then things become ugly. Then he thinks, "This woman deceived me" and she thinks, "This man deceived me." Nobody can deceive you unless you are ready to be deceived, remember. Nobody has ever deceived anybody unless

they were ready to be deceived, waiting to be deceived.

You cannot deceive a person who knows himself, because there is no way. If you say something he will laugh. He will say, "Don't be worried about it—I already know who I am. You can drop that subject and go ahead with whatever you have to say. Don't be bothered about me—I myself know who I am."

Once you have an inner richness of life, you don't seek wealth, you don't seek power. Psychologists have become aware that when people start becoming impotent, they start seeking sexual, phallic symbols to compensate. If a person becomes impotent then he may try to have the biggest car—that is a phallic symbol.

He would like to have the most powerful car in the world; his own power is lost, his own sexual energy is gone, and he would like a substitute. While pushing his car to the maximum speed, he will feel good—as if he is making love to his woman. The speed will give him power. He will identify with the car. Psychologists have been watching the phenomenon for many years, that people who have a certain inferiority complex always become ambitious. In fact, almost nobody goes into politics unless he is deeply rooted in an inferiority complex. Politicians are basically people with inferiority complexes. They have to prove their superiority in some way; otherwise, they will not be able to live with their inferiority complex. What I am trying to point out is that whatever you miss within, you try to accumulate something outside as a substitute for it.

If you don't miss your life within, you are enough unto yourself. And only then are you beautiful. And only then you *are*.

Buddha said, "People cleave to their worldly possessions and selfish passions so blindly as to sacrifice their own lives for them. They are like a child who tries to eat a little honey smeared on the edge of a knife. The amount is by no means sufficient to appease his appetite, but he runs the risk of wounding his tongue."

Nothing is enough in this life to fulfill your desires, to fulfill your appetite. This world is a dream world—nothing can fulfill because only reality can be fulfilling. Have you watched? In a dream, you feel hungry in the night and in your dream you go to the fridge and open it and you eat to your heart's content. Of course, it helps in

a way—it does not disturb your sleep; otherwise, the hunger will not allow you to sleep, you will have to wake up. The dream creates a substitute; you continue to sleep, you feel, "I have eaten enough." You have deceived your body. The dream is a deceiver. In the morning you will be surprised—you are still hungry—because a feast in the dream is equivalent to a fast. Feasting and fasting, both are the same in a dream because a dream is unreal. It cannot fulfill your hunger. To quench real thirst real water is needed. To fulfill you, a real-life reality is needed.

Buddha says you go on taking the risk of wounding yourself, but no fulfillment comes out of this life. Maybe here and there you have a taste of honey—sweet, but dangerous, unfulfilling. And the honey is smeared on the edge of a knife; there is every danger you will wound your tongue. Look at so many old people: You will not find anything else but wounds; their whole being is nothing but wounds and ulcers. When a person dies, you don't see blossoming flowers in his being; you see stinking wounds.

If a person has lived and not been deceived by his dreams and illusory desires, the older he grows the more beautiful he becomes. In his death he is superb. Sometimes you may come across an old man whose old age is more beautiful than his youth ever was. Then bow down before that old man—he has lived a true life, a life of inwardness, a life of "interiorness." Because if life is lived truly, then you go on becoming more and more beautiful and a grandeur starts coming to you, a grace. Something of the unknown starts abiding in your surroundings—you become the abode of the infinite, of the eternal. It has to be so because life is an evolution.

If when you are no longer young and you become ugly, that simply means in your youth you tasted honey on too many knives—you have become wounded. Now you will suffer cancerous wounds. Old age becomes a great suffering. And death is rarely beautiful, because rarely have people really lived. If a person has truly lived—like a flame burning from both ends—then his death will be a tremendous phenomenon, an utter beauty. You will see his life aglow when he is dying, at the maximum, at the optimum. In the last moment he will become such a flame; his whole life will become a concentrated perfume in that moment, a great luminosity will arise in his being. Before he leaves, he will leave behind him a memory.

That's what happened when Buddha left the world. That's what happened when Mahavira left the world. We have not forgotten them, not because they were great politicians or people of power—they were nobodies, but we cannot forget them. It is impossible to forget them. They had not done anything as far as history is concerned. We can almost omit them from history, we can leave them out of history and nothing will be lost. In fact, they never existed in the main current of history, they were by the side of it—but it is impossible to forget them. Their last moments have left a glory to humanity. Their last glow has shown us our own possibilities, our infinite potentialities.

SEEING AND BELIEVING

Buddha says again and again to his disciples, "*Ihi passiko*: come and see!" They are scientific people; Buddhism is the most scientific religion on the earth. Hence, it is gaining more and more ground in the world every day. As the world becomes more intelligent, Buddha will become more and more important. It is bound to be so. As more and more people come to know about science, Buddha will have great appeal, because he will convince the scientific mind—because he says, "Whatsoever I am saying can be practiced. And I don't say to you, 'Believe it,' I say, 'Experiment with it, experience it, and only then if you feel it yourself, trust it.' Otherwise there is no need to believe."

blowing out
the candle

IT IS SIGNIFICANT to understand that there is only one person, Gautam Buddha, who has used nothingness, emptiness, for the ultimate experience. All other mystics of the world have used fullness, wholeness, as the expression, the indication of the ultimate experience.

Why did Gautam Buddha choose a negative term? It is significant to understand—for your own spiritual growth, not for any philosophical reasons. I do not speak for philosophical reasons. I speak only when I see there is some existential relevance.

The idea of fullness, the idea of God, the idea of perfection, the idea of the absolute, the ultimate—all are positive terms. And Gautam Buddha was amazed to see the cunningness of human mind....

The innocent mystics have used the positive words because that was their experience. Why bother about the misery, which is no more? Why not say something about that which is now? The innocent mystics have spoken out of their "isness." But throughout the centuries the cunning minds of people around the world have taken advantage of it.

To the cunning mind, the idea of fullness, and the positive terms indicating it, became an ego trip: "I have to become God. I have to attain the absolute, the Brahma; I have to achieve the ultimate liberation." The "I" became the center of all our assertions. The trouble is that you cannot make the ultimate experience a goal for the ego. Ego is the barrier; it cannot become the bridge.

All the positive terms have been misused. Rather than destroying the ego, they have become decorations for the ego. God has become a goal; you have to achieve the goal. You become greater than God.

Remember, the goal cannot be greater than you. The achieved cannot be greater than the achiever. It is a very simple fact to understand.

All the religions have fallen because of this simple innocence of the mystics.

Gautam Buddha was the most cultured, the most educated, the most sophisticated person ever to become a mystic. There is no comparison in the whole of history. He could see where the innocent mystics had unknowingly given opportunities for cunning minds to take advantage. He decided not to use any positive term for the ultimate goal, in order to destroy the ego and any possibility of the ego taking any advantage.

He called the ultimate, nothingness, emptiness—*shunyata*, zero. Now, how can the ego make "zero" a goal? God can be made a goal, but not zero. Who wants to become zero?—that is the fear. Everybody is avoiding all possibilities of becoming a zero, and Buddha made it an expression for the ultimate!

His word is *nirvana*.

He chose a tremendously beautiful word, but he shocked all the thinkers and philosophers by choosing the word *nirvana* as the most significant expression for the ultimate experience. *Nirvana* means "blowing out the candle."

Other mystics have said that you are filled with enormous light, as if thousands of suns together have suddenly risen inside you, as if the sky full of stars has descended within your heart. These ideas appeal to the ego. The ego would like to have all the stars, if not inside the chest, then at least hanging on the coat outside the chest. "Enormous light"... the ego is very willing.

To cut the roots, Buddha says the experience is as if you were to blow out a candle. There was a small flame on the candle giving a small light—even that is gone, and you are surrounded with absolute darkness, abysmal darkness.

People used to say to him, "If you go on teaching such things, nobody is going to follow you. Who wants darkness, enormous darkness? You are crazy. You say that the ultimate experience is an ultimate death. People want eternal life, and you are talking about ultimate death?"

But he was a consistent man, and you can see that for forty-two years he hammered on the genius of the East without ever compromising with the ego. He also knows that what he is calling darkness is too much light; that's why it looks like darkness. If one thousand suns rise in you, what do you think?—that you will feel enormous light? You will feel immense darkness, it will be too dazzling. Just look at one sun for a few seconds and you will feel your eyes are going blind. If one thousand suns are within you, inside the mind, the experience will be of darkness, not of light.

It will take a long time for you to get accustomed, for your eyes to become strong enough to see—slowly, slowly—darkness turning into light, death turning into life, emptiness turning into fullness. But he never talked about those things. He never said that darkness would ever turn into light. And he never said that death would become a resurrection at some later point, because he knows how cunning your ego is. If that is said, the ego will say, "Then there is no problem. Our aim remains the same; it is just that we will have to pass through a little dark night of the soul. But finally, we will have enormous light, thousands of suns."

Gautam Buddha had to deny that God existed—not that he was against God, a man like Gautam Buddha cannot be against God. And if Gautam Buddha is against God, then it is of no use for anybody to be in favor of God. His decision is decisive for the whole of humanity; he represents our very soul. But he was not against God. He was against the ego, and he was constantly careful not to give the ego any support to remain. If God can become a support, then there is no God.

One thing becomes very clear: although he used, for the first time, all negative terms, the man must have had tremendous charismatic qualities. He influenced millions of people. His philosophy is such that anyone listening to him would freak out. What is the point of all the meditations and all the austerities, renouncing the world, eating one time a day...and ultimately you achieve nothingness, you become zero! We are already better off than that—we may be miserable, but we *are* at least. Certainly, when you are completely a zero there cannot be any misery—zeros are not known to be miserable—but what is the gain?

Yet he convinced people, not through philosophy, but through his individuality, through his presence. He gave people the experience itself, so they could understand. It is emptiness as far as the world is concerned, it is emptiness for the ego, and it is fullness for the being.

There are many reasons for the disappearance of Buddha's thought from India, but this is one of the most significant. All other Indian mystics, philosophers, and seers have used positive terms. For centuries before Buddha, all of India was accustomed to thinking only in the positive; the negative was something unheard of. Under the influence of Gautam Buddha they followed him, but when he died his following started disappearing—because the following was not intellectually convinced; it was convinced because of his presence. Because of the eyes of Gautam Buddha they could see: "This man if he is living in nothingness then there is no fear, we would love to be nothing. If this is where becoming a zero leads, if by being nothing such lotuses bloom in the eyes and such grace flows, then we are ready to go with this man. The man has a magic."

But his philosophy alone will not convince you, because it has no appeal for the ego.

Buddhism survived in China, in Ceylon, in Burma, in Japan, in Korea, in Indochina, in Indonesia—in the whole of Asia except India—because the Buddhists who reached there dropped the negative terms. They started speaking in positive terms. Then the "ultimate," the "absolute," the "perfect"—the old terms returned. This was the compromise. So as far as I am concerned, Buddhism died with Gautam Buddha. Whatever exists now as Buddhism has nothing to do with Buddha because it has dropped his basic contribution, which was his negative approach.

I am aware of both traditions. I am certainly in a better position than Gautam Buddha was. Gautam Buddha was aware of only one thing— that the ego can use the positive.

And it is his great contribution, his courageous contribution, that he dropped the positive and insisted on the negative, emphasized the negative—knowing perfectly well that people were not going to follow this because it had no appeal for the ego.

To me, now both traditions are available. I know what happened to the positive—the ego exploited it. I know what happened to the negative. After the death of Gautam Buddha, the disciples had to compromise, compromise with the same thing which Gautam Buddha was revolting against.

So I am trying to explain both approaches together—emptiness as far as the world is concerned and fullness as far as the inner experience is concerned. This is a total

> *If you think in terms of the sacred, you will find your life overflowingly full*

approach, it takes note of both: that which has to be left behind, and that which is to be gained. All other approaches up to now have been half-and-half. Mahavira, Shankara, Moses, Mohammed, all used the positive. Gautam Buddha used the negative. I use both, and I don't see any contradiction. If you understand me clearly, then you can enjoy the beauty of both viewpoints. You need not be exploited by your ego or be afraid of death and darkness and nothingness. They are not two things. It is almost as if I were to put a glass of water in front of you, half-full and half-empty, and ask you whether the glass is empty or full. Either answer would be wrong, because the glass is both half-full and half-empty. From one side it is empty, from another side it is full.

Half of your life is part of the mundane world, the other half is part of the sacred. It is unfortunate, but there is no other way—we have to use the same language for both the mundane and the sacred.

So one has to be alert. To choose the mundane will be missing something essential; if you think in terms of the mundane, you will find the sacred life empty. If you think in terms of the sacred, you will find it overflowingly full.

ZEN

its history and teachings

Zen is an extraordinary development. Rarely does such a possibility

become an actuality because many hazards are involved. Many

times before, the possibility existed—a certain spiritual happening

might have grown and become like Zen, but it was never realized.

Only once in the whole history of human consciousness has a thing

like Zen come into being. It is very rare.

First I would like you to understand what Zen is. Try to follow me slowly through the growth of Zen—how it happened.

Zen was born in India, grew in China, and blossomed in Japan. The whole situation is rare. Why did it happen that it was born in India, but could not grow there and had to seek a different soil? It became a great tree in China, but it could not blossom there; again it had to seek a new climate, a different climate. And in Japan it blossomed like a cherry tree in thousands of flowers. It is not coincidental; it is not accidental; it has a deep inner history. I would like to reveal it to you.

India is an introverted country. Japan is extroverted. And China is just in the middle of these two extremes. India and Japan are absolute opposites. So how come the seed was born in India and blossomed in Japan? They are opposites; they have no similarities; they are contradictory. Why did China come just in the middle, to givesoil to it?

A seed is an introversion. Try to understand the phenomenon of the seed, what a seed is. A seed is an introverted phenomenon, it is centripetal—the energy is moving inward. That's why it is a seed, covered and closed from the outer world completely. In fact, a seed is the loneliest, most isolated thing in the world. It has no roots in the soil, no branches in the sky; it has no connection with the earth, no connection with the sky. It has no relationships. A seed is an absolute island, isolated, caved in. It does not relate. It has a hard shell around it; there are no windows, no doors. It cannot go out, and nothing can come in.

The seed is natural to India. The genius of India can produce seeds of tremendous potentiality, but cannot give them soil. India is an introverted consciousness. India says the outer doesn't exist, and even if it seems to exist, it is made of the same stuff that dreams are made of. The whole genius of India has been in trying to discover how to escape from the outer, how to move to the inner cave of the heart, how to be centered in oneself. And how to realize that the whole world that exists outside consciousness is just a dream—at the most beautiful, at the worst a nightmare. Whether beautiful or ugly, in reality it is a dream, and one should not bother much about it. One should awaken and forget the whole dream of the outer world.

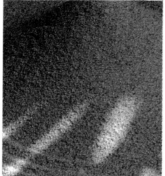

The whole effort of Buddha, Mahavira, Tilopa, Gorakh, Kabir—their whole effort through the centuries—has been to find out how to escape from the wheel of life and death: how to enclose yourself; how to completely cut yourself off from all relationships; how to be unrelated, detached; how to move in and to forget the outer. That's why Zen was born in India.

Zen means the same as *dhyan* and is a Japanese change of this word. *Dhyan* is the whole effort of Indian consciousness, and means to be so alone, so into your own being, that not even a single thought exists. In fact, in English, there is no direct translation of the word. Contemplation is not the word. Contemplation means thinking, reflection. Even meditation is not the word because meditation involves an object to meditate upon; it means something is there. You can meditate on Christ, or you can meditate on the cross. But dhyan means to be so alone that there is nothing to meditate upon. No object, just simple subjectivity exists—consciousness without clouds, a pure sky.

When the word reached China it became *ch'an*. When *ch'an* reached Japan, it became *Zen*. It comes from the same Sanskrit root, *dhyan*.

India can give birth to dhyan. For millennia, the whole Indian consciousness has been traveling on the path of dhyan—how to drop all thinking and how to be rooted in pure consciousness. With Buddha the seed came into existence. Many times before Gautam Buddha, the seed came into existence, but it couldn't find the right soil so it disappeared. And if a seed is given to the Indian consciousness it will disappear,

The future of humanity will go closer to the approach of Zen, because the meeting of East and West is possible only through something like Zen, which is earthly and yet unearthly

because the Indian consciousness will move more and more inward, and the seed will become smaller and smaller and smaller, until a moment comes when it becomes invisible.

A centripetal force makes things smaller, smaller, smaller—atomic—until suddenly they disappear. Many times before Gautam Buddha the seed of dhyan was born— and to become a *dhyani* was to become a great meditator. In fact, Buddha is one of the last in a long series. He himself remembers twenty-four buddhas before him. Then there were twenty-four Jaina *teerthankaras*, and they all were meditators. They did nothing else, they simply meditated, meditated, meditated, until they came to a point where only they were, and everything else disappeared, evaporated.

The seed was born with Parasnath, Mahavira, Neminath, and others, but then it remained with the Indian consciousness. The Indian consciousness can give birth to a seed, but cannot become the right soil for it. It goes on working in the same direction and the seed becomes smaller and smaller, molecular, atomic—and disappears. That's how it happened with the Upanishads; that's how it happened with the Vedas; that's how it happened with Mahavira and all the others.

With Buddha it was also going to happen. Bodhidharma saved him. If the seed had been left with the Indian consciousness it would have dissolved. It would never have sprouted, because a different type of soil is needed for sprouting—a balanced soil. Introversion is a deep imbalance; it is an extreme.

Buddha himself is reported to have said, "My religion will not exist for more than five hundred years, then it will disappear." He was aware that it always happened that way. The Indian consciousness goes on grinding it into smaller and smaller and smaller pieces, then a moment comes when it becomes so small that it is invisible. It is simply no longer part of this world; it disappears into the sky.

Bodhidharma escaped with the seed to China. He did one of the greatest things in the history of consciousness: he found the right soil for the seed that Buddha had given to the world.

Bodhidharma's experiment was great. He looked and observed all around the world, deeply, for a place where this seed could grow.

China is a balanced country, not like India, not like Japan. The golden mean is the path there. Confucian ideology is to remain always in the middle: neither be an introvert nor an extrovert; neither think too much of this world nor too much of that world—just remain in the middle. China has not given birth to a religion, just to morality. No religion has been born there; the Chinese consciousness cannot give birth to a religion. It cannot create a seed. All the religions that exist in China have been imported; they have all come from the outside. Buddhism, Hinduism, Mohammedanism, and Christianity have all come from the outside. China is a good soil but it cannot originate any religion, because to originate a religion one has to move into the inner world. To give birth to a religion one has to be like a feminine body, a womb.

India is introverted, a feminine country; it is like a womb, very receptive. But if a child remains in the womb forever and forever and forever, the womb will become the grave. The child has to move out from the mother's womb, otherwise the mother will kill the child inside. He has to escape, to find the world outside, a greater world.

> *A seed is a miser, confined to himself, and a flower is a spendthrift*

The womb may be comfortable—it is! Scientists say we have not yet been able to create anything more comfortable than the womb. The womb is just a heaven. But even the child has to leave that heaven and come outside the mother. Beyond a certain time the

mother can become very dangerous. Then the womb can kill, because it will have become an imprisonment. It is good for a time, when the seed is growing, but then the seed has to be transplanted to the outside world.

Bodhidharma looked around, observed the whole world, and found that China had the best soil; it was a middle ground, not extreme. The climate was not extreme, so the tree could grow easily. And China had balanced people. Balance is the right soil for something to grow: too cold is bad, too hot is bad. In a balanced climate, neither too cold nor too hot, the tree can grow.

Bodhidharma escaped with the seed, escaped with all that India had produced. Nobody was aware of what he was doing, but it was a great experiment. And he was proved right. In China, the tree grew—grew to vast proportions.

But although the tree became vaster and vaster, no flowers grew. Flowers did not come, because flowers need an extroverted country. Just as a seed is an introvert, so a flower is an extrovert. The seed is moving inward; the flower is moving outward. The flower is like male consciousness. It opens to the outer world and releases its fragrance to this outside world. Then the fragrance moves on the wings of the wind to the farthest possible corner of the world. To all directions, the flower releases the energy contained in the seed. It is a door. Flowers would like to become butterflies and escape from the tree. In fact, that is what they are doing, in a very subtle way. They are releasing the essence of the tree, the very meaning, the significance of the tree to the world. They are great sharers. A seed is a miser, confined to himself, and a flower is a spendthrift.

Japan was needed. Japan is an extroverted country. The very style of life and consciousness is extroverted. Look… in India nobody bothers about the outside world very much—about clothes, houses, the way one lives. Nobody bothers. That is why India has remained so poor. If you are not worried about the outside world, how can you become rich? If there is no concern to improve the outside world you will remain poor. And the Indian is always very serious, always getting ready to escape from life, with buddhas talking about how to become perfect dropouts from existence itself—not only from society, but ultimate dropouts from existence itself! The existence is too boring. For the Indian eye, life is just a gray color—nothing interesting in it, everything just boring, a burden. One has to carry it somehow because of past karma. Even if an Indian falls in love, he says it is because of past karma; one has to pass through it. Even love is like a burden one has to drag.

India seems to be leaning more toward death than life. An introvert has to lean toward death. That's why India has evolved all the techniques for how to die perfectly, how to die so perfectly that you are not born again. Death is the goal, not life. Life is for fools, death is for those who are wise. However beautiful a Buddha or a Mahavira may be, you will find them closed; around them a great aura of indifference exists. Whatever is happening, they are not concerned at all. Whether it happens this way or that way makes no difference; whether the world goes on living or dies, it makes no difference. In this tremendous indifference, flowering is not possible; in this inner-confined state, flowering is impossible.

Japan is totally different. With the Japanese consciousness it is as if the inner doesn't exist; only the outer is meaningful. Look at Japanese dresses. All the colors of flowers and rainbows, as if the outer is very meaningful. Look at an Indian when he is eating, and then look at the Japanese. Look at an Indian when he takes his tea, and then the Japanese. A Japanese creates a celebration out of simple things. Taking tea,

he makes it a celebration. It becomes an art. The outside is very important: clothes are very important, relationships are very important. You cannot find more outgoing people in the world than the Japanese—always smiling and looking happy. To the Indian they will look shallow; they will not look serious. Indians are the introverted people and the Japanese are the extroverts: they are opposites.

A Japanese is always moving in society. The whole Japanese culture is concerned with how to create a beautiful society, how to create beautiful relationships—in everything, in every minute thing—how to give them significance. Their houses are so beautiful. Even a poor man's house has a beauty of its own: it is artistic, it has its own uniqueness.

It may not be very rich, but still it is rich in a certain sense because of the beauty, the arrangement, the mind that has been brought to every small, tiny detail. Where the window should be, what type of curtain should be used, how the moon should be invited from the window, and from where. Very small things, but every detail is important.

To the Indian, nothing matters. If you go to an Indian temple, it is without any windows; there is nothing, no hygiene, no concern with air, ventilation—nothing. Even temples are ugly, and anything goes—dirt, dust, nobody bothers. Just in front of the temple you will find cows sitting, dogs fighting, people praying. Nobody bothers. No sense of the outer, they are not at all concerned with the outer.

Japan is very concerned with the outer—just at the other extreme. Japan was the right country. And the whole tree of Zen was transplanted in Japan, and there it blossomed in thousands of colors. It flowered.

born in

laughter

Zen is the ultimate flowering of consciousness. It started with

Gautam Buddha giving a lotus flower to Mahakashyapa.

the seed of zen

A man once took a flower and, without a word, held it up before the men seated in a circle about him. Each man in his turn looked at the flower, and then explained its meaning, its significance, all that it symbolized. The last man, however, seeing the flower, said nothing, only smiled. The man in the center then also smiled, and without a word handed him the flower. This is the origin of Zen.

BUDDHA WAS to give a talk one day, and thousands of disciples had come from miles around. When Buddha appeared he was holding a flower. Time passed, but Buddha said nothing, he just looked at the flower. The crowd grew restless, but Mahakashyap, who could restrain himself no longer, laughed. Buddha beckoned him over, handed him the flower, and said to the crowd, "All that can be given with words I have given to you; but with this flower, I give Mahakashyap the key to all the teachings."

The key to all teachings, not only for a Buddha but for all masters—Jesus, Mahavira, Lao Tzu—cannot be given through verbal communication. The key cannot be delivered through the mind; nothing can be said about it. The more you say the more difficult it becomes to deliver, because you and a buddha live in such different dimensions—not only different but diametrically opposite—that whatsoever a buddha says will be misunderstood.

I have heard that one evening three slightly deaf women met on the road. The day was very windy, so one woman said,

"Windy, isn't it?"

The other said, "Wednesday? No, it's Thursday."

And the third said, "Thirsty? I am also, so let's go to the restaurant and have a cup of tea."

This is what happens when a buddha says something to you. He says, "Windy?" You say, "Wednesday? No, it's Thursday."

The physical ear is okay, but the spiritual ear is missing. A buddha can talk only to another buddha—this is the problem—and with another buddha there is no need to talk. A buddha has to talk with those who are not enlightened. With them the need exists to talk and communicate, but then communication is impossible.

Two ignorant persons can talk. They talk much; they do nothing except talk. Two enlightened persons cannot talk—it would be absurd. Two ignorant persons talking is meaningless because there is nothing to convey. They don't know anything that can be said, that should be said, but they go on talking. They are chattering. They cannot help it; it's just a mad catharsis, a release.

Two enlightened persons cannot talk because they know the same. Nothing needs to be said. Only one enlightened person and one unenlightened person can have a meaningful communication, because one knows and the other is still in ignorance. A meaningful communication, I say. I don't say that the truth can be conveyed. But some hints, some indications, some gestures can be communicated, so that the other becomes ready to take the jump. The truth cannot be conveyed but the thirst can be given. No teaching worth the name can give the key through words.

Buddha talked—it's difficult to find another person who talked as much. Scholars have been studying all the scriptures in existence that are in the name of Buddha, and it seems an impossible accomplishment because after his enlightenment he lived only forty years, walking from one village to another.

He walked all over the province of Bihar in India, which was named Bihar because Buddha walked there. *Bihar* means the walking paths of Buddha. The whole province is called Bihar because this is the boundary where Buddha walked—his *bihar*, his wanderings.

He continually walked; only in the rainy season did he rest. So much time was wasted in walking, and then also he had to sleep. So the scholars who have been calculating say, "This seems impossible. Sleeping, walking, doing other daily routines—there are so many scriptures, how could he have talked so much? If he was continuously talking for forty years, without a gap of a single moment, only then could this much have been talked." He must have talked so much—almost continuously—yet still he says the key cannot be conveyed through words.

This story is one of the most significant, because from this was born the tradition of Zen. Buddha was the source, and Mahakashyap was the first, the original master of Zen. Buddha was the source, Mahakashyap was the first master, and this story is the source from which the whole tradition—one of the most beautiful and alive that exists on earth, the tradition of Zen—started.

Try to understand this story. Buddha came sone morning and, as usual, a crowd had

gathered; many people were waiting to listen to him. But one thing was unusual—he was carrying a flower in his hand. Never before had he carried anything in his hand. People thought that someone must have presented it to him. Buddha came; he sat under the tree. The crowd waited and waited and he did not speak. He wouldn't even look at them, he just went on looking at the flower. Minutes passed, then hours, and the people became very restless.

It is said that Mahakashyap couldn't contain himself. He laughed out loud. Buddha called him, gave him the flower and said to the gathered crowd, "Whatsoever can be said through words I have said to you, and that which cannot be said through words I give to Mahakashyap. The key cannot be communicated verbally. I hand over the key to Mahakashyap."

This is what Zen masters call "transference of the key without scripture"—beyond scripture, beyond words, beyond mind. He gave the flower to Mahakashyap, and nobody could understand what happened. Neither Mahakashyap nor Buddha ever commented upon it again. The whole chapter was closed. Since then, in China, in Tibet, in Thailand, in Burma, in Japan, in Ceylon—everywhere—Buddhists have been asking for these twenty-five centuries, "What was given to Mahakashyap? What was the key?"

The whole story seems to be very esoteric. Buddha was not secretive; this was the only incident.... Buddha was a very rational being. He talked rationally, he was not a mad ecstatic, he argued rationally, and his logic was

perfect—you could not find a loophole in it. This was the only incident where he behaved illogically, where he did something that was mysterious. He was not a mysterious man at all. You cannot find another master who was less mysterious.

Jesus was very mysterious. Lao Tzu was absolutely mysterious. Buddha was plain, transparent; no mystery surrounds him, no smoke is allowed. His flame burns clear and bright, absolutely transparent, smokeless. This was the only thing that seemed mysterious; hence many Buddhist scriptures never relate this anecdote; they have simply dropped it. It seemed as if someone had invented it. It didn't make any sense with Buddha's life and teaching.

But for Zen this is the origin. Mahakashyap became the first holder of the key. Then six holders of the key lived in succession in India, up through Bodhidharma, who was the sixth holder of the key.

To me, if all the scriptures of Buddha disappear nothing is lost. Only this anecdote should not disappear. This is the most precious, yet scholars have dropped it from Buddha's biography. They say, "This is irrelevant; it doesn't fit with Buddha." But I say to you, most of what Buddha did was just ordinary, anybody could do it, but this is extraordinary, this is exceptional. Only a buddha can do this.

What happened that morning? Let us penetrate into it. Buddha came, sat, and started looking at the flower. What was he doing? When Buddha looks at anything, the quality of his consciousness is transferred. And a flower is one of the most receptive things in the world. Hence, Hindus and Buddhists go with flowers to put at their master's feet or in the temple, because a flower can carry something of your consciousness.

A flower is receptive and, if you are aware of the new research in the West, you will understand it. Now they say plants are more sensitive than human beings. A flower is the heart of the plant; the whole being comes into it. Much research is going on in Russia, in the

US, in the UK, about the sensitivity of plants, and something wonderful has been discovered.

One man, a scientist, was studying plants—how they feel, whether they feel anything or not, whether they have emotions or not. He was sitting with a plant with electrodes fixed to it to detect any movement in its inner being, any sensation, any emotion. He thought, "If I cut this plant, if I tear down a branch or cut it from the earth, what will happen?" Suddenly, the needle writing the graph jumped. He had not done anything, he had just had a thought: "If I cut this plant...." The plant became afraid of death and the needle jumped, recording that the plant was trembling. Even the scientist became frightened because he had not done anything—just a thought and the plant received it. Plants are telepathic.

Not only this, but if you think of cutting one plant, all the other plants surrounding the area become emotionally disturbed. Also, if someone has cut a plant and he comes into the garden, all the plants become disturbed because this man is not good and they carry the memory. Whenever this man enters the garden the whole garden feels that a dangerous person is coming in. Now a few scientists think that plants can be used for telepathic communication, because they are more sensitive than the human mind.

In the East it has always been known that a flower is the most receptive thing. When Buddha looked at the flower and continued to look at the flower, something of him was transferred to that flower. Buddha entered the flower. The quality of his being—the alertness, the awareness, the peace, the ecstasy, the inner dance—touched the flower. With Buddha looking at the flower—so at ease, at home, without any desire—the flower must have danced in its inner being. Buddha looked in order to transfer something to the flower. Only the flower and he existed—for a long period of time, the whole world dropped. Only Buddha and the flower were there. The flower entered Buddha's being, and Buddha entered the flower's being.

Then the flower was given to Mahakashyap. It was not just a flower now. It carried buddhahood; it carried the inner quality of Buddha's being. And why to Mahakashyap? There were other great scholars. History records ten great disciples; Mahakashyap was only one, and he was included in the ten only because of this story; otherwise, he would never have been included.

Nothing much is known about Mahakashyap. Great scholars like Sariputta were there—you could not find a more keen intellect. Moggalayan was also there; a great scholar, he had all the Vedas in his memory, and nothing that had ever been written was unknown to him. A great logician in his own right, he had thousands of disciples. And there were others. Ananda was there, Buddha's cousin-brother, who for forty years was continuously moving with him. But no, someone who was unknown before— Mahakashyap—suddenly became very important. The whole gestalt changed. Whenever Buddha was speaking, Sariputta was the significant man because he could understand words more than anybody else, and when Buddha was arguing, Moggalayan was the significant man. Nobody thought about Mahakashyap very much. He remained in the crowd, was part of the crowd.

But when Buddha became silent, the whole gestalt changed. Now Moggalayan and Sariputta were not significant; they simply dropped out of existence as if they were not there. They became part of the crowd. A new man, Mahakashyap, became the most important. A new dimension opened. Everybody was restless, thinking, "Why is Buddha not speaking? Why is he keeping silent? What is going to happen? When will it end?" They became uncomfortable, restless.

But Mahakashyap was not uncomfortable or restless. Instead, for the first time he was at ease with Buddha; for the first time he was at home with Buddha. When Buddha was talking he may have been restless. He may have thought, "Why this nonsense? Why go on talking? Nothing is conveyed, nothing is understood; why go on knocking your head against the wall? People are deaf. They cannot understand...." He must have been restless when Buddha was talking, and now for the first time he was at home. He could understand what silence was.

Thousands were there and everybody was restless. He couldn't contain himself, looking at the foolishness of the crowd. They were at ease when Buddha was talking; now they were restless when he was silent. When something could be delivered they were not open; when

nothing could be delivered they were waiting. Through silence Buddha could give something immortal, but they could not understand. So he couldn't contain himself and laughed aloud— he laughed at the situation, the absurdity.

Mahakashyap laughed at the foolishness of people. They were restless and thinking, "When will Buddha stand up and drop this whole silence so that we can go home?" He laughed. Laughter started with Mahakashyap and has been going on and on in the Zen tradition. There is no other tradition that can laugh. Laughter looks so irreligious, profane, that you cannot think of Jesus laughing, you cannot think of Moses laughing. It's difficult even to conceive of Moses having a belly laugh, or of Jesus laughing uproariously. No, laughter has been denied. Sadness, somehow, has become religious.

One of the famous German thinkers, Count Keyserling, has written that health is irreligious. Illness has a religiousness about it because an ill person is sad, desireless—not because he has become desireless, but because he is weak. A healthy person will laugh, wants to enjoy, will be merry—he cannot be sad. So religious people have tried in many ways to make you ill: go on a fast, suppress your body, torture yourself. You will become sad, suicidal, crucified on your own. How can you laugh? Laughter comes out of health. It's an overflowing energy. That's why children can laugh and their laughter is total. Their whole body is involved in it—when they laugh you can see their toes laughing. The whole body— every cell, every fiber of the body—is laughing

and vibrating. They are so full of health, so vital; everything is flowing.

A sad child is an ill child and a laughing old man is still young. Even death cannot make him old; nothing can make him old. His energy is still flowing and overflowing; he is always flooded. Laughter is a flooding of energy.

In Zen monasteries they have been laughing and laughing and laughing. Laughter becomes prayer only in Zen, because Mahakashyap started it. Twenty-five centuries ago, on a morning just like this, Mahakashyap started a new trend, absolutely new, unknown to the religious mind before—he laughed. He laughed at the foolishness, the stupidity. And Buddha didn't condemn him; on the contrary, he called him near, gave him the flower, and spoke to the crowd.

And when the crowd heard the laughter they must have thought, "This man has gone mad. This man is disrespectful to Buddha, because how can you laugh in front of a buddha? When a buddha is sitting silently, how can you laugh? This man is not paying respect."

The mind will say that this is disrespect. The mind has its rules, but the heart does not know them; the heart has its own rules, but the mind has never heard about them. The heart can laugh *and* be respectful. The mind cannot laugh, it can only be sad and then be respectful. But what kind of respect is this, which cannot laugh? A new trend entered with Mahakashyap's laughter, and down the centuries the laughter has continued.

Only Zen masters and Zen disciples laugh. All over the world, religions have become ill because sadness has become so prominent. Temples and churches look like graveyards; they don't look festive, they don't give a sense of celebration. If you enter a church, what do you see there? Not life, but death— Jesus crucified on the cross completes the sadness there. Can you laugh in a church, dance in a church, sing in a church? Yes, there is singing, but it is sad and people sit with long faces. No wonder nobody wants to go to church—it's just a social duty to be fulfilled. No wonder nobody is attracted to the church—it is a formality. Religion has become a Sunday thing. For one hour you can tolerate being sad.

Mahakashyap laughed in front of Buddha and since then the Zen monks and masters have been doing things that so-called religious minds cannot even conceive. If you have seen any Zen book you may have seen Zen masters depicted or painted. No painting is realistic. If you look at Bodhidharma's portrait or Mahakashyap's portrait, they are not true to their faces, but just looking at them you will have a feeling of laughter. They are hilarious; they are ridiculous.

Look at Bodhidharma's pictures. He must have been one of the most beautiful men; that he was otherwise is not possible, because whenever a man becomes enlightened a beauty descends, a beauty that comes from the beyond. A blessing comes to his whole being. But look at Bodhidharma's picture. He looks ferocious and dangerous. He looks so dangerous that you will be scared if he comes to visit you in the night—never again in your life will you be able to sleep! He looks so dangerous, as if he is going to kill you. It was just disciples laughing at the master, creating a ridiculous portrait that looks like a cartoon.

> *Silence and laughter are the keys*
>
> *—silence within,*
>
> *laughter without*

All Zen masters are depicted in a ridiculous way. Disciples enjoy it. But those portraits carry a message that Bodhidharma is dangerous, that if you go to him he will kill you, that you cannot escape him, that he will follow you and haunt you. Wherever you go, he will be there; unless he kills you he cannot leave you. That is the message depicted with all Zen masters, even Buddha.

If you look at Japanese and Chinese paintings of Buddha, they don't look like the Indian Buddha. They have changed him totally. If you look at Indian paintings of Buddha, his body is proportionate, as it should be. He was a prince, then a buddha—a beautiful man, perfect, proportionate. A big-bellied Buddha? He never had a big belly. But in Japan, in his paintings and his scriptures, he is painted with a big belly because a man who laughs must have a big belly. Belly laughter—how can you do it with a small belly? You cannot do it. They are joking with Buddha and they have said such things about Buddha. Only very deep love can do that, otherwise it looks insulting.

The Zen master Bankei always insisted on having a painting of Buddha hanging behind him, and talking to his disciples he would say, "Look at this fellow. Whenever you meet him, kill him immediately; don't give him a chance. While meditating he will come to disturb you. Whenever you see his face in meditation, just kill him then and there; otherwise, he will follow you." And he used to say, "Look at this fellow! If you repeat his name"—because Buddhists go on repeating, *Namo Buddhaya, namo Buddhaya*—"if you

repeat his name, then go and wash your mouth." This statement seems insulting. It is Buddha's name and Bankei says, "If you repeat it, the first thing to do is wash your mouth. Your mouth has become dirty."

But he is right—because words are words; whether one is the name of Buddha or not makes no difference. Whenever a word crosses your mind, your mind has become dirty. Wash out even Buddha's name.

And this man, keeping the portrait of Buddha always behind him, would bow down to it every morning. So his disciples asked, "What are you doing? You go on telling us to kill this man, not to allow him to stand in the way. You say, 'Don't take his name; don't repeat it; if it comes to you, wash out your mouth.' And now we see you bowing down to him!"

Bankei said, "All this has been taught to me by this fellow, so I have to pay him respect."

Mahakashyap laughed—and his laughter carried many dimensions within it. In the second dimension, laughter at the foolishness of the whole situation, at the Buddha silent and nobody understanding him, everybody expecting him to speak. His whole life Buddha had been saying that the truth cannot be spoken, and still everybody expected him to speak. In the second dimension, he laughed at Buddha also, at the whole dramatic situation he had created, sitting there with a flower in his hand, looking at the flower, creating so much uneasiness and restlessness in everybody. At this dramatic gesture of Buddha he laughed and he laughed.

The third dimension was to laugh at his own self. Why couldn't he understand before now? The whole thing was easy and simple. And the day you understand, you will laugh too, because there is nothing to be understood. There is no difficulty to be solved. Everything has always been simple and clear. How could you miss it?

With Buddha sitting silent, the birds singing in the trees, the breeze passing through, and everybody restless, Mahakashyap understood. What did he understand? He understood that there is nothing to be understood, there is nothing to be said, there is nothing to be explained. The whole situation is simple and transparent.

Nothing is hidden in it. There is no need to search, because all that is, is here and now, within you. He laughed at his own self also, at the whole absurd effort of many lives just to understand this silence—he laughed at so much thinking.

Buddha called him, gave him the flower, and said, "Hereby, I give you the key." What is the key? Silence and laughter are the keys—silence within, laughter without. And when laughter comes out of silence, it is not of this world; it is divine.

When laughter comes out of thinking it is ugly; it belongs to this ordinary, mundane world; it is not cosmic. Then you are laughing at somebody else, at somebody else's cost, and it is ugly and violent.

When laughter comes out of silence you are not laughing at anybody's cost, you are simply laughing at the whole cosmic joke. And it really is a joke! That's why I go on telling jokes…because jokes carry more than any scriptures. It is a joke because inside you, you have everything—yet you are searching everywhere! What else should a joke be? You are a king and acting like a beggar in the streets—not only acting, not only deceiving others, but also deceiving yourself that you are a beggar. You have the source of all knowledge and you are asking questions; you have the knowing self and think that you are ignorant; you have the deathless within you and are afraid and fearful of death and disease. This really is a joke, and if Mahakashyap laughed, he did well.

But, except for Buddha, nobody understood. He accepted the laughter and immediately realized that Mahakashyap had attained. The quality of that laugh was cosmic; he understood the whole joke of the situation. There was nothing else to it. The whole thing is as if the divine is playing hide-and-seek with you. Others thought Mahakashyap was a fool, laughing in front of Buddha. But Buddha thought this man had become wise. Fools always have a subtle wisdom in them, and the wise always act like fools.

In the old days all great emperors always had one fool in their court. They had many wise men, counselors, ministers, and prime ministers, but always one fool. Even though many of them were intelligent and wise, emperors all over the world in the East and the West had a court jester, a fool. Why? Because there are things so-called wise men will not be able to understand, that only a foolish man can understand, because the wise can be so foolish that their cunningness and cleverness close their minds.

A fool is simple, and was needed because many times the so-called wise would not say something because they were afraid of the emperor. A fool is not afraid of anybody else. He will speak whatsoever the consequences. A fool is a man who will not think of the consequences. A clever man always thinks first of the result, then he acts. Thought comes first, then action. A foolish man acts; thought never comes first. Whenever someone realizes the ultimate, he is not like a wise man. He cannot be. He may be like a fool but he cannot be like a wise man. When Mahakashyap laughed he was a fool, and Buddha understood him. Later on, Buddhist priests didn't understand him, so they dropped the anecdote.

This anecdote has been dropped from Buddhist scriptures because it is sacrilegious to laugh before Buddha. To make it the original source of a great tradition as Zen is not good. This is not a good precedent that a man laughed before Buddha, and also not a good thing that Buddha gave the key to this man and not to Sariputta, Ananda, Moggalayan, and others who were important, significant. And finally, it was they, Sariputta, Ananda, and Moggalayan, who recorded the scriptures.

Mahakashyap was never asked. Even if they had asked he would not have answered. Mahakashyap was never consulted whether he had something to say to be recorded.

When Buddha died, all the monks gathered and started recording what happened and what did not. Nobody asked Mahakashyap. This man must have been discarded by the community. The whole community must have felt jealous. The key had been given to this man who was not known at all, who was not a great scholar or pundit. Nobody knew him before, and suddenly that morning he became the most significant man because of the laughter, because of the silence.

And in a way they were right, because how can you record silence? You can record words, you can record what happened in the visible, but how can you record what has not happened in the visible? They knew the flower had been given to Mahakashyap, nothing else.

But the flower was just a container. It had something in it—buddhahood, the touch of Buddha's inner being, the fragrance that cannot be seen, that cannot be recorded. The whole thing seems as if it never happened, or as if it happened in a dream.

Those who recorded the scriptures were men of words, proficient in verbal communication, in talking, discussing, arguing. But Mahakashyap is never heard of again. This is the only thing known about him, such a small thing that the scriptures must have missed it. Mahakashyap has remained silent, and silently the inner river has been flowing. To others the key has been given, and the key is still alive, it still opens the door.

These two are the parts: the inner silence—the silence so deep that there is no vibration in your being; you are, but there are no waves; you are just a pool without waves, not a single wave arises; the whole being silent, still; inside, at the center, silence—and on the periphery, celebration and laughter. Only silence can laugh, because only silence can understand the cosmic joke.

So your life becomes a vital celebration, your relationship becomes a festive thing. Whatsoever you do, every moment is a festival. You eat, and eating becomes a celebration; you take a bath, and bathing becomes a celebration; you talk, and talking becomes a celebration. Relationship becomes a celebration. Your outer life becomes festive; there is no sadness in it. How can sadness exist with silence? But ordinarily you think otherwise: you think if you are silent you will be sad.

Ordinarily you think, how can you avoid sadness if you are silent? I tell you that the silence that exists with sadness cannot be true. Something has gone wrong. You have missed the path; you are off the track. Only celebration can give proof that a real silence has happened.

Buddha must have known Mahakashyap. He must have known when he was looking at the flower silently and everybody was restless, he must have known that only one being there, Mahakashyap, was not restless.

Buddha must have felt the silence coming from Mahakashyap, but he would not call him up. When he laughed, then Buddha called him and gave him the flower. Why? Silence is only the half of it.

Mahakashyap would have missed if he had been innocently silent and didn't laugh. Then the key would not have been given to him. He was only half grown, not yet a fully grown tree, not blossoming. The tree was there, but flowers had not yet come. Buddha waited.

Now, I will tell you why Buddha waited for so many minutes, why for one or two or three hours he waited.

Mahakashyap was silent but he was trying to contain laughter, he was trying to control laughter. He was trying not to laugh because it would be so unmannerly: What would Buddha think? What would the others think? But then, the story says, he couldn't contain himself anymore. It had to come out as a laugh. The flood became too much, and he couldn't contain it anymore.

When silence is too much it becomes laughter; it becomes so overflooded that it starts overflowing in all directions. He laughed. It must have been a mad laughter, and in that laughter there was no Mahakashyap. Silence was laughing; silence had come to a blossoming.

Then immediately Buddha called Mahakashyap: "Take this flower—this is the key. I have given to all others what can be given in words, but to you I give that which cannot be given in words. The message beyond words, the most essential, I give to you."

Buddha waited for those hours so that Mahakashyap's silence could overflow and become laughter.

the lion's

roar

Bodhidharma did one of the greatest things in the history of consciousness: he found the right soil for the seed that Buddha had given to the world.

bodhidharma
goes to china

In these fourteen centuries that have followed Bodhidharma, hundreds of Zen masters of great clarity, insight and awakening, have appeared, but no one even comes close to the depth, the subtlety, the beauty, and the immense perception of Bodhidharma. As I look into Bodhidharma, I don't find any other single individual in the whole history of mankind—Gautam Buddha included—who can be said to have condensed religion into its simplest possibility, expressed religion into its absolute purity. It is obvious that this man is going to be misunderstood, condemned, ignored. The greatest peak of consciousness that man has achieved, mankind has not been kind enough to remember. Perhaps there are heights our eyes cannot see, but we should try our best. One never knows.

BODHIDHARMA WAS BORN fourteen centuries ago as a son of a king in the south of India where there was a big empire, the empire of Pallavas. He was the third son of his father. But seeing everything—he was a man of tremendous intelligence—he renounced the kingdom. He was not against the world, but he was not ready to waste his time in mundane affairs, in trivia.

His whole concern was to know his self-nature, because without knowing it, you have to accept death as the end. All true seekers, in fact, have been fighting against death. Bertrand Russell has said that if there were no death, there would be no religion. There is some truth in this. I will not agree totally, because religion is a vast continent. It is not only a response to death, it is also the search for bliss, it is also

the search for truth, and it is also the search for the meaning of life. It is many more things. But certainly Bertrand Russell is right: if there were no death, very few, very rare people would be interested in religion. Death is a great incentive.

Bodhidharma renounced the kingdom, saying to his father, "If you cannot save me from death, then please don't prevent me. Let me go in search of something that is beyond death."

Those were beautiful days, particularly in the East. The father thought for a moment and he said, "I will not prevent you, because I cannot prevent your death. You go on your search with all my blessings. It is sad for me but that is my problem; it is my attachment. I was hoping for you to be my successor, to be the emperor of the great Pallavas empire, but you have chosen

something higher than that. I am your father, so how can I prevent you? And you have put in such a simple way a question which I had never expected. You say, 'If you can prevent my death, then I will not leave the palace. But if you cannot prevent my death, then please don't prevent me from leaving, either.'"

You can see Bodhidharma's great intelligence. And although he was a follower of Gautam Buddha, in some instances he shows higher flights than Gautam Buddha himself. For example, Gautam Buddha was afraid to initiate a woman into his commune of disciples, but Bodhidharma was initiated by a woman who was enlightened. Her name was Pragyatara. Perhaps people would have forgotten her name; it is only because of Bodhidharma that her name still remains known. But only the name—we don't know anything else about her. It was she who ordered Bodhidharma to go to China.

Buddhism had reached China six hundred years before Bodhidharma. It was something magical; it had never happened anywhere, at any time, and Buddha's message immediately caught hold of the whole Chinese people. The situation was such that China had lived under the influence of Confucius and was tired of it because Confucius was just a moralist, a puritan. He did not know anything about the inner mysteries of life.

There were people like Lao Tzu, Chuang Tzu, and Lieh Tzu, contemporaries of Confucius, but they were mystics, not masters. They could not create a counter-movement against Confucius in the hearts of the Chinese people. So there was a vacuum. Nobody can live without a soul, and once you start thinking that there is no soul, your life starts losing all meaning. The soul is your integrating concept; without it you are cut away from existence and eternal life. Just like a branch cut from a tree is bound to die—it has lost the source of nourishment—the very idea that there is no soul inside you, no consciousness, cuts you away from existence. One starts shrinking; one starts feeling suffocated.

Confucius was a great rationalist. These mystics—Lao Tzu, Chuang Tzu, Lieh Tzu— knew that what Confucius was doing was

wrong, but they were not masters. They remained in their monasteries with their few disciples.

When Buddhism reached China, it immediately entered into the very soul of the people, as if they had been thirsty for centuries and Buddhism had come as a rain cloud. It quenched their thirst so immensely that something unimaginable happened. Buddhism simply explained itself, and the beauty of the message was understood by the people. They were thirsty for it; they were waiting for something like it. The whole country, which was the biggest country in the world, turned to Buddhism. When Bodhidharma arrived six hundred years later, there were already thirty thousand Buddhist temples, monasteries, and two million Buddhist monks in China. Two million Buddhist monks is not a small number; it was five percent of the whole population of China.

Pragyatara, Bodhidharma's master, told him to go to China because the people who had reached there before him had made a great impact, although none of them were enlightened. They were great scholars, disciplined people, loving and peaceful and compassionate, but none of them were enlightened. And now China needed another Gautam Buddha. The ground was ready.

Bodhidharma was the first enlightened man in the Buddhist tradition to reach China. There are many legends about the man; they all have some significance. The first legend is that when he reached China—it took him three years—the Chinese emperor, Wu, came to receive him. Bodhidharma's fame had preceded him. Emperor Wu had done great service to the philosophy of Gautam Buddha. Thousands of scholars were translating Buddhist scriptures from Pali into Chinese, and the emperor was the patron of that great work of translation. He had built thousands of temples and monasteries, and he was feeding thousands of monks. He had put his whole treasure in the service of Gautam Buddha.

Naturally, the Buddhist monks who had arrived before Bodhidharma had been telling the emperor that he was earning great virtue, that he would be born as a god in heaven. So his first question to Bodhidharma was, "I have made so many monasteries, I am feeding thousands of scholars, I have opened a university for the studies of Gautam Buddha, I have put my whole empire and its treasures in the service of Gautam Buddha. What is going to be my reward?"

He was a little taken aback seeing Bodhidharma, not having thought that the man would be like this. He looked ferocious. He had very big eyes, but a very soft heart—just a lotus flower in his heart. But his face was as dangerous looking as you can conceive. Just the sunglasses were missing; otherwise he looked like a Mafia guy! With great fear, Emperor Wu asked the question, and Bodhidharma said, "Nothing, no reward. On the contrary, be ready to fall into the seventh hell."

The emperor said, "But I have not done anything wrong—why the seventh hell? I have been doing everything that the Buddhist monks have been telling me."

Bodhidharma said, "Unless you start hearing your own voice, nobody can help you, Buddhist or non-Buddhist. And you have not yet heard your inner voice. If you had heard it, you would not have asked such a stupid question.

"On the path of Gautam Buddha there is no reward because the very desire for reward comes from a greedy mind. The whole teaching of Gautam Buddha is desirelessness. And if you are doing all these so-called virtuous acts—making temples and monasteries and feeding thousands of monks—with a desire in your mind, you are preparing your way to hell. If you are doing these things out of joy, to share your joy with the empire, and there is not even a slight desire anywhere for any reward, the very act is a reward unto itself. Otherwise you have missed the whole point."

Emperor Wu said, "My mind is so full of thoughts. I have been trying to create some peace of mind, but I have failed and because of these thoughts and their noise, I cannot hear what you are calling the inner voice. I don't know anything about it."

Bodhidharma said, "Then at four o'clock in the morning, come alone without any bodyguards to the temple in the mountains where I am going to stay. And I will put your mind at peace, forever."

The emperor thought, "This man is really outlandish, outrageous!" He had met many monks; they were so polite, but, "This one does not even bother that I am an emperor of a great country. And to go to him in the darkness

"Strange, because I have been asking," the emperor thought, "of many wise people who have come from India, and they all gave me methods, techniques, which I have been practicing, but nothing is happening. And this strange fellow, who looks almost mad, or drunk, and has a strange face with such big eyes that he creates fear.... But he seems to be sincere too. He is a wild phenomenon! It is worth the risk. What can he do? At the most he can kill me." Finally, he could not resist the temptation to go, because the man had promised, "I will put your mind at peace forever."

Emperor Wu reached the temple at four o'clock, early in the morning in darkness, alone, and Bodhidharma was standing there with his staff, just on the steps. He said, "I knew you would be coming, although the whole night you debated whether to go or not to go. What kind of an emperor are you? So cowardly, being afraid of a poor monk, a poor beggar who has nothing in the world except this staff. And with this staff I am going to put your mind to silence."

The emperor thought, "My God, who has ever heard that with a staff you can put somebody's mind to silence! You can finish him, hit him hard on the head—then the whole man is silent, not just the mind. But now it is too late to go back."

And Bodhidharma said, "Sit down here in the courtyard of the temple." There was not a single person around. "Close your eyes. I am sitting in front of you with my staff. Your work is to catch hold of the mind. Just close your eyes and go inside looking for it—find where

of early morning at four o'clock, alone.... This man seems to be dangerous!" Bodhidharma always used to carry a big staff with him.

The emperor could not sleep the whole night, "To go or not to go? Because that man can do anything. He seems to be absolutely unpredictable." On the other hand, he felt deep down in his heart the sincerity of the man, that he was not a hypocrite. "He does not care a bit that you are an emperor and he is a beggar. He behaves as an emperor, and in front of him you are just a beggar. And the way he has said, 'I will put your mind at peace forever'....

it is. The moment you catch hold of it, just tell me, 'Here it is.' And my staff will do the rest."

It was the strangest experience any seeker of truth or peace or silence could have ever had. But now there was no way out. Emperor Wu sat with closed eyes, knowing perfectly well that Bodhidharma seemed to mean what he said. He looked all around— there was no mind. That staff did its work!

For the first time he was in such a situation. The choice... if you find the mind, one never knows what this man is going to do with his staff. And in that silent mountainous place, in the presence of Bodhidharma, who has a charisma of his own....

There have been many enlightened people but Bodhidharma stands aloof, alone, like an Everest. His every act is unique and original. His every gesture has his own signature; it is not borrowed.

Emperor Wu tried hard to look for the mind and he could not find it. It is a small strategy. Mind exists only because you never look for it; it exists only because you are never aware of

it. When you are looking for it, you are aware of it, and awareness surely kills it completely.

Hours passed and the sun was rising in the silent mountains with a cool breeze. Bodhidharma could see on the face of Emperor Wu such peace, such silence, such stillness... as if he were a statue. He shook him and asked him, "It has been a long time. Have you found the mind?"

Emperor Wu said, "Without using your staff, you have pacified my mind completely. I don't have any mind and I have heard the inner voice about which you spoke. Now I know that whatever you said was right. You have transformed me without doing anything. Now I know that each act has to be a reward unto itself; otherwise, don't do it. Who is there to give you the reward? This is a childish idea. Who is there to give you the punishment? Your action is punishment and your action is your reward. You are the master of your destiny."

Bodhidharma said, "You are a rare disciple. I love you. I respect you, not as an emperor, but as a man who has the courage just in a

single sitting to bring so much awareness, so much light that all darkness of the mind disappears."

Wu tried to persuade Bodhidharma to come to the palace. But Bodhidharma said, "That is not my place. You can see I am wild, I do things I myself don't know beforehand that I'm going to do. I live moment to moment, spontaneously. I am very unpredictable. I may create unnecessary trouble for you and your court, your people. I am not meant for palaces; just let me live in my wildness."

He lived on a mountain whose name was Tai. The second legend is that Bodhidharma was the man who created tea—the name *tea* comes from the mountain *Tai*, because it was created there. All the words for tea, in any language, are derived from the same source, *tai*.

The way Bodhidharma created tea cannot be historical, but it is significant. He was meditating almost all the time, and sometimes in the night he would start falling asleep. So, just to stay awake and teach a lesson to his eyes, he pulled out all his eyelashes and threw them on the temple ground. The story is that out of those eyelashes, the tea bushes grew. Those were the first tea bushes. That's why when you drink tea, you cannot sleep. Tea is immensely helpful during meditation. Today the Buddhist world drinks tea as part of meditation, because it keeps you alert and awake.

Although there were two million Buddhist monks in China, Bodhidharma could find only four who were worthy to be accepted as his disciples. He was so choosy, it took him almost nine years to find his first disciple, Hui-k'o.

For nine years—and that is a historical fact based on ancient references, almost contemporary to Bodhidharma which all mention that fact—for nine years, after sending Wu back to the palace, Bodhidharma sat facing a wall inside the temple. He made it a great meditation. He would simply look at the wall. After looking at a wall for a long time, you cannot think. Slowly, slowly, just like the wall, the screen of your mind also becomes empty. Bodhidharma had a second reason. He declared, "Unless somebody who deserves to be my disciple comes, I will not look at the audience."

People used to come and sit behind him. It was a strange situation. Nobody had spoken in this way before; he would speak to the wall. People would be sitting behind him but he would not face the audience because, he said, "The audience hurts me more, because it is just *like* a wall. Nobody understands, and to look at human beings in such an ignorant state hurts deeply. But to look at the wall, there is no question...a wall, after all, is a wall. It *cannot* hear, so there is no need to feel hurt. I will turn to face the audience only if somebody proves by his action that he is ready to be my disciple."

Nine years passed. People could not figure out what to do, what action would satisfy him. They could not figure it out. Then came a young man, Hui-k'o. He cut off one of his hands with a sword, threw the hand before Bodhidharma, and said, "This is the beginning. Either you turn, or my head will be falling before you. I am going to cut my head off too." Bodhidharma turned and said, "You are really a man worthy of me. No need to cut the head off; we have to use it." This man, Hui-k'o, was his first disciple. When Bodhidharma finally intended to leave China, he called his four disciples—three more he had gathered after Hui-k'o. He said to them, "In simple words, in small sentences, telegraphic, tell me the essence of my teachings. I intend to leave tomorrow morning to go back to the Himalayas, and I want to choose from you four, one as my successor."

The first man said, "Your teaching is of going beyond mind, of being absolutely silent, and then everything starts happening of its own accord."

Bodhidharma said, "You are not wrong, but you don't satisfy me. You just have my skin."

The second one said, "To know that I am not, and only existence is, is your fundamental teaching."

Bodhidharma said, "A little better, but not up to my standard. You have my bones; sit down."

And the third one said, "Nothing can be said about it. No word is capable of saying anything about it."

Bodhidharma said, "Good, but you have said already something about it. You have contradicted yourself. Just sit down; you have my marrow."

The fourth was his first disciple, Hui-k'o, who simply fell at Bodhidharma's feet, without saying a word, tears rolling down from his eyes. Bodhidharma said, "You have said it. You are going to be my successor."

But during the night, Bodhidharma was poisoned by some disciple out of revenge for not having been chosen as the successor. So they buried him, and the strangest legend is that after three years he was found by a government official, walking out of China toward the Himalayas with his staff in his hand, and one of his sandals hanging from the staff—and he was barefoot. The official had known him, had been to see him many times, had fallen in love with the man, although he was a little eccentric. He asked, "What is the meaning of this staff, and one sandal hanging from it?" Bodhidharma said, "Soon you will know. If you meet my people just tell them that I'm going into the Himalayas forever."

The official rushed immediately, as fast as he could, to the monastery on the mountain where Bodhidharma had been living. There he heard that Bodhidharma had been poisoned and had died…and there was the tomb. The official had not heard about it because he was posted on the boundary of the empire. He said, "My God, but I have seen him, and I cannot be deceived because I have seen him many times before. He was the same man, those same ferocious eyes, the same fiery and wild outlook, and on top of it, he was carrying one sandal on his staff."

The disciples could not contain their curiosity, and they opened the tomb. All they found there was just one sandal. And then the official understood why he had said, "Soon you will know."

We have heard so much about Jesus' resurrection. But nobody has talked much of the resurrection of Bodhidharma. Perhaps he was only in a coma when they buried him, and then he came to his senses, slipped out of the tomb, left one sandal there and put another sandal on his staff and according to the plan, he left.

He wanted to die in the eternal snows of the Himalayas. He wanted there to be no tomb, no temple, no statue of him. He did not want to leave any footprints behind him to be worshiped; those who loved him should enter into their own being. "I am not going to be worshiped," he said. And he disappeared almost in thin air. Nobody heard anything more about him—what happened, where he died. He must be buried in the eternal snows of the Himalayas.

a marriage
with tao

Zen is a crossbreed between Buddha's thought and Lao Tzu's thought. It is a great meeting, the greatest that ever took place.

sosan, the third zen patriarch

Zen goes beyond Buddha and beyond Lao Tzu. It is a culmination, a transcendence, both of the Indian genius and of the Chinese genius. The Indian genius reached its highest peak in Gautam the Buddha and the Chinese genius reached its highest peak in Lao Tzu. And the meeting between the essence of Buddha's teaching and the essence of Lao Tzu's teaching merged into one stream so deeply that no separation is possible now. Even to make a distinction between what belongs to Buddha and what to Lao Tzu is impossible, the merger has been so total. It is not only a synthesis, it is an integration. Out of this meeting Zen was born. Zen is neither Buddhist nor Taoist and yet it is both.

SOSAN IS THE third Zen Patriarch. Nothing much is known about him, and this is as it should be because history records only violence. History does not record silence—it cannot record it. All records are of disturbance. Whenever someone becomes truly silent, he disappears from all records; he is no longer a part of our madness. So it is as it should be.

Sosan remained a wandering monk his whole life. He never stayed anywhere; he was always passing by, going along, moving. He was a river; he was not a pond, static. He was a constant movement. That is the meaning of Buddha calling his monks *bhikkhus*, "wanderers": not only in the outside world, but also in the inside world they should be homeless, because whenever you make a home you become attached to it. They should

remain rootless; there is no home for them apart from this whole universe.

Even when it was recognized that Sosan had become enlightened, he continued his old beggar's way. Nothing was special about him. He was an ordinary man, a man of Tao.

One thing I would like to remind you of: Zen is a crossbreed. And just as more beautiful flowers can come out of crossbreeding, and more beautiful children are born out of crossbreeding, the same has happened with Zen.

Zen is a crossbreed between Buddha's thought and Lao Tzu's thought. It is a great meeting, the greatest that ever took place. That's why Zen is more beautiful than Buddha's thought and more beautiful than Lao Tzu's thought. It is a rare flowering of

the highest peaks and the meeting of those peaks. Zen is neither Buddhist nor Taoist, but it carries both within it.

India is a little too serious about religion—there is a long past, a great weight on the mind of India, and religion has become serious. Lao Tzu remained a laughingstock—he is known as the old fool. He is not serious at all; you cannot find a more non-serious man. When Buddha's thought and Lao Tzu's thought met, India and China met, and Zen was born. Sosan was near the original source when Zen was coming out of the womb. He carries the fundamentals.

His biography is not relevant at all, because whenever a man becomes enlightened he has no biography. He is no longer confined to his form, so when he was born and when he died are irrelevant facts.

That's why in the East we have never bothered about biographies, about historical facts. That obsession has never existed in the East. That obsession has come from the West only recently, now that people have become more interested in irrelevant things.

When a Sosan is born, what difference does it make—this year or that? When he dies, how is it important? Sosan is important, not his entry into this world and the body, not his departure. Arrivals and departures are irrelevant. The only relevance is in the being.

In his lifetime, Sosan only uttered a few words. Remember, they are not just words, because they come out of a mind that has gone beyond words. They are not speculations; they are authentic experiences. Whatsoever he says, he knows. He is not a man of knowledge; he is a wise man. He has penetrated the mystery and whatever he brings forth is significant. It can transform you completely. If you listen to him, the very listening can become a transformation, because whatsoever he is saying is the purest gold.

When Sosan speaks, he speaks on a different plane. He is not interested in speaking; he is not interested in influencing anybody; he is not trying to convince you of some theory or philosophy or ism. No, when he speaks, his silence blooms. When he speaks, he is saying that which he has come to know and would like to share with you. It is not to convince you, remember—it is just to share with you. If you can understand a single word

of his, you will feel a tremendous silence being released within you.

We will be talking about Sosan and his words. If you listen attentively, suddenly you will feel a release of silence within you. These words are atomic, they are full of energy. Whenever a person who has attained says something, the word is a seed and for millions of years the word will remain a seed and will seek a heart.

If you are ready, ready to become the soil, then these tremendously powerful words of Sosan—these living seeds—will enter your heart if you allow it, and you will be totally different through them. Don't listen to them from the mind, because their meaning is not of the mind; the mind is absolutely impotent to understand them. They don't come from the mind, they cannot be understood by the mind. They come from a no-mind. They can be understood only by a state of no-mind.

So while listening, don't try to interpret. Don't listen to the words but to the gaps between the lines, not to what he says but to what he means—the significance. Let that significance hover around you like a fragrance. Silently it will enter you; you will become pregnant. But don't interpret. Don't say, "He means this or that," because that interpretation will be yours. Don't interpret—listen. When you interpret you can't listen, because the consciousness cannot do two opposite things simultaneously. If you start thinking, listening stops. Just listen as you listen to music—a different quality of listening in which there is no meaning in the sounds.

This is also music. This Sosan is a musician, not a philosopher. This Sosan is not saying words, he is saying more—more than the words. They have significance but they don't have any meaning. They are like musical sounds.

When you sit near a waterfall, you listen to it, but do you interpret what the waterfall says? It says nothing, yet it speaks. It says much that cannot be said.

What do you do near a waterfall? You listen, you become silent and quiet, you absorb. You allow the waterfall to go deeper and deeper within you. Then everything becomes quiet and silent within. You become a temple—the unknown enters through the waterfall.

What do you do when you listen to the songs of the birds, or wind passing through the trees, or dry leaves being blown by the breeze? What do you do? You simply listen.

This Sosan is not a philosopher, he is not a theologian, he is not a priest. He does not want to sell any idea to you, he is not interested in ideas. He is not there to convince you, he is simply blooming. He is a waterfall, or he is a wind blowing through the trees, or he is a song of the birds—no meaning, but much significance. You have to absorb that significance, only then will you be able to understand.

So listen, but don't think. Then it will be possible for much to happen within you, because I tell you: this Sosan, about whom nothing much is known, was a man of power, a man who has come to know. When he speaks he carries something of the unknown to the world of the known. With him enters the divine, a ray of light into the darkness of your mind.

Before we enter into his words, remember the significance of the words, not the meaning; the music, the melody, not the meaning; the sound of his soundless mind, his heart, not his thinking. You have to listen to his being, the waterfall.

How to listen? Just be silent. Don't bring your mind in. Don't start thinking, "What is he saying?" Just listen without deciding this way or that, without saying whether he is right or wrong, whether you are convinced or not. He does not bother about your conviction; you also need not bother about it. Simply listen and delight. Such persons as Sosan are to be delighted in; they are natural phenomena.

A beautiful rock—what do you do with it? You delight in it. You touch it, you move around it, you feel it, the moss on it.

What do you do with clouds moving in the sky? You dance on the earth, you look at them, or you just keep quiet and lie down on the ground and watch them float.

And they fill you. Not only the outer sky— by and by, the more you become silent, they fill your inner sky also.

Suddenly you are not there; only clouds are moving, in and out. The division is dropped, the boundary is no more. You have become the sky and the sky has become you.

Treat Sosan as a natural phenomenon. He is not just a man, he is godliness, he is Tao, he is a buddha. This Sosan is not for logic, he is for life. Now, try to understand the significance of his words. He says:

The Great Way is not difficult for those who have no preferences.

When love and hate are both absent everything becomes clear and undisguised.

Make the smallest distinction, however, and heaven and earth are set infinitely apart.

If you wish to see the truth, then hold no opinion for or against.

The struggle of what one likes and what one dislikes is the disease of the mind.

Just as Chuang Tzu says, "Easy is right," Sosan says, "The Great Way is not difficult." If it appears difficult, it is you who make it difficult. The Great Way is easy. How can it be difficult? Even trees follow it, rivers follow it, rocks follow it. How can it be difficult? Even birds fly in it and fish swim in it. How can it be difficult? People make it difficult, the mind makes it difficult—and the trick to make any easy thing difficult is to choose, to make a distinction.

Love is easy, hate is easy, yet you choose. You say, "I will only love, I will not hate." Now everything has become difficult. Now you cannot even love! To breathe in is easy, to breathe out is easy. You choose. You say, "I will only breathe in, I will not breathe out." Now everything has become difficult.

The mind can ask, "Why breathe out? Breath is life. Simple arithmetic: go on breathing in, don't breathe out, and you will become more and more alive. More and more life will be accumulated. You will become a great treasure of life. Breathe in only; don't breathe out because breathing out is death."

Remember, the first thing a child has to do when he is born is to breathe in. And the last thing a man does when he dies is to breathe out. Life begins with breathing in and death begins with breathing out. Each moment when you breathe in you are reborn; each moment when you breathe out you are dead, because breath is life. That's why Hindus have called it *prana: prana* means life. Breath is life.

The simple logic, simple arithmetic; there is not much trouble, you can make it plain: more and more breathe in and don't breathe out, then you will never die. If you breathe out you will have to die. And if you do it too much you will die soon! Simple arithmetic, it seems so obvious. So what is a logician supposed to do? A logician will only breathe in, never breathe out.

Love is breathing in, hate is breathing out. So what to do? Life is easy if you don't decide, because then you know breathing in and breathing out are not two opposite things; they are two parts of one process. Those two parts are organically connected, you cannot divide them. And if you don't breathe out...? The logic is wrong. You will not be alive—you will be simply, immediately, dead.

Try it—just breathe in and don't breathe out. You will understand. You will become very, very tense. Your whole being would like to breathe out because this is leading to death. If you choose, you will be in difficulty. If you don't choose, everything is easy. Easy is right.

If you are in difficulty, it is because of too many teachers who have poisoned your mind, who have been teaching you: "Choose this—don't do this, do that." Their dos and don'ts have killed you, yet they look logical. If you argue with them they will win the argument. Logic will help them: "Look! It is so simple. Why breathe out if it brings death?"

The same thing has happened with sex, in some traditions, because people think death enters with sex. They seem to be right, because sex energy gives birth to life, so the more sex energy moves out, the more life is moving out. It is logical, absolutely Aristotelian, but foolish. You cannot find greater fools than logicians. It is logical that life energy comes from sex—a child is born because of sex, sex is the source of life—so keep it in. Don't allow it to go out, otherwise you will be dead. Thus the world has become afraid.

But this is the same as keeping the breath in; if you suppress it, the whole being wants to throw it out. So your so-called celibates, who try to keep their sex energy in, find that the whole body wants to throw that energy out.

Their entire lives become sexual—their minds become sexual, they dream of sex, they think of sex all the time. Sex becomes their obsession because they are trying to do something that is logical, of course, but not true to life.

If you want more life, breathe out more, so you create a vacuum inside and more breath comes in. Don't think about breathing in, simply exhale as much as you can and your whole being will inhale. Love more—that is breathing out—and your body will gather energy from the whole cosmos. You create the vacuum and the energy comes.

It is like this in every process of life. You eat, but then you become a miser, you become constipated. The logic is right: don't breathe out. Constipation is choosing to breathe in and being against breathing out. Almost every civilized person is constipated; you can measure civilization through constipation. The more constipated a country the more civilized because the more logical. Why breathe out? Just go on breathing in. Food is energy. Why throw it out? You may not be aware of it, but this is the unconscious mind being logical and Aristotelian.

Life is a balance between throwing out and inviting in. You are just a passage. Share! Give, and more will be given to you. Be a miser, don't give, and less will be given to you because you don't need it.

Remember, and watch your life processes. If you are interested in understanding enlightenment ultimately, remember to give so that more is given to you, whatsoever it is.

Breathe out, exhale more. That is what sharing means, what giving means.

But the mind has its own logic, and Sosan calls that logic the disease.

The Great Way is not difficult... You make it difficult, *you* are difficult. The Great Way is easy...*for those who have no preferences*.

Don't prefer—just allow life to move. Don't say to life, "Move this way, go to the north, or go to the south." Don't say anything; simply flow with life. Don't fight against the current; become one with the current.

The Great Way is easy for those who have no preferences, and you have preferences about everything! About everything you bring in your mind. You say, "I like, I don't like, I prefer this, I don't prefer that." But when you have no preferences—when all 'for' and 'against' attitudes are absent, both love and hate are absent, you have neither likes nor dislikes—you simply allow everything to happen. Then, Sosan says, "Everything becomes clear and undisguised."

Make the smallest distinction, however, and heaven and earth are set infinitely apart.

But your mind will say, "You will become an animal if you don't prefer. If you don't choose then what will be the difference between you and a tree?" There will be a difference, a great difference—not a difference that brings the mind in but a difference that comes through awareness. The tree is choiceless and unconscious. You will be choiceless and *conscious*. That is what choiceless awareness means, and that is the greatest distinction: you will be *aware that you are not choosing*.

This awareness gives such profound peace...you become a buddha, you become a Sosan, a Chuang Tzu. The tree cannot become a Chuang Tzu. Chuang Tzu is like the tree, and something more. He is like the tree as far as choice is concerned, he is absolutely unlike the tree as far as awareness is concerned. He is fully aware that he is not choosing.

Sosan says: *When love and hate are both absent....*

Love and hate both color your sight and then you cannot see clearly. If you love a person, you start seeing things that are not there. No woman is as beautiful as you think she is when you love her, because you project. You have a dream girl in mind and that dream girl is projected. Somehow the real girl functions only as a screen. That's why every love comes to frustration sooner or later, because how can the girl go on playing the screen? She is a real person; she will assert herself, she will say, "I am not a screen!" How long can she go on fitting in with your projection? Sooner or later you feel the projection doesn't fit. In the beginning she yielded to you, in the beginning you yielded to her. You were a projection screen for her, and she was a projection screen for you.

Mulla Nasruddin's wife said to him, "You don't love me as much as you loved me before, when you were courting me."

Nasruddin said, "Darling, don't pay much attention to those things—it was just campaign propaganda. I'll forget what you said if you forget what I said. Now let's get real."

> *Drop all burdens.*
> *The higher you want to reach,*
> *the less burdened you must be*

Nobody can play a screen for you forever because it is uncomfortable. How can somebody adjust to your dream? He has his own reality, and that reality asserts itself.

If you love a person, you project things that are not there. If you hate a person, again you project things that are not there. In love the person becomes a god, in hate the person becomes a devil—and the person is neither a god nor a devil, the person is simply himself or herself. These devils and gods are projections. If you love, you cannot see clearly. If you hate, you cannot see clearly.

When there is no liking and no disliking, your eyes are clear; you have clarity. Then you see the other as he is or she is. When you have a clarity of consciousness the whole existence reveals its reality to you. That reality is divine, that reality is truth.

What does it mean? Does it mean that a man like Sosan will not love? No, but his love will have a totally different quality; it will not be like yours. He will love but his love will not be a choice. He will love but his love will not be a projection. He will love but his love will not be a love for his own dream. He will love the real.

That love toward the real is compassion. He will not project this way or that. He will not see a god in you or a devil. He will simply see you. And he will share because he has enough— and the more one shares, the more it grows. He will share his ecstasy with you.

When you love, you project. You love not to give, you love to take, you love to exploit. When you love a person you start trying to fix the person according to your ideas. Every husband is doing that, every wife is doing that, every friend. They go on trying to change the other, the real—and since the real cannot be changed, they will only get frustrated. The real cannot be changed, so only your dream will be shattered and you will feel hurt. You don't listen to reality.

Nobody is here to fulfill your dream. Everybody is here to fulfill his own destiny, his own reality.

A man like Sosan loves but his love is not an exploitation. He loves because he has so much that he is overflowing. He is not creating a dream around anybody. He shares with whoever comes on his path. His sharing is unconditional, and he does not expect a thing from you.

If love expects anything, then there will be frustration. If love expects something, then there will be unfulfillment. If love expects something, there is going to be misery and madness.

"No," says Sosan, "neither love nor hate. Simply look at the reality of the other." This is Buddha's love: to see the reality of the other— not to project, not to dream, not to create an

image, not to try to fix the other according to your image.

Sosan says: *"When love and hate are both absent, everything becomes clear and undisguised."*

Mind has to love and hate, and mind has to go on fighting between these two. If you don't love and don't hate, you go beyond mind. Where is the mind then? When choice disappears within you, the mind disappears.

But even if you say, "I would like to be silent," you will never be silent because you have a preference. This is the problem.

People say, "I would like to be silent. I don't want these tensions anymore." I feel sorry for ·them—sorry because what they are saying is stupid. If you "don't want tensions anymore"

you will create new ones, because not-wanting is going to create a new tension. If you want silence too much, if you are striving for it too much, your silence itself will become a tension. Now you will be more disturbed because of your effort to catch hold of silence.

What is silence? It is a deep understanding of the phenomenon that if you prefer, you will be tense. Even if you prefer silence, you will be tense. Understand, feel it—whenever you prefer, you become tense; whenever you don't prefer, there is no tension and you are relaxed. When you are relaxed, your eyes have clarity; they are not crowded with clouds and dreams. No thoughts move in the mind; you can see the true. And when you can see the true, you are liberated. Truth liberates.

"Make the smallest distinction, however, and heaven and earth are set infinitely apart," says Sosan. The smallest distinction, the slightest choice, and you are divided. Then you have a hell and a heaven, and between these two you will be crushed.

"If you wish to see the truth, then hold no opinion for or against," says Sosan. Move without opinion. Move naked, with no clothes, with no opinions about truth, because truth abhors all opinions. Drop all your philosophies, theories, doctrines, scriptures! Drop all rubbish! Become silent, unchoosing, your eyes ready to see what is, not in any way hoping to see your wishes fulfilled.

Don't carry wishes. It is said the path to hell is completely filled with wishes—good wishes, hopes, dreams, rainbows, ideals. The path to heaven is absolutely empty.

Drop all burdens. The higher you want to reach, the less burdened you must be. If you go to the Himalayas you have to unburden yourself completely. Finally, when you reach the Gourishankar, the Everest, you have to drop everything.

You have to go completely naked, because the higher you move the more weightless you need to be. And opinions are weights on you. They are not wings, they are like paperweights. Be opinionless, without any preference... "If you wish to see the truth then hold no opinion for or against."

Don't be a theist and don't be an atheist if you really want to know what truth is. Don't say, "There is a God" and don't say, "There is no God," because whatever you say will become a deep desire and you will project whatever is hidden in the desire.

If you want to see God as a Krishna with a flute on his lips, someday you will see him—not because Krishna is there, only because you had a seed of desire that you projected on the screen of the world. If you want to see Jesus crucified, you will see that. Whatsoever you want will be projected, but it is just a dream world—you are not coming nearer to the truth.

Become seedless within: no opinion, no thought for or against, no philosophy. Simply go to see that which is. Don't carry any mind. Go mindless.

"If you wish to see the truth then hold no opinion for or against. The struggle of what one likes and what one dislikes is the disease of the mind."

This is the disease of the mind: what one likes and what one does not like, for and against. Why is the mind divided? Why can't you be one? You would like to be one, you want to be one, but you go on watering the divisions, the preferences, the likes and dislikes. The more you use the mind, the more it is strengthened, the stronger it becomes. Don't use it.

Difficult, because you will say, "What will happen to our love? What will happen to our belonging? What will happen to our beliefs? What will happen to our religion, church, and temple?" They are your burdens. Be freed of them, and let them be freed of you. They are keeping you here, rooted, and truth would want you to be liberated.

Liberated you reach, with wings you reach, weightless you reach.

Says Sosan: "The struggle of what one likes and what one dislikes is the disease of the mind."

How to overcome it? Is there any way to overcome it? No, there is no way. One has simply to understand it. One has simply to look at the facticity of it. One has just to close one's eyes and look at one's own life—watch it, and you will feel the truth of Sosan. And when you feel the truth, the disease drops. There is no medicine for it because if medicine is given to you, you will start liking the medicine. Then the disease will be forgotten but the medicine will be liked, and then the medicine becomes a disease.

No, Sosan is not going to give you any medicine, any method. He is not going to suggest what to do. He is simply going to insist again and again and again, a thousand and one times, that you understand how you have created this mess around you, how you are in such misery. Nobody else has created it; it is your mind's disease of preference, of choosing.

Don't choose. Accept life as it is in its totality. You must look at the total: life and death together, love and hate together, happiness and unhappiness together, agony and ecstasy together.

If you look at them together, then what is there to choose? If you see they are one, then from where can choice enter? If you see that agony is nothing but ecstasy, ecstasy nothing but agony; if you can see that happiness is nothing but unhappiness; love is nothing but hate, hate is nothing but love—then where to choose? How to choose?

Then choice drops. *You* are not dropping it. If *you* drop it, that will become a choice—this is the paradox. You are not supposed to drop it, because if you drop it that means you have chosen for and against.

Now your choice is for totality. You are for totality and against division, but the disease has entered. It is subtle.

Simply understand, and the very understanding becomes dropping. Never drop it. Simply laugh... and ask for a cup of tea.

PLATE NUMBER ONE

TENDING THE OX—A ZEN ALLEGORY

Tending the ox is an ancient symbol in the history of Zen. There exist ten paintings in China; the tenth painting has been a cause of great controversy. I would like you to understand those ten paintings.

The ten paintings are immensely beautiful. In the first, the ox is lost. The man to whom the ox belongs is standing, looking all around in the thick forest, and he cannot see where the ox has gone. He is simply bewildered, confused. It is getting late, the sun it setting; soon it will be night, and then going into the thick forest to find the ox will become more and more difficult.

In the second picture he finds hoofprints of the ox. He feels a little happier; perhaps there is a possibility of finding the ox—he has found the hoofprints. He follows them.

In the third picture he sees the back of the ox standing in the thick forest. It is difficult to see, but he can figure out that it is the back of his ox. In the fourth he has reached the ox; he can see the ox now, its whole body. He rejoices.

In the fifth painting he takes hold of the ox's horns. It is a great struggle to bring it back home, but he wins. In the sixth picture he is riding on the ox, coming back toward his home. These are beautiful paintings!

In the seventh picture the ox is tied down in his place. In the eighth picture the man is so full of joy that he starts playing on his flute. The ninth picture is an empty frame—there is nothing painted in it.

PLATE NUMBER TWO

In the tenth picture, which is the cause of a great controversy, the man is going with a bottle of wine toward the marketplace, almost drunk. You can see, he cannot even walk. This tenth picture has caused a great controversy which has been raging for two thousand years.

One sect, which is the major sect of mahayana, believes that the ninth is the last picture. It represents the no-mind; you have achieved the goal. The ox is your innermost self which you have lost, and the whole series of pictures is in search of your inner self. You have found the self in the ninth. There is immense silence and peace. It is nirvana; it is no-mind.

Beyond the ninth... the people who say this is the end of the journey think that somebody has added the tenth picture, which seems to be absolutely irrelevant. But the people who belong to a certain small sect of Zen believe in the tenth picture, too. They say that when one has become enlightened this is not the end. This is the highest peak of consciousness, it is the greatest achievement, but one has to come back to the human world, to the ordinary world. One has to again become part of the greater humanity. Only then can he share, only then can he provoke others to the search. And certainly when he comes from such height, he is absolutely drunk with ecstasy. That bottle of wine is not an ordinary wine. It is symbolic of an ecstatic state.

When these pictures were brought to Japan, just twelve or thirteen hundred years ago, only

PLATE NUMBER THREE

PLATE NUMBER FOUR

nine pictures were brought. The tenth was troublesome; it was left in China.

I was puzzled when I first looked at the Japanese pictures. They seem to be complete. Once you have achieved nirvana, what more is there? And then I found in an old Chinese book ten pictures. I was immensely happy that somebody had the insight two thousand years ago that a buddha is not a buddha if he cannot come back to ordinary humanity, if he cannot again become simple, innocent, carrying his nirvana, carrying his ecstasy in the bottle of wine, utterly drunk with the divine but still going toward the marketplace.

I could see that whoever painted the tenth picture was right. Up to the ninth picture, it is simply logical. Beyond the ninth, the tenth is a great realization.

According to me, up to the ninth a man is only a buddha; with the tenth he also becomes a Zorba. And this has been my constant theme: I have been insisting that the tenth picture is authentic, and if it were not there, I was going to paint it. Without it, ending in nothingness looks a little sad, looks a little serious, looks empty.

All this effort of finding yourself, meditating, going beyond the mind, realizing your being and ending up in desert of nothingness...no, there must be something more to it, something more beyond it, where flowers blossom, where songs arise, where dance is again possible—of course, on a totally different level.

These pictures of tending the ox have been found to be tremendously significant in explaining the whole path step by step.

PLATE NUMBER FIVE

PLATE NUMBER SIX

PLATE NUMBER SEVEN

PLATE NUMBER NINE

PLATE NUMBER EIGHT

PLATE NUMBER TEN

rinzai, master of the

irrational

Rinzai became known as "the master of shouts."

He used shouting as a method to bring silence to people.

zen goes to japan

Rinzai was one of the loveliest masters in the history of Zen. He brought Zen from China to Japan, but he had lived with the Chinese masters. He carried the same flame that Bodhidharma took from India to China. He had something of the same greatness, beauty, and the same absurd approach to awakening.

RINZAI IS ONE of the most loved masters in the tradition of Zen. The first transmission of the light happened between Gautam Buddha and Mahakashyapa. The second great transmission happened between Bodhidharma and his successor, Hui-k'o. Bodhidharma took the ultimate experience of consciousness from India to China.

Rinzai introduced the same consciousness, the same path of entering into oneself, from China to Japan. These three names—Mahakashyapa, Bodhidharma, and Rinzai—stand like great peaks of the Himalayas.

Rinzai became known as "the master of shouts." He used shouting as a method to bring silence to people—a sudden shout. They are asking about God, they are asking about heaven, they are asking about great philosophical or theological problems...and the master suddenly shouts!

The mind gets a shock, almost an electric shock. For a moment you are not, only the shout is. For a moment the mind stops, time stops—and that is the secret of meditation.

Rinzai would shout at the disciples to give them a first experience of their centering. You are both a circumference and a center. You live on the circumference; the shout pushes you to the center.

Once you experience being at the center you suddenly see the whole world changing. Your eyes are no longer the same; your clarity and transparency are absolute. You see the same green leaves greener, the same roses rosier, the same life as a festival, as a ceremony. You would love to dance.

Then the disciples learned that the shout could help them reach to their very center. It was a strange sight when Rinzai started accepting disciples near the river. The disciples

> *Once you experience being at the center, you suddenly see the whole world changing*

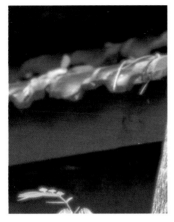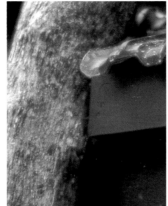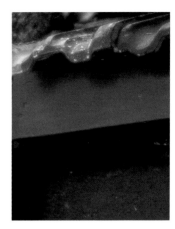

would be shouting and the valley would resound with shouts.

You could tell from miles away that you were getting closer to Rinzai. It was not only that he was shouting, but that shouting was a method to throw you from the circumference to the center.

Many mystics around the world have used sounds, but usually in a superficial way. Rinzai used shouts in a tremendously deep way. His shouts would become like a sword entering into you, piercing to the very center.

Another example is Jalaluddin Rumi's technique of whirling to find the center. If you whirl for hours, you will see slowly that something at the very center is not moving at all, and that is you. Your body is whirling, but your consciousness is a pillar of light.

Rumi attained his first enlightenment by whirling for thirty-six hours continuously. People thought he was mad. Even today a small group of his followers continues. They are called whirling dervishes. But the point is the same: whirling, your body becomes a cyclone, and your witnessing self becomes the center. Everything moves around you, but the center remains unmoving. To know this unmoving center is to know the master key of all the mysteries of life.

Rinzai had no idea about Rumi, neither did Rumi have any idea about Rinzai, but both were working on the same strategy—how to get to the center. As your consciousness becomes deeper, as it becomes an easy thing to go to the center just like you go into your house and come out again, you have become a buddha. Then slowly, slowly your center starts changing your circumference. First you cannot be violent; then you cannot be destructive; then you are love. Not that you love—you *are* love. Then you are silence, then you are truth, all that is old in you has disappeared. That was your circumference, that was the cyclone, and now it is gone. Now, only the center remains.

Rinzai said:

If you meet a buddha, cut him down; if you meet a patriarch, cut him down; if you meet an

arhat, cut him down; if you meet your parents, cut them down; and if you meet your relatives, cut them down.

Only thus will you be liberated, and if you are not held by externals, you will be disengaged and comfortably independent.

After this mountain monk has said that there is no dharma externally, students who do not understand this immediately make their interpretation of the internal. They then sit against the wall with the tongue touching the palate, to be in a motionless position and regard this as the Buddha Dharma of the patriarchs.

The greatest mistake is that if you take immobility as the right state, you will mistake the darkness for your master. This is what an ancient meant when he said, "In complete darkness, an abyss is dreadful."

If you take the moving state as the right one, all plants and straws can move. Are they Tao? Therefore, the moving is the element wind, and the unmoving is the element earth. Both the moving and the unmoving have no nature of their own. If you want to catch it in the moving, it will go to the unmoving; and if you want to catch it in the unmoving, it will go to the moving.

The moving and unmoving are two kinds of states, but the man of Tao can make use of both.

One of the fundamentals of Zen that makes it a unique religion, like no other religion in the world, is that it does not want to exclude anything from your life. Your life has to be all-inclusive; it has to comprehend all the stars and the sky and the earth. Zen is not a path of renouncing the world.

People are taught to sit silently with their tongue touching their palate, so even inside their mouth they cannot make any movement of the tongue, and the whole body should be like a statue—only then can you realize the truth. But it is only half of the truth, and a half truth is more dangerous than a total lie; at least a lie is total.

Life is both rest and movement.

If you go to Bodhgaya, where Gautam Buddha became enlightened, there stands a temple in memory of his enlightenment, by the side of the tree where he used to sit and meditate. That was his routine: for one hour he would sit under the tree and meditate, then for one hour he would walk by the side of the tree. Even the places where he moved are marked by stones to reveal a small path.

One hour he would walk and meditate, showing perfectly that life, if it is unmoving, is dead. And life, if it has no rest, will end very soon.

Life is a balance between rest and movement. When harmony is achieved between rest and movement, you come to the very center of your life, which is always with you whether you are sitting or moving, whether you are awake or asleep. Its existence is absolutely certain, but not discovered by reading scriptures. You have to experience it, then you can do anything. Then there is no problem for you, because whatever you do will be done out of a buddha nature.

The meditation that Buddha gave to the world is perhaps one of the most significant. There are many meditations, many ways to enter into yourself, but Buddha's is sharp, almost like a sword—it cuts everything that hinders. Even in a split second, you can reach to your ultimate destiny. But for that, Rinzai says: "If you meet a buddha...." He does not mean the actual Buddha, because where will you meet him now? Even when Rinzai was alive, Buddha had been dead for almost fifteen hundred years. So what is the meaning?

"If you meet a buddha, cut him down...."

It is a meditation process. When you go deeper into yourself, you are bound to meet figures who are very close to your heart. If you have loved Buddha, you are going to meet Buddha before you meet yourself. It will be just an image, but in the silences of the heart that image will be so radiant that there is a possibility you may sit down at the side of the road with of the image and forget that this is not the goal.

"If you meet a buddha, cut him down"—immediately! "If you meet a patriarch, a master, cut him down"—immediately! "If you meet an arhat, cut him down; if you meet your parents, cut them down; and if you meet your relatives, cut them down. Only thus will you be liberated...."

It is an inner psychological process, making you free from the master, from the parents, from the friends. It has nothing to do with the outside world, it is your inner world where images go on gathering. And unless all these images are dissolved, you cannot see yourself. They are hindering your perception. Rinzai's description of the Buddhist meditation is excellent.

"And if you are not held by externals, you will be disengaged and comfortably independent."

Now you have destroyed all the images, your dreams, your love affairs. You have made the path clean, but you may still be attached to externals. You may be ready to cut away your parents' image and be free of it, but what of the desire for power in the world, the desire to be the richest man in the world? A thousand and one desires surround you in the external world. The second step is easier. Rinzai begins with the hardest because he knows if you can do the hardest, the easier can be done without any difficulty.

"After this mountain monk has said that there is no dharma externally, students who do not understand this immediately make their interpretation of the internal."

It is very easy to misunderstand a master. In fact, it is easier to misunderstand a master than anyone else, because he is speaking a new language, giving new meanings to words, talking about spaces you have never been to. It is human to be mistaken, to misunderstand.

He says: "After this mountain monk has said that there is no dharma externally...." There is no religion externally. Going to the temple or to the church or to the synagogue, reading scriptures, ancient holy books—these are all externals and there is no dharma as far as externals are concerned. They are dead skeletons, remnants of somebody who attained, but now it is too difficult to decode the scriptures. The man is no longer there— only the skeleton of the man, which cannot speak, which cannot explain, which cannot help you in any way.

You can go on carrying scriptures, but those scriptures will be your interpretations, not the meaning of the masters.

You can go to the temples outside, but what are you doing? Going to manmade temples, full of manmade gods, and you are worshipping those stone gods. And you are not alone; almost the whole world is worshipping something or other as a god. But in this way you cannot find the essence of dharma. It is a very upside down, disturbed, and perverted situation when man starts worshipping gods he has created himself.

You have to know the source of life—the source from which you spring, just as roses spring. It is not a question of prayer, it is a question of intense exploration inside to find your roots. You will be surprised: your roots are the roots of the moon, of the sun, of the stars—of all existence.

You are just a small branch of a vast tree. Once you know it, there is no fear of death. You cannot die—you belong to immortality. There is no more desire. What more can you have? You have the whole universe in your hands. You are already everything you could have dreamed, desired, asked to be. A great contentment descends over you. In this contentment are all the qualities of blissfulness, of ecstasy, of all that is a continuous dance, a festivity, a ceremony.

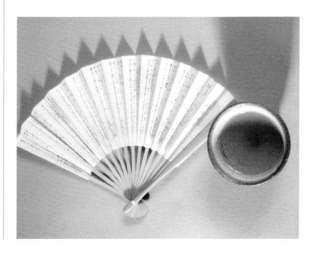

Rinzai says, "But I can be misunderstood. When I say there is no dharma externally, people might then sit against the wall with the tongue touching the palate, to be in a motionless position and regard this as the buddha dharma of the patriarchs."

Just sitting...how long can you go on sitting? When you stand up, Bodhidharma or Buddha or Rinzai will say, "What happened to the buddha?" The Buddha was sitting; your form of the buddha experience was sitting, but when you stand it will disappear. Walking, you will be walking away from sitting.

Rinzai is trying to say things in simple terms, and he had to be very simple because he was the man who brought Zen from China to Japan. He was talking to absolutely unconcerned people who had never heard about meditation.

"The greatest mistake is that if you take immobility as the right state, you will mistake the darkness for your master."

Immobility is only a rest period. Existence is motion, continuous motion. Yes, there are moments of rest, but if you choose the moments of rest as the whole truth, you are accepting darkness as your master. You are cutting life in two: darkness and light. Have you watched one thing? Darkness is stable. It never goes anywhere, it is always here. You bring light and you cannot see darkness. You take the light away and darkness is already there. It does not come running in from the street; it is never late, not even a single moment. If it had gone out for an evening walk, or to have a look at what was happening around the world, there would be a gap. When you had taken the lights away, the darkness would not be there yet. But there is never a gap. The reason is that darkness is always here even when light is here; it is just because of the light that you cannot see the darkness. Even in the motion, the action, the gesture of a buddha, there is a certain restfulness. That restfulness brings a grace to it, a beauty to it.

Rinzai says: "This is what an ancient meant when he said, 'In complete darkness, an abyss is dreadful.'"

Meditation is not meant to divide your life and your existence in two parts and then to choose one, the internal. A perfect meditation is all-inclusive. It transforms you, and with your transformation your vision of things is transformed, but nothing is excluded.

If you take the moving state as the right one, all plants and straws can move. Are they Tao? Therefore, the moving is the element wind, and the unmoving is the element earth, and both the moving and the unmoving have no nature of their own. If you want to catch it in the moving, it will go to the unmoving....

They are continuously changing places: day becoming night, night becoming day; life becoming death, death becoming life. Don't hold onto anything. It will immediately change into something else.

The movement and the non-movement are both in your hands. You are the watcher, neither the moving nor the unmoving.

You simply are.

You have never moved, so the question of unmoving does not arise. The question of movement or no movement is irrelevant to your witnessing consciousness. Your witnessing consciousness is existential. It is here. If your meditation does not bring you to this state of watchfulness, it is a false meditation. If it brings you to any god, you are fooling yourself; you are dreaming. If it brings you to Jesus Christ, then... Jesus Christ! Rinzai is saying if you meet Jesus Christ, give him another cross immediately! "That is your work, what else are you all doing here?" Even Buddha is not spared—and they are all disciples of Buddha.

If you meet the Buddha on the way, cut his head immediately. Nothing is more important than your own internal watchfulness. That is the very stuff the universe is made of.

flowers
bloom

Anything can be used to find the truth. Even a warrior can use his sword, fighting with another warrior; there is no need for him to sit and meditate.

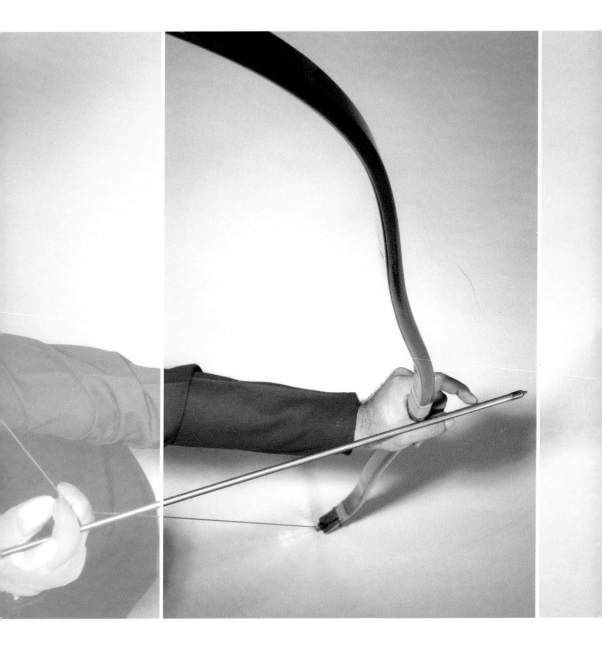

the japanese contribution to zen

Zen has given birth to many things. No other religious movement in the world has been so creative, so productive. It has created art that has a quality of its own, it has created poetry, it has created literature, it has created drama, it has created sculpture. Whatever it has created, it has left unmistakably the mark of meditativeness on it; it has turned things into meditation which nobody had ever imagined could even be associated with meditation.

ZEN WAS BORN in India in the absurd laughter of Mahakashyapa, a close disciple of Gautam Buddha. He had many disciples even closer than Mahakashyapa; Mahakashyapa is mentioned only once and that mention is of when he laughed.

This is the only mention of Mahakashyapa in the whole Buddhist canon. It is a vast literature, and for centuries, twenty-five centuries, people have been asking the question, "Why did Mahakashyapa laugh? And why was his laughter accepted? Not only accepted, but raised to the highest point of communication." Something transpired in that silent giving of the flower to Mahakashyapa. Zen became a new stream, flowing from Gautam Buddha to Mahakashyapa.

The next great name is Bodhidharma. His master told him to go to China, not to convert China to Buddhism... "But in China there is already a fragrance existing, created by Lao Tzu, Chuang Tzu, Lieh Tzu. Truth is nobody's monopoly. It will be good if you take the treasure that Mahakashyapa has given from generation to generation to China. And let these two beautiful streams of mystics meet." Just as in crossbreeding the child is stronger, the same happens when two streams of thought, or of no-thought, meet, merge. Something new, far deeper than either, far greater than either arises.

It took Bodhidharma three years to reach China. He went to China and the crossbreeding happened. What was Zen in Buddhism was made even more simple, so that the Chinese could understand and use it. It flourished in China, and great masters arose out of the mystic experience. From China it was taken to Japan. Again a new crossbreeding.... And in Japan it is manifested in many dimensions.

There are two ways to disappear as a personality: one we can call "grounding" and one we can call "centering."

Mahakashyapa and Bodhidharma used centering: going within to the point where nothing remains but a pure presence, no person. The same approach became even more beautiful with the great heritage of Chuang Tzu, Lieh Tzu, and Lao Tzu. They were also people of centering. They were exploring their interiority to find themselves, and what they found was an absolute absence of anybody—even the finder disappeared. Out of that state came neither the found nor the finder, neither the seeker nor the sought, but an absolute silence, alive, full of its own music, full of its own dance. Seeing this, Mahakashyapa had laughed—"Buddha goes on saying to people 'Seek yourself, find yourself' and he is tricking them." It is a perfectly legitimate statement, to "seek yourself." But Mahakashyapa knew that when you find yourself, you are no longer there! It is a strange situation; except for laughter, nothing can express it.

There is an old definition of a philosopher: on a dark night, in a dark house where there is no light—and the philosopher, moreover, is blind—he is looking for a black cat which

is not there. But the search continues. And if suddenly light comes in and his eyes are cured and he thinks of all the trouble that he was taking to find the cat which does not exist, what else is there to do except to laugh at himself?

Fools laugh at others. Wisdom laughs at itself.

In Japan the crossbreeding had a tremendous manifestation. Zen had come far from its beginnings in Mahakashyapa's laughter—a long journey. On the journey it gathered many new manifestations, many new revelations, many new methods. In Japan it finally turned out to be the peak. The peak is that anything can be used to find the truth. Even a warrior can use his sword, fighting with another warrior; there is no need for him to sit and meditate. The archer can find it in his archery; the painter can find it in his painting; the sculptor can find it in his sculpture.

What was in India only pure meditation grew in Japan into many branches. Indians cannot conceive how a warrior, a fighter with a sword, can be meditative, or how archery can be a meditative method, because Indians have

never tried it. Zen needed Mahakashyapa's laughter to travel from India to China and from China to Japan. On this long travel of a thousand years it gathered much insight.

One German professor, Herrigel, was reading about Zen and could not believe how the art of archery could be a form of meditation. There seems to be no relationship. Gautam Buddha sitting in the lotus posture meditating, that seemed to be perfect. But to conceive that an archer or a swordsman, whose effort is to kill the other, can be meditative...?

Herrigel went to Japan. For three years he was in Japan, and there he found the secret. He learned archery. He himself became an archer, a master archer, a hundred percent successful in hitting the target. But his Zen master said, "This is not the point. The point is not there in the target; the point is within you. Are you grounded?"

He said, "In the West we have practiced archery for hundreds of years and nobody has thought about grounding. What is grounding?"

The master said, "Grounding means you become almost part of the earth and allow the gravitation to flow in you, to flood you— particularly below the navel, two inches below to be exact. The gravitation comes from all around, and settles two inches below your navel."

But Herrigel asked, "What has this to do with archery? I have to concentrate on the target." The master said, "Forget about the target; first be grounded. And when you shoot your arrow, be relaxed, so that the gravitation shoots it, not you."

He said, "You are making strange statements. I will have to shoot. How can the gravitation shoot an arrow?"

Three years and Herrigel never missed a single target; he was a master archer. But his master would say, "No, you have still missed. I am not watching your target—who cares about your target? I am watching you; you are the target."

Why two inches below the navel? That is the center of life. It was from there that you were connected with your mother. It was from there that for nine months you were supplied with everything that you needed, and you didn't have to do anything at all—you were simply relaxed.

Grounding means bringing this life center within you into contact with the gravitational force, so that the gravitational force starts filling it. And a moment comes when you don't shoot at the target. Certainly you aim, but it is as if the arrow shoots itself. The gravitational force is enough to take it to the target.

Three years later Herrigel finally gave up. He said, "You are driving me crazy. Day and night I am thinking about how to do it." And the master said, "That's what I have been telling you! Don't *think* about how to do it, let it *happen*. Just have enough energy so it happens."

Finally Herrigel decided to go back. Three years are enough, and not even a single time had the master said, "Good." He always said, "You missed again." Every day Herrigel would come and every day he would be a failure. He told the master, "I am sorry, but I could not get the point. Tomorrow I am leaving, so I will come to say good-bye."

Next day he came. The master was teaching another disciple and Herrigel was sitting on the bench, simply watching, because it was not his business anymore; he was finished with it. If he could not get it in three years, he cannot get it in three lives. It is beyond any logic, what the master is saying.

So he was sitting relaxed, watching—watching the master because the master was showing the new disciple. And suddenly he saw the point. The master was so relaxed, it was not his hands that were shooting the arrow; it was so clear that some inner force was at work. Spontaneously he stood up, went to the master, took the bow and arrow, and shot the arrow.

For the first time the master said, "I can certify it—you have achieved. You were trying with your mind, tense. Today it was accidental—you were sitting relaxed, it was not your business, you were finished with it... And because you were finished with it, your eyes were clear, your heart was silent. You were watching in deep peace and silence, and you could see. For three years I was trying to show it to you, but could not because you were in a hurry to learn quickly and go back to Germany. Just now there was no hurry—you had already decided to go back to Germany.

"I can certify that you have achieved not only the art of archery, but simultaneously the art of grounding."

The moment you become grounded, as the trees are grounded—with deep roots in the earth—when your body is receiving forces from the earth and you are available, relaxed, allowing them to fill your life center, the mind stops functioning, time stops. So just by the side, meditation happens. People around the world have wondered, "What has meditation to do with archery?" But it happens. It can happen with anything. The question is that the mind should stop, time should stop; you should be relaxed and allow life to take possession of you.

I have always loved the story of a king who was passing through a village. He loved archery; he himself was a master archer. He could not believe that in that small village there lived someone who was certainly a greater archer than himself. He had not been one hundred percent; once in a while the target was missed. But there he saw circles on trees and exactly in the middle an arrow—on many trees.

He said, "This is… even the best archer cannot manage this. It seems so perfect. I want to meet the man." So he called the people and asked, "Who is the archer?" They

all laughed. They said, "Forget about him. He is the village idiot."

He said, "You don't understand. You bring him. His archery is perfect."

The villagers said, "You don't understand his archery. First he shoots the arrow and then he makes a circle around it. Naturally, he is perfect, always perfect. And we have told him, 'This is not the right way. First you should make the circle on the tree and then shoot. In that way one can miss. This is a simple way, you never miss.'"

Japan has been a warrior race, so naturally when Zen reached Japan it became associated with all kinds of swordsmanship, the art of archery, and other things. But they have retained the essential of Zen in it. Even Mahakashyapa would not be successful in archery, but that does not mean that he is not the originator.

I don't think Gautam Buddha would be able to pass Aikido examinations. He would be bound to fail. But that does not mean that Aikido is only a faraway echo of Gautam Buddha's experience of his own being. There is no contradiction.

Just remember one thing: whatever you are doing—chopping wood you can be a meditator, or carrying water from the well you can be a meditator—meditation is simply a silent thread inside you. You can do anything, and that silent thread should not be disturbed. Be careful that your awareness remains and then you can do anything.

In Zen, and only in Zen, something of great import has happened. That is, there isn't any distinction between ordinary life and religious life; rather, it has bridged them both. And Zen uses ordinary skills and methods for meditation. That is something of tremendous import. Because if you don't use ordinary life as a method to meditation, your meditation is bound to become something of an escape.

In India this has happened, and India has suffered badly. The misery that you see all around, the poverty, the horrible ugliness of it, is because India always believed religious life to be separate from ordinary life. So people who became interested in religion renounced the world. People who became interested in God closed their eyes, sat in the caves in the Himalayas, and tried to forget that the world existed. They tried to create the idea that the world is simply an illusion, illusory, a dream. Of course, life suffered much because of it.

All the greatest minds of India became escapists, and the country was left to the mediocre. No science could evolve; no technology could evolve.

But in Japan, Zen has done something very beautiful. That's why Japan is the only country where East and West are meeting: Eastern meditation and Western reason are in a deep synthesis in Japan. Zen has created the whole situation there. In India you could not conceive that swordsmanship could become a method for meditation, but in Japan they have done it. And in doing so, they have brought something new to religious consciousness.

Anything can be converted into a meditation because the whole thing is awareness. And of course, in swordsmanship more awareness is needed than anywhere else because life will be at stake every moment. When fighting with a sword you have to be constantly alert—a single moment's unconsciousness and you will be gone. In fact, a real swordsman does not function out of his mind; he cannot function out of his mind because mind takes time. It thinks, calculates. When you are fighting with a sword, where is time? There is no time. If you miss a single fragment of a second in thinking, the other will not miss the opportunity: the other's sword will penetrate into your heart or cut off your head.

So thinking is not possible. One has to function out of no-mind, one has to simply *function*, because the danger is so much that you cannot afford the luxury of thinking. Thinking needs an easy chair. You just relax in the easy chair and go off on mind trips.

But when you are fighting and life is at stake and the swords are shining in the sun and at any moment a slight unawareness and the other will not lose the opportunity, you will be gone forever, there is no space for thought to appear, one has to function out of no-thought. That's what meditation is all about.

If you can function out of no-thought, if you can function out of no-mind, if you can function as a total organic unity, not out of the head, if you can function out of your gut, it can happen to you. You are walking one night and suddenly a snake crosses the path. What do you do? Do you sit there and think about it? No, suddenly you jump out of the way. In fact, you don't decide to jump, you don't think about it

logically that "here is a snake; and wherever there is a snake there is danger; therefore, I should jump." That is not the way it happens—you simply jump! The action is total. The action is not corrupted by thinking. It comes out of the very core of your being, not out of your head. Of course, when you have jumped out of the danger you can sit under a tree and think about the whole thing—that's another matter! Then you can afford the luxury.

If the house catches fire, what do you do? Do you wonder whether to go out or not to go out—"to be or not to be"? Do you consult a scripture about whether it is right to do it? Do you sit silently and meditate upon it? You simply get out of the house. And you will not be worried about manners or etiquette—you will jump out of the window.

Just two nights ago a girl entered here at 3 A.M. and started screaming in the garden. Asheesh jumped out of his bed, ran—and only then realized that he was naked. Then he came back. That was an act out of no-mind, without any thought. He simply jumped out of the bed. Thought came later on. Thought followed, lagged behind. He was ahead of thought. Of course, it caught hold of him so he missed an opportunity. It would have become a *satori*— a glimpse of enlightenment—but he came back and put on his gown. Missed!

Swordsmanship became one of the basic methodologies in Zen, because it is so dangerous that it doesn't allow thinking. It can lead you toward a different type of functioning, a different type of reality, a separate reality. You know of only one way to function: to think first and then to act. In swordsmanship, a different type of existence becomes open to you: you act first and then you think; thinking is no longer primary.

This is the beauty—when thinking is not primary, you cannot err. You have heard the proverb, "To err is human." Yes, it is true, it is human to err because the human mind is prone to error. But when you function out of no-mind you are no longer human; you are part of the whole, and then there is no possibility of erring. The whole never errs, only the part; only the part goes astray.

When you start functioning out of nothingness, with no syllogism, with no thinking, with no conclusions—your conclusions are limited, they depend on your experience, and you can err—when you put aside all your conclusions, you are putting aside all your limitations also. Then you function out of your unlimited being, and it never errs.

It is said that sometimes in Japan two Zen people will fight who have both attained satori through swordsmanship. They cannot be defeated. Nobody can be victorious because they both never err. Before the other attacks, the first has already made preparations to receive it. Before the other's sword moves to cut off his head, he is already prepared to defend himself, and the same happens with the other. Two Zen people who have attained satori can go on fighting for years, but it is impossible for them to err. Nobody can be defeated and nobody can be victorious.

A TEMPLE FOR TEA— A ZEN CEREMONY

In Japan they have developed the tea ceremony. In every Zen monastery and in the house of every person who can afford it, there is a small temple for drinking tea. Now, tea is no longer an ordinary, profane thing; they have transformed it into a celebration. The temple for drinking tea is made in a certain way—in a beautiful garden, with a beautiful pond; swans on the pond, flowers all around...guests come and they have to leave their shoes outside. It is a temple.

As you enter the temple, you cannot speak; you have to leave your thinking and thoughts and speech outside with your shoes. You sit down in a meditative posture. The hostess, the woman who prepares tea for you, moves so gracefully, as if she is dancing, putting cups and saucers before you as if you are a god. With such respect, she bows down, and you receive it with the same respect.

The tea is prepared in a special samovar that makes beautiful sounds, a music of its own. It is part of the tea ceremony that everybody should listen first to the music of the tea. So everybody is silent, listening...birds chirping outside in the garden, and in the samovar the tea is creating its own song. A peacefulness surrounds all....

When the tea is ready and it is poured into everybody's cups, you are not to drink it the way people are doing everywhere else. First you will smell the aroma of the tea. You will sip the tea as if it has come from the beyond, you will take time—there is no hurry. An ordinary

thing—plain tea—and they have made it a
beautiful religious festival. Everybody comes
out of it nourished, refreshed.

anecdotes of

the absurd

The truth cannot be contained by any word whatsoever.

The truth can only be experienced. The truth can be lived,

but there is no way to say it.

the illogical life

Zen is unique because no other religion exists on anecdotes. They are not holy scripture; they are simply incidents that have happened. It is up to you...if you understand them, they can open your yes and your heart. These small anecdotes in their very smallness, just like dewdrops, contain the whole secret of the ocean. If you can understand the dewdrop, there is no need to understand the ocean—you have understood it.

Once a beginner asked a Zen master, "Master, what is the first principle?"

Without hesitation the master replied, "If I were to tell you, it would become the second principle."

THE FIRST PRINCIPLE cannot be said. The most important thing cannot be said, and that which can be said will not be the first principle. The moment truth is uttered it becomes a lie; the very utterance is a falsification. So all the scriptures of all the religions contain the second principle, not the first principle. They contain lies, not the truth, because the truth cannot be contained by any word whatsoever. The truth can only be experienced. The truth can be lived, but there is no way to say it.

The word is a far, faraway echo of the real experience. It is so far away from the real that it is worse than the unreal because it can give you a false confidence. It can give you a false promise. You can believe it, and that is the problem. If you start believing in some dogma, you will go on missing the truth. Truth has to be known by experience. No belief can help you on the way; all beliefs are barriers. All religions are against religion—it has to be so by the very nature of things. All churches are against God. Churches exist because they fulfill a certain need. The need is that people do not want to make any efforts; they want easy shortcuts. Belief is an easy shortcut.

The way to truth is hard; it is an uphill task. One has to go through total death—one has to destroy oneself utterly; only then is one newborn. The resurrection comes only after the crucifixion.

To avoid the crucifixion we have created beliefs. Beliefs are cheap. You can believe and yet remain the same. You can go on believing, and it doesn't require any basic change in your life pattern. It does not require any change in your consciousness, and unless your consciousness changes, the belief is just a toy. You can play with it, you can deceive yourself with it, but it is not going to nourish you.

Visualize a child playing in the garden of his house, playing with imaginary lions, and then suddenly he has to face a real lion who has escaped from the zoo. Now he does not know what to do. He is scared out of his wits. He is paralyzed; he cannot even run. He was perfectly at ease with the imaginary, but with the real he does not know what to do.

That is the situation of all those people who go on playing with beliefs, concepts, philosophies, theologies. They ask questions just to ask questions. The answer is the last thing they are interested in. They don't want the answer. They go on playing with questions, and each answer helps them to create more questions. Each answer is nothing but a jumping board for more questions.

The truth is not a question. It is a quest! It is not intellectual; it is existential. The inquiry is a gamble, a gamble with your life. It needs tremendous courage. Belief needs no courage. Belief is the way of the coward. If you are a Christian or a Hindu or a Mohammedan, you are a coward. You are avoiding the real lion; you are escaping from the real lion.

If you want to face the real, then there is no need to go to any church, there is no need to go to any priest, because the real surrounds you within and without. You can face it—it is already there.

I have heard:

A Zen master, Shou-shan, was asked by a disciple, "According to the scriptures, all

beings possess the Buddha-nature; why is it that they do not know it?"

Shou-shan replied, "They know!"

This is a rare answer, very rare, a great answer. Shou-shan said, "They know! But they are avoiding it." It is not a question of how to know the truth. The truth is here; you are part of it. The truth is now; there is no need to go anywhere. It has been there since the beginning, if there was any beginning, and it will be there until the end, if there is going to be any end. You have been avoiding it. You find ways to avoid it. When somebody asks, "What is the way to truth?" in fact he is asking, "What is the way to avoid the truth?" He is asking, "How can I escape?"

You may not have heard:

Says that old rascal Bodhidharma: "All know the way, few walk it, and the ones who don't walk cry regularly, 'Show me the way! Where is the way? Give me a map! Which way is it?' "

Those who don't walk go on regularly crying and shouting, "Where is the way?" Yet all know the way because life is the way, experience is the way. To be alive is the way; to be conscious is the way. You are alive; you are conscious. This is the first principle. But it cannot be said, and I am not saying it! And you are not hearing it.

The truth, by its very nature, is a dumb experience. All experiences are dumb because they happen only in deep silence. If you love a woman, the love happens in deep silence. If you create poetry, it descends on you in deep silence. If you paint a picture, you disappear. The painter is *not*, when the painting is born; there is not even a witness to it. It happens in utter silence and utter aloneness. If you are there, then the painting cannot be of any value. If the poet is there, then the poetry will be nothing but a technical thing. It will have all the rules fulfilled, it will follow the grammar, the rules of melody, but there will be no poetry. It will be a dead corpse. It will not be a real woman; it will be a nun.

I have heard:

At an isolated part of the beach of Cannes a beautiful French girl threw herself into the sea. A young man off at a distance noticed it and dashed into the water to save her, but it was too late. He dragged the seminude body ashore and left it on the sand while he went in search of an official. When he returned he was horrified to see a man making love to the corpse.

"Monsieur!" he exclaimed, "that woman is dead!"

"Sacrè bleu!" muttered the man, jumping up. "I thought she was a nun."

To be a monk or to be a nun is to be dead. There are millions of ways to die and not live.

Truth surrounds you. It is in the air, it is in the fragrance of the flowers, it is in the flow of the river, it is in the green leaves, it is in the stars, it is in the dust, it is in you. Only truth is! But you go on avoiding it and you go on asking questions. How to attain to truth? Where is the map? Which way is it? And even if the map is given to you, the map does not help you in any way. In the first place, the map cannot be given, because the truth goes on changing. It is not a stagnant phenomenon; it is continuously changing. It is alive; it is breathing. It is never the same; it is never the same for two consecutive moments.

Says old Heraclitus, "You cannot step in the same river twice." In fact, you cannot even step once; the river is flowing, the river is flowing so fast. And not only is the river flowing, you are flowing. You cannot step in the same river twice: the river changes. You cannot step in the same river twice because *you* change.

Truth is dynamic. Truth is not something dead. That's why it cannot be contained in words. The moment you utter it, it has passed, it has gone beyond, it is no more the same. The moment you say it is so, it is no more so. Words lag behind.

To be with truth there is only one possibility: drop words. Language lags behind. Language is lame. Only silence can go with truth, hand in hand. Only silence can move with truth. Only silence can be so fast, because silence has no weight to carry.

Words are loaded; they carry weight. So when you are carrying words, great theologies in your head, great abstractions, then you cannot walk with truth. To walk with truth one has to be weightless. Silence is weightless; it has nothing to carry. Silence has wings. So only in silence is the truth known, and only in silence is the truth transferred, transmitted.

The tyro asked the Master:

"Master, what is the first principle?"
He must have been a tyro, a beginner; otherwise the question is foolish, the question is stupid. Either a stupid person or a philosopher can ask it. The question is meaningless because "first" means the most fundamental. The mind cannot contain it, because it contains the mind! The "first" means the basic; it was before the mind, so how can the mind comprehend it? Mind came out of it, mind is a by-product of it. The child cannot know the father; the father can know the child. The reality can know you, but you cannot know the reality. The part cannot know the whole; the whole can know the part. And the part cannot contain the whole. Now the mind is a very tiny part. It cannot contain the vastness of reality. Yes, the person who asked must have been a beginner.

"What is the first principle, Master?"
And the Master said:
"If I were to tell you, it would become the second principle."

Then it will be an echo, a reflection, a mirror image. Do you know who you are? You don't know, but you know your mirror image. You know your name, you know your address, you know the name of your family, the country, the religion, the political party you belong to. You know your face reflected in the mirror. You don't know your real face. You have not encountered your original face yet.

The Zen masters persist in telling their disciples, "Look into your original face—the face that you had before even your father was born, the face that you will have when you are dead, the face that is yours, originally yours."

All that we know about our face is not really about our face. It is the mask of the body, the mask of the mind. We don't know who lives in the body. We know truth as secondhand, borrowed.

Whenever something is borrowed it becomes ugly. Only the firsthand experience is beautiful, because it liberates. The secondhand thing is ugly because it becomes a bondage. If you become religious, you will be liberated. If you become a Christian or a Hindu or a Mohammedan, you will be in bondage. Mohammed was liberated because for him Islam was a firsthand experience.
So was Jesus liberated because for him his experience was authentically *his* experience. Buddha was liberated; he came upon the experience. It was not handed to him by somebody else, it was not borrowed, it was not thought out, it was not a logical syllogism, it was not an inference. It was an experience!

Beware of inference. You have been taught inference to avoid experience. There are people who say, "God exists because if God is not there, who will create the world? God must exist because the world exists."

Just the other day I was reading a story about a rabbi:

A man came to the rabbi. The man was an atheist, and he said, "I don't believe in God, and you talk about God. What is the proof?" And the rabbi said, "You come back after seven days, and come wearing a new suit." The man
said, "But what does that have to do with my question?" The rabbi said, "It has something to do with it. Just go to the tailor, prepare a new suit, and come after seven days."

The man came, reluctantly, because he could not see any relationship between his question and the answer that had been given. But he still came; he was wearing a new suit. The rabbi said, "Who has made this suit?" And the man said, "Have you gone mad? What type of a question are you asking? Of course, the tailor." The rabbi said, "The suit is here; it proves that the tailor exists. Without the tailor, the suit would not be here. And so is the case with the world. The world is here: there must be a tailor to it, a creator."

This is inference.

Change the scene. In a small Indian village a mystic is sitting with his disciples. Silently they are sitting; there is tremendous silence. It is a *satsang*—the disciples are drinking in the presence of the Master. And along comes an atheist, a scholar, a well-known logician, and he says, "I have come to ask one question. What is the proof of God?" The mystic opens his eyes, and he says, "If you want the proof of God, look into the eyes of the devotees. There is no other proof."

God exists in the eyes of the devotees. God exists in the vision of the lovers. It is an experience of the deepest core of your being, the heart. There is no other proof. God is not a concept. God is a reality, an experience, a deep subjective experience, the deepest there is. All else is peripheral.

❝ You enter into the temple, taking your shoes off,

and Zen believes,

'Where you leave your shoes, leave yourself too' ❞

God is the experience of your innermost center. When you are centered you know.

But you have been taught to believe in the God of the philosophers. That is a way to avoid the real God! The real God is very wild! The real God is very crazy! The real God is unknown and unknowable. And the real God cannot be controlled. The real God can possess you; you cannot possess the real. That is the fear: the mind is always afraid of anything that can possess it. The mind goes on playing games with words, ideas, philosophies. It can remain the master there. With the false, the mind is the master; with the real, the mind becomes a slave, and the mind does not want to become a slave. So the mind is completely contented with the secondhand.

Your God is secondhand. Your love, too, is secondhand. Your poetry is secondhand. Your dance is secondhand. Your singing is secondhand. And of course all these second-hand things make *you* secondhand; then you lose all originality.

Religion has nothing to do with logic. Religion has something to do with the first principle. Logic deals with the secondhand.

Logic deals with the junkyard, the used—used by many people. Logic deals with inference. And remember, it is good as far as the human world of intellectual garbage is concerned; the moment you go beyond that boundary, logic fails utterly, it falls flat on the ground.

I have heard a beautiful anecdote:

The safari had struck camp in dangerous territory and to protect themselves from wild animals they built a high fence around the camp. To be quite sure, they dug a deep ditch around the fence. One evening a member of the group, who was a professor of philosophy and a world-known logician, carelessly went out for an evening stroll without his gun and was attacked by a lion. He ran back to the camp with the lion after him and fell into the ditch. His friends inside heard a terrible yelling and screaming from outside, and when they ran out to look they saw the poor man—the poor philosopher—running round and round in the ditch closely followed by the lion. "Watch out, he is right behind you," they yelled down to him.

> *Zen is not interested in dogma. It is interested in helping you to contact your own being*

"That's all right," the philosopher yelled back. "I am one round ahead of him."

Logic is meaningless as far as life is concerned. Life is not logical at all; life is illogical. Logic is man-made, manufactured by the human mind. Life is absurd.

So if you go through inference you will reach the secondhand. If you go through experience you will reach the firsthand.

Religion is radical. Churches are not radical. The word *radical* means "belonging to the roots." Religious is radical, religion is rebellion. Churches are not rebellious; they are orthodox. Hence, I will repeat again, all churches are against religion. All so-called religious people are against religion. They deal in a false entity; they deal in counterfeit coins. That's why so many people look religious and there is not even a trace of religion on the earth. So many people talk about God, but it remains an empty talk.

Have you ever felt God? You have heard the word again and again and again. You are bored with the word. It has almost become a dirty word. From childhood people have been conditioning you for the word. Have you ever had any glimpse of God?

This is something very strange. How can we miss him? If he is the totality, if he is all over the place, how can we miss him? How did it ever become possible for us to miss him? We must have been doing great work to miss him. We must be doing much work to miss him. We must be avoiding him. We must be creating many barriers and hindrances and obstacles so that he cannot reach us.

And then these empty words: God, love, peace, prayer. All beautiful words have become empty. All ugly things are very real. War is real; love is unreal. Madness is real; meditation is unreal. Beauty is not there at all; ugliness, everywhere. You can come across the ugly any moment. But God is beauty, God is truth, God is love.

So what has happened? We have been trained for empty words, and we have become contented with these empty words.

Drop this contentment! If you want to know what is, become discontented with all that you have been taught, become discontented with all that you have been educated for! Become discontented with your education, with your society, with the power structures around you, the churches, the priests. Become discontented! Become discontented with your own mind. Only in that discontent comes a moment when you become capable of dropping all this mind and all this nonsense with it... and suddenly God is there, the first principle is there.

A naive young man who had lived a sheltered life finally decided he could not take any more. He arranged an appointment with his doctor and poured out the whole story.

"It is this girl I have been going with," he said. "I suspected she was fast, but I never dreamed she was a sex maniac. Every night now for weeks and weeks on end, I keep trying to break off the romance, but I haven't got the will power. What can I do? My health just can't stand the pace."

"I see," said the doctor grimly. "Tell me just what happens; you can trust me."

"Well, every night I take her driving in my car. We park in some secluded street. Then she asks me to put my arms around her. And then, every night, she reaches over and holds my hand."

"And then?"

"What do you mean 'and then'?" gasped the youth. "Is there more?"

That's what has happened to religion. The moment the word *religion* is uttered you remember the long faces in the churches, the sad-looking priests, the serious theologians, trying to split hairs, chopping abstract words, nobody knows why, for what. Religion is broke. The religion of the philosophers is bankrupt. The religion of the intellectuals is relevant no more; it has lost all relevance.

The old religion is dead! And it is good that it is dead. The old God is dead! And it is good that it is dead because now the door opens and we can search for a new God: a God more real, not conceptual, more existential, not philosophical, a God who can be seen, loved, lived, a God who can transform your life, a God who is life and nothing else.

A different kind of religion is needed in the world, a gut-level religion, a religion which has blood and life, a religion whose heart still beats. The old religion is dead, and people are worshiping the corpse. The people carrying the corpse, by and by, become just like the corpse they are carrying.

The first principle is a gut-level religion, a religion that you can experience in your innermost core, in the interiority of your being. You are the shrine for the first principle. No Bible, no Koran, no Veda. You are the shrine for the first principle. The only way to reach to the real is to go within, to go in. Turn in.

That's what meditation is all about. That's why Zen is not interested in dogma. It is interested in helping you to contact your own being.

When the fifth patriarch of Zen, Hung-jen, was asked why he had chosen Hui-neng as his successor out of the five hundred monks in his monastery, he replied: "Four hundred and ninety-nine of my disciples understood Buddhism very well, and only Hui-neng had no understanding of it whatsoever. He is not a man to be measured by any ordinary standard. Hence, the robe of authentic transmission was given to him."

Because he has "no understanding of it whatsoever." An intellectual understanding is not an understanding. It is a deception, an illusion, a dream, a substitute. Because you

are missing the real and because you are not courageous enough to accept the fact that you are missing the real, you substitute it. It is a plastic flower. You substitute the real with a false thing and then you feel good. You start thinking that you have it. And you don't have it! Your hands are empty.

Those four hundred ninety-nine disciples of Hung-jen were all scholars. For years they had studied all the scriptures. They had all the scriptures on their tongue. And he had chosen a man who has no understanding whatsoever. The man he had chosen, Hui-neng, was not known at all in the monastery. Nobody even was aware that he existed there.

When Hui-neng had come to the Master, the Master had asked him one thing: "Do you really want to know? Do you? Do you want to know about truth, or do you want to know truth itself?" And Hui-neng said, "What will I do by knowing *about* the truth? Give me the real thing." And the Master said, "Then go to the kitchen and clean the rice for the mess—and never come again to me. Whenever the right moment has come I will call you."

Twelve years passed, and Hui-neng was still working in the kitchen, at the back. People did not even know about him. Nobody knew his name. Who bothers to think about a man who works in the kitchen from the morning till late in the night? The monastery was not aware. There were great scholars, famous people, celebrities in the ashram: all over China their names were known. Who bothered about Hui-neng?

Twelve years passed, and then one day the Master declared, "My time has come and I will be leaving this world, so I have to choose a disciple as my successor. Anybody who thinks himself ready, capable of becoming my successor, should write four lines in front of my door to show his understanding." The greatest scholar went there in the night and wrote four lines, beautiful lines, the very essence of the *second* principle. You cannot reach higher through the mind than that. He wrote: "The mind is like a mirror. Dust gathers on it. Clean the dust, and you know what is." Perfectly true, absolutely okay. What more can there be?

The whole monastery was agog. People were discussing, debating whether the Master would choose this man as the successor or not. And everybody was trying to improve upon it, but nobody could find anything wrong in it. There was nothing wrong....

That is one of the most difficult things about the intellect. What is wrong in a plastic flower? Nothing is wrong. In a way—in many ways—it may be better than a real flower. A real flower is born in the morning and by evening it is gone. A plastic flower is more stable, more permanent—gives the idea of the eternal! The real flower is momentary. The real flower is born and dies, and the plastic flower knows no death. It is the closest that you come to the eternal. And what is wrong in it? It can have as much color as the real—more color because it is in your hands to make it so. You can make it perfumed, too. But something basic is missing; it is dead.

Nobody could find anything wrong. And people were trying to improve it, but they were all intellectuals. You cannot improve more than that; this is the last point the mind can reach. And it seems logical: "The mind is like a mirror. Dust gathers on the mirror, and then it cannot reflect"—that's what has happened to the mind.

Then a group of monks were discussing it, and they passed Hui-neng, who was doing his work in the kitchen. He heard it—they were talking about these beautiful lines, the essence of all the scriptures—and he laughed. For twelve years nobody had ever seen him laughing. He laughed. The monks looked at him and said, "What? Why are you laughing?" And he said, "It is all nonsense. It is not true." They could not believe their ears. This man, the rice cleaner, for twelve years just cleaning rice.... Nobody had ever seen him even meditating.

How can you see Deeksha meditating? Impossible.

One never knows.... This man, has he become enlightened or something? But they could not believe it, and they were scholars, so they laughed at the absurdity of it, and said, "All the great scholars are there, and you, a rice cleaner! For twelve years nobody has seen you reading scripture, studying, sitting by the side of the Master, inquiring about anything—can you improve upon it?"

Hui-neng said, "I can, but there is one problem. I cannot write. I knew twelve years ago, I used to write a little bit, but I have forgotten."

The mind is not a mirror. Where can the dust gather? One who comes to know this has known, has become enlightened, has looked into the deepest core of his being.

When these words were written on the door of the Master, the Master became very angry. Listen carefully—the Master became very angry. He said, "Bring this Hui-neng immediately, and I am going to beat him." The scholars were very happy; they said, "That's how it should be. Bring that fellow."

Hui-neng was brought, and the Master took him inside and told him, "So you have got it! Now you escape from this monastery. This is my robe; you are my successor. But if I tell it to people, they will kill you. It will be too much against their egos to accept a rice cleaner as the head of the monastery. You simply escape. That's why I was angry. Excuse me. I had to be. Escape from this monastery and go as far away as possible. You are my successor, but these people will kill you."

Scholars are very ambitious and political. Go to any university and you will see. Go to any academy and you will see. You will never see men anywhere else backbiting so much as in a university. Each professor against all, and each trying to pull everybody else down, and each thinks he is the only one capable of being the vice-chancellor or the chancellor. And all are fools.

Hui-neng escaped. Within two or three days people got the idea that something had happened. Hui-neng was missing, and the Master's robe was missing. They started searching for him. The greatest scholar, who had

This happens; this unlearning happens. Unlearning is the process of becoming enlightened. Because you have learned wrong ways, and those wrong ways are the barriers, they have to be unlearned. You are born enlightened, and then you are forced into unenlightenment. You are conditioned for an insane society. Then you are forced to adjust to an insane society. If you remain miserable there is no wonder in it. You will remain miserable because this is not your real nature. This is not the flowering of your being.

So he said, "I cannot write. I have completely forgotten. If you can write, I can say something; you go and write it." Then he simply said, "The mind is not a mirror at all. Where can the dust gather? One who knows it knows it."

written the first lines, went in search. Hui-neng was caught in a forest, and when caught he said, "You can take this robe. I am not interested in this robe at all; this is absolutely unnecessary. I was happy cleaning rice. Now I am trying to escape and hide for no reason. You take this robe."

He dropped the robe on the ground, and the scholar tried to pick it up, but it was too heavy. He could not pick it up.

He fell on the ground perspiring, and said to Hui-neng, "Excuse me. I had come for the robe, but the robe is not ready to go with me. I am incapable. And I know that I am incapable because all that I know are words and words and words. Excuse me…and teach me something."

Hui-neng said, "Teaching is your problem; you have taught yourself too much. Now unteach, unlearn. Now drop all that you know. Knowledge is your barrier in knowing."

That's why the Master said "…and only Hui-neng had no understanding of it whatsoever." When you don't have any intellectual understanding, there arises a great understanding which is not of the mind, but which is of your total being. That understanding gives you the first principle, the first taste of tao.

I have heard:

A wealthy horse-owner died and left a large fortune to a university. A provision in the will, however, was that the school must confer the degree of Doctor of Divinity upon his favorite horse. Since the university was anxious to receive the money—it was a really big sum—the Dean set a date for the animal to receive a degree of DD.

This unusual occasion was attended by the press, and one of the reporters asked the Dean, "What is your reaction to this strange arrangement?"

"Well," replied the Dean, "in my experience I have awarded many degrees. However, I must admit that this is the first time I have awarded a degree to a whole horse."

All others were donkeys, not whole horses.

The mind cannot have any contact with reality. To live in the mind is to live like an idiot. To live with the mind, in the mind, as the mind, is to live a stupid life. The moment you become a little loosened from the mind: celebration. The moment you become a little loosened from the mind: joy. You become a little loosened from the mind: and God.

Suddenly the doors are open. They have never been closed; only your mind was blocking the way.

Thoughts don't allow you to see or, even if they allow, they distort. Or they interpret. They never allow the reality to come to you raw. They decorate it, they change it, they color it. They make it digestible to you. They make it according to you. And you are false, you are a mask, so when reality is cut according to you it becomes unreal.

That's why the Master said to the disciple, "If I tell you the first principle it will become the second principle. You are asking the question from the head." It was an intellectual question: "What is the first principle?" If the Master answered it, the head would take the answer, spin philosophy around it, and cause it to become the second principle.

The real, the true cannot be conveyed through words. It can be conveyed—yes, it can be conveyed—but the way to convey it is different. It is like measles: you catch them. Nobody can give them to you, but you can catch them. Truth cannot be taught but it can be caught.

Look at me. I have the measles. Now, if you don't resist, you will catch it, so lower your resistance. If you resist, you may not catch it. If you are really stubborn and hard and you close your being utterly, if you are not vulnerable at all, you will not catch it. But I cannot give it to you. You can catch it, or you can not catch it, but I cannot give it to you.

It cannot be given, but it can be taken, and that is the whole art of being with a master: to learn how to take. Because he will not give. He cannot give. He makes it available. A master is a catalytic agent; he is a presence. Something is possible around him. You have to be vulnerable,

The mind can give you the second principle. The first principle is possible only through no-mind. Meditation means a state of no-mind. Meditation does not mean "to think about." Meditation means not to think at all. It does not mean, of course, to fall asleep. It means to fall *awake*. It means thoughts should disappear and only pure consciousness should be there, a presence, a luminous presence: you see; there is clarity, transparency.

have an attitude of surrender, an attitude of receptivity: you have to be feminine.

Hui-k'o, another Zen master, made his way northward to H'sin-yeh, where he began teaching, and among those who came to hear him speak was Tao-ho, a noted teacher, a well-known author, and a famous scholar on Buddhist philosophy.

But Hui-k'o's teaching was not like that of any other Buddhist school's, and Tao-ho was very much disturbed....

The teaching was absurd, almost sacrilegious, because Hui-k'o used to say, "Kill your parents." A beautiful saying—but don't take it literally. The parents are within you. You can ask the T.A. (Transactional Analysis) people. The parents are within you. The mother, the father—their conditioning is within you. They control you from within. So when Hui-k'o said, "Kill your parents; only then come to me," he was uttering a great insight.

That's what Jesus said. Christians have not yet been able to explain it. He said, "Unless you hate your mother, unless you hate your father, you cannot come to me." Hate? And the utterance is coming from the man who says, "God is love"?

Hui-k'o also used to say, "If you meet the Buddha on the way, kill him immediately!" Because when you start meditating you will meet your parents; you will meet all the people who have been related to you. You will have to kill them; you will have to disassociate yourself from them; you will have to learn aloneness. And finally you will meet the Buddha, your Master, and you have to kill the Master, too.

These are dangerous things to say, and so is the way he used to say them. The scholar Tao-ho became very angry. He said, "This man will destroy all religion." That's what people say about me.

He determined to destroy this unholy doctrine and to that end dispatched several of his best students to dispute with Hui-k'o....

Hui-k'o is the successor of Bodhidharma, and of course he was a worthy successor of a great Master. He was a great disciple. Hui-k'o was attacked by this man Tao-ho in many ways. Tao-ho used to send his disciples to dispute with and to defeat Hui-k'o. Tao-ho awaited their return with high expectations of hearing that they had won a notable victory over the hated interloper, but they did not come back....

Not a single person ever came back. Whosoever went to Hui-k'o simply disappeared. These people are dangerous people. One should avoid them completely if one truly wants to avoid them. You may go as an antagonist, and you may fall in love with them. And these people are like dragons; once you are close to them they will suck you in.

Tao-ho sent out other emissaries, and still others, but none came back to report the expected victory. It was only after some time had passed that he met some of his messengers and said to them: "I had opened your eyes to the Tao; why were you such faithless emissaries?"

One of them spoke up for the rest: "The original eye is perfect in itself, but your teaching has rendered us half blind."

"The original eye is perfect in itself." Each child is born with that original eye—it is perfect—that innocent eye. It is perfect! It needs no improvement! And the effort of all the masters down through the ages has been one; whatsoever the society has done, they have to undo. Whatsoever the society has put into your mind, they have to take away. They have to dehypnotize you, they have to uncondition you. They have to make your childhood again available to you.

But remember, religion is not a teaching; it is not a learning. You can catch it. Yes, it is like measles. And you have to be in a mood to catch it. That mood is what is meant by being a disciple. A disciple shows a gesture, a great gesture, a *mahamudra*, that "I am ready, Master," that "I am open," that "I will not resist. If you are going to kill me, I am ready. Whatsoever you are going to do to me, I am available—my availability is total." That's all a disciple has to do. And the Master has to do nothing; he has just to be there.

The Master there—the one who has become enlightened, the one who has come to know his real nature—his presence, and the availability of the disciple, and something catches fire, something simply happens. That is the first principle. It cannot be asked, it cannot be answered. That which can be asked and that which can be answered will be the second principle; it will be a carbon copy, an echo.

Of course, the priests won't like such a rebellious meaning to be given to religion. They will not like people to become awake. Neither will the politicians like it.

The politician and the priest represent the ancient conspiracy against the innocence of humanity. They corrupt. Their business depends on this: that you remain unconscious, that you do not become aware. Because the moment you are aware, you are freedom—freedom from all politics and freedom from all religions. You are religious, but free from all religions. You cannot say that you are a Mohammedan, you cannot say that you are a Hindu.

To call Zen people Buddhist is wrong. It is as wrong as to call Sufis Mohammedans. It is as wrong as to call Hassidim Jews. The real people are simply real people. Zen, Sufi, or Hassid, there is neither Buddhist nor Mohammedan nor Jew.

But the priest will not like it. It will be destroying his business. It will be dismantling his shop, his whole market.

Two waiters were standing at a table over which a loaded customer had fallen asleep. Said one, "I have already awakened him twice. Now I am going to awaken him for the third time."

"Why don't you chuck him out?" asked the other waiter.

"The devil I will," said the first waiter. "I've got a good thing going for me. Every time I wake him up he pays his bill."

If humanity remains asleep, if humanity remains unconscious and hypnotized, then the politician can remain in power and the priest can go on exploiting you. If humanity becomes awake, then there will be no need for priests and politicians. There will be no need for any country or state, and there will be no need for any church, any Vatican, any pope. The need will disappear. There will be a totally different quality to human consciousness.

That quality needs to be born. We have come to the point in the evolution of human consciousness where this new consciousness is tremendously needed, desperately needed— this new consciousness which makes man free from politics and free from religion.

Let me remind you again and again, that will be the only religious world: free from religions, but not free from religion; free from churches and dogma, but not free from the first principle; free from all the second principles.

> *When you are happy,*
>
> *you start disappearing*

A girl told her friend she had just become engaged to a traveling salesman.

"Is he good looking?" asked the friend.

"Look, he would never stand out in a crowd."

"Does he have money?" continued the friend.

"If he does, he won't spend it."

"What about his bad habits. Does he have any?"

"Well, he drinks an awful lot," said the future bride.

"I don't understand you," said the friend. "If you can't say anything nice about him, then why are you marrying him?"

"He is on the road all the time," she replied, "and I will never see him."

That's the only good thing about it—and that is the good thing about the god of the priests: you will never see him. That's why you go on following the priest. To avoid God, you follow the priest. To avoid God, you read the Bible. To avoid God, you chant Vedas. To avoid God, you become scholars, thinkers. To avoid God, you are doing everything that is possible.

But why do you want to avoid God? Why in the first place do you want to avoid God? There are reasons. The very idea of God creates tremendous fear because God will mean death to your ego. You will not exist if God is there.

The great Indian mystic Kabir has said, "Look at the irony of it. When I was, God was not; now God is, I am not. Anyway, the meeting has not happened." Because for the meeting, two are needed. "When I was, God was not; now God is, I am not."

The fear is that you will have to lose yourself. You are afraid of death; that's why you are afraid of God. And that's why you are afraid of love, and that's why you are afraid of all that is great.

You are too attached to this false ego which never gives anything but misery and pain, but at least gives you a feeling that you are. Just watch. Meditate over it.

If you want to be, then you will always fall into the trap of the priest. In fact, you are not. The whole idea is a false notion. How can you be? The waves exist, but not separate from the ocean. So we exist: not separate from the ocean of consciousness. That's what God is. The leaves exist, but not separate from the tree. Everything exists, but nothing exists separately.

No man is an island and no part can exist independently. We exist in deep interdependence. We are members of one another, of each other. We penetrate each other. This whole existence is a great penetration. Trees penetrate you; you penetrate the trees. Stars penetrate you;

you penetrate the stars. You penetrate the earth; the earth penetrates you. Everything is penetrated.

God is this totality. You cannot exist separately. If you want to exist separately, then you are a politician. All politics are nothing but the shadow of the ego. Then you will live in misery and in madness.

But if you look, if you watch deeply, you will be surprised. You are not! Not that you have to dissolve! Simply you are not. It is just a false notion that you have been carrying, the notion that you are. Any moment of silence and you will suddenly see there is emptiness within you, nothingness within you. Buddha has called this nothingness *anatta*, nonbeing, *shunya*, nothingness. If you look within, you will not find yourself. That's why people don't look within; they are afraid.

Once it happened that I was traveling with Mulla Nasruddin on a train. Came the ticket collector and Nasruddin became very hectic. He looked in his suitcase, he turned over all the things, he looked in the bed, turned over everything, he looked in his many pockets, and he started perspiring and he could not find the ticket. I saw that he had not looked in one pocket, so I told him, "Nasruddin, you have not looked in that pocket." He said, "Don't mention that." I said, "But why? The ticket may be there." He said, "Don't mention it at all. If I look in it and the ticket is not found, I will fall dead. I will drop dead! I cannot look in that pocket! If the ticket is not there, then I am finished. There is a hope that it may be there."

That's why people don't look inside: a hope one may be there. The day you look in, you are not. The day you look in, suddenly there is vast emptiness…and it is tremendously blissful, beautiful, peaceful. You are not there; then there is no noise.

That's what Hui-neng means when he says, "There is no mirror of the mind. Where can the dust gather? To know this is to know all."

Look within. People think, "We are bad," but you are not, so how can badness gather? People think, "We are good," but how is it possible? You are not there; how can you be good? People think, "We are moral and immoral and this and that," but everything hangs on the idea of "I." To be good the "I" is needed first; to be virtuous the "I" is needed first. To be a sinner or to be a saint the "I" is needed first. Without the "I" you will not have anything to hang anything upon. Where will you hang your goodness, your sin, or your saintliness?

That's why Zen insists there is nobody who is a sinner and there is nobody who is a saint, nothing is good and nothing is bad. All distinctions are ego-created. Distinctions are created so that the ego can exist through the distinctions. When you look within there is neither saint nor sinner, neither good nor bad, neither life nor death. All distinctions disappear.

In that nothingness one becomes one with God. One *is* one with God—one has been from the very beginning. So the fear is that if you want to know God, you will have to disappear; so you don't look into your own being. The fear is that if you look within yourself you may become happy.

People say that they want to become happy, but I rarely come across a person who really wants to be happy. People cling to their misery. Again the same game. With the misery you have something to do. With the misery, some occupation. With the misery you can avoid yourself, you are engaged. With joy there is nothing with which to be engaged, there is nowhere to go. In joy you again disperse and disappear. In misery you are there—you are very much there. Misery gives you a solid experience that you are. When you are happy, you start disappearing. When you are really happy, you are not, again you are not. In a state of bliss, again you disappear.

You talk about heaven, but you go on creating hell because only in hell can you exist. You cannot exist in heaven. George Bernard Shaw is reported to have said, "If I am not going to be the first in heaven, then I would not like to go to heaven. I would like to be in hell, but I would like to be first; I don't want to be second." Hell is okay, but the ego says, "Be first, be a leader." Hell is okay if the ego remains; heaven is not okay if the ego has to be dropped.

You would like to be in heaven with your ego. You are asking the impossible. That cannot happen.

The religion that exists on the earth is false, it is a make-believe, it is just for the name's sake, but it fulfills your demand. It fulfills a certain demand, that you want to pretend that you are religious. You don't want to become religious but you want to

pretend. And you want to pretend in such
a way that not even you yourself can catch
yourself pretending.

You want to pretend in such a way that you
don't ever come across your pretensions, so
a great structure is created. And that great
structure is the church. Avoid that structure
if you really want to become religious. And
unless you are religious you are not!

Now let me tell you this paradox: You
are only when you are not, because you are
only when the ego has disappeared and you
are God. That is the first principle. I am not
telling it to you, and you are not hearing it
from me.

It happened:

*The car suddenly broke down in the middle
of nowhere. He crawled underneath to see
what the trouble was. She crawled underneath
to hold the flashlight for him.*

*It was quite cozy under there and, after a
while, they forgot about car repairs. Suddenly
a voice said, "And just what do you two think
you are doing?"*

*Looking up, they saw the local
village constable.*

*"Why, we are—er—repairing the back
axle," the young man stammered.*

*"Well, while you are down there, you had
better look at the brakes as well," replied the
law. "Your car has been at the bottom of the hill
for the past half hour."*

That's what has happened to churches.
Jesus is not there; Buddha is not there. People
are doing something else in the name of Jesus,

in the name of Buddha, and they are thinking
Buddha is there. Church is the last place
where you can meet Jesus, and the Buddhist
temple is the last place where you can meet a
buddha. But you go to the church, you go to
the temple…and you think you are going to
Buddha and to Jesus.

You are great pretenders. You want to
pretend. You want to be respectable. You
want to show to everybody that "We are
religious people." So we have created a
Sunday religion; every Sunday you go. Six
days for the world; one day—not the whole
day, just one or two hours—for God. Just in
case something goes wrong or maybe really
God is or maybe one survives death. These
are all perhapses. And a perhaps never
changes anybody's life; only a certainty
changes somebody's life.

Hence, my insistence, if you cannot find
a living master, go on searching and searching.
There are always living masters somewhere
or other; the earth is never empty of them.
But never go to the places where
conventionally you expect them. There they
are not. Jesus was not in the synagogue.
Buddha was not in any Hindu temple; he
was born a Hindu, but he was not in any
Hindu temple. Jesus was a Jew, but he was
not in the synagogue. And so has been the
case always. Don't go on worshiping ideas.
Find a living reality.

The moment you find a living reality,
become vulnerable, become open. And you
will have the first principle, which cannot be
said, but you can get it.

zen

dialogues

All these Zen anecdotes and dialogues say the same thing

again and again. But they say it very beautifully. From different

standpoints, from different attitudes, they point to the same

moon... hoping that perhaps, if last night you did not see it,

today it may be possible from some other aspect.

tales of enlightenment

These stories belong to a world, to a time, when people were simple. They were not cunning or complex; they were innocent. Hence there was a possibility of immediate awakening. Zen has become more and more difficult for the simple reason that man has become more and more complex. Today it is almost impossible to conceive how sudden enlightenment can be possible, how in a single flash of lightning one can be transformed totally. The knowledgeable person can only understand the way of gradualness; his whole education is a process of graduation.

ZEN IS SPECIAL in many ways compared to other traditions of the mystics. But what stands out, unique, are the strange, small dialogues in Zen: just reading them you cannot see how those small dialogues can bring enlightenment to someone.

Secondly, Zen itself gives no explanations. That is one of the reasons a living tradition of enlightenment has not overtaken the world. I would like you to understand these small dialogues which apparently mean nothing, but in a certain circumstance produced by other Zen methods can bring awakening. The dialogues are remembered down the centuries, and the people on the path of Zen enjoy them immensely.

However, for outsiders they remain a mystery because the context is never told; in what reference the awakening happened is never discussed.

Behind these small dialogues there is a long discipline of meditation and understanding—maybe years and years of work. But only the dialogue is known to the outside world. You don't know those who are discussing with each other; they are not ordinary people. The awakening is possible only if they have a background that can make the small piece of dialogue—which in itself is nothing—of tremendous importance. But when you read them, you cannot believe how these dialogues can make somebody enlightened—because you are reading them and you are not becoming enlightened!

Something is missing in your perspective. My effort will be to give you the entire context and to explain not only the words of the dialogue but also the individuals who are engaged in these small dialogues. Only then will you see that they are not small things, they are the very essence. The people involved have reached to

the ultimate point; these dialogues are just a little push. They were almost ready... it can be said that even without these dialogues they were going to become enlightened, maybe a week later. These dialogues have cut no more than a week from the time of their being enlightened.

Now that Zen has become fashionable all around the world there is so much written about it. But nobody I have come across up to now... and I have seen almost everything that has been written about Zen by people who don't have any enlightenment, but who are impressed by the beauty of the people who have been following Zen. They have picked up things that make no sense, are almost nonsense, and they don't have the capacity to give you the background.

Remember, everything depends on the background: long years of preparation, long years of waiting and longing, long years of silent patience and meditating. The dialogue comes at the apex, at the very end. If you can understand the whole process, then it will be clearer to you how the dialogue can bring enlightenment to someone.

Unless people know the whole process, Zen will remain just entertainment to the world. What is enlightenment to Zen people falls down to a state of entertainment. These dialogues are not the whole process. It is just like an iceberg: a small piece is showing above the sea—one-tenth of the iceberg—and nine-tenths is underneath. Unless you understand that nine-tenths, the one-tenth will not give you any insight.

The first dialogue:

In the old days the venerable Yen Yang asked Chao Chou, "What is it like when not bringing a single thing?"

Chou said, "Put it down."

Yen Yang said, "Since not a single thing is brought, put what down?"

Chou said, "If you can't put it down, pick it up."

At these words, Yen Yang was greatly enlightened.

Now, if you hear only this small anecdote, you cannot imagine how it can possibly bring great enlightenment.

First, in the context of the Zen approach—in the eyes of Gautam Buddha and Bodhidharma—the world is nothing but emptiness. And when they use the word *emptiness*, they have their own meaning; it is not the ordinary meaning that you can find in a dictionary. If everything is removed from your room—all the furniture, the photographs hanging on the wall, the chandelier and everything—and nothing is left behind, anybody will say, "This room is empty." This is the ordinary meaning of the word. But from the perspective of Gautam Buddha, this room is empty of things but it is full of space. In fact, when things were there, they were hindering the space. The very word *room* means "space." So it is overflowing now with space, with nothing to hinder, nothing to prevent and obstruct the space.

Space is not a negative thing like the word *emptiness* connotes. Everything in the world has come out of space and everything disappears into space. Space seems to be the reservoir of all that is....

Scientists have discovered black holes in space. It is the most amazing story that science has to tell. The scientists themselves feel mystified, but what can they do? They have come across a few places in space where the moment any star, even the biggest, comes into that area, you can no longer see it: it has become pure nothingness. The pull of these few places is so tremendous that anything that comes close to them is immediately pulled into the black hole and disappears from the world. Every day, many stars disappear into black holes; that is the basic idea.

But then, certainly, scientists started thinking: if there are black holes, there must be white holes, too. If everything goes on disappearing into the black holes, one day everything will have disappeared. But every day new stars are being born—from where do they come? It is still an assumption, a hypothesis, that from wherever they come, that place should be called a white hole.

My own understanding is that the black hole and the white hole are just two sides of the same phenomenon; they are not separate. It is just like a door: you can go in, you can go out. On one side of the door is written "Push" and on the other side is written "Pull."

The black hole de-creates; it is a death. Not only do you get tired and old, now they say even metal gets tired; even for machinery, working twenty-four hours a day is too much. You are creating too much tension in the metal. It needs a little rest to recover itself; otherwise, soon it will not be functional anymore. Even machines become old, just as people do.

Stars become old, just like everything else. When a star or a planet has become too old and cannot hold itself together anymore, it disappears into a black hole. Its death has come. It is a de-creation. The function of the black hole is to disperse all constituents of the planet or star—to return them to their original form.

The original form is electricity, energy, so matter melts into energy. Energy cannot be seen, you cannot see it. Have you ever seen electricity? You have seen a byproduct of electricity, like your light bulb, but you have not seen electricity itself. When it is passing through a wire, do you see anything? And if the bulb is removed, the electricity is still there, but do you see it?

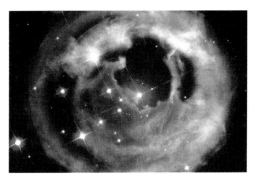

No energy can be seen. No energy is visible, so when the mass of a vast star or planet falls back into the original source, it becomes pure energy. That is why you cannot see it: it has disappeared. Perhaps it was time for a long rest. And once it is rested, then the basic constituents can again come together, can again form a new body and get out into the universe from the other side of the black hole—that is, the white hole.

This is significant. It means the universe is continuously renewing itself in the same way as every individual is born, grows old, dies, and then somewhere else is born in a new form, fresh, young. This is the process of rejuvenation.

Existence itself is full of space. Space looks empty to us, but it is not empty, it is a potential for things to happen. Everything has come out of it—how can you call it empty? Can you call a mother's womb empty? It

has the potential of giving birth to life. It appears empty because its potentiality has not been transformed into actuality.

Gautam Buddha was the first man to use the word *emptiness* in the sense of spaciousness, infinite space. Everything is just a form, and the thing that is creating the form is invisible. Only the form is visible; the energy that makes it is invisible.

The Zen disciple meditates continuously on the emptiness of existence, on the spaciousness of existence. All forms are empty; no form has a self. Only existence has a self. All others are only dreams lasting for a few years—and in the eternity of time, a few years are not much to brag about; they don't matter at all. The meditator continually goes on and on realizing the nature and the flavor of nothingness.

One day he understands that everything phenomenal that appears will disappear— today it exists, tomorrow it may be gone—it is nothing eternal. And unless something is eternal, it is not real.

Getting deep into this meditation will change your whole life. Anger comes and you know that it is just an energy form; you don't pay attention to the person against whom you are angry. The meditator pays his whole attention to anger itself. The form disappears, and the energy contained in the form is absorbed by the meditator.

As things go on disappearing—sadness, tensions, unhappiness, misery—you go on becoming more and more powerful, because everything is falling back into the form of energy. In this state, try to understand the anecdote.

The second dialogue:

Master Shui Lao asked Ma Tsu, "What is the true meaning of the coming from the West?"

Ma Tsu then knocked him down with a kick to the chest: Shui Lao was greatly enlightened. He got up, clapping his hands and laughing loudly, and said, "How extraordinary! How wonderful! Instantly, on the tip of a hair, I've understood the root source of myriad states of concentration, and countless subtle meanings." Then he bowed and withdrew.

Afterward, he would tell the assembly, "From the time I took Ma Tsu's kick up until now, I haven't stopped laughing."

A sudden rain shower after a long dry spell can be an immense joy...not only to the earth, which is thirsty, waiting for it—but also to the trees and to all the people. Such small experiences can release in you the ultimate experience...just the beauty of them, the splendor, unexpected, unpredictable. Suddenly you are surrounded with tremendous peace, silence—not empty, but full of songs and dances, and the whole existence rejoicing.

As one goes deeper on the path, as one releases oneself from the prison of one's own mind, ordinary experiences start taking on extraordinary colors. An ordinary flower looked at silently becomes a wondrous experience. What a marvel that a small flower can exist with such beautiful colors, with a little fragrance of its own, an individuality of its own. The greatest philosopher cannot fathom the meaning of the smallest flower.

But the mystic is not a philosopher; he does not bother to fathom meanings, to measure meanings, to think about things. He simply rejoices in them. When it rains, he dances, he joins hands with the rain. When trees are rejoicing, becoming fresh, one starts feeling the same freshness. Only one thing is needed, and that is the offering of this small story...release.

This small dialogue is intended to convey a simple thing to you: you are the prison, you are the prisoner, and you are the one who has imprisoned you. You are playing a game with yourself. One part of you functions as the jailer, another part functions as the jail, and your innermost core is crushed between these two parts. You become a prisoner; it is not that somebody else is making you a prisoner.

It would have been a great calamity if human consciousness were imprisoned by somebody else. Then freedom would not be in your own hands; then freedom would be in somebody else's hands. It is marvelous that you are yourself imprisoning your being; hence, the release can happen instantly. It is only a question of a little understanding, a little intelligence.

Many intellectuals in the world who have become aware of Zen in the past century were, in the beginning, simply laughing at the craziness of these people, because it did not make sense to their reasoning minds. Somebody hits you and you become enlightened...the mind cannot believe it. There seems to be no reason why a certain hit would destroy all your ignorance.

Even today, Zen is being studied in the West on a vast scale; it has become one of the universal phenomena. But the very idea of studying it goes against it: you cannot study Zen. You can have it, but you cannot get it from someone else. And the simple reason is that you have it already. It is just a question of forgetfulness. It will be helpful for you to be reminded. Perhaps in everybody's life there are moments when you know that a certain name, a certain person, a certain face is known to you. The expression exists in all languages that it is "just on the tip of my tongue."

Then who is preventing you? Why don't you tell it? You know perfectly well it is there, but it needs some release, and perhaps a hit may do it. You have only forgotten—perhaps a good hit will help you to forget to remember it, because the effort to remember a thing makes your mind tense, and the more you try to remember, the more tense you become.

Tension means narrowing of the mind. It becomes so narrow that nothing can pass through it. A good hit and the mind opens... because you have forgotten that you were trying to remember something, and suddenly that which was on your tongue is no more a secret; now you know it fully well. Something like this has been happening in transmissions of a higher and deeper level.

But Zen is not a study. There is no way to make it a subject of studies in the universities; that would be stupid. There is no way to find someone who has it who can give it to you. It is not that the people who have it are miserly or not generous—just the contrary. They are the

most generous people; if they could give it to you they would not bother whether you want it or not, they would give it to you.

But the very nature of the experience is such that it does not come from outside; it happens within you. The people who have experienced it are in constant search of creating a situation around you so that what is asleep becomes awake. Once you understand it, Zen will not look crazy; it will not look irrational. It will look super-rational—beyond the capacities of the mind.

Hindus, Mohammedans, Christians, and Jews have created a difficult situation for millions of people. They have been giving people the idea that it will be delivered to you by a savior, it will be given to you by a messenger; all you have to do is to believe and wait. Jesus will redeem you, or Mohammed, or Krishna.

What I want to point out very clearly is that the idea that somebody else, it does not matter who—Jesus, Moses, Krishna, or Mohammed—the idea that somebody else will do it on your behalf is absolutely wrong. But this idea has prevailed and it is easy to

accept it, it is simple to be imprisoned by it because somebody else is taking the responsibility.

In this world, people are easily ready to give responsibility to somebody else. They think that by giving away responsibility they are free of the burden. They are absolutely wrong. Responsibility *is* freedom, and the moment you give responsibility to somebody else you have also given your freedom.

Now two thousand years have passed and Christians are waiting for the savior to come. I tell you he is never going to come, for the simple reason that what he has promised he cannot deliver. Krishna has promised that he will be coming, but it is strange that nobody wonders why these people did not redeem humanity while they were here. What is the point of postponing it for the future, for the next time they come?

People were as much in misery then as they are now, people were as ignorant as they are now—so what was the reason to postpone? Jesus could have redeemed the whole world; Krishna could have enlightened everybody. But it was a subtle game: they

took the responsibility and helped you to remain a prisoner till they come back. Just go on praying...one day he is going to come.

This has taken away not only your responsibility but also your freedom. It has taken away your individuality and your uniqueness.

I love Gautam Buddha for the simple reason that he is the first man in the long history of humanity who refused to take the responsibility of redeeming anybody. He seems to be the most courageous man—because it is so easy to gather followers if you take responsibility. But rather than taking responsibility, he was saying that there is no way for anybody else to redeem you.

Let it sink deep in your heart. Only you are capable of awakening, because only you are capable of falling asleep. Nobody else is responsible for your sleep—how can somebody else be responsible for your awakening? All those who have promised to redeem you have reduced you to something less than human beings. Jesus was calling himself the shepherd and people the sheep and I sometimes wonder why not even a single person stood up and said, "This is very insulting." Not that people must not have felt it, but it was very cheap, and "this fellow is taking all the responsibility, that is good—so we need not bother about it. We can go round and round in our trivia and he will take care of our spirituality." It was a good chance to get rid of the whole affair. It seems hurtful to say it, but I cannot say anything that is not true. All these people behaved more like businessmen; they were concerned with having more and more customers.

Gautam Buddha seems to be the only man who was not interested in having followers, who was not interested in being a shepherd, who was not interested in reducing people to sheep. On the contrary, his whole life he insisted on only one thing: You are just like me; the difference is very small. One day I was asleep, today I am awake. Today you are asleep, tomorrow you may be awake—and if you are intelligent you can be awake this very moment.

Gautam Buddha, rather than talking about hypothetical nonsense, took on the existential problem directly: the problem is your release. And the problem is simple because the release is within your own hands: you have just forgotten who you are. By telling you who you are, you will not understand, and the danger is that by telling you who you are, you may become a parrot. In India you will find a whole country full of parrots. Everybody is talking about the soul, enlightenment, awakening, nirvana. They have all been repeating beautiful sentences from scriptures. Buddha does not want to make you a parrot; hence, he says there is no way to give you the truth, for the simple reason that you already have it.

So all that can be done is somehow to create situations to wake you up and, if it is needed, to give you a good slap at the right moment. Anybody's slap won't do, only a master's—and only a disciple who has been working on the way for years, or maybe for lives, comes to a point just on the boundary line, where a little push…and he has reached to the other shore. So there are disciplines in Buddhism, but those disciplines are not going to give you the truth. They are only going to bring you to the point where some insightful and compassionate master will be needed to create a device which releases you.

Have you seen young birds? They see their parents flying all around, and they also flutter their wings. But they are afraid—naturally, because they have never flown—and they cannot believe that going out of their cozy nest is safe.

The vast sky and no experience of flying frighten them—although they are capable of flying, they have the wings, and they will rejoice to fly in the sky under the warm sun.

Finally the parents of those small birds have to push them. That is a device—that is a Zen device. But the parents have to wait until their wings are strong enough; they do many things which to me seem to be exactly what the Zen master does for the disciple. The mother will fly in front of them, showing that if she can fly, why can't they? The young birds flutter their wings to gain confidence, to become acquainted with the fact that they also have wings—it's true!

But to take the jump…. They come to the very edge of their nest. They weigh all the pros and cons. There is a great longing to take the jump, but there is also a fear because they are going into the unknown. Who knows—they may fall flat on the earth and be finished. The mother goes to the other tree, and from there she starts calling them: Come on! It is irresistible. They try, but some invisible boundary prevents them.

When the parents see that they are perfectly capable and it is only fear that is preventing them, one day, without informing them, suddenly—a Zen push!

Of course, in the beginning they flutter haphazardly, but they know now that although they are not flying as they should, they can keep themselves up in the air. Then the mother starts calling to them from other trees. First they go to close trees, then they start going to farther trees, and one day they are gone forever into the infinite; they never come back. Then the whole sky has become theirs.

I have always thought that the Zen devices of transmitting must have come from such sources. Zen monasteries are in the forests, and some genius master may have seen the situation of a bird being pushed. There is no logical sense to it, you cannot convince the bird intellectually, and a push is not rational. Only in principle is it sudden enlightenment. In practice, in reality, the small bird has to grow strong wings, wait for the right moment, and has to be under the protection of a right master. Any hurry can be fatal.

If somebody is awakened before his ripening time, before his maturity, that enlightenment can be dangerous. He may not be able to survive it, it may be too much. He was not yet able to contain it, to absorb it, to relish it.

Intellectuals all over the world have asked, "If it is sudden, then why is it not happening to us? Then why does somebody have to meditate for years if it is sudden?" They have not understood that *in principle* it is

sudden. When it happens, it will happen suddenly—but before that happening, a certain maturity is needed. That means enlightenment in itself is sudden, but the preparation for it is gradual.

Gradualness and suddenness are not necessarily opposite; that gradualness can be a preparation for suddenness. Both can be part of a synthetic process. It takes time, different times for different people. According to their love, according to their trust, according to their longing, according to their passion, according to their readiness to risk all, the time element will differ.

When one comes to a master, one has so much garbage that the master has to remove it gradually, because to him it is garbage, but to the disciple it is knowledge. To the master it is chains; to the disciple, these are his ornaments. So it takes time…the master throwing the garbage out and the disciple collecting it back, and hiding it in deeper places where the master cannot reach, until there is a recognition that the master and the disciple stand in the same space. Then anything will do, even a little push…. So you have to just remain alert and aware—not aware of anything special, not of any object, but just alert, as if something great is going to happen and you don't know what. As if a great guest is going to come and you are standing at your door waiting. You don't know who is coming… you don't know whether he is coming or not. You don't have any confirmation—but greatly alert, you are standing at the door. A pure awareness…

Master Shui Lao asked Ma Tsu, "What is the true meaning of the coming from the West?" This is a special way of asking the question, "What is the true meaning of Bodhidharma coming from the West?" because to China, India is the West. "What was the special reason for Bodhidharma coming to China?" In other words, the question is, "What has he come to transmit?" It took him three years to reach that far, and it took him nine years to transmit it. What was it?

Ma Tsu then knocked him down with a kick to the chest: Shui Lao was greatly enlightened. He got up, clapping his hands and laughing loudly, and said, "How extraordinary! How wonderful! Instantly, on the tip of a hair, I have understood the root source of myriad states of concentration, and countless subtle meanings." Then he bowed and withdrew.
Afterward he would tell the assembly, "From the time I took Ma Tsu's kick, up until now, I have not stopped laughing."

Remember that Master Shui Lao is not an ordinary disciple; he is already recognized as a great master, although he is only a great teacher. But the difference is subtle and can be known only by those who are beyond the master and the teacher. He was known as a master himself…and he was not just a teacher; he had come gradually closer and closer to being a master but he needed a last push. He was fluttering his wings… he was waiting, but on the verge of flying into the sky.

> *The master is there not only to teach you certain doctrines; he is there to release you from the prison that you yourself have made*

Master Shui Lao asked Ma Tsu… Ma Tsu is one of the strangest masters in the assembly of strange masters of Zen. Shui Lao is asking a simple question: "Why did Bodhidharma come to China? What special transmission was there that he had to deliver?"

Ma Tsu then knocked him down with a kick to the chest: Shui Lao was greatly enlightened.

Now incidents like this make intellectuals confused. What has happened? Ma Tsu has shown him that Bodhidharma has come to kill your ego, to release you from the fear of death. He kicked him in the chest, knocked him down. It was so strange and so sudden, it was not expected. He had asked a simple, routine question; any intellectual could have explained why Bodhidharma had come to China—to spread Buddhism, to spread the message of the great master.
Nobody could have thought that Ma Tsu would do this to the poor questioner, but it only seems sudden and unpredictable to us; Ma Tsu could have seen the ripeness of

the man, his maturity…that he needed just a small push, that this moment should not be missed. Kicking him on the chest and knocking him down may have completely stopped the functioning of his mind, because it was so unexpected and so strange. In that stopping of the mind is the release. Suddenly the goose is out! Shui Lao became enlightened.

He got up, clapping his hands and laughing loudly, and said, "How extraordinary! How wonderful! Instantly, on the tip of a hair, I have understood the root source of myriad states of concentration, and countless subtle meanings." Then he bowed—in deep respect—and withdrew. Afterward, he would tell the assembly—he became himself a great master—*"From the time I took Ma Tsu's kick, up until now, I have not stopped laughing."*

How can one stop laughing? This great affair is so ridiculous!

It is like a dog who, on a winter morning in the warm sun, sitting silently looking at his tail, becomes interested in catching it. He tries in many ways, and the more he tries, the more he becomes challenged, because the tail jumps immediately. The faster he jumps, the faster the tail jumps—and the difference remains the same. Standing by the side you will laugh: "This stupid dog! That tail belongs to him; there is no need to catch hold of it—and there is no way…."

Your enlightenment belongs to you, there is no need to seek and search. You *are* it. It is

not an achievement, it is only a recognition—hence, the laughter.

Naturally, people who have not been accustomed to the tradition of Zen will be shocked by such behavior. If I suddenly knock somebody over the head here and now, will you understand? You will think, "This man has gone mad." You will think, "We already knew that he was mad; now he has crossed all the boundaries."

But people who are not in a deep resonance with Zen will not be able to understand it—Hindus or Mohammedans or Christians or Jews—because there is nothing like that in their whole history. Their history is more or less intellectual gymnastics.

Zen is absolutely existential. The master is there not only to teach you certain doctrines; he is there to release you from the prison that you yourself have made. Whatever arbitrary, expedient methods are needed, he is not going to be worried about what people will think of them; he will use them.

There have never been more compassionate beings than Zen masters. It is a great compassion of Ma Tsu; otherwise, who cares?—he could have just answered the question and the whole thing would be over. He took so much effort, hit the man, knocked him down....

And it is not only Ma Tsu who is compassionate: Shui Lao also knows tremendous understanding. If it had happened to somebody who was not ready, he would have started fighting or he would have become angry, saying "This is absolutely absurd! I am asking a question and you are hitting me." But he took the hit in the same way as Mahakashyapa had taken the lotus flower from Gautam Buddha—with even more beauty: *"How extraordinary! How wonderful!"*—and with great reverence—... *he bowed down and withdrew.*

No other question... everything is solved. He has been kicked out of the nest; now his wings are open in the sky.

the mystery of

the koan

...the koan of the goose in a bottle. "If a man puts a gosling in a bottle and feeds him until he is full-grown, how can the man get the goose out without killing it or breaking the bottle?"

insoluble puzzles

The very function of the koan is to tire your mind to such a point that it gives up. If there were an answer, the mind would find it. It does not matter whether you are very intelligent, or not very intelligent—no intelligence of any category can find the answer.

ZEN IS NOT a religion, not a dogma, not a creed; Zen is not even a quest, an inquiry; it is non-philosophical. The foundation of the Zen approach is that all is as it should be, nothing is missing. This very moment everything is perfect. The goal is not somewhere else; it is here, it is now. Tomorrows don't exist. This very moment is the only reality. Hence, in Zen there is no distinction between methods and goals, means and ends.

All the philosophies of the world and all the religions of the world create duality; however they may go on talking about non-duality, they create a split personality. That has been the greatest calamity that has befallen humanity: all the do-gooders have created schizophrenia in people. When you divide reality into means and goals, you divide humanity itself, because for humans, the closest reality is themselves.

An individual's consciousness becomes split. He lives here but not really; he is always there, somewhere else. He is always searching, always inquiring; never living, never being. Always doing—getting richer, more powerful, getting spiritual, getting holier, more saintly—always more and more. This constant hankering for more creates a tense, anguished state; meanwhile he is missing all that is made available by existence. He is interested in the far away, yet God is close by. His eyes are focused on the stars, yet God is within him.

Let me tell you the story of how one of the most famous Zen koans started:

A great and philosophical official, Riko, once asked the strange Zen Master, Nansen, to explain to him the koan of the goose in the bottle.

"If a man puts a gosling into a bottle," said Riko, "and feeds him until he is full-grown, how can the man get the goose out without killing it or breaking the bottle?"

Nansen gave a great clap with his hands and shouted, "Riko!"

"Yes, Master," said the official with a start.

"See," said Nansen, "the goose is out!"

It is only a question of seeing; it is only a question of becoming alert, awake; it is only a question of waking up. The goose is in the bottle if you are in a dream; the goose has never been in the bottle if you are awake. And in the

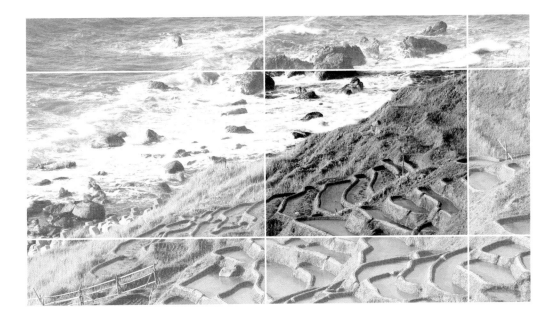

dream there is no way to take the goose out of the bottle. Either the goose will die or the bottle will have to be broken, and neither alternative is allowed. A fully-grown goose in a small bottle.... How can you take it out? This is called a koan.

A koan is not an ordinary puzzle; it is not a puzzle because it cannot be solved. A puzzle is that which has a possibility of being solved; you just have to look for the right answer. You will find it—it only needs intelligence to find the answer to the puzzle; but a puzzle is not insoluble.

A koan is insoluble; you cannot solve it, you can only *dissolve* it. And the way to dissolve it is to change the very plane of your being from dreaming to wakefulness. In the dream the goose is in the bottle and there is no way to bring it out of the bottle without breaking the bottle or killing the goose—in the dream. Hence, as far as the dream is concerned, the

puzzle is impossible; nothing can be done about it. But there is a way out that has nothing to do with the puzzle, remember. You have to wake up. That has nothing to do with the bottle and nothing to do with the goose, either. You have to wake up. It has something to do with *you*. That's why Nansen did not answer the question.

Riko asked, "If a man puts a gosling into a bottle and feeds him until he is full-grown, how can the man get the goose out without killing it or breaking the bottle?"

Nansen didn't answer. On the contrary, he gave a great clap with his hands and shouted, "Riko!"

Now, this is not an answer to the question—this has nothing to do with the question at all—it is irrelevant, inconsistent. But it solves it; in fact, it dissolves it. The moment Nansen shouted, "Riko!" the official, with a start, said,

"Yes, Master." The whole plane of his being was transformed by a simple strategy.

A Zen master is not a teacher; he does not teach you, he simply devises methods to wake you up. That clap is a method; that clap simply brought Riko into the present. And it was so unexpected.... When you are asking such a spiritual koan you don't expect the master to answer you with a loud clap and then to shout your name.

Suddenly Riko was brought out of the past, out of the future. Suddenly for a moment, he forgot the problem. Where is the bottle and where is the goose? There was only the master, in a strange posture, clapping and shouting for Riko. Suddenly the problem was dropped. He had slipped out of the problem without even knowing that he slipped out of it. He had slipped out of the problem as a snake slips out of its old skin. For a moment, time stopped. For a moment, the clock stopped. For a moment, the mind stopped. For a moment, there was nothing. The master, the sound of the clap—and a sudden awakening. In that very moment the master said, "See! See, the goose is out!" it is dissolved.

A koan can only be dissolved but can never be solved. A puzzle can never be dissolved but it can be solved. So remember, a koan is not a puzzle.

When people who are accustomed to continual thinking, to logical reasoning, start studying Zen, they take a false step from the beginning. Zen cannot be studied; it has to be lived; it has to be imbibed—it is a transmission beyond words, a transmission of the lamp. The lamp is invisible.

When you enter into the world of Zen there is no-mind. Zen is equivalent to no-mind. It is not freedom of the mind, it is freedom *from* the mind, and there is a lot of difference, an unbridgeable difference. The mind is not free, you are free of the mind. The mind is no longer there, free or unfree; the mind has simply ceased. You have gone through a new door that was always available to you but you had never knocked on it—the door of being, the door of eternity.

Zen, the very word *zen* comes from the Sanskrit word *dhyana*. *Dhyana* means "meditation," but the word *meditation* does not carry its total significance. *Meditation* gives the impression that mind is doing something: mind meditating, concentrating, contemplating, but mind is there. *Dhyana* means a state of no-mind—no concentration, no contemplation, no meditation, in fact—just silence, a deep, profound silence where all thoughts have disappeared. When there is no ripple in the lake of consciousness; the consciousness is functioning just like a mirror reflecting all that is—the stars, the trees, the birds, the people, all that is—simply reflecting it without any distortion, without any interpretation, without bringing in any prejudices.

That's what your mind is: your prejudices, your ideologies, your dogmas, your habits. Mind can never be free. Freedom and mind never meet. Mind means bondage; mind is a prison. In the mind you live an encapsulated life, surrounded by all kinds of thoughts, theories, systems, philosophies, the history of humanity, all kinds of superstitions—Hindu,

Mohammedan, Christian, Buddhist, Jaina, political, social, economic, religious. Either your mind is made up of the bricks of the Bible, the Koran, the Gita...or maybe *Das Kapital* or the *Communist Manifesto*. You may have made your prison differently from others, you may have chosen a different architect, but the prison is the same.

The architect can be Sigmund Freud, Karl Marx, Albert Einstein—you can choose: prisons come in all shapes and all sizes and the interior decoration is up to you. You can put beautiful paintings inside, you can carpet it wall to wall, you can paint it according to your likes and dislikes. You can make a few changes here and there, a window on the left or on the right, a curtain of this material or that. But a prison is a prison. Mind *as such* is a prison, and everybody is living in a prison. Unless you get out of the prison you will never know what freedom is. Your prison can be cozy, comfortable, convenient; it can be well decorated, golden, studded with diamonds, and it will be difficult to leave it. You have worked so hard to create it, it is not going to be easy. But a prison is a prison; made of gold or made of mud, it makes no difference. You will never know the infinity of freedom; you will never know the beauty and the splendor of freedom; your splendor will die in the bottle. You will never know that the goose is always out.

zen in

the west

People in the West who have written about Zen don't know

what effort Zen people have been making before they relax.

Much has to be done before you can come to a point where

relaxation is possible. And that relaxation is not from you—

it happens: because the whole energy has moved, nothing

remains behind to be restless; a rest comes.

a new approach to existence

People are translating Zen books, people are commenting on Zen books, but all their commentaries and all their talks about Zen are intellectual. They are fed up with Christianity and they are in search of something fresh and new, but although they have found in Zen fresh insights, their approach remains Western, the approach of intellect. Their approach remains Socratic, Aristotelian. They are beautiful people, but their Zen is only a mind phenomenon; they have not experienced it. It is not their own truth; they have borrowed it from different sources.

THE WESTERN intelligentsia have become acquainted with Zen, have even fallen in love with Zen, but they are still trying to approach Zen from the mind. They have not yet come to the understanding that Zen has nothing to do with mind. Its tremendous job is to get you out of the prison of the mind. It is not an intellectual philosophy. It is not a philosophy at all. Nor is it a religion, because it has no fictions, no lies, no consolations. It is a lion's roar. The greatest thing that Zen has brought into the world is freedom from oneself.

All the religions have been talking about dropping your ego. But it is a weird phenomenon: they want you to drop your ego, and the ego is just a shadow of God. God is the ego of the universe, and the ego is your personality. Just as God is the center of existence according to religions, your ego is the center of your mind, of your personality. They have all been talking about dropping the ego, but it cannot be dropped unless God is dropped. You cannot drop a shadow or a reflection unless the source of its manifestation is destroyed.

So religions have been saying continuously, for centuries, that you should get rid of the ego—but for wrong reasons. They have been asking you to drop your ego so you can surrender to God, so you can surrender to the priests, so you can surrender to any kind of nonsense, any kind of theology, superstition, belief system.

Zen goes beyond the ego and beyond the self. Except Zen, no religion has come to the point of going beyond the self, beyond your spirit, beyond your individuality. Zen is essentially freedom from oneself. You have heard about other freedoms, but freedom from oneself is the ultimate freedom—not to be,

and to allow existence to express itself in all its spontaneity and grandeur. But it is existence—not you, not me. It is life itself dancing—not you, not me.

Only Zen has refined, in these twenty-five centuries, methods and devices to make you aware that you are not, that you are only arbitrary, just an idea.

As you go beyond the mind, even the idea of "I am" disappears. When the "I" also disappears and you start feeling a deep involvement in existence, with no boundaries, only then has Zen blossomed in you.

In fact, that is the state, the space of the awakened consciousness. But it has no "I" at the center.

To make it clear to you, Socrates says, "Know thyself." Gautam Buddha says, "Know—just know, and you will not find thyself." Enter deeper into your awareness, and the deeper you go, your self starts melting. Perhaps that is the reason why none of the religions except Zen have tried meditation—because meditation will destroy God, will destroy the ego, will destroy the self. It will leave you in absolute nothingness. It is only the mind that makes you afraid of nothingness. I receive this question almost every day: "Why are we afraid of nothingness?" You are afraid because you don't know nothingness. You are afraid only because you figure out intellectually,

"What is the point? If in meditation you have to disappear, then it is better to remain in the mind." At least you *are*—maybe illusory, maybe just an idea, but at least you are. What is the point of making all this effortless effort just to disappear into nothingness?

The mind makes you reluctant to go beyond the boundaries of the mind, because beyond the boundaries of the mind you will exist no more. That will be the ultimate death.

A Gautam Buddha dies ultimately, you die only temporarily. Maybe a few minutes, a few seconds, and you enter into another womb. Some idiots are always making love around the world, twenty-four hours, and you don't have to travel far away, just in the neighborhood.

Around the clock millions of couples are making love, so whichever is the closest couple, here you die and there you are born. The gap is very small.

Mind is afraid, and it seems logical, obvious: What is the point? Why should one do such a thing in which he disappears?

Gautam Buddha was told again and again, "You are a strange fellow. We came here to realize our self, and your meditation is to *unrealize* our self."

Socrates was a great genius, but confined to the mind: "Know thyself." There is no self to be known. That is the Zen message to the world. There is nothing to know. You have only to be one with the whole. There is no need to be afraid....

Think for a moment: When you were not born, was there any anxiety, any worry, any angst? You were not there, there was no problem. You are the problem, the beginning of the problem, and as you grow, more and more problems.... But before your birth, was there any problem?

Zen masters continuously ask the newcomers, "Where were you before your father was born?" An absurd question, but of immense significance. They are asking you, "If you were not, there was no problem. So what is the worry?" If your death becomes the ultimate death and all boundaries disappear, you will not be there, but the existence will be there. The dance will be there, but the dancer will not be there. The song will be there, but the singer will not be there.

This is only possible to experience by falling deeper, beyond the mind, to the very depth of your being, to the very source of life from where your life is flowing. Suddenly you realize the image of yourself was arbitrary. You are imageless; you are infinite. You were living in a cage. The moment you realize your sources are infinite, the cage disappears and you can open your wings into the blue sky and disappear. This disappearance is freedom from oneself. But this is possible not through intellect, it is possible only through meditation. Zen is another name for meditation.

Hundreds of beautiful books have appeared in the West since a strange man, D.T. Suzuki, introduced Zen to the West. He did a pioneer job, but he was not a Zen master, or even a man of Zen. He was a great scholar, and his impact spread through all the countries to the intelligentsia. He immediately had great appeal.

The old religions are crumbling, particularly in the West. Christianity is just a name; the empire is crumbling. They are trying to hold onto it, but it is not possible. This creates a great anxiety: "We are worthless...nobody needs us...existence doesn't care." At that moment D.T. Suzuki appeared on the horizon in the West. He was the first man to talk about Zen in the Western universities and colleges, and his work was immensely attractive to intelligent people, because they had lost faith in organized religions.

D.T. Suzuki appeared in the West with a new approach to existence. He appealed to people because he was a man of great scholarship, profound scholarship, and he brought to the Western mind a new concept of religion. But it

remained a concept; it remained an argument in the mind; it never went deeper than that.

A parallel exists in China. Before Bodhidharma appeared in China, China was already converted to Buddhism. Bodhidharma went there fourteen hundred years ago, but Gautam Buddha's philosophy and religion had reached China two thousand years ago, six hundred years before Bodhidharma went there. In those six hundred years scholars had converted the whole of China to Buddhism.

In those days it was easy to convert the whole country. You simply converted the emperor, and then his whole court was converted, then his whole army was converted, then his whole bureaucracy was converted. And when the emperor and the whole bureaucracy and the army and all the so-called wise people of the emperor's court were converted, the masses simply followed.

The masses have never decided anything for themselves. They simply follow the people who proclaim themselves great, in power, in intelligence, in riches. If these people are converted, the masses simply follow.

So in those six hundred years, thousands of Buddhist scholars reached China and converted China—the emperors, the governors. But it was not the true message of Gautam Buddha yet. Although China had become Buddhist, Buddha had not yet appeared. Bodhidharma was sent by his master, who was a woman. She said, "Scholars have prepared the way, now you go. You are immensely needed there." Bodhidharma was the first buddha to enter China, and he brought a totally different vision, not of the mind but of no-mind. For six hundred years in China, Buddhism had been only an intellectual exercise, good gymnastics. But as Bodhidharma entered China, he changed the whole idea about Zen.

❝ Zen means to be so alone that there is nothing to meditate upon. No object, just simple subjectivity exists— consciousness without clouds, a pure sky ❞

People were talking about Zen as if it were another philosophy, which it is not; as if it were another religion, which it is not. It is a rebellion against mind, and all your religions and philosophies are part of the mind.

This is the only rebellion against mind, against self, the only rebellion of withdrawing all the limits that imprison you and taking a quantum leap into nothingness. But this nothingness is very alive. It is life; it is existence. It is not a hypothesis. And when you take the jump, the first experience is that you are disappearing. The last experience is that you have become the whole.

Why have so many Western intellectuals been drawn to an examination of Zen? They are feeling a great vacuum, and they want to fill it. You cannot live with a vacuum. The vacuum is empty, and out of that emptiness, life becomes sad, serious.

All the religions have been filling your vacuum with lies. Now those lies are exposed. Science has done much in exposing those lies, and great meditators and mystics, have done tremendous work around the world in exposing the lies of religions.

The contemporary person stands in a strange position: the old has fallen, it was a deception, and the new has not yet arrived. So there is a gap, an interval, and the Western intelligentsia is trying to find something which will not be a lie, which will not just give you consolation, but which will transform you, which will be a deep revolution in your being.

Zen certainly is the right approach toward existence, the ultimate truth. Without believing in anything, without being a follower or a believer, you enter into your own interiority and into the immense nothingness of the whole. It is the same nothingness from where you have come and to where you are going again.

When the source and the goal become one, you will have a great celebration. In that celebration you will not be, but all of existence will be participating. The trees will be showering flowers, the birds will be singing songs, and the oceans and the rivers will all be rejoicing.

The whole existence becomes your home the moment your heart melts into the universal heart. That is where Zen is happening. In that melting into the universe, you are back to

as sweet, but if you have not tasted sugar, you hear the word *sweet* but don't understand what it is. The only way is for somebody to put some sweetness into your mouth.

The master's function in Zen is to force nothingness into your experience or, in other words, to bring you to your own nothingness. The master devises methods and when they become old and routine he drops them, finds new methods, new ways.

It has been twenty-five centuries since Gautam Buddha gave a lotus flower to Mahakashyapa, without a single word, and told his congregation, "What I could say I have told you. What I cannot say—although I want to, but it is simply not possible—I am transferring to Mahakashyapa." That lotus flower was a symbol: unless you open up like a lotus flower in the early morning sun when the dewdrops are shining like pearls on the lotus leaves.... It is a silent transmission of the lamp. Nothing is said.

Mahakashyapa came for the first time close to Buddha, took the lotus flower, touched his feet, went back and sat silently under his tree. Mahakashyapa is the first patriarch of Zen. So the lineage of Zen, the family of Zen, is a branch, a silent branch of Buddhism. They love Gautam Buddha, because Zen really originated in his disappearance. He transferred it to Mahakashyapa, and then it was the responsibility of Mahakashyapa to go on finding people to whom he could transfer it.

So since that moment, twenty-five centuries ago, it has been transferred without any

the original source, fresh, eternal, timeless, spacious. The only thing needed is freedom from the self. That is the essence of Zen. You have heard about many freedoms: political freedom, psychological freedom, economic freedom—there are many kinds of freedom. The ultimate freedom is Zen, freedom from yourself. That is not to be accepted as a belief, it has to be experienced. Only then will you know. It is a taste. Anybody can describe sugar

arbitrary means, without any language, from master to disciple; from one who has come home to one who is just wandering around and cannot find the way.

The master functions as a friend. He holds your hand and takes you on the right path, helps you to open your eyes, helps you become capable of transcending the mind. That's when your third eye opens, when you start looking inward. Once you are looking inward, the master's work is finished. Now it is up to you.

You can travel that small gap between your mind and no-mind in a single moment of tremendous intensity and urgency. Or you can travel slowly, hesitantly, stopping, being afraid that you are losing grip of your mind, you are losing grip of your individuality, that all boundaries are disappearing. What are you doing? You may think for a moment, "This may bring a breakdown, I may not be able to come back to my mind again. And who knows what is going to happen ahead? Things are disappearing...."

If you pay too much attention to the things that are disappearing, you may stop out of fear. The master helps you focus your mind on things that are happening, not on things that are disappearing. He forces you to look at the blissfulness, at the silence that is descending on you. Look at the peace, look at the joy, look at the ecstasy. He continuously emphasizes that which is happening, not that which is going away—the anxiety, the despair, the angst, the anguish; he does not allow you even to take note of them. What is disappearing is not worth keeping. Keep looking at what is appearing out of nothingness.

So you gather courage, you become more daring. You know that nothing is going to be wrong. With every single inch of movement, something greater is happening. Finally, as you enter the source of your being, the center of your being, the universe falls upon you, as if the whole ocean has fallen into a dewdrop.

Once you have experienced this beatitude, this ecstasy, this divine drunkenness, who cares about individuality? Who cares about the self? What has the self given to you except anxiety, except hell? And this nothingness is so pure, without boundaries. For the first time you find the infinity, the eternity, and all the mysteries of existence are suddenly opening their doors to you. And they go on opening... door after door....

There is no end to this journey; it is an endless pilgrimage. You are always arriving and arriving and arriving, but you never arrive. Each moment you are going deeper into bliss, deeper into ecstasy, deeper into truth, and there is no full stop.

> 66 *There is no end to this journey; it is an endless pilgrimage. You are always arriving and arriving and arriving, but you never arrive* 99

A Zen Manifesto is absolutely needed, because old religions are falling apart, and before they fall apart and humanity goes completely bananas, Zen has to be spread wide around the earth. Before the old house falls down, you have to create a new house.

And this time don't commit the same mistake. You have been living in a house which was not there; hence, you were suffering rain, winter, sun, because the house was imaginary. This time enter into your original home, not into any man-made temple, any man-made religion. Enter into your own existence. Why be continuously a carbon copy?

This time is valuable. You are born in a fortunate moment, when the old has lost its validity, its proof, when the old is simply hanging around you because you are not courageous enough to get out of the prison. Otherwise, the doors are open—in fact, there have never been any doors, because the house you are living in is completely imaginary. Your gods are imaginary, your priests are imaginary, your holy scriptures are imaginary. This time don't commit the same mistake. This time humanity has to take a quantum leap from the old rotten lies to the fresh, eternally fresh truth.

This is the Manifesto of Zen. D.T. Suzuki said, "Zen must be seized with bare hands, with no gloves on." His statement is rationally beautiful. You should seize Zen with your bare, naked hands, with no gloves on. He means that you should enter into the world of

Zen without any beliefs, without any security, without any safety, without any gloves. You should enter into Zen with naked hands, with nudity.

But his statement is still intellectual. He was neither a master of Zen nor even a man of Zen. If he had been a master of Zen, he could not have said it. A master of Zen cannot say that Zen must be seized. It is not a question of seizing Zen. This is the old language of the mind, of "conquering nature." Now it becomes conquering Zen.

Zen is your reality. Whom are you going to seize? Whom are you going to conquer? You *are* Zen.

And what does he mean by "with bare hands"? Hands will not reach there, bare or with gloves on. Hands symbolize movement outward; they always point toward the outside. All your senses open to the outside; they are all extrovert. Your ears hear the sound that is coming from the outside, your eyes see colors, light that is coming from the outside, your hand goes on grabbing—that is outside you. None of your senses can reach to the inside. For the inside there is a different sensitivity, the third eye. There are no hands.

Just between your two eyebrows, exactly in the middle, is the place which can look inward. When you are with closed eyes, trying to look inward, rushing toward your center, you are hitting on the third eye continuously. Because it has not been opened for centuries, it has forgotten how to open.

There are no hands, and there is no question of conquering. It is your nature. The very idea

that Zen must be seized creates a duality: you are the person who is going to seize Zen, and Zen is something other than you. It creates a duality. That's what gives me a clear-cut idea whether the person is intellectualizing or has had the experience.

Mind is dual; it always divides things into polar opposites: the conqueror and the conquered, the observer and the observed, the object and the subject, the day and the night. It divides things that are not divided. Neither is the day divided from the night, nor is birth divided from death. They are one energy. But mind goes on dividing everything into polarities, opposites. Nothing is opposite in existence; every contradiction is only apparent. Deep down all contradictions are meeting together.

So when somebody says, "Seize, conquer," he is still talking in the language of the mind and is still being violent. The words show it.

Zen has to be neither the object nor the subject. It is a transcendental experience. Duality of all kinds is transcended: the observer and the observed become one, the knower and the known become one. So it is not a question of conquering or seizing, it is a question of relaxing into yourself.

It is not a fight or a war, it is pure resting, sinking into your rest deeply. And as you sink deeper and deeper you find you are melting. The moment you come to oneness with existence, you have arrived at your nature. It can be possible only through relaxation, through rest.

Zen is the only existential approach in the world.

afterword

ZEN IS LIKE a telegram. Have you noticed that when you write a letter, it becomes longer and longer? It is easy to start the letter but difficult to end it. When you send a telegram, just ten words, it is a condensed message. Your ten-page-long letter will not have the same effect as the ten words of a telegram. The more condensed the meaning, the more striking. The more spread the meaning, the less impressive.

Zen believes in the essentials. It has no nonsense around it; no rituals, in which all other religions have got lost; no chanting, no mantras, no scriptures—just small anecdotes. If you have the right awareness, they will hit you directly in the heart. It is a condensed and crystallized teaching, but a person must be prepared for it. The only preparation is meditative awareness.

You cannot teach Zen in universities for the simple reason that the students don't have meditative awareness, and there are no books on Zen that can make meaningful that which looks absurd.

You will be surprised that in many Zen universities they are teaching Zen through my books, because my books at least make an effort to make the absurd appear sensible.

I try to provide a context and the right background for those who are not born in the Zen tradition. Zen books themselves are fragmentary. They are telegrams—urgent, immediate, not giving any explanation, but simply giving the essence, the perfume of thousands of flowers. You have to be alert and meditative to absorb them.

If you can absorb them, in the world's literature there is nothing more important than Zen anecdotes. In everything they are unique. They are small paintings, and just watching them, you will fall into such peace.

There are great poetries, but not of the same significance as the small haikus from Zen. I have always loved Basho, one of the haiku masters. His haikus say so much that even a thousand-page holy scripture does not say—it is all so much prose. A haiku of Basho is:

The ancient pond...

When you hear the haiku, you have to visualize it. It is so small that it is not a question of understanding, it is a question of entering into it. *The ancient pond...* Experience the feel of an ancient pond, visualize it.

The ancient pond
A frog jumps in
Plop

And the haiku is complete.

But Basho has said so much: the ancient pond, the ancient trees, the ancient rocks around it.... and there must be silence.... and a frog jumps in. For a moment the silence is disturbed, *plop*. And again the silence is restored.... perhaps deeper than it was before. What does he want to say in this haiku? He is saying, This ancient world...and your existence is just a *plop*, a little sound in the silence. And then you are gone, and the silence deepens. In this way he makes the whole world ephemeral, dreamlike—nothing solid in it, only great silence.

That great silence is your very being. It is also the very being of the whole universe.

TAO
the great rebellion

Taoist masters only talk about "the Way." Tao means the Way—

they don't talk about the goal at all. They say: The goal will take

care of itself; you need not worry about the goal.

If you know the Way, then you know the goal, because the goal is not at the very end of the Way, the goal is all along the Way—each moment and each step it is there. It is not that when the Way ends you have arrived at the goal; each moment, wherever you are, you are at the goal if you are on the Way. To be on the Way is to be at the goal. Hence, Taoists don't talk about the goal, they don't talk about God, they don't talk about *moksha*, *nirvana*, enlightenment—no, not at all. Very simple is their message: You have to find the Way.

Things become a little more complicated when the masters say: The Way has no map, the Way is not charted, the Way is not such that you can follow somebody and find it. The Way is not like a superhighway; the Way is like a bird flying in the sky—it leaves no footprints behind. The bird has flown but no tracks are left to follow. The Way is a pathless path. It is not ready-made, available; you cannot just decide to walk on it, you will have to find it. You will have to find it in your own way; nobody else's way will do. Buddha has walked, Lao Tzu has walked, Jesus has walked, but their ways are not going to help you because you are not Jesus, and you are not Lao Tzu, and you are not Buddha. You are you, a unique individual. Only by walking, only by living your life, will you find the Way. This is something of great value.

That's why Taoism is not an organized religion—it cannot be. It is an organic religiousness, but not an organized religion. You can be a Taoist if you simply live your life authentically and spontaneously; if you have the courage to go into the unknown on your own, as an individual; if, not leaning on anybody, not following anybody, you simply go into the dark night not knowing whether you will arrive anywhere or whether you will be lost. If you have the courage, that choice is there. It is risky. It is adventurous.

Christianity, Hinduism, and Mohammedanism are superhighways: you need not risk anything—you simply follow the crowd. With Tao you have to go alone, you have to be alone. Tao respects the individual, not the society. Tao respects the unique, not the crowd. Tao respects freedom, not conformity. Tao has no tradition. Tao is a rebellion, and it is the greatest rebellion possible.

道

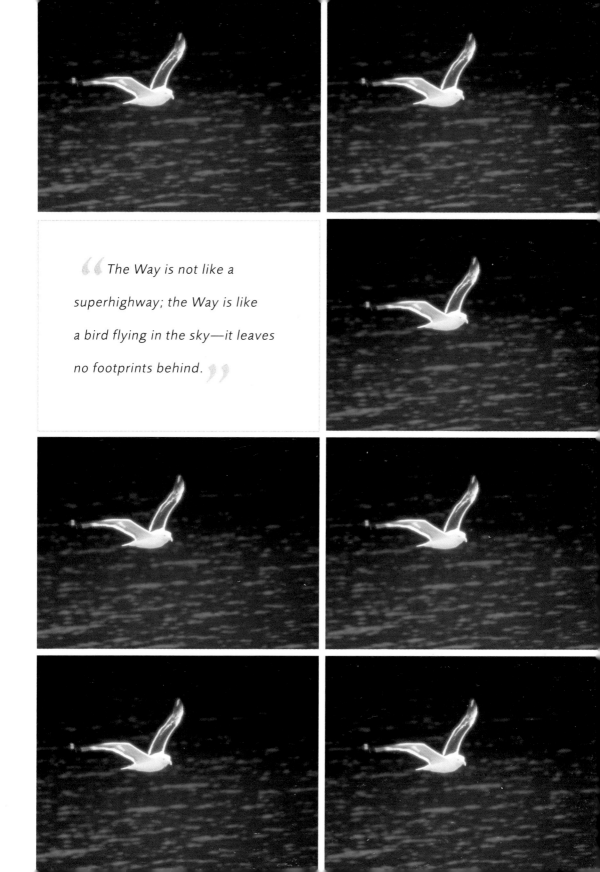

" The Way is not like a superhighway; the Way is like a bird flying in the sky—it leaves no footprints behind. "

the principles

of tao

Tao is one, but the moment it becomes manifest, it has to become

two. Manifestation has to be dual: it cannot be singular. It has to

become matter and consciousness; it has to become man and

woman. It has to become day and night; it has to become life and

death. You will find these two principles everywhere. The whole

of life consists of these two principles, and behind these two

principles is hidden the One. If you continue to remain involved in

these dualities, in the polar opposites, you will remain in the world.

If you use your intelligence, if you become a little more alert and

start looking into the depths of things, you will be surprised—the

opposites are not really opposites, but complementaries. And

behind them both is one single energy: that is Tao.

道

the ultimate synthesis

Tao means transcendence—transcendence of all duality, transcendence of all polarity, transcendence of all opposites. Tao is the ultimate synthesis—the synthesis of man and woman, positive and negative, life and death, day and night, summer and winter.

OW DOES THIS synthesis become possible? How does one grow into that ultimate synthesis? A few things have to be understood.

First, the principle of yin—the principle of femininity—is like a ladder between hell and heaven. You can go to hell through it or you can go to heaven through it; the direction will differ but the ladder will be the same. Nothing happens without the woman. The energy of the woman is a ladder to the lowest and to the highest, to the darkest valley and to the lightest peak. This is one of the fundamental principles of Tao. It must be understood in detail. Once it is rooted in your heart, things will become very simple.

It will be good to go into the symbolism of Adam and Eve. The world does not start with Adam, it starts with Eve. Through Eve, the serpent persuades Adam to disobey. The serpent cannot persuade Adam directly. There is no direct way to persuade the man; if you want to reach him, you must go through the woman. The woman functions as a medium for the serpent. On the other hand, when Christ is born, he is born of the Virgin Mary. The Christ child is born of virgin femininity, out of virgin yin. The highest enters through the woman. The lowest and the highest have both been expressed through the woman.

Adam means "red earth." God made Adam out of red earth. Adam is the principle of dust unto dust. The man is the outer principle, the principle of extroversion: the man is the physical body. Try to understand these symbols. The man is the physical body, and God created Eve out of man's physical body. Eve was something higher. First the man had to be created, then the woman. The feminine was more subtle, more refined—a greater synthesis. Eve was created out of a rib because she could not be created directly from the earth.

To understand these symbols, consider that you cannot eat mud, but you can eat apples—apples are on a higher plane. They come from the mud in the sense that the tree grows out of the mud—so the apple is nothing but earth transformed. You can eat

道

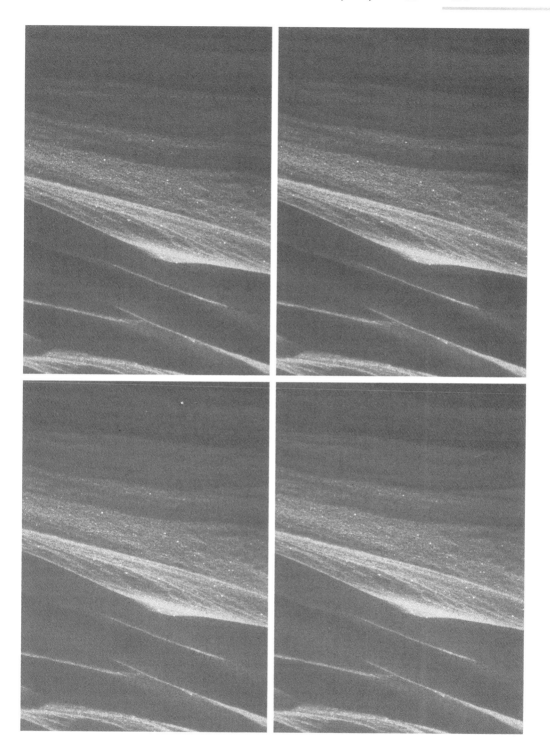

> *Tao has no tradition. Tao is a rebellion, and it is the greatest rebellion possible.*

the apple and digest it, but if you try to eat the earth, you will die. The apple is from the earth, but it is a superior synthesis—better tasting, more digestible.

God created Adam—and man has taken it to mean that because God created the man first, he *is* first. No, the man was created first because he is very close to the earth. Then the woman was created—and since she is not as close to the earth; she was created out of Adam as a higher synthesis.

The name *Eve* is also significant. *Eve* means "the heart." Adam means the earth and Eve means the heart. God told Adam to name things, so he named everything. When he came to name Eve, he simply said, "She is my heart—Eve." *Eva* or *Eve* can be further translated into modern jargon to mean the psyche. Man is the body principle; woman is the psychic principle. Man is body; woman is mind. Everything happens through the mind.

If you are to do something wrong, your mind has to be convinced first; if you are to do good, your mind has to be convinced about that first. Everything happens first as an idea, only—then can it be actualized.

Your body cannot be persuaded to do anything unless your mind is ready. Even if an illness enters your body, it enters through the mind. Anything that ever happens, happens through the mind.

The woman is the principle of the inner—not, certainly, of the innermost, but of the inner. She is in the middle. The innermost is called the soul, the outermost is called the body, and just between the two is the psyche, the mind.

> " *Through Eve, Adam disobeyed.*
>
> *Adam followed Eve on this adventure*
>
> *into the world.* "

    That is the meaning of the whole parable of Adam and Eve. The serpent persuaded Eve since only the mind can be persuaded, convinced, seduced. Then the mind can persuade the body easily. In fact, the body follows the mind like a shadow. Once your mind has a thought, it is bound to be translated into actuality.

Through Eve, Adam fell. Through Eve, he was expelled from the garden of God. Through Eve came this great adventure we call the world. Through Eve, Adam disobeyed. Adam followed Eve on this adventure into the world.

The parable about Jesus is the same, with a different emphasis. Jesus is born to the Virgin Mary. Why a virgin? If you understand rightly, virgin means a mind that is absolutely pure, uncontaminated by thought. Thoughts are represented by the serpent because the ways of thoughts are serpentine. If you watch your own thoughts, you will understand. They walk without legs just like serpents; they wriggle within you. They are cunning and clever and deceptive— like the serpent. They hide in dark holes in your unconscious and whenever they have an opportunity they sneak up on you. In the night, in the dark night, they come out; in the daylight they hide. When you are alert, those thoughts

disappear; when you are not so alert, they come out and start influencing you.

The Virgin Mary is a mind in meditation; Eve is a mind full of thoughts, full of serpents. Jesus enters into the world through the Virgin Mary, through purity, through innocence. Thought is cunning; thoughtlessness is innocent.

When you understand these beautiful parables, you will be surprised: We have not done justice to them. They are not historical facts; they are great metaphors of the inner being of man. Through Eve, Adam fell, and through the Virgin Mary, Jesus rose and entered again into the world of godliness.

One thing more. It is said that the sin of Adam was disobedience. God had said not to eat the fruit of a certain tree, the Tree of Knowledge— but the serpent persuaded Eve and Eve persuaded Adam. It was disobedience.

You will be surprised to learn the Hebrew meaning of the name Mary. The Hebrew word for Mary is *mariam*, which— means "rebellion." Through disobedience, Adam fell, and through rebellion, Jesus rose.

Disobedience means a reaction, going against, against God. Rebellion means negating the negative, going against the world, going against the serpents. Eve listened to the serpents and went against God. Mary rebelled against the serpents and listened to God.

Disobedience is political; rebellion is religious. Disobedience only brings disorder. Rebellion, real rebellion, brings a radical change in being—a 180-degree turn, a conversion.

But both Adam and Jesus happened through the feminine principle.

yin and yang

In Taoist language, the feminine principle is called yin and the male principle is called yang. Yang is ambition, yang is aggression, yang is desire and projection. Yang is political—yin is religious. Whenever you are ambitious, it is impossible for you to be religious; whenever you are religious, it is impossible for you to be political. The two don't go together. They don't mix. They cannot mix—their very natures are like water and oil. Ambition and meditation can never mix.

THE POLITICIAN FUNCTIONS through the male principle and the sage functions through the feminine principle. That's why the sages become so soft, so feminine, so round, so beautiful. A certain grace surrounds them. And the beauty is certainly not only of the body—sometimes it happens that the body may not be beautiful at all.

In early Christianity, there was a legend that Jesus was the ugliest person in the world. By and by Christians dropped that idea; they didn't like it. But it has something beautiful in it. It said that his body was ugly, yet when you came across Jesus, you would be suddenly surprised, overtaken, possessed, overwhelmed by his beauty. If you had seen a picture of him, you would have seen only his ugliness, but if you had gone to him, entered his actual presence, you would have forgotten all about his ugliness because so much beauty was flowing. So much beauty was pouring out, raining from him, that you would not even remember that he was ugly. So those who had not seen him used to think that he was ugly, and those who had seen him used to say that he was the most beautiful person of all.

The body is not the question. The sage does not live in the body or as the body, he lives *through* the body. The politician is nothing *but* the body, the extrovert. The body is extrovert, the psyche is introvert, and when you transcend both, Tao arises. When you are neither extrovert nor introvert—when you are not going to the outer nor into the inner, when you are not going anywhere—there is tremendous stillness. There is no movement, because there is no motivation. Your inner flame is no longer wavering because there is no direction to go in, no purpose to fulfill. There is nowhere else to be and nobody else to be; you are absolutely content in the moment. Then you have transcended man and woman and the polarity. In that transcendence is Tao.

This transcendence has been taught in different ways all over the world. Different terms have been used. The explanation of one term will help you to understand. The term is "israel." It is not the name of a certain

道

> **❝ If you are dominated by the sun, you will be aggressive, ambitious and political. If you are dominated by the moon, you will be cool, non-aggressive, receptive, peaceful, silent. ❞**

race—and it is not a name of a certain individual. Israel is exactly what Tao is. Israel is made up of three symbols: *is-ra-el*. *Is* comes from the Egyptian word *isis*. Isis is the Egyptian moon goddess and Ishtar is the Babylonian moon goddess. Thus *is* is the principle of yin, the feminine.

Yoga recognizes three passages in the human being: the moon, the sun, and the transcendental. Through one nostril, you breathe the moon energy; through the other nostril, you breathe the sun energy. Deep inside, when both types of breathing stop, then you transcend.

Ra is the Egyptian sun god. The symbol *Ra* represents the masculine principle, yang. And *El* comes from Elohim, the same root from which the Mohammedans derive "Allah." The Hebrew word for God is Elohim; "el" comes from there. It represents the meeting of the feminine and the masculine and their transcendence—Tao. Israel means Tao exactly.

If you are dominated by the sun, you will be aggressive, ambitious, political—and burning with desire and passion. If you are dominated by the moon, you will be cool, non-aggressive, receptive, peaceful, silent. But both have to be transcended because both are lopsided. You have to come to the moment when you can say, "I am neither man nor woman." That's when you can become a Buddha or a Christ or a Krishna—when you are neither man nor woman, neither moon nor sun, neither *is* nor *ra*, neither yin nor yang, but simply *is*, purely *is*. All formulations have disappeared.

This transcendence develops only gradually. First you have to drop the principle of *ra*—the principle of the sun, the male energy—and you have to move into the feminine, into the female *is*. And from there you have to move into the beyond. Remember that everything happens through the feminine principle—so whether you are going beyond or you are going below makes no difference—it is the ladder.

With only the body, the sun energy, the male, you will become a rapist. You will rape life; you will not be a lover. Science comes out of sun energy; science is male-oriented. That's why the East has not developed it. The East has lived through the moon principle—passive, silent, easygoing, not trying to conquer—in deep love with nature, not trying to fight. The East has never been a rapist; the West has raped nature. Hence the problems of ecology have arisen: nature is being destroyed.

With the feminine principle, with the moon principle, there is love. You will love. You will not rape. Sometimes the physical act may look the same, but the innermost quality is different. You can rape even your wife if you don't love

her. The physical act of making love to or raping a woman may be similar, but the inner quality differs greatly.

With the sun energy, science is born: it is the rape of nature. With the moon energy, poetry, art, painting, dance, and music are born: it is love playing with nature. The East has lived through art, music, dance, drama. The West has been trying to use male energy too much. The West has lost balance, but

so has the East—no society has yet evolved which can be called Israel, which can be called Tao, which has transcended both or synthesized both in such harmony that the antagonism has disappeared.

Tao is the goal: to create a human being who is fully integrated, totally integrated, and to create a human society that is totally integrated as well.

no goal, no technique

All technique is against nature, against Tao. Effort as such is against Tao. If you can leave everything to nature, then no technique is needed, because that is the ultimate technique. If you can leave everything to Tao, that is the deepest surrender possible. You are surrendering yourself, your future, your possibilities. You are surrendering time itself and all effort. This means infinite patience, awaiting.

ONCE YOU surrender everything to nature, there is no effort; you just float. You are in a deep let-go. Things happen to you, but you are not making any effort for them—you are not even seeking them. If they happen, it is okay; if they don't happen, it is okay—you have no choice. Whatsoever happens, happens; you have no expectations and, of course, no frustrations.

Life flows by; you flow in it. You have no goal to reach, because with a goal effort enters. You have nowhere to go, because if you have somewhere to go, effort will come in; it is implied. You have nowhere to go, nowhere to reach, no goal, no ideal, nothing to be achieved —you surrender all. In this surrendering moment, in this very moment, all will happen to you.

Effort will take time; surrender will not take time. Technique will take time; surrender will not take time. That's why I call surrender the ultimate technique. It is a non-technique. You cannot practice it—you cannot practice surrender. If you practice, it is not surrender. Then you are

relying on yourself; then you are not totally helpless; then you are trying to do something— even if it is surrender, you are *trying* to do it. Then technique will come in, and with technique time enters, future enters. Surrender is non-temporal; it is beyond time. If you surrender, this very moment you are out of time, and all that *can* happen will happen. But then you are not searching for it, not seeking it; you are not greedy for it. You have no mind for it at all: whether it happens or not, it is all the same to you.

Tao means surrender—surrender to nature. Then you are not. Tantra and yoga are techniques. Through them you will reach a place of surrender, but it will be a long process. Ultimately after every technique you will have to surrender— but with techniques it will come in the end. With Tao, in Tao, it comes in the beginning. If you can surrender right now, no technique is needed.

You have to be deconditioned. If you are in Tao, then no technique is needed. If you are healthy, then no medicine is needed. Every medicine is against health. But you are ill;

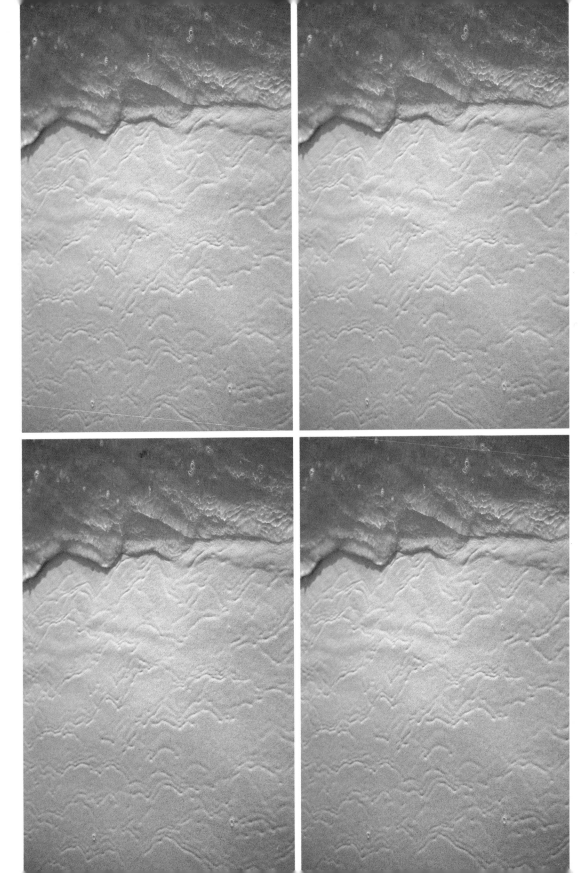

道

medicine is needed. This medicine will kill your illness. It cannot give you health, but if the illness is removed, health will happen to you. No medicine can give you health. Basically every medicine is a poison—but you have gathered some poison; you need an antidote. It will balance, and health will be possible.

Technique is not going to give you your divinity, it is not going to give you your nature. All that you have gathered around your nature it will destroy. It will only decondition you. You are conditioned, and right now you cannot take a jump into surrender. If you can take it, it is good—but you cannot take it. Your conditioning will ask, "How?" Then techniques will be helpful.

When one lives in Tao, then no yoga, no tantra, no religion is needed. One is perfectly healthy; no medicine is needed. Every religion is medicinal. When the world lives in total Tao, religions will disappear. No teacher, no Buddha, no Jesus will be needed, because everyone will be a Buddha or a Jesus. But right now, as you are, you need techniques. Those techniques are antidotes.

You have gathered around yourself such a complex mind that whatsoever is said and given to you, you will complicate it. You will make it more complex, you will make it more difficult. If I say to you, "Surrender," you will ask, "How?" If I say, "Use techniques," you will ask, 'Techniques? Are not techniques against Tao?" If I say, "No technique is needed; simply surrender and godliness will happen to you," you will immediately ask, "How?"—your mind.

If I say, "Tao is right here and now. You need not practice anything, you simply take a jump and surrender," you will say, "How? How can I surrender?" If I give you a technique to answer you your mind will say, "But is not a method, a technique, a way, against Tao? If divinity is my nature, then how can it be achieved through a technique? If it is already there, then the technique is futile, useless. Why waste time with the technique?" Look at this mind!

Once it happened that a man, the father of a young girl, asked composer Leopold Godowsky to come to his house and give an audition to his daughter. She was learning piano. Godowsky came to their house; patiently he listened to the girl playing. When the girl finished, the father beamed, and he cried in happiness and asked Godowsky, "Isn't she wonderful?"

Godowsky is reported to have said, "She has an amazing technique. I have never heard anyone play such simple pieces with such great difficulty."

This is what is happening in your mind. Even a simple thing you will make complicated and difficult for yourself. This is a defense measure, because when you create difficulty you need not do it—first the problem must be solved, and *then* you can do it.

Remember, you can go on in this vicious circle continuously forever and ever. You will have to break it somewhere and come out of it. Be decisive, because only with decision is your humanity born. Only with decision do you become human. Be decisive. If you can surrender, surrender. If you cannot surrender, don't create philosophical problems, use some technique. Either way, the surrender will happen to you.

the watercourse way

There are few Taoist temples, so to find a Taoist statue is very rare. Most statues are in the mountains —standing in the open, carved out of the mountain with no roof, no temple, no priest, no worship.

THERE WAS A STATUE of Lao Tzu, the founder of Tao, and a young man had been hoping for years to go to the mountains and see that statue. He loved the words, the way Lao Tzu has spoken, the style of life that he lived, but he had never seen any of his statues. Years passed, and there were always many things preventing the young man from following his desire to see the statue.

Finally one night he decided that he had to go—it was not that far, only a hundred miles. But he was a poor man, and he would have to walk. In the middle of the night—he chose a time in the middle of the night so that his wife and the children and family would be asleep and no trouble would arise—he took a lamp in his hand, because the night was dark, and walked out of the town. As he reached the first milestone outside the town, a thought arose in him: "My God, one hundred miles! And I only have two feet—it is going to kill me. I am asking the impossible. I have never walked one hundred miles, and there is no road."

It was a small footpath into the mountains—dangerous, too. So he thought, "It is better to wait till the morning. At least there will be light and I can see better; otherwise I will fall somewhere, off this small footpath, and without even seeing the statue of Lao Tzu, I will simply be finished! Why commit suicide?" So he stopped and sat down just outside the town.

As the sun was rising, an old man came by. He saw this young man sitting there and he asked, "What are you doing here?" The young man explained. The old man laughed. He said, "Have you not heard the ancient saying? Nobody has the power to take two steps together; you can take only one step at a time. The powerful, the weak, the young, the old— it doesn't matter. The saying goes, 'Just step by step, one step at a time, a man can go ten thousand miles.' And this is only a hundred miles! Who is saying that you have to go continuously? You can take your time; after ten miles you can rest for a day or two days and enjoy. This is one of the most beautiful valleys, among the most beautiful mountains, and the trees are so full of fruits, fruits that you may not have even tasted. Anyway, I am going; you can come along with me.

I have been on this path thousands of times, and I am at least four times your age. Stand up!"

The old man was so authoritative—when he said "Stand up!" the young man simply stood. And the old man said, "Give your things to me. You are young and inexperienced; I will carry your things. You just follow me, and we will take as many rest stops as you want."

What the old man had said was true—as they entered deeper into the forest and the mountains, it became more and more beautiful. There were many wild, juicy fruits to eat and whenever the young man wanted to rest, the old man was ready. He was surprised that the old man himself never said it was time to rest. But whenever the young man wanted to rest, he was always willing to rest with him— a day or two, and then they would start the journey again.

Those one hundred miles just came and went by, and they reached one of the most beautiful statues of one of the greatest men who has ever walked on the earth. Even his statue was something special—it was not just a piece of art; it was created by Taoist artists to represent the spirit of Tao.

The Tao philosophy is one of letting go. You are not to swim, but to flow with the river, to allow the river to take you wherever it is going, because every river ultimately reaches the ocean. There is no need to be tense or to worry—you will reach the ocean.

In that lonely spot the statue was standing, and there was a waterfall just by its side— because Tao is called the watercourse way. Tao flows just as water goes on and on flowing with no guidebooks, no maps, no rules, no discipline. Strangely enough, it flows in a very humble way, always seeking the lower position everywhere. It never goes uphill. It always goes downhill, and it reaches to the ocean, to its very source. The whole atmosphere surrounding the statue was representative of the Taoist idea of let-go.

The old man said, "Now begins the journey."

The young man said, "What? I was thinking, one hundred miles and the journey is finished."

The old man said, "That is just the way the masters have been talking to people. But the reality is now—from this point a journey of a thousand and one miles begins. And I will not deceive you, because after a thousand and one miles you will meet another old man—perhaps me—who will say, 'This is just a stopover; go on.' Going on is the message."

The journey is endless, but the ecstasy goes on deepening. At each step, you are more; your life is livelier, your intelligence is aflame. And nobody stops. Once the seeker has reached to his being, he himself becomes capable of seeing what lies ahead—treasures upon treasures. Persuasion is needed only up to the point of being; those first one hundred miles are the most difficult. After those one hundred miles, it may be a thousand and one miles or an infinity—it makes no difference.

Now you know that in reality there is no goal; the very talk of the goal was for the beginners, was for children. The journey is the goal.

The journey itself is the goal.

It is infinite. It is eternal.

You will find stars, unknown spaces, unknowable experiences, but you will never come to a point where you can say, "Now I have arrived." Anybody who says, "I have arrived" is not on the path. He has not traveled; his journey has not begun; he is just sitting on the first milestone.

Each departure is a little painful, but the pain will be forgotten immediately—because more and more blissfulness will be showered on you. Soon you will learn this: there is no need to feel pain when you depart from one overnight stay. You become accustomed to

THE WAY

Tao means the way with no goal. Simply, the Way. It was courageous of Lao Tzu, twenty-five centuries ago, to tell people that there is no goal and we are not going anywhere. We are just going to be here, so make the time as beautiful, as loving, as joyous as possible. He called his philosophy Tao, and Tao means simply the Way.

Many asked him, "Why have you chosen the name Tao? Because you don't have any goals in your philosophy."

He said, "Specifically for that reason I have chosen to call it 'the Way,' so that nobody forgets that there is no goal, there is only the Way."

The Way is beautiful; the way is full of flowers. And the Way becomes more and more beautiful as your consciousness becomes higher. The moment you have reached the peak, everything becomes so sweet, so ecstatic, that you suddenly realize that this is the place; this is home. You were unnecessarily running here and there.

So cancel all the tickets you have booked! There is nowhere to go.

leaving because you know that the journey is endless. The treasure becomes greater and greater; you are not losing. Stopping anywhere will be a loss. So there is no stop, no full stop, not even a semicolon....

lao tzu:

"the old guy"

Lao Tzu is just a spokesman of life. If life is absurd, Lao Tzu is absurd;

if life has an absurd logic to it, Lao Tzu has the same logic to it. Lao

Tzu simply reflects life. He doesn't add anything to it, he doesn't

choose out of it; he simply accepts whatsoever it is. It is simple to

see the spirituality of Buddha—it is impossible to miss it, he is so

extraordinary. But it is difficult to see the spirituality of Lao Tzu. He

is so ordinary, just like you. You will have to grow in understanding.

Buddha passes by you and you will immediately recognize that a

superior human being has passed; he carries the aura of a superior

human being around him. It is difficult to miss him, almost impossible

to miss him. But Lao Tzu...he may be your neighbor. You may

have been overlooking him because he is so ordinary—he is so

extraordinarily ordinary, and that is the beauty of it.

道

道

absolute tao

Let me tell you the story of how the verses of Lao Tzu's **Tao Te Ching** *came to be written, because that will help you to understand them. For ninety years Lao Tzu lived—in fact, he did nothing except live. He lived totally. Many times his disciples asked him to write, but he would always say: The Tao that can be told is not the real Tao. The truth that can be told becomes untrue immediately.*

Lao Tzu says: *The Tao that can be told of is not the absolute Tao.*

SO HE WOULD NOT say anything; he would not write anything. Then what were his disciples doing with him? They were only being with him. They lived with him; they moved with him; they simply imbibed his being. Being near him, they tried to be open to him; being near him, they tried not to think about anything; being near him, they became more and more silent. In that silence he would reach them—he would come to them and he would knock at their doors.

For ninety years he refused to write anything or to say anything. His basic attitude was that truth cannot be taught. The moment you say something about truth, it is no longer true—the very saying falsifies it. You cannot teach it. At the most you can indicate it, and that indication should be your very being, your whole life; it cannot be indicated in words. Lao Tzu was against words; he was against language.

It is said that he used to go for a morning walk every day, and a neighbor used to follow

him. Knowing that Lao Tzu was a man of absolute silence, the neighbor also always kept silent. Even a "hello" was not allowed; even talking about the weather was not allowed. To say, "How beautiful a morning!" would be too much chattering. Lao Tzu would walk for miles and the neighbor would follow him.

For years this went on, but once it happened that a guest was staying with the neighbor and he also wanted to come, so the neighbor brought him. The guest did not know Lao Tzu or his ways. He started to feel suffocated because his host was not talking, and he couldn't understand why they were so silent— the silence became heavy on him.

If you don't know how to be silent, silence can become heavy. It is not that by saying things you communicate—no. It is by saying things that you unburden yourself.

In fact, through words, communication is not possible; just the opposite is possible—you can avoid communication. You can create a screen of words around you so that your real situation cannot be known. You clothe yourself with words.

That man started feeling naked and suffocated and awkward; it was embarrassing. So he simply said, when the sun was rising, "What a beautiful sun. Look...! What a beautiful sun is born, is rising! What a beautiful morning!"

That's all he said. But nobody responded because the neighbor, his host, knew that Lao Tzu wouldn't like it. And of course Lao Tzu wouldn't say anything at all.

When they came back, Lao Tzu told the neighbor, "Tomorrow, don't bring this man. He is a chatterbox." Yet the guest had only said those few words in a two- or three-hour walk. Lao Tzu said, "He talks uselessly—because I also have eyes, I can see that the sun is being born and it is beautiful. What is the need to say it?"

Lao Tzu lived in silence. He avoided talking about the truth that he had attained and he rejected the idea that he should write it down for the generations to come.

At the age of ninety he took leave of his disciples. He said, "Now I am moving towards the hills, towards the Himalayas. I am going there to get ready to die. It is good to live with people, it is good to be in the world while you are living, but when one is getting nearer to death it is good to move into total aloneness, so that you move toward the original source in your absolute purity and loneliness, uncontaminated by the world."

The disciples felt very sad, but what could they do? They followed him for a few hundred

> " *The truth cannot be said for many reasons. The first and most basic is that truth is always realized in silence.* "

miles, but by and by Lao Tzu persuaded them to go back. He was crossing the border alone and the guard on the border imprisoned him. The guard was also a disciple, and he said, "Unless you write a book, I am not going to allow you to move beyond the border. This much you must do for humanity. Write a book. That is the debt you have to pay, otherwise I won't allow you to cross." So for three days, Lao Tzu was imprisoned by his own disciple.

It was beautiful. It was loving. He was forced—and that's how the small book of Lao Tzu, *Tao Te Ching*, was born. He had to write it, because the disciple wouldn't allow him to cross the border otherwise. Since the guard had the authority and could create trouble for him, Lao Tzu had to write the book. In three days he finished it.

This is the first sentence of the book:

The Tao that can be told of is not the absolute Tao.

This is the first thing Lao Tzu had to say: whatsoever can be said cannot be true. This is the introduction for the book. It simply makes you alert: Now some words will follow, but don't become a victim of the words. Remember the wordless. Remember that which cannot be communicated through language, through words. The Tao can be communicated, but it can only be communicated from being to being. It can be communicated when you are with the master, just with the master doing nothing, not even practicing anything.

Why can't the truth be said? What is the difficulty? The truth cannot be said for many reasons. The first and the most basic reason is that truth is always realized in silence. When your inner talk has stopped, then truth is realized. And that which is realized in silence, how can you express it through sound? It is an experience. It is not a thought.

If it were a thought it could be expressed; there would be no trouble in that. Howsoever complicated or complex a thought may be, a way can be found to express it. The most complex theory of Albert Einstein, the theory of relativity, can also be expressed in a symbol. There is no problem with that. The listener may not be able to understand it; that is not the point. It can be expressed.

It is said that when Einstein was alive, only a dozen persons in the whole world understood him and what he was saying. But even that is enough. If even a single person can understand, it has been expressed. And even if a single person cannot understand right now, maybe after many centuries there will come a person who can understand it. Then too it has been expressed. The very probability that somebody can understand it means that it has been expressed.

But truth cannot be expressed because the reaching of it is through silence, soundlessness, thoughtlessness. You reach it through no-mind; the mind drops. How can you use something that, as a necessary condition, has to drop before truth can be reached? Mind cannot understand truth, mind cannot realize truth, so how can mind express it? Remember it as a rule: If mind can attain something, mind can express it; if mind cannot attain it, mind cannot express it.

All language is futile. Truth cannot be expressed.

Then what have all the scriptures been doing? Then what is Lao Tzu doing? Then what are the Upanishads doing? They all try to say something that cannot be said in the hope that a desire may arise in you to know about it. Truth cannot be said, but in the effort of saying it, a desire can arise in the listener to know that which cannot be expressed.

A thirst can be provoked. The thirst is there; it needs a little provocation. You are already thirsty—how can it be otherwise? You are not blissful, you are not ecstatic—you are thirsty. Your heart is a burning fire. You are seeking something that can quench the thirst but, not finding the water, not finding the source, by and by you have tried to suppress your thirst itself. That is the only way; otherwise, it is too much—it will not allow you to live at all. So you suppress the thirst.

A master like Lao Tzu knows well that truth cannot be said, but the very effort to say it will provoke something, bring the suppressed thirst to the surface. Once the thirst surfaces, a search, an inquiry starts. And he has moved you.

The Tao that can be told of is not the absolute Tao.

At the most it can be relative.

For example, we can say something about light to a blind man, knowing well that it is impossible to communicate anything about light because he has no experience of it. But something can be said about light—theories about light can be created. Even a blind man can become an expert in the theories of light. About the whole science of light he can become an expert—there is no problem in that—but he will not understand what light is. He will understand what light consists of; he will understand the physics of light, the chemistry of light. He will understand the poetry of light, but he will not understand the facticity of it, what light *is*. The *experience* of light he will not understand. So all that is said to a blind man about light is only relative: it is something about light; it is not light itself. Light cannot be communicated.

Something can be said about God, but God cannot be said. Something can be said about love, but love cannot be said. That "something" remains relative. It remains relative to the listener's understanding, intellectual grip, training, and desire to understand. It depends on and it is relative to the master's way of expressing, the devices used to communicate. It remains relative—relative to many things—but it can never become the absolute experience. This is the first reason that truth cannot be expressed.

The second reason that truth cannot be expressed is because it is an experience. No *experience* can be communicated, leave truth aside. If you have never known love, when somebody mentions love, you will hear the word but you will miss the meaning. The word is in the dictionary—even if you don't understand, you can look in the dictionary and know what it means. But the meaning is in you. Meaning comes through experience. If you have loved someone then you know the meaning of the word "love." The literal meaning is in the dictionary, in the language, in the word. But the experiential meaning, the existential meaning, is in *you*. If you have known the experience, immediately the word "love" is no longer empty; it contains something.

If I say anything at all, it is empty unless you bring your experience to it. When your experience comes to it, it becomes significant; otherwise, it remains empty—words and words and words.

How can truth be expressed when you have not experienced it? Even in ordinary life, an unexperienced thing cannot be told. Only words will be conveyed. The container will reach you, but the content will be lost. An empty word will travel toward you; you will hear it, and you will think you understand because you know its literal meaning, but you will miss it. The real, authentic meaning comes through existential experience. You have to know it; there is no other way. There is no shortcut. Truth cannot be transferred. You cannot steal it, you cannot borrow it, you cannot purchase it, you cannot rob it, you cannot beg it—there is no way. Unless you have it, you cannot have it.

The Tao that can be told of is not the absolute Tao.

Remember this condition.

three types of people

Lao Tzu says: When the highest type of people hear the Tao, they try hard to live in accordance with it. When the mediocre type hear the Tao, they seem to be aware and yet unaware of it. When the lowest type hear the Tao, they break into loud laughter—if it were not laughed at, it would not be Tao.

THE GREATEST MYTH is that of humankind. There exists nothing like it. There are as many humankinds as there are people; there is not one kind. Every individual is so different from every other that humanity does not exist. It is just a word, an abstraction. You appear to be similar to others but you are not, and that myth has to be thrown away—only then can you penetrate deeper into the reality of human beings.

No ancient psychology ever believed that humanity existed. In fact, if we are going to classify, then all the ancient psychologies classify man in three divisions. In India, they have divided humanity into three parts: *Satwa*, *Rajas*, and *Tamas*. Lao Tzu has not given these names, but he also divides humanity into three types, exactly the same way.

These three divisions are arbitrary—we have to classify in order to understand; otherwise, there are as many humankinds as there are men and women, every man and woman is a world in himself or herself. But this classification helps to understand many things that would be impossible to understand without it. Try to understand the classification as clearly as possible.

When the highest type of people hear the Tao, they try hard to live in accordance with it. When the mediocre type hear the Tao, they seem to be aware and yet unaware of it. When the lowest type hear the Tao, they break into loud laughter—if it were not laughed at, it would not be Tao.

The first is *Satwa*, the second is *Rajas*, and the third is *Tamas*.

The highest type of person, when he hears about Tao, suddenly feels in tune with it. It is not an intellectual understanding for him: his total being vibrates with a new song; a new music is heard. When he hears the truth, suddenly something fits and he is no longer the same—just hearing, he becomes totally a different type of individual. Not that he has to use his intellect to understand it—that would be a delayed understanding. The highest type of person understands immediately, with no time gap. If he hears a truth, in just the hearing

itself, he has understood. His total being understands it, not only the intellectual part. Not only the soul, not only the mind, but even the body vibrates in a new unknown way. A new dance has entered into his being, and now he can never be the same.

Once he has heard the truth he can never be the old way again; a new journey has started. Now nothing else can be done, he has no choice but to move. He has heard about light and he has been living in darkness: now unless he achieves the light, there will be no rest for him. He will become deeply discontented. He has heard that a different type of existence is possible: now unless he attains it, he cannot be at ease, he cannot be at home anywhere. Wherever he is, the constant call from the unknown will be knocking at the door. Waking he will hear it; sleeping he will hear it; dreaming—and the knock will be

there—he will hear it. Eating he will hear it; walking he will hear it; in the market, he will hear it—it will be haunting him all the time.

That's why Krishnamurti always said that there is no need to do anything. In fact, for the first-rate type of person there is no need to do anything—just by hearing, by right listening, one attains. But where to find the first-rate person? They are very rare. Unless a Krishnamurti comes to listen to Krishnamurti, it won't happen. But why should a Krishnamurti go to listen to a Krishnamurti? It is absurd; it has no meaning. A person with that kind of perceptivity can become awakened just by listening to the song of a bird, just by listening to the breeze passing through the trees, just by listening to the sound of water flowing—that's enough, because from everywhere the truth speaks. If you are perceptive, whatsoever you hear you have heard the truth, you have heard

the Tao. Nothing else exists. All sounds are divine, all messages are divine, everywhere is the divine signature. For the first-rate mind the path is not a path at all; the person simply enters the temple without any path, there is no need for any bridge.

Lao Tzu says that when the highest type of person hears the Tao there is an immediate perception, an immediate understanding. Just by looking at the master who has attained, just by hearing his word, or just by hearing his breathing, silent, peaceful, sitting by his side, he understands.

Once this type of person understands, then they are not trying to attain truth; they are simply trying to refine their mechanism. They have understood the truth—it exists; they have heard it. Hindus call their scriptures *Shrutis*. The word *shruti* means "that which has been heard." All the scriptures are "that which has been heard."

Once a man of the first-rate intelligence hears truth, he understands it.

Once it happened that a Sufi master suddenly called one of his disciples. Many disciples were sitting in the hall, but he called only one: "Come near to me."

He was standing near the window, and it was a full-moon night. All the disciples watched in wonder. Why had he called the one? Then the old man indicated something outside the window to the young man and said, "Look!" And from that day the young man changed completely.

The others asked, "What happened? There was nothing we know, only the full-moon night. The full moon was there, of course; the night was beautiful, of course; but what has happened to you seems to be completely out of proportion. You are completely transformed. What happened?"

The young man said, "I heard the master, and I was so silent because he called me, I was so without thoughts, so peaceful, that when he indicated the moon something opened inside me: a window. I had a perception that I had never had. I looked at the moon with new eyes; I looked at the moonlight with a new being. Of course, I have seen the view from a faraway state of my mind and I will have to work hard to reach it, but now it exists. Now I know it is a certainty. Now there is no doubt. But I will still have to reach that state because I have looked through the eyes of the master. Those eyes were not mine; he gave his to me; for a single moment, I borrowed them. I have looked through his being. It was not my being, the window was not mine, it was his window, and he allowed me to look through it. But now I know that a different type of existence is possible—is not only possible, is absolutely certain. Now it may take many lives for me to reach that goal, but the goal is certain. No doubt exists in me now, now doubt cannot disturb me—now my journey is clear."

When the highest type of people hear the Tao, they try hard to live in accordance with it.

They hear, they understand, then they try hard to live in accordance with it. They have looked through the window of the master and they have become certain that now it is an absolute fact; it is not a philosophy, not a metaphysics. It is existential. They have felt it, they have known it, but they will have to go a long way before the same perception becomes their own.

They have heard truth, they have understood it, but they will have to move a long way before the truth becomes their being.

The highest type try hard to live in accordance with it—not that by living in accordance with it and trying hard one achieves it, no. Just by trying hard, nobody achieves it—but by trying hard, by and by you come to feel that the effort itself is a barrier in the final stages of the transformation. By trying hard, you come to know that even trying hard is a barrier, and you drop it. Because when you are trying hard to live in accordance with Tao, that life cannot be a spontaneous life, it can be only a forced phenomenon, a discipline, not a freedom. It will become bondage, because all efforts are of the ego. Even the desire to achieve truth comes from the ego. You will drop that, too.

Remember, you can drop effort only when you have made the effort to its utmost. You cannot say, "If that's the case, then I should drop the effort from the very beginning. Why make it?" You will miss the whole point. That's what happened to those who listened to Krishnamurti. He says that no effort is needed. That is right, but it is right only for those who have been making a great effort with their total being. It is true only for *those* people—*they* can drop it.

To become artlessly artful is not possible for those who have not moved through any discipline. Finally an artist has to become completely oblivious of his art; he should forget whatsoever he has learned. But you can forget only that which you have learned. If the art of an artist is effortful, then his art is not perfect.

In Zen they used many methods to teach meditation. They used art also—painting, calligraphy, and other forms. A student would learn painting for ten or twelve years until becoming absolutely technically perfect—not even a single error existed in the technology of the art. Once the artist had become technically perfect, the master would say, "Now you drop it. For two or three years, completely forget it. Throw away your brushes, forget everything you know about painting, and when you have forgotten it completely, then come to me."

Two, three, four, five years, sometimes even more, are needed to forget. It is very difficult. It is difficult first to learn a thing, and more difficult to unlearn it once you have learned it. The second part is essential, fundamental; otherwise, you will be a technician, not an artist.

It is said that a great archer trained his disciple to perfection in archery, and then told him, "Now you forget everything about it." For twenty years the disciple used to come and go to the master, but the master would not say anything, so the disciple had to wait patiently. By and by he completely forgot everything about archery—twenty years is a long time— and he had become almost an old man.

Then one day he came and as he entered the master's room he saw a bow, but he did not recognize what it was. The master came to

him, embraced him, and said, "Now you have become a perfect archer; you have forgotten even the bow. Now go out and look at the flying birds and with just the idea that they should drop, they will."

The archer went out and he couldn't believe it. He looked at the birds flying, almost a dozen birds, and they fell immediately to the ground. The master said, "Now there is no more to do. I was just showing you that when you forget the technique only then will you become perfect. Now the bow and arrow are not needed; they are needed only for amateurs."

A perfect painter does not need the brush and the canvas; a perfect musician does not need the sitar or the violin or the guitar. No, that is for the amateur.

I came across an old musician—he is dead now—who was one hundred and ten years old. He could create music with anything,

anything whatsoever. He would be passing by two rocks and he would create music with them; he would find a piece of iron and he would start playing with it and you would hear beautiful music, such as you have never heard. This was a musician. Even his touch was musical. If he touched you, you would see that he had touched the innermost instrument of your inner harmony and music—suddenly you would start vibrating.

When anything becomes perfect, the effort that was made to learn it has to be forgotten, otherwise the effort remains heavy on the mind. So it is not by trying hard to live in accordance with Tao that the highest type achieve it—no. They try to live in accordance with it, and by and by they start understanding that to live in accordance with nature, no effort is needed. It is like floating in the water: nobody can just float, first you have to learn to

道

> *" A perfect swimmer becomes part of the river; he is a wave in the river. How can the river destroy the wave? "*

swim. Don't go to the river or you will be drowned. A person has to learn to swim and when the swimming becomes perfect, he need not swim, he can just be in the river, floating; he can lie in the river as if he is lying in his bed. Now he has learned how to be in accordance with the river; now the river cannot drown him; now he has no more enmity with the river. In fact, he no longer exists separate from the river. A perfect swimmer becomes part of the river; he is a wave in the river. How can the river destroy the wave? When he floats in accordance with the river, he is no longer fighting, resisting, doing something. He is in tune with the river and he can simply float. But don't try this unless you know how to swim; otherwise, you may be drowned.

The same thing happens with Tao. You make a great effort to live in accordance with the truth, and by and by you understand that your great effort helps a little, but hinders a lot. To live in accordance is to let go, it is not to fight with nature. To live in accordance with nature is to be one with nature; there is no need to struggle. Effort is struggle; effort means that you are trying to do something according to you.

Science is effort; Tao is effortlessness. Science is violence to nature. That's why scientists continually talk in terms of conflict and conquering. It is a fight, as if nature is your enemy and you have to dominate it. Science has a deep political relationship with nature, a deep war, an enmity. Tao is not a fight at all; in fact, it is understanding that you are part of nature. How can the part fight with the whole? And if the part tries to fight with the whole and then becomes anxiety-ridden, what can you expect? It is natural. If the part tries to fight with the whole, if my hand tries to fight with my whole body, the hand will become ill. How can the hand fight with the body? The body supplies the blood, the body supplies the nourishment, how can it fight with the body? The hand fighting with the body is foolish.

Man fighting with nature is foolish. We can live only in accordance with nature. Tao is surrender; science is a war. Science strengthens the ego and the whole problem is how to drop the ego. Through effort it cannot be dropped.

So remember this:

When the highest type of people hear the Tao, they try hard to live in accordance with it.

That is their first standpoint. Once they understand, they hear, they feel, they taste the affinity with it, and they start the hard effort to live accordingly. But as they grow in it, they begin to understand that effort is not needed—rather, effortlessness. Finally they drop effort and become one with nature.

Somebody asked Lao Tzu, "How did you attain?"

A LEAF FALLS AND SETTLES

If history is to be written rightly then there should be two kinds of histories: the history of doers—Genghis Khan, Tamerlane, Nadirshah, Alexander, Napoleon Bonaparte, Ivan the Terrible, Joseph Stalin, Adolf Hitler, Benito Mussolini; these are the people who belong to the world of doing. There should be another history, a higher history, a real history—of human consciousness, of human evolution: the history of Lao Tzu, Chuang Tzu, Lieh Tzu, Gautam Buddha, Mahavira, Bodhidharma; totally different kind of history.

Lao Tzu became enlightened sitting under a tree. A leaf had just started falling— it was in the autumn, and the leaf was zig-zagging with the wind, slowly. He watched the leaf. The leaf came down to the ground, settled on the ground, and as he watched the leaf falling and settling, something settled in him.

From that moment, he became a non-doer. The winds come on their own, and existence takes care.

Lao Tzu was the contemporary of the great thinker, moralist, and law giver, Confucius.

Confucius belongs to the other history, the history of the doers. Confucius had great influence over China—and has influence even today.

Chuang Tzu and Lieh Tzu were the disciples of Lao Tzu. These three people have reached to the highest peaks, but nobody seems to be impressed by them. People are impressed when you do something great. Who is impressed by somebody who has achieved a state of non-doing?

道

He said, "I was sitting under a tree and I had done all that could be done, all that was humanly possible, and I was completely frustrated. Much had happened through it, but not all; something was lacking, missing, and the missing link was the most difficult to find, elusive. Then while I was sitting under a tree, a leaf, a dry leaf, fell from the tree slowly, and moved in the wind. The wind was going north, the leaf moved north; then the wind changed course, started moving toward the south, and the leaf started moving toward the south, then the wind stopped—and the leaf fell down on the earth, with not a single complaint, with no struggle, with no direction of its own. If the wind was going south, it was going south; if the wind was going north, it was going north; if the wind stopped, it fell down on the earth and rested beautifully.

"Then again there was some wind and again it rose high in the sky—but there was no problem. Suddenly I understood. The message hit home. From that day I became a dry leaf and the missing link that had been was so elusive was elusive no more." The missing link was only this: you can attain many things through effort, but you cannot attain Tao through effort. Finally you have to leave effort—and suddenly everything fits, you are in accordance. Then you don't give direction, then you are no longer a director; you don't say to the winds: Go south, because I am on a journey toward the south. You have no destination; the destiny of the whole is your destiny; you are not separate. You no longer think in terms of individuality; you have become part of the whole and wherever the whole is going you are going. If the whole changes its mind, you change your mind; if the whole stops the journey, it is beautiful; if the whole runs, you run with it. That is what "in accordance" means.

With not a bit of mind of your own, when you have become a no-mind, the whole lives through you, lives you, moves through you, moves you. Now you don't breathe, the whole breathes you. Everything is a benediction, a blessing. How can you be tense then? Worried about what? All worries exist because you have brought an individual destiny into your mind against the destiny of the whole—you are moving upstream.

This is the secret of your failure—you are moving upstream. You are worried, tense, in anguish, in anxiety, almost going mad—anybody will go mad if they are constantly going upstream because the fight is so hard and so meaningless. One day you will feel tired and then it will look like a frustration, a failure. The wise man leaves this upstream nonsense; he simply allows the river to take him wherever it is going. If it is going anywhere, good; if it is not going anywhere, good.

Suddenly you are still, silent. Only then, never before, does real meditation happen and all effort is dropped. But you have to make the effort first, otherwise you will never understand that it has to be dropped.

When the mediocre type hear the Tao they seem to be aware and yet unaware of it.

That's what the mediocre mind is—a little bit aware. A little understanding and a little

non-understanding, a little part lighted and a little part in darkness, divided. To be divided is to be mediocre. To be divided against yourself is to be mediocre because it dissipates your energy; it can never allow you to be overflowing, celebrating existence. If you are trying to create a fight between your right and left hand, how can you be happy? The fight itself will kill you and there will be no result from it, because how can the left win, or how can the right win? Both hands are yours.

Any type of inner conflict makes you mediocre, and those who teach you to be divided are your enemies. They say, "This is bad and that is good." Immediately division enters. They say, "This is lower, that is higher."

Immediately division enters. They say, "This is sin and that is virtue." Immediately division enters. You are split. The whole of humanity is schizophrenic and everybody has become mediocre.

To be one is to be blissful; to be divided is to be in misery. To be one is to be in heaven; to be divided is to be in hell. The more divided, the greater will be the hell—and you will be a crowd—not only two, but many. Psychologists say that humans have become polypsychic: a person has not one mind now, he has many minds. In small matters also you have many minds—whether to eat this or to eat that, whether to order this or that? It is as if you have lost all possibility of being decisive, because you can only be decisive if you are one, a unit.

How can you be decisive? When one voice says this, another voice immediately contradicts and says that; one voice says

go east; another says go west. If you are pulled against yourself in so many directions, your whole life will be a sad failure, a long tale of frustration and nothing else—"a tale told by an idiot, full of sound and fury, signifying nothing."

Significance is possible only when there is unity within. The highest type of people can attain unity, the lowest type also have a certain type of unity, but the mediocre ones are in the greatest danger.

You can see wise persons like Buddha or Lao Tzu in unity—bliss surrounds them, they move surrounded by a subtle ecstasy, and if you look at them you can see they are drunk with the divine. They walk on the earth but they are not here. But you can sometimes also feel the same type of vibe around an idiot. A certain innocence surrounds him—he laughs, and you can glimpse the sage in the idiot because he is also one. He is not a sage, he has not attained anything, but at least he is not divided.

A sage has gone beyond the mind while an idiot is below the mind. In this one thing they are equal: neither of them have any mind. There are vast differences, but there is also this one similarity. If you don't understand, a sage can sometimes look like an idiot—and sometimes, in your ignorance, you can worship an idiot for a sage. I have come across many idiots being worshipped—they have a certain quality; at least they are one. They don't have much mind—in fact, they don't have a mind at all, they have no thoughts.

BE USELESS

Lao Tzu was wandering with his disciples and they came to a forest where hundreds of carpenters were cutting trees, because a great palace was being built. The whole forest had been almost cut, but only one tree was standing there, a big tree with thousands of branches—so big that ten thousand persons could sit under its shade. Lao Tzu asked his disciples to go and inquire why this tree had not been cut yet when the whole forest had been cut and was deserted.

The disciples went and asked the carpenters, "Why have you not cut this tree?"

The carpenters said, "This tree is absolutely useless. You cannot make anything out of it because every branch has so many knots in it. Nothing is straight. You cannot make pillars out of it. You cannot make furniture out of it. You cannot use it as fuel because the smoke is so dangerous to the eyes—you might go blind. This tree is absolutely useless. That's why."

They came back. Lao Tzu laughed and he said, "Be like this tree. If you want to survive in this world be like this tree—absolutely useless. Then nobody will harm you. If you are straight, you will be cut, you will become furniture in somebody's house. If you are beautiful, you will be sold in the market, you will become a commodity. Be like this tree, absolutely useless. Then nobody can harm you. And you will grow big and vast, and thousands of people can find shade under you."

> ❝ *I can give you the flower, but how can I give you the fragrance? You have to cleanse your nose and become more sensitive.* ❞

I lived in a town for many years, and near that town lived a saint who was famous, and people used to come from all over India to see him. He was a perfect idiot, but he had a certain beauty around him—no anxiety, no problems. A few problems might have existed for him, but because people started worshipping him, even those problems were not there. People would bring food and everything else for him so even the problem of basic survival was not there. They even made a beautiful house for him.

Yet if you watched him, you could see that he didn't understand a thing. I went to see the man many times and I watched him closely. He was absolutely mentally damaged—he could not utter a single word—but people thought that he had taken a vow of silence for his whole life. There was no glimmer in his eyes of any alertness, but still there was a similarity. People have been deceived many times. Of course, these poor people can't deceive you; it is your own gullibility. You are deceived by your own self. Many times it has happened that very rare souls have been thought to be idiotic, because there is a similarity to what happens with the idiot.

The idiot is one part, the superhuman being is one part, and then there is the middle part, the mediocre, which is the majority in the world.

"The mediocre part," says Lao Tzu, "... seems to be aware and yet unaware of it." When you talk about truth, the mediocre mind understands it intellectually but does not understand it totally. That person says, "Yes, I can understand what you are saying but still I miss something. What do you mean?" The word is heard, but the meaning is lost. The mediocre person can understand intellectually—he may be educated, he may be a graduate, even have a PhD. He understands what you are saying because he understands language, but something is being lost. He understands the word, but the word is not the message. The message is subtle; it can come with the word, but it is not the word.

The word is like a flower and the meaning is like the fragrance that surrounds it. If your nose is not functioning well, I can give you a flower but I cannot give you the fragrance. If your mind is not functioning totally, I can give you a word but I cannot give you the meaning. The meaning has to be detected by you, decoded by you. I can give you the flower, but how can I give you the fragrance? If your nose is not functioning, if your nose is insensitive, then nothing can be done—I can give you a thousand and one flowers, but you will not smell the fragrance.

Many people come to me and say, "Whatsoever you say, we understand, but nothing happens. We have understood

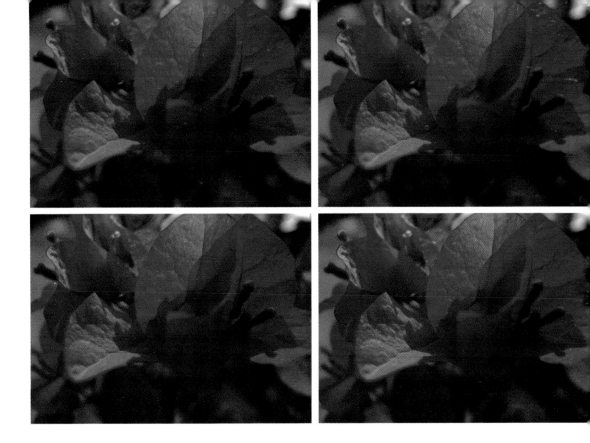

everything you have said, we have read your books many, many times, we have underlined almost every line—but nothing is happening."

I can give you the flower, but how can I give you the fragrance? You have to cleanse your nose and become more sensitive. That is where meditation can be helpful: it makes you more sensitive, more alert. It pushes you toward the first type, and by and by you start feeling—not only understanding, but feeling. Feeling is needed. I don't mean that you should become sentimental. Sentimentality is not feeling; sentimentality is a false coin. There are people who can weep and cry for nothing and they think they are the feeling type. They are not. They are only sentimental.

Feeling is a mature quality; sentimentality is an immature quality. A person of feeling will do something; a person of sentimentality will create more trouble. For example, if somebody is ill or dying, the person of feeling will go to the hospital and try to help the one who is dying. The man or woman of sentimentality will start crying and weeping. They will create more trouble for the dying person—they will not even allow the person to die in silence. Sentimentality is chaos; feeling is substantial growth. When I talk about love, if you have feeling, then not only your head understands, but also your heart starts throbbing in a different way. The fragrance has reached you.

Meditation can help you by throwing out all the dust and dirt that you have collected within you, all that is stopping your sensitivity.

The doors of your perception are covered with dirt. You would like to see rightly, but there are so many suppressed tears that they won't allow a clear eye. You would like to smell the flower, but you cannot, because the whole of civilization has been suppressing your nose. You may not be aware that the nose is the most suppressed part of the body. Humans have lost the sense of smell almost completely.

Horses and dogs are more sensitive than humans. What is happening to your nose? Why has it gone dead? There is a subtle mechanism working here because smell is deeply concerned and connected with sex. Have you seen animals smelling each other before they make love? They will never make love unless they smell first, because through scent they feel if their body energies will meet or not, whether they are meant for each other or not. Smelling is a kind of antenna. A dog moves, smells: if the female dog suits his sense of feeling and sense of smell, only

then does he make the effort; otherwise, they move on their separate ways. He is not worried at all. That female dog is not for him; he is not for her.

Smell is the most sexual sense in the body and when civilization decided to suppress sex, automatically civilization decided to suppress smell also. Whenever a woman wants to make love, she suddenly starts emitting subtle scents around herself and that would be dangerous in a world where sex is not accepted. If you walk on the street with your wife and, looking at some other man, she starts emitting the scent, you will know it immediately! Then your wife cannot deceive you; she cannot say that she had not even looked at that man. But as it is now, the wife herself cannot know that her body is throwing off a certain scent, neither can the man to whom she has become suddenly attracted. Your noses are completely closed; you don't smell. And in that way things are beautifully settled, no trouble arises.

So if you really want to smell the flower— if you want not only to carry the flower but to enjoy the scent as well—then you will have to come to a more natural state of non-repressed sexuality. Otherwise it will not be possible. If all your five senses are covered with dust and dirt and suppressed, they will create a mediocre mind, because the mind is nothing but a collective reservoir of all the five senses. When you are mediocre, then you can go on becoming more and more scholarly, but you will remain a fool because you will not be alive.

Have you watched the phenomenon that pundits are the most dead people you can ever see? Professors and scholars are the most dead people. They don't see, they don't smell, they don't taste—they are almost dead since all their senses are dead. Only their head functions, alone, without any support from the body. If you cut off their body they would not be worried, only don't disturb their head. They will, on the contrary, be very happy if the head can function without the body. Then they can go on and on in their scholarly trips with no trouble from the body. No illness will disturb them; no hunger will disturb them.

A scholar does not know even his hunger. He lives in the head. Scholars are always mediocres, perfect mediocres, and the problem for the mediocre is that he understands—that deceives him, because he thinks that he understands, it is finished. Yet he doesn't understand a bit; he remains unaware. His understanding is only of the head, not of the total being. And unless understanding is of the total being, it is not understanding at all. Intellectual understanding is not understanding at all; that is a misnomer.

When the lowest type hear the Tao, they break into loud laughter.

The lowest type think this truth, this Tao, is some sort of joke. They are so shallow that nothing about the depth appeals to them and the laughter is a protection. The shallow people laugh because now you are being funny. They know well that there is no truth at all, that nothing like truth exists; it is just an invention of cunning people to exploit other people. The loud laughter is a protection because they are also afraid, afraid that the thing may exist. Through laughter they brush it away, they throw it away. Through laughter they show derision, condemnation, the belief that the whole thing is nonsense. At the most you can laugh at it and nothing else. You will come across the lowest type everywhere. If a lowest type sees a Lao Tzu he will laugh: "This man has gone mad; one more man is lost to humanity and has gone mad."

If the lowest man sees you meditating, he will laugh, he will think that you seem to be a little eccentric. What are you doing? Why are you wasting your time? If he can laugh ,he can feel very good about himself that he is not as mad or as foolish as this meditating person is.

Says Lao Tzu:

If it were not laughed at, it would not be Tao.

Lao Tzu says, *If the third type does not laugh when it hears about truth, it will not be truth.* So this is a definite indication: whenever truth is asserted the lowest type will immediately laugh. It shows two things certainly: one, that truth has been asserted, and second, that a third, a lowest person, has heard about it. Between truth and the lowest person, laughter happens; between the mediocre person and the truth an intellectual type of understanding happens; between the first type of person and truth a deep understanding of total being happens—the person's total being throbs with an unknown adventure, a door has opened into a new world.

LAO TZU AND CONFUCIUS

It is said that Confucius went to see Lao Tzu. Lao Tzu was an old man and Confucius was younger. Lao Tzu was almost unknown and Confucius was almost universally known. Kings and emperors used to call Confucius to their courts; wise men used to come for his advice; he was the wisest man in China in those days. But by and by he must have felt that although his wisdom might be of use to others, he was not blissful; he had not attained anything. He had become an expert, maybe helpful to others, but not helpful to himself.

So he started a secret search to find someone who could help him. Ordinary wise men wouldn't do, because they came to him for his advice. Great scholars wouldn't do; they came to ask him about their problems. But there must be someone somewhere—life is vast. He sent his disciples to find someone who could be of help to him, and they came back with the information that there lived a man—nobody knew his name—known as "the old guy."

Lao Tzu means "the old guy." It is not his name; nobody knows his name. He was such an unknown man that nobody knows when he was born or to whom, nor who his father was or who his mother was. He lived for ninety years but only rare human beings had come across him who had different eyes and perspectives from which to understand him. He was only for the rarest—so ordinary a man, but only for the rarest of human minds.

Hearing the news that a man known as "the old guy" existed, Confucius went to see him. When he met Lao Tzu, he could feel that here was a man of great understanding, great intellectual integrity, great logical acumen—a genius. He could feel that something was there, but he couldn't catch hold of it. Vaguely, mysteriously, there was something; this man was no ordinary man, although he looked absolutely ordinary. Something was hidden; he was carrying a treasure.

Confucius asked, "What do you say about morality? What do you say about how to cultivate good character?"—because he was a moralist and he thought that if you cultivated a good character that was the highest attainment.

Lao Tzu laughed loudly and said, "If you are immoral, only then does the question of morality arise. If you don't have any character, only then do you think about character. A man of character is absolutely oblivious of the fact that anything like character exists. A man of morality does not know what the word *moral* means. So don't be foolish! And don't try to cultivate. Just be natural."

The man had such tremendous energy that Confucius started trembling. He couldn't withstand him and so he escaped. He became afraid, as one becomes afraid near an abyss. When he came back to his disciples, who were waiting outside under a tree, the disciples could not believe it. This man

道

had been going to emperors, the greatest emperors, and they had never seen any nervousness in him. Now he was trembling, and cold sweat was pouring from all over his body. They couldn't believe it—what had happened? What had this man Lao Tzu done to their teacher? They asked him, and he said, "Wait a little. Let me collect myself. This man is dangerous."

About Lao Tzu, he said to his disciples, "I have heard about great animals like elephants, and I know how they walk. I have heard about animals hidden in the sea, and I know how they swim. And I have heard about great birds who fly thousands of miles across the earth, and I know how they fly. But this man is a dragon. Nobody knows how he walks. Nobody knows how he lives. Nobody knows how he flies. Never go near him—he is like an abyss. He is like a death."

And that is the definition of a master: a master is like death. If you come near him, too close, you will feel afraid; trembling will take over. You will be possessed by an unknown fear, as if you are going to die. It is said that Confucius never went again to see this old man.

chuang tzu:
natural and ordinary

Chuang Tzu was one of the most natural men the world has seen. He has not given any discipline, he has not given any doctrine, he has not given any catechism. He has simply explained one thing: that if you can be natural and ordinary, just like the birds and the trees, you will blossom, you will have your wings open in the vast sky.

道

道

easy is right

Chuang Tzu says:

Easy is right. Begin right and you are easy.
Continue easy, and you are right.
The right way to go easy is to forget the right way
and forget that the going is easy.

EASY IS RIGHT. Nobody has dared to say it, ever. On the contrary, people make the "right" as difficult as possible. To everyone that has been conditioned by different traditions, the wrong is easy and the right is arduous. It needs training, it needs discipline, it needs repression, it needs renouncing the world, it needs renouncing pleasures....

Lies are easy, truth is difficult—that is the common conditioning of humanity.

But Chuang Tzu is certainly a man of tremendous insight. He says, *Easy is right.*

Then why have people been making the

> **A state of awareness is just like a cat: even when she is asleep she is alert.**

right difficult? All the saints have been making the right difficult. There is a psychology behind it: only the difficult is attractive to your ego. The more difficult the task, the more the ego feels challenged.

Climbing Everest was difficult; hundreds of people died in the attempt before Edmund Hillary reached the top alive. For a whole century, groups upon groups of mountaineers had been making the effort. And when Edmund Hillary reached the top, there was nothing to be found! At the very peak there is only space enough for one person to stand there, on the highest point. He was asked, "What prompted you? Knowing perfectly well that dozens of mountaineers have lost their lives over the years, and not even their bodies have been found... why did you try this dangerous project?"

He said, "I had to try. It was hurting my ego. I am a mountaineer, I love climbing mountains, and it was humiliating that Everest existed and nobody had been able to reach there. It

道

is not a question of finding anything... I feel immensely happy."

What is this happiness? You have not found anything! The happiness is that your ego has become more crystallized. You are the first man in the whole of history who has reached the peak of Everest; now nobody can take your place. Anybody else who reaches there will be second, third...but you have made your mark on history; you are the first. You have not found anything but a deep nourishment for your ego.

All the religions make the right difficult, because the difficult is attractive—attractive to the ego. But the ego is not the truth; the ego is not right. Do you see the dilemma? The ego is attracted only to the difficult. If you want people to become saints you have to make your right, your truth, your discipline very difficult. The more difficult it is, the more egoists will be attracted, almost magnetically pulled.

But the ego is not right. It is the worst thing that can happen to a person. It cannot deliver to you the right, the truth; it can only make your ego stronger. Chuang Tzu is saying in a simple statement, the most pregnant statement: *Easy is right*. Because for the easy, the ego has no attraction. If you are moving toward the easy, the ego starts dying. When there is no ego left, you have arrived at your reality—at the right, at the truth.

Truth and right have to be natural. Easy means natural; you can find the real and the true without any effort. "Easy is right" means *natural* is right, *effortlessness* is right, *egolessness* is right.

Begin right and you are easy; continue easy and you are right.

They are just two sides of the same coin. If, beginning to live a right life, you find it difficult, then remember: it is not right. If, living the right, your life becomes more and more easy, more and more a let-go, a flowing with the stream, then it is right.

Going against the stream is difficult, but going with the stream is not difficult. So either choose the easiest things in life, the most natural things in life, and you will be right; or if you want to begin the other way, remember the criterion that the right has to produce easiness and relaxation in you.

Continue easy and you are right. Never forget for a moment that the difficult is food for the ego, and the ego is the barrier that makes you blind, makes you deaf, makes your heart hard to open, and makes it impossible for you to love, to dance, to sing.

Continue easy. Your whole life should be an easy phenomenon. Then you will not be creating the ego. You will be a natural being. The ordinary is the most extraordinary. The people who are trying to be extraordinary

have missed the point. Just be ordinary; just be nobody.

All your conditionings corrupt you. They say, To be easy is to be lazy, to be ordinary is humiliating. If you don't try for power, for prestige, for respectability, then your life is meaningless—that idea has been forced into your mind.

Chuang Tzu in his simple statements is taking away all your conditionings. *Continue easy and you are right*. Never for a moment get attracted to the difficult. It will make you "somebody"—a prime minister, a president— but it will not make you divine. Easy is divine.

I have heard about a wealthy American man. He had been striving all his life to be on the top and he had reached it, and had all the things the world can offer. But he felt stupid inside, because there was nothing on the top.

If Edmund Hillary was intelligent enough, he must have felt stupid standing on Everest. Why had he been striving so hard? The man who walked on the moon must have felt a little embarrassed, although there was nobody who could see his face. This man had come to the top as far as money was concerned, and as far as money could purchase, he had purchased everything. Now he was feeling stupid.

"What is the point of it all?" Inside he felt hollow. He had no time to give to his inner growth, no time even to be acquainted with himself.

He dropped all his riches and rushed to the East to find the truth, because three-quarters of his life was almost gone—just the tail end remained; the elephant had passed by. But if

NO WAY

It is said that the first time Chuang Tzu entered the hut where Lao Tzu, his would-be master, was living, Lao Tzu looked at him and said, "Remember one thing: never ask me how to become enlightened." The poor fellow had come for that very purpose. But Lao Tzu made it clear: "Only on this condition will I accept you as my disciple."

There was a moment of silence. Chuang Tzu thought, "It is strange. I have come to become enlightened; that is the very purpose of becoming a disciple. And this old fellow is asking such an absurd thing: if you want to be my disciple, promise me that you will never ask about how to become enlightened."

But it was already too late. He had fallen in love with the old man. He touched his feet and he said, "I promise I will never ask how to become enlightened, but accept me as your disciple."

Immediately came a hard slap, "You idiot! If you are not going to become enlightened, then for what purpose are you becoming a disciple? I was asking this promise because I could see in you such beautiful intelligence that you might have immediately realized the point of my asking. You are enlightened; there is no way to become enlightened. There is no need. In fact even if you want to become unenlightened, there is no way."

道

..ething might be possible, then there were a few days left. He rushed from one master to another, but nobody could satisfy him because whatever they said was another trip for the ego, and he was well acquainted with that trip.

It does not matter whether you are accumulating money or whether you are accumulating virtue, whether you are becoming respectable here or you are becoming respectable hereafter—it does not matter, it is the same game. Whether you are becoming a world-famous celebrity or a world-worshipped saint, there is no difference: both are ego trips.

All these gurus were trying to give him difficult disciplines and arduous ways of finding the truth; they were all saying, "It may not be possible in this life, but start anyhow. In the next life maybe.... The journey is long, the goal is a faraway star."

But now nobody could deceive him. He had understood that just "becoming somebody special" is an exercise in stupidity.

Finally he heard about a saint who lived in the Himalayas. The people said, "If you are not satisfied with him, you will never be satisfied with anybody. Then forget the whole thing."

So, tired and tattered, after walking for miles, finally he found the old man. He was happy upon seeing the old man, but he was shocked. Before he could say anything, the old man asked, "Are you an American?"

He said, "Yes, I am."

The old man said, "Very good. Have you got any American cigarettes with you?"

He said, "My God, where am I? I have come to seek truth, to find the right..." He pulled out his cigarettes and the old man took one and started smoking.

The American said, "You have not even asked me why I have come here, tired, hungry..."

The old man said, "That does not matter."

The American said, "I have come to find the truth!'

The old man said, "Truth? You do one thing—go back where you came from. And next time when you come, bring a lot of American cigarettes, because here in this place it is difficult to find cigarettes. I am an easygoing man. I don't make any effort; people come on their own. But I like the best cigarettes."

"But," the man asked, "...what about my search?"

The old man said, "Your search? This is the discipline for you: go back, buy as many cigarettes as you can, and come back and remain here with me."

The man asked, "Any discipline?"

The old man said, "I am an ordinary old man—no discipline, no religion, no philosophy—I only like to smoke cigarettes. You come here, and slowly, slowly you will also become just as ordinary as I am. And I tell you, to be ordinary, with no pretensions, is the right."

And as the man turned to go back, puzzled, the old man said, "Listen, at least leave your wristwatch here, because I don't have any wristwatch so I never know the time. And anyway, you are going back, so you can buy yourself another wristwatch."

Chuang Tzu would have liked this old man. *Easy is right. Begin right and you are*

道

easy. That has to be the criterion. If you feel uneasiness, tension, then what you have started cannot be right.

Continue easy and you are right.

And the last part is something never to be forgotten. *The right way to go easy is to forget the right way*—because even to remember it is an uneasiness. *The right way to go easy is to forget the right way and forget that the going is easy.* What is the need of remembering these things?

Relax to such a point... be as natural as the trees and the birds. You will not find in the birds that somebody is a saint and somebody is a sinner; you will not find in the trees that somebody is virtuous and somebody is full of vices. Everything is easy—so easy that you need not remember it.

Chuang Tzu was one of the most natural men the world has seen. He has not given any discipline, he has not given any doctrine, he has not given any catechism. He has simply explained one thing: that if you can be natural and ordinary, just like the birds and the trees, you will blossom, you will have your wings open in the vast sky.

You don't have to be a saint. Saints are tense—more tense than sinners. I have known both, and if there is a choice I will choose the sinners as a company rather than the saints. Saints are the worst company, because their eyes are full of judgment about everything: "You should do this and you should not do that." And they start dominating you, condemning you, humiliating you, insulting you, because what they are doing is the right, and what you are doing is not

the right thing. They have poisoned your nature so badly that if real criminals are to be found, they will be found in your saints, not in your sinners. Your sinners have not done much harm to anybody.

I have visited jails, met criminals, and I was surprised that they are often the most innocent people. Perhaps because they are the most innocent they have been caught—the cunning ones are doing far greater crimes, but they are not caught. Every law has loopholes. The cunning ones find the loopholes first; the innocent ones get caught because they don't have that cunningness.

It is a strange world in which we are living. The criminals are the rulers, the criminals are politicians, the criminals become presidents, vice presidents, prime ministers—because, except for a criminal, who wants power? An authentic human being wants peace, love, to be left alone, and the freedom to be himself. The very idea of dominating others is criminal.

Chuang Tzu is right: if you feel any tension, whatever you are doing is not right. And he is the only man who has given such a beautiful criterion:

Easy is right.

Begin right and you are easy.

Continue easy, and you are right.

The right way to go easy is to forget the right way and forget that the going is easy.

Relax into nobodiness. Be natural. Become part of this relaxed universe—so relaxed that you forget all about easiness and you forget all about rightness.

THE HAPPY TURTLE

Two messengers came from the Emperor. Chuang Tzu was fishing, and they came to him and said, "The Emperor wants you to become the prime minister of the country."

Chuang Tzu said, "Do you see that turtle there, wagging its tail in the mud?"

They said, "Yes, we see."

"And do you see how happy he is?"

They said, "Certainly. He looks tremendously happy."

And then Chuang Tzu said, "I have heard that in the king's palace there is a turtle, three thousand years old, dead, encaged in gold, decorated with diamonds, and he is worshipped. If you ask this turtle who is wagging his tail in the mud to change his role, to become that turtle in the palace—dead, but encaged in gold, decorated with diamonds, and worshipped by the emperor himself—will this turtle be ready to accept that?"

The messengers said, "Certainly not. This turtle will not be ready."

So Chuang Tzu said, "Why should I be ready? Then be gone! I am happy in my mud, wagging my tail, and I don't want to come to the emperor's palace."

道

the value of that which is useless

Life is dialectical, and that is why it is not logical. Logic means that the opposite is really opposite, and life always implies the opposite in itself. In life, the opposite is not really the opposite, it is the complementary. Without it nothing is possible. For example, life exists because of death. If there is no death, there cannot be any life. Death is not the end and death is not the enemy—on the contrary, because of death, life becomes possible. So death is not somewhere in the end, it is involved here and now. Each moment has its life and its death; otherwise, existence is impossible.

Hui Tzu said to Chuang Tzu:

"All your teaching is centered on what has no use."

Chuang Tzu replied:

"If you have no appreciation for what has no use, you cannot begin to talk about what can be used. The earth, for example, is broad and vast, but of all this expanse a man uses only a few inches upon which he happens to be standing at the time.

"Now suppose you suddenly take away all that he is not actually using, so that all around his feet a gulf yawns, and he stands in the void with nowhere solid except under each foot, how long will he be able to use what he is using?"

Hui Tzu said: "It would cease to serve any purpose."

Chuang Tzu concluded: "This shows the absolute necessity of what is supposed to have no use."

THERE IS LIGHT; there is darkness. For logic they are opposites and logic will say: If it is light, there cannot be any darkness; if it is dark, then there cannot be any light. But life says quite the contrary. Life says, If there is darkness it is because of light; if there is light, it is because of darkness. We may not be able to see the other when it is hidden just around the corner.

There is silence because of sound. If there is no sound at all, can you be silent? How can you be silent? The opposite is needed as a background. Those who follow logic always go wrong because their life becomes lopsided. They think of light, then they start denying darkness; they think of life, then they start fighting death.

One tradition says that God is light, and another tradition says that God is darkness.

Both are wrong, because both are logical: they deny the opposite. And life is so vast, it carries the opposite in itself. The opposite is not denied, it is embraced.

Once somebody said to Walt Whitman, one of the greatest poets ever born, "Whitman, you are contradicting yourself. One day you say one thing, another day you say just the opposite."

Walt Whitman laughed and said, "I am vast. I contain all the contradictions."

Only small minds are consistent, and the narrower the mind, the more consistent. When the mind is vast, everything is involved: light is there, darkness is there, God is there, and the devil too, in his total glory.

If you understand this mysterious process of life, which moves through the opposites, which is dialectical—where the opposite helps, gives balance, gives tone, makes the background— then only can you understand Chuang Tzu— because the whole Taoist vision is based on the complementariness of the opposites.

The two words, yin and yang, are opposites: male and female. Just think of a world that is totally male or a world that is totally female—it will be dead.

The moment it is born, it will be dead; there cannot be any life in it. If it is a female world— women, women, and women, and no men— the women will commit suicide!

The opposite is needed because the opposite is attractive. The opposite becomes the magnet to pull you; the opposite brings you out of yourself; the opposite breaks your prison; the opposite makes you vast.

> *Whenever the opposite is denied there will be trouble. And that is what we have been doing, hence so much trouble in the world.*

Whenever the opposite is denied there will be trouble. And that is what we have been doing, hence so much trouble in the world.

Man has tried to create a society which is basically male, that is why there is so much trouble—the woman has been denied: she has been thrown out. In past centuries the woman was never to be seen anywhere. She was hidden in the back chambers of the house, not even allowed in the drawing room. You couldn't meet her on the streets, you couldn't see her in the shops. She was not part of life. The world went ugly, because how can you deny the opposite? The world became lopsided; all balance was lost. The world went mad.

In many cultures the woman is still not allowed to move in life; she is really not yet a part, a vital part of life. Men move in male-oriented groups—the exclusive men's club where boys meet, the market, politics, the scientific group. Everywhere it is lopsided. The man dominates, that is why there is so much misery. And when one of the polar opposites dominates, there will be misery because the other feels hurt and takes revenge. So every woman takes her revenge in the house. When

she cannot go out and move in the world and take revenge on humanity, on mankind, she takes revenge on her husband. There is constant conflict.

Why is the wife always in conflict? It is not the person; it is not a personal thing. It is the revenge of the woman, of the female, of the denied opposite. And this man in the house, the husband, is the representative of the whole male world, the male-oriented world that she is fighting.

By negating the opposites you invite trouble—and on every path, on every level, in every dimension, it is the same thing.

Chuang Tzu says that if you deny the useless, then there will be no use in the world. If you deny the useless, the playful, the fun, there cannot be any work, any duty. This is difficult because our whole emphasis is on the useful.

If somebody asks you what a house consists of, you will say the walls. And Chuang Tzu would say, just like his master Lao Tzu, that a house consists not of walls but of doors and windows. Their emphasis is on the other part. They say that walls are useful, but their use depends on the useless space behind the walls. A room is space, not walls. Of course, the space is free and the walls have to be purchased. When you purchase a house, what do you purchase? The walls, the material, the visible. But can you live in the material? Can you live in the walls? You have to live in the room, in the vacant space.

So really, what is a house? Emptiness surrounded by walls. And what is a door? There is nothing—"door" means there is nothing, no wall, just emptiness. But you

cannot enter the house if there is no door; if there is no window, then no sun will enter, no breeze will blow. You will be dead and your house will become a tomb.

Chuang Tzu says: Remember that the house consists of two things: the walls, the material—the marketable, the utilitarian —and the emptiness surrounded by the walls, the non-utilitarian, which cannot be purchased, which cannot be sold, which has no economic value. How can you sell emptiness? But you have to live in the emptiness—if a man tries to live only in the walls he will go mad; it is impossible to do. But we try to do the impossible. In life, we have chosen the utilitarian.

For example, if a child is playing and you say, "Stop! What are you doing? This is useless. Do something useful. Learn, read, at least do your homework, something useful. Don't wander around, don't be a vagabond." If you continue insisting on this to a child, by and by you will kill the useless—then the child will have become just useful, and when a person is simply useful, he is dead. You can use him, he is a mechanical thing now—a means, not an end unto himself.

You are truly yourself when you are doing something useless—painting, but not to sell, just to enjoy; gardening, just to enjoy; lying down on the beach, not to do anything, just to enjoy. Useless fun, sitting silently next to a friend.

Much could be done in these moments. You could go to the shop or the market; you could earn some money. You could change time into money. You could add to your bank balance, because these moments will not come back and foolish people say that time is money. They know only one use for time: to convert it into more and more money. In the end you die with a big bank balance, but inside you are totally poor, because the inner richness arises only when you can enjoy the useless.

What is meditation? People ask, "What is the use of it? What will we gain out of it? What is the benefit of it?" Meditation…and you ask about the benefit? You cannot understand it because meditation is useless. The moment I say "useless," you feel uncomfortable because the whole mind has become so utilitarian, so commodity-oriented, that you always ask for a result. You cannot concede that something can be a pleasure unto itself.

Useless means you enjoy it but there is no benefit from it; you are deeply merged in it and it gives you bliss. But when you are deeply in it, you cannot accumulate that bliss, you cannot make a treasury out of it.

In the world, two types of people have existed: the utilitarians, who become scientists, engineers, doctors; and the other branch, the complementary type, of poets and vagabonds—useless, not doing anything useful. But they provide the balance, they give grace to the world. Think of a world full of scientists and not a single poet—it would be absolutely ugly, not worth living in. Think of a world with everyone working in the shops and offices: not a single vagabond. It would be hell. The vagabond gives beauty.

Two vagabonds were arrested. The judge asked the first one, "Where do you live?"

The man said, "The whole world is my home, the sky is my shelter; I go everywhere, and there is no barrier. I am a free man."

Then the judge asked the other, "And where do you live?"

The second vagabond said, "Next door to him."

These people give beauty to the world, they bring a perfume. A Buddha is a vagabond; a Mahavira is a vagabond. This man, this vagabond, answered that the sky was his only shelter. That is what is meant by the word *digamber*. Mahavira, the last great master of the Jains, is known as "*digamber*." *Digamber* means naked, with only the sky for clothing, nothing else. The sky is the shelter, the home.

When the world becomes too utilitarian, you create many things, you possess many things, you become obsessed with things—but the inner is lost, because the inner can flower only when there are no outer tensions, when you are not going anywhere, when you are just resting. Then the inner flowers. The greatest has always happened when you are not doing anything. Only the trivial happens when you are doing something.

Soren Kierkegaard, the Danish philosopher, has written something very penetrating. He said, "When I started praying, I would go to the church and talk to God...." That is what Christians are doing all over the world. They talk to God in a loud voice, as if God is dead. And as if God is just a foolish entity, they advise him what to do and what not to do. Or, as if God is just a foolish monarch, they persuade him or bribe him to fulfill the desires that are in them.

But Kierkegaard said, "I started talking, then suddenly I realized that this was useless. How can you talk to God? One has to be silent. What is there to be said? And what can I say that will help God to know more? He is omnipotent, he is omniscient, he knows all, so what is the purpose of my telling him?"

And Kierkegaard said, "I talked to him for many years, then suddenly I realized that this was foolish. So I stopped talking, I became silent. Then after many years I realized that even silence wouldn't do. Then the third step was taken, and that was listening. First I was talking, then I was not talking, and then I was listening."

Listening is different from just being silent, because just being silent is a negative thing—listening is a positive thing. Just being silent is passive, while listening is an alert passiveness: waiting for something, not saying anything, but waiting with the whole being. Listening has an intensity. And Kierkegaard said, "When this listening happened, then for the first time prayer happened."

But it seems listening is absolutely useless, especially listening to the unknown; you don't know where it is. Silence is useless, talking seems to be useful. Something can be done through talking; by talking you do many things in the world. So you think that if you want to become religious you will also have to do something.

But Chuang Tzu said: Religion begins only when you have understood the futility of all doing, and you have moved to the polar opposite of nondoing, inactivity, of becoming passive, becoming useless.

THE DONKEY'S SHADOW

It is said about Chuang Tzu that one evening he was talking to his disciples and many of them were fast asleep, as disciples are. It must have been late at night and they were tired, and Chuang Tzu was saying difficult things that were beyond them. When something is beyond you, it seems better to rest and sleep than to bother with it.

Suddenly Chuang Tzu became aware that many of the disciples were fast asleep and it was useless. Some were even snoring and disturbing him. So he told a parable. He said: "Once it happened that a man had a donkey and he was traveling on a pilgrimage to some holy place. But he was very poor, and it came to pass that he was hungry. No money was left, so he sold the donkey on which he was riding to another traveler, who was rich. But the next afternoon, when the sun was very hot, the first owner rested in the shadow by the side of the donkey.

"The second owner said, 'This is not good. You have sold the donkey to me.'

"The first owner said, 'I have sold the donkey, but not the shadow.'"

Everybody became alert—suddenly nobody was asleep, nobody was snoring. When you talk about donkeys, donkeys hear it immediately! Chuang Tzu said, "Now I come back to my point...."

But all the disciples said, "Wait! Please finish the story." Now everybody was throbbing with excitement: "What happened? Then what happened?"

Chuang Tzu said, "It was a parable, not a story. You are more interested in donkeys than you are in me." Chuang Tzu left the story there, he never completed it. It was not meant to be completed, it was just an indication that the human mind is more interested in stupidities than in higher values; it is more interested in foolish things.

Chuang Tzu and his master Lao Tzu were always talking about the useless; they even praised men who were useless.

Chuang Tzu talks about a man, a hunchback. All the young people of the town were forcibly entered into the military, because they were useful. Only this one man, the hunchback, who was useless, was left behind. Chuang Tzu said: Be like the hunchback, so useless that you are not slaughtered in the war.

They praise the useless because they say that the useful will always be in difficulty. The world will use you; everybody is ready to use you, manipulate you, and control you. If you are useless nobody will look at you; people will forget about you. They will leave you in silence; they will not bother about you. They will simply become unaware that you exist.

It happened to me. I am a useless man. In my childhood days I would be sitting down

next to my mother. She would look around her and say, "I would like to send someone to fetch vegetables from the market, but there is no one to send"—and I would be sitting there right next to her! She would say, "I don't see anyone around," and I would laugh inside myself—she couldn't send me to the market —I was so useless that she was not aware that I was there.

Once my aunt came to stay, and she was not aware of my uselessness. My mother was saying, "Nobody is available to go to the market. All the children have gone out and the servant is ill, so what can I do? Some one has to be sent."

My aunt said, "Why not send Raja? He is sitting there, not doing anything."

So I was sent. I asked the market vendor there, "Give me the best vegetables you have got, the best bananas, the best mangoes." Looking at me and hearing the way I was talking, he must have thought I was a fool, because nobody ever asks for the best. So he charged me double and gave me all the rotten things he had, and I came home very happy.

My mother threw them away and said, "Look! This is why I say nobody is here."

Chuang Tzu insists: Be alert and don't be very useful; otherwise, people will exploit you. Then they will start managing you and then you will be in trouble. And if you can produce things, they will force you to produce all your life. If you can do a certain thing, if you are skillful, then you cannot be wasted.

He says that uselessness has its own intrinsic utility. If you can be useful for others, then you have to live for others. Useless, nobody looks at you, nobody pays any attention to you; nobody is bothered by your being. You are left alone. In the marketplace you can live as if you are living in the Himalayas. In that solitude you grow. Your whole energy can move inward.

Chuang Tzu says, "If you have no appreciation for what has no use, you cannot begin to talk about what can be used." The useless is the other aspect of the useful. You can talk about the useful only because of the useless. It is a vital part. If you drop it completely, then *nothing* will be useful. Things are useful because there are things that are useless.

But this is what has happened to so many people in the world. We cut out all playful activities, thinking that then the whole of our energy will move into work. But now work has become a bore.

You have to move to the opposite pole— only then will you be rejuvenated. The whole day you are awake and at night you fall asleep. What is the use of sleep? It is wasting time— and not just a little time. If you live to ninety years of age, for thirty years of your life you will be asleep, eight hours every day, one third of each day. What is the use of it?

But at the end of the whole day's work, when you fall asleep you move from the useful to the useless. And that is why in the morning you feel so fresh, so alive, so unburdened. Your legs have a dancing quality, your mind can sing, your heart can again feel—all the dust of work is thrown off, the mirror is again clear. You have clarity in the morning. How does it come? It comes through the useless.

That is why meditation can give you the greatest glimpses, because it is the most useless thing in the world. You don't do anything—you simply move into silence. It is greater than sleep, because in sleep you are unconscious and whatever happens, happens unconsciously. You may be in paradise, but you don't know it. In meditation you move knowingly. You become aware of the path: how to move from the useful world of the outer to the useless world within. Once you know the path, at any moment you can move inward. Sitting in a bus, you do not need to do anything; traveling in a car or train or an airplane, you are not doing anything. Everything is being done by someone else; you can close your eyes and move into the useless, the inner. Suddenly everything becomes silent, and suddenly everything becomes cool, and suddenly you are at the source of all life.

Meditation has no value on the market. You cannot sell it, you cannot say, "I have great meditation. Is anybody ready to buy it?" Nobody will buy it. It is not a commodity; it is useless.

Chuang Tzu says:

"If you have no appreciation for what has no use, you cannot begin to talk about what can be used. The earth, for example, is broad and vast, but of all this expanse a man uses only a few inches upon which he happens to be standing at the time. Now suppose you suddenly take away all that he is not actually using, so that all around his feet a gulf yawns, and he stands in the void with nowhere solid except under each foot, how long will he be able to use what he is using?"

This is a beautiful metaphor. You are sitting in a chair, and you are using only a small space, two by two. You are not using the whole earth; the rest of the earth is useless. Says Chuang Tzu, Suppose the whole earth is taken away, only two by two is left for you? Suppose you are standing with each foot using a only few inches of earth—suppose only that is left, and the rest of the earth is taken away—how long will you be able to use this small part that you are using?

A gulf, an infinite abyss, yawns around you—you will get dizzy immediately and you will fall into the abyss. The useless earth supports the useful—and while the useless is vast, the useful is very small. This is true on all levels of being: the useless is vast and the useful is very small. If you try to save only the useful and forget the useless, sooner or later you will get dizzy. And this has already happened, you are already dizzy and falling into the abyss.

All over the world, thinking people have a problem: life seems to be meaningless. Ask Sartre, Marcel, Jaspers, Heidegger—they say life is meaningless. Why has life become so meaningless? It never used to be so. Buddha never said it; Krishna could dance, sing, enjoy himself; Mohammed could pray and thank God for the blessing of life. Chuang Tzu is happy, as happy as a person can possibly be. These people never said that life was meaningless.

What has happened to the modern mind? Why does life seem so meaningless?

The whole earth has been taken away and you are left only the part on which you are sitting or standing. You are getting dizzy. All around you, you see the abyss and the danger. You cannot use the earth on which you are standing now, because you can use it only when the useless is joined with it. The useless has to be there.

What does it mean? Your life has become only work and no play. The play is the useless, the vast; the work is the useful, the trivial, the small. You have filled your life completely with work. Whenever you start doing something, the first thing that comes to the mind is, what is the use of it? If there is some use, you do it.

Sartre sets one of his stories in the twenty-first century. A very rich man says, "Love is not for me, it is only for poor people. As far as I am concerned my servants can do it."

Of course, why should a Henry Ford waste time making love to a woman? A cheap servant can do that; Ford's time is more valuable. He should put it to some greater use.

It is possible! Looking at the human mind as it is, it is possible that in the future only servants will make love. When you can send a servant, why bother yourself? When everything is thought of in terms of economics, when a Ford or a Rockefeller can make so much better use of their time, why should they waste their time with a woman? They can send a servant; that will be less trouble.

It looks absurd, but it has already happened in many dimensions of life. You

> *Life seems meaningless because the meaning arises in a balance between the useful and the useless.*

are not an active participant in fun; others do it for you. You go to see a football match: others are playing and you are just watching. You are a passive spectator, not involved. You go to a movie and watch others making love, creating war, violence, everything while you are just a spectator in the seat. It is so useless you need not bother to do it. Anyone else can do it, you can just watch. Work *you* do—fun, others do for you.

Life seems meaningless because the meaning arises in a balance between the useful and the useless. You have denied the useless completely. You have closed the door. Now only the useful is there, and you are burdened too much by it. It is a sign of success that by the age of forty you have ulcers. If you are now fifty and still the ulcers have not appeared, you must be a failure. What have you been doing all your life? You must have been wasting time. By fifty you really ought to have had your first heart attack. And by sixty the really successful man is gone—and he never lived. There was no time to live. He had so many more important things to do, there was no time to live.

Look all around you, look at successful people—politicians, rich men, big industrialists—what is happening to them? Don't look at the things they possess, look at them directly, because if you look at the things you will be deceived. Things don't have ulcers, cars don't have heart attacks, and houses are not hospitalized. Look at the person bereft of all his possessions; look directly at him, and then you will feel his poverty. Then even a beggar may be a rich man; then even a poor man may be richer as far as life is concerned.

Success fails, and nothing fails like success, because the person who succeeds is losing his grip on life—on everything. The person who succeeds is really bargaining, throwing away the real for the unreal, throwing away inner diamonds for colored pebbles on the shore; collecting the pebbles and losing the diamonds. But because you look with the eyes of ambition, you look at the possessions. You never look at the politician; you look at the post, the prime ministership. You look at the power. You never look at the person who is sitting there absolutely powerless, missing everything, not even having a glimpse of what bliss is. He has purchased power, but in purchasing it he has lost himself. The inner self is being lost for futile possessions. You can deceive others, but how will you be able to deceive yourself? In the end you will look at your life and you will see that you have missed it because of the useful.

The useless must be there. The useful is like a garden: neat, clean. The useless is like a vast forest: it cannot be so neat and clean. Nature has its own beauty and when everything is neat and clean, it is already dead. A garden cannot be alive, because you prune it, cut it, manage it. A vast forest has vitality, a powerful soul. Go into a forest and you will feel the impact; get lost in a forest and you will see the power of it. In a garden you cannot feel the power; it is not there, because the garden is man-made. It is beautiful, but it is cultivated, managed, and manipulated.

A garden is a false thing—the real thing is the forest. The useless is like a vast forest and the useful is like a garden you have created around your house. Don't cut into the forest. Let your garden be a part of the vast forest that is not your garden, but nature's garden.

Chuang Tzu emphasized uselessness so much because you have emphasized the useful too much. That emphasis is needed just to give you balance. You have gone too much to the left; you have to be pulled to the right.

But remember, because of this overemphasis you can easily move to the other extreme. And that happened to many followers of Chuang Tzu. They became addicted to the useless and missed the point. Chuang Tzu emphasized the useless only because you have become so addicted to usefulness. But I must remind you—because mind can move to the opposite and remain the same—that the real thing is transcendence. You have to come to a point where you can use the useful and the non-useful, the purposeful and the purposeless. When you are beyond both, they both serve you.

道

A real, a perfect man, a man of Tao, has no addictions. He can move easily from one extreme to another because he remains in the middle. He uses both wings.

Chuang Tzu should not be misunderstood, that is why I say this. People like Chuang Tzu are dangerous because you can misunderstand them, and there is more possibility for misunderstanding than understanding. The mind says, "Okay, enough of this shop, enough of this family...now I will become a vagabond." That is misunderstanding. You will carry the same mind, you will become addicted to being a vagabond. Then you will not be able to come back to the shop, to the market, to the family. Then you will be afraid of it.

In the same way, medicine can become a new disease if you get addicted to it. So the doctor has to see that you get rid of the disease but don't become addicted to the medicine; otherwise, he is not a good doctor.

First you have to get rid of the disease, and immediately afterward you have to get rid of the medicine; otherwise, the medicine will take the place of the disease and you will cling to it always.

Mulla Nasruddin was teaching his small son, who was seven years old, how to approach a girl, how to ask her to dance, what to say and what not to say, how to persuade her. The boy went away and half an hour later came back and said, "Now teach me how to get rid of her!" That has to be learned too, and that is the difficult part. To invite is very easy, but to get rid of is difficult. You know it well through your own experience. Remember, the useless has its own attraction. If you are very troubled by the useful, you may move to the other extreme too much. You may lose your balance. What is needed is a deep balance, standing in the middle, free from all the opposites. You can use the useful and you can use the non-useful; you can use the purposeful and the non-purposeful and still remain beyond both. You are not used by them. You have become the master.

THE RASCAL SAINT

Few people had the courage to remain with Chuang Tzu. He was always creating embarrassing situations; saints were not supposed to do such things. For example, he was seen one day in the capital riding on a donkey with his disciples following him. The whole town was laughing—people were gathered on both sides of the road— because he was not sitting in the right way. The donkey was going forward, and Chuang Tzu was sitting backward on the donkey, facing his disciples!

The townspeople were laughing and the disciples were very embarrassed. Finally one disciple said, "Why are you doing this? You are making a fool of yourself, and along with you we are being ridiculed unnecessarily. People think we are idiots!"

Chuang Tzu said, "There is something great implied in it—I have thought it over. If I sit the way people normally sit on donkeys, then my back will be facing you, and that is insulting.
I don't want to insult anybody, not even my own disciples.

"The other possibility is that you could walk in front of me, but then you will be insulting me—and that is not right either, the disciples insulting the master. So this is the solution that I have found.

"Let the fools laugh—but I am facing you and you are facing me. That's how a master and disciple should be: I am respectful toward you, and you are respectful toward me.

"And the donkey has no objection— why should we bother about what some people think?"

Now this kind of man is rare, unique, difficult to find. He attained to the highest clarity, consciousness, love, compassion— but he remained a rascal to the very end.

道

lieh tzu:

a master storyteller

Lieh Tzu is one of the most perfect expressions of the

inexpressible. Truth cannot be expressed: that inexpressibility

is intrinsic to truth. Thousands and thousands of people have

tried to express it—very few have succeeded even in giving

a reflection of it. Lieh Tzu is one of those few; he is rare.

道

道

expressing the inexpressible

Lieh Tzu's approach is that of an artist—the poet, the storyteller—and he is a master storyteller. His experience has flowered into parables; that seems to be the easiest way to hint at that which cannot be said. A parable is a great device; it is not just an ordinary story. Its purpose is not to entertain you; its purpose is to say something that there is no other way to say.

LIFE CANNOT BE put into a theory: it is so vast, infinite. A theory by its very nature is closed. A theory has to be closed; if it is a theory it cannot be open-ended, otherwise, it will be meaningless. A parable is open-ended: it says something and yet leaves much to be said—it only hints. That which cannot be said can be shown. A parable is a finger pointing to the moon. Don't cling to the finger—it is irrelevant—look at the moon. Parables in themselves are beautiful, but their purpose is not in clinging to them—they go beyond; they are transcendental. If you dissect the parable you will not come to much understanding.

It is like the navel in the body—if you ask a surgeon what the purpose of the navel is and he dissects the body, he will not find any purpose. The navel seems to be useless.

What is the purpose of the navel? It was purposeful when the child was in the womb; its purpose was to connect the child to the mother. But now that the child is no longer in the womb—the mother may have died, the child has grown old—now what is the purpose of the navel? The navel has a transcendental purpose; the purpose is not in itself. You will have to look everywhere to find what it indicates. It indicates that the person was once a child, that the child was once in the womb of a mother, that the child was connected to the mother. The navel is just a mark left on the body by the past.

Just as the navel shows something about the past, a parable shows something about the future. It shows that there is a possibility of growing, of being connected with existence. Right now that is only a possibility; it is not actual. If you just dissect the parable, it becomes an ordinary story. If you don't dissect it but drink the meaning of it, the poetry of it, the music of it—forget the story and just look for the significance of it—soon you will see that it indicates a future, indicates something that can be, but is not yet. It is transcendental.

So the first thing to understand about Lieh Tzu is that he is not a theoretician. He will

not give you any theories; he will simply give you parables.

A theory can be dissected—its meaning is in it, it has no transcendence, the meaning is immanent. A parable cannot be dissected—dissect it, and it will die. The meaning is transcendental. You have to live a parable, then you will come to its meaning. It has to become your heart, your breathing; it has to become your inner rhythm.

To understand a man like Lieh Tzu, you will have to live an authentic life. Only then, through your own experience, will you be able to feel what he means by his parables. It is not that you can learn the theories and become informed; the information will not help. Unless you know, nothing is going to help. If these parables create a thirst in you to know, a great desire to know, a great hunger to know; if these parables lead you on an unknown journey, on a pilgrimage—only then, by treading the path, will you become acquainted with the path.

Western scholars have been puzzled about Lieh Tzu—about whether he ever existed or not. There are great treatises about him; they worked hard for years to find out whether this man really existed. To the Eastern mind this whole scholarship looks stupid because it does not matter whether he existed or not. If you ask me whether he existed or not, I say it is all the same. Whoever wrote these beautiful stories was Lieh Tzu—whoever the person was, one thing is certain: *somebody* wrote them. That much is certain because these stories exist.

Now, whether somebody by the name of Lieh Tzu really wrote the stories that are attributed to him or somebody by some other name wrote them, how does it make any difference? It will not add anything to the stories; they are already perfect. It will not take anything away from the stories; nothing can be taken away. Whether Lieh Tzu was an historical person or not, how is that going to affect the stories? The stories are beautiful; they have intrinsic value. One thing is certain, somebody wrote them—why be bothered about the writer's name, whether it was Lieh Tzu or something else?

It is possible that they were written by many people—then too there is no problem. Whoever wrote any one of these stories must have touched the consciousness of Tao; otherwise, they could not have been written. One person or many people may have written them, but whenever these stories were written, somebody had penetrated the consciousness of Tao; somebody had understood what life is, somebody had a vision.

In the West this question of authorship is felt to be significant. People have written books and books about whether Shakespeare ever existed or not—as if it makes any difference! The plays that Shakespeare wrote are so beautiful—why not look into the plays and love and enjoy them? It seems to be going astray to ask whether Shakespeare existed or not. And the problem arises because it is thought that Shakespeare was an uneducated man, so how could he write such beautiful things?

Have you ever known very educated men to write beautiful things? It is thought by some that it was not Shakespeare but Lord Bacon who was the real author. But I cannot trust this because I have read Lord Bacon's other books—they have nothing to compare with Shakespeare. Lord Bacon is just ordinary. He may have been a very learned man, he may have been a great scholar, but his books are ordinary rubbish. Just because he is Lord Bacon and has a famous name, who is deceived? Have you ever heard the name of any book by Lord Bacon? How could Lord Bacon write these Shakespearian plays? Under his name he has not written a single masterpiece, so how could he write one under a pseudonym? And if he could write such beautiful plays as the Shakespearian plays are, under a pseudonym, then what was he doing when he was writing under his own name? It doesn't seem right.

So whether Shakespeare was known as Shakespeare or not is not the point. Some consciousness certainly existed that gave birth to these beautiful plays. What is wrong with calling that consciousness Shakespeare?

In the East, we have never bothered about these things. We say, "What does it matter who wrote something?" If the books are beautiful, very beautiful, tremendously significant, and if we have enjoyed them down the centuries and we have loved them and contemplated them, the authorship is irrelevant.

Whether or not Lieh Tzu really existed is uncertain. He does not seem to be an historical person at all because he has not left any trace. Either he was not an historical person or he was a great horse. My preference is for the second—he was a great horse who never

raised any dust and who never left any tracks behind. He effaced himself completely. Only one small book exists—the *Book of Lieh Tzu* —with a few small parables.

This book says nothing about Lieh Tzu. But why should we bother? Lieh Tzu may have been a woman; he may not have been a man. Who knows? He may not have been Chinese; he may have been Tibetan. Who knows? He may not have *been* at all. It does not matter. But the parables matter. These parables are doors. So please don't chase after the non-essential. Look into the spirit of the essential. Don't be bothered by the gross; go into the subtle.

道

the nature of knowing

One of the most fundamental questions that has always faced humanity, and that will always encounter every human being ever born, is the nature of knowledge. What is real knowing? Only through knowing does one attain liberation, only through knowing does one come to know oneself, only through knowing is the truth revealed.

MAN IS BORN IN IGNORANCE. The darkness is tremendous. Naturally, the first question that any intelligent being will ask is how to find light. What is light? We are born in darkness not knowing who we are. What greater darkness can there be? We are not even aware of who we are, from where we come, or to where we are going. We are groping somehow, drifting somehow. We are accidental. We don't yet have a destiny. We are unconscious. We have not yet attained to the light of inner being that can enlighten our path. In this darkness, if failure happens, it is natural. In this darkness, if frustration happens, what more can you expect? In this darkness, if you only die and never live, it seems logical.

The fundamental question is: What is the nature of knowledge? What is real knowledge? We know many things and yet remain ignorant. We know many things but the fundamental thing is missing. It is as if we have made a big building and the foundation is missing.

HITTING THE TARGET

Lieh Tzu was studying archery and he hit the target. He sought advice from Kuan-Yin who asked him, "Do you know why you hit the target?"

"No."

"It won't do yet."

Lieh Tzu went away to practice and after three years again reported to Kuan-Yin.

"Do you know why you hit the target?"

"I know."

"It will do. Hold onto this awareness and do not lose it."

This applies not only to archery, but also to ruling oneself. Therefore the sage scrutinizes not the fact of survival or ruin, but its reasons.

Humanity knows much—the knowledge has grown every day—and yet deep down we remain as ignorant as ever. We must have misunderstood the very nature of knowledge.

Before we enter this symbolic and very significant parable, a few things have to be understood.

First, unless you know yourself, all knowing is useless. Unless you know yourself, all knowing is only pseudo-knowing—you appear to know but you don't really know; it is a deception. You know science, you know *things*, you know the world—but you don't know yourself. If the knower himself is in deep darkness, all his knowledge is superficial. It cannot even be skin deep. Scratch the surface of knowledge and soon you will find ignorance coming out. Just scratch a little and knowledge will not be of any help. You will find each person as ordinary and ignorant as any other.

If you insult Albert Einstein, he becomes as angry as anybody else. If Albert Einstein fails,

he feels as frustrated as anybody else. If Bertrand Russell succeeds he is as happy as anybody else. There is no basic difference, because the innermost core remains the same. Bertrand Russell, of course, knows more than you, but the knowledge is quantitative. He is not more of a *knower* than you; the knowledge is not yet *qualitative*. As far as your being is concerned, he is the same as you. He has more information but not more knowing. More information is not more knowing—and more knowing does not necessarily mean more information.

Buddha may not know as much as Bertrand Russell knows—but Buddha is a knower and Bertrand Russell is not. Buddha's knowledge is not about things; his knowledge is about his own being. His knowledge is not an accumulation of information; his knowledge is an explosion, an inner explosion of light.

That's why we call it enlightenment.

He has become more aware—that is his knowing. He no longer walks unalert and inattentive. If you hit him, he will not react the way an unconscious man will react. He will *respond*, but he will not *react* at all. And his response will not be because you have insulted him; his response will be out of his awareness. His response will not be mechanical—that's why I say it will not be a reaction.

A reaction is a mechanical thing; anybody can push your buttons and you react mechanically. You don't have any control over your own mechanism. If somebody insults you, you are insulted. The other person is the master: he pushed a button and you fell under his control. If somebody appreciates you, you are flowing and happy; if he pushes another button, you are under his control.

You can praise Buddha or you can condemn Buddha, but it will not make any difference. You can try to push the buttons, but Buddha will not react. He is not a machine anymore.

Once Buddha was insulted. He was passing through a village and many people gathered and insulted and condemned him. Their anger was almost righteous, because Buddha was destroying the very foundation of their rotten culture. He was destroying the laws that Manu had prescribed for the Hindus. He was destroying the foundation of this class-divided society—a society divided into castes, *varna*. And he was destroying the foundation of the ancient sannyas, because in the ancient days a sannyasin meant a very old man. After seventy-five years of age, you had to become a sannyasin—when life had already ebbed, you were supposed to become a sannyasin, renounce everything, and take up the spiritual life. But Buddha was initiating young people, even young children.

He was destroying two basic fundamentals of Hindu society. The first was *ashrama*, the four stages of life—sannyas is the fourth stage, the last. And the second was the four-caste system, *varna*. In this system the Brahmin is the highest caste and the Sudra is the lowest, and in between is the Vaishya and the Kshatriya. Buddha was destroying this system because he said that anyone who knows Brahma is a Brahmin—not by birth, but by knowing, by being. He said that everybody is born as a Sudra, as an untouchable, the lowest— Brahmins included. At birth, nobody is higher and nobody is lower; at birth everybody is born

as an animal. Then if you work, grow, seek and search, and refine your consciousness, by and by, slowly, you move higher—from the Sudra you become a Vaishya.

A Vaishya is a businessman. He is a little higher, has a few more values in life, thinks sometimes about music, sometimes about poetry. The Sudra is one who thinks only of the body—he eats, sleeps, and that is all. Eat, drink, and be merry—that is his whole circle of life. If you are doing only that you are a Sudra, the lowest category of human being.

Everybody is born that way. You cannot expect a small child to be interested in music, poetry, philosophy and religion. When a child is born he is a hedonist, an Epicurean. He sleeps for eighteen to twenty hours—what more can you expect? Whenever he feels hungry he awakes and cries and weeps—and finds food and nourishment. Then again he falls asleep. He eats, drinks, and sleeps. Every child is a Sudra.

As you start growing, new dimensions open in your being. You start becoming interested in things that are not only of the body. A little of the mind, a little of psychology enters into your being. You are no longer just a physique. Then you are a Vaishya. Then you are moving in the bigger business of life: you are a businessman. Not a very high state, but better than the Sudra.

Then comes the Kshatriya, the warrior. He becomes a little more interested in higher things. He starts searching for truth, for beauty, for love. His interest is higher than the businessman's. And he is ready to

> *As you start growing, new dimensions open in your being.*

stake his life, he is ready to lose his life, for these higher values. He is ready to gamble; he is courageous. Courage enters him. The businessman is not courageous; if everything goes well, he may enjoy music, he may enjoy poetry, he may sit in his home, centered and secure—and think about the truth, too. But he will not put himself in much danger; he will not take risks.

The warrior, the Kshatriya, takes risks. He puts his life at stake. He becomes a gambler. The businessman is never a gambler. He thinks first about the profit and he goes only so far. He takes risks, but only limited risks, and he always worries about profit and loss. The warrior risks all. He goes deep into life. That is the third stage.

The Brahmin is the highest, the one who goes deeper into the mystery of life, reality, existence. And he is never satisfied unless he comes to know what ultimate truth is. That is what Brahmin means—one who comes face-to-face with the ultimate truth, the absolute truth.

Buddha said that these are not divisions of birth, these are the qualities that you have to evolve into. Everybody has to evolve from the Sudra and everybody has to go to the Brahmin. Buddha destroyed the whole idea of the caste structure. He said that a sannyasin has nothing to do with age or how old you are. Age has nothing to do with sannyas; it is not a chronological thing. If sannyas is not concerned with time, how can it be concerned with age? Sannyas is a movement into the timeless for anybody who is ready. Sometimes a child will enter into sannyas. Shankara entered into sannyas when he was only nine years of age. If he had waited according to the old Hindu concept, he would have never become a sannyasin, because by the age of thirty-three he was dead. Humanity would have missed something tremendous.

Buddha said that sannyas can be entered whenever somebody is ready. And there are different qualities of people, different intensities, different passions. At the age of nine, someone may be more alert than most people are, even at the age of ninety. You cannot decide outright by a person's age; you have to look into the inner intensity of the person.

It is your life. If you want to risk it, it is your freedom. You have to be allowed. Buddha allowed young people to be initiated into sannyas.

These two systems were the foundations of the Hindu society, and both were destroyed in Buddha's approach. People were against him, naturally. He was always in danger. But he created a great revolution in human consciousness.

In this story, Buddha was passing through a village of Brahmins. They gathered around him and they insulted him very much. He listened silently. They pushed and pushed

道

the buttons, but nothing happened. So they became a little embarrassed—when you insult somebody and he stands there unperturbed, you become embarrassed. He seems to be beyond you. In fact, you cannot reach him because he is at such a height.

They asked, "Are you listening? Why are you standing silently? We are insulting and condemning you. Have you gone dumb? Have you gone deaf? Can't you speak? Can't you hear what we are saying?"

Buddha said, "I can feel and see your worries and your embarrassment, but I am sorry. You should have come ten years earlier

if you wanted me to react. Now it is too late. Now these buttons don't work. I have gone beyond them."

It is as if a child is playing with a toy and you snatch the toy away and he cries and weeps. One day he will not be a child, and then if you snatch his toy away he will not cry and weep. In fact, he will give it to you, he will present it to you and say, "You can take it, you can have it. I am finished with it."

That's what Buddha said. He said, "It is too late. I am finished with it. I have gone beyond."

This is knowing, real knowing. Knowing is a qualitative change in your being. It is a

transformation of your being, it is a metanoia. As you move higher, the altitude changes. With knowledge, the so-called knowledge, you remain the same, but you go on accumulating more. You know more—but *you* remain the same.

The so-called knowledge is like money. You hoard money—but that doesn't change you. How can it change you? Your bank balance grows, but that doesn't mean you are growing with it. You may hoard millions of dollars, but how is that going to help your growth? You remain the same. That's why you will see that even rich people remain beggars. The money is there, but their inner beggary remains the same. They remain the same way—miserly.

Sometimes they become even more miserly, because when you don't have so much, you are not so worried about losing it. When you have it, you become worried about losing it. Rich people become poorer; their poverty is tremendous. They cannot share. They are always afraid. Their inner poverty does not change at all; it remains the same. It has to be so. If you are aggressive, changing your clothes will not make you become non-aggressive. If you are angry, changing the style of your hair will not make you peaceful. So the amount of money you have does not make any difference to your inner being.

In the same way, the amount of knowledge you have makes no difference. You can go to the university, attain all the degrees possible, visit libraries, read and study, and collect much knowledge—but it will be just on the outside, on the periphery of your mind. It will be just in your memory; it will not change the quality of your consciousness. And unless your consciousness changes, nothing is attained.

So the first thing to be understood is that knowledge and knowing are different. Knowledge is information; knowing is understanding. Knowledge is gathered from the outside; knowing is a growth inside. Knowledge is borrowed; knowing is yours, authentically yours. Knowledge is learned; knowing is not learned from anybody.

You have to become more alert so that you can see more, so that you can feel more, so that you can be more. Knowing is being; knowledge is just a peripheral accumulation.

Another thing: When you are full of knowledge, when you have hoarded much knowledge, your ego will be strengthened. You will think, "I know so much." And the ego is one of the barriers toward reality. It is not a bridge: it disconnects, it does not connect. When you are a person of knowing, ego disappears—because a person of knowing comes to know that there is nothing you can know. How can you know? Life is so mysterious, so tremendously mysterious, there is no way to truly know it.

If you can know only yourself, that is more than enough, more than anyone can expect. If a small light starts burning in your heart and your inner being becomes lighted, that is more than enough. And that is what is needed. In that light you become aware that the reality is an ultimate mystery—that's what we mean when we use the word *God*. *God* means exactly what *nature* means with only one difference. In the concept of nature it is implied that what is not known now will be known later on—but it can be known. It is knowable. That is the intrinsic meaning of nature.

Nature is theoretically knowable. Scientists talk about nature because we have known something of it, and one day everything will be known. By using the word *God* or *godliness* we bring another dimension into it. We say that something is known and more will be known—more will always be known—yet something will always remain unknowable, something will be forever elusive.

The mystery is vast; the mystery is infinite. And we are part of it—how can the part know the whole totally? It is impossible. The part cannot know the whole totally, the part can only know so far.

A person of knowing understands the mystery of life. That's why Buddha is silent about life. He does not say a single word about it.

Lao Tzu kept quiet for his whole life until he was forced to write his experiences. But the first sentence he wrote in the *Tao Te Ching* was that the Tao, the truth that can be said, is

道

> " *Tao says that any activity can be turned into a sacred activity—any activity whatsoever, even archery, even swordsmanship.* "

not the real Tao. The Tao that can be uttered or expressed is already false.

The truth cannot be said because you can say only things that have been known totally, known perfectly. Truth is never known totally. You feel it, you live it, you have great experiences of it—great visions, great mysteries open—but each mystery brings you to another mystery. As each door opens you see that a thousand and one doors are still waiting, unopened. Each door brings you to new doors. So how can you express it?

A person of knowing will say, "I don't know," or "I don't know the all, I know only a little bit. I know only myself." But that is enough—that is more than enough. That is the highest one can aspire to.

The person of knowledge claims to know everything and hence proves ignorant. Only an ignorant person claims to know; the knower always admits not knowing. That is the sign, the indication, of real knowing.

One thing more: When you know something, you divide reality into the knower, the known, and the knowledge. The reality immediately becomes divided into three things. That's the meaning of the symbol of the trinity in Christianity. If you *know*, God becomes three. The moment you know, God becomes three; the one is no longer one. Knowledge divides. That is the meaning of the concept of the *trimurti* in Hinduism—God has three faces. The moment you know, he has three faces. Knowledge divides.

It seems that three is basic. If you dissolve into reality there is one, but the moment you turn it over and look at it, it turns into three. Certainly, because then you are one thing, that which you know is another, and between the two is knowledge—the knower, the known, and the knowledge.

Knowledge divides—and that which divides cannot lead you to ultimate truth. Knowing unites. In knowing, one does not know who is the knower, who is the known, and what is knowledge. That's why in knowing, you become a mystic. In knowing, you become one with reality; in knowing, you lose all distinctions, differences, boundaries, definitions. In knowing, you become undefined—as undefined as reality itself.

Now here is a parable.

Lieh Tzu was studying archery, and hit the target. He sought advice from Kuan-Yin who asked him, "Do you know why you hit the target?"

Each word has to be understood. Have the taste of each single word—because each single word is significant. These parables are not just to be read in one stroke and forgotten about; these parables were written to meditate upon.

These are meditative devices.

Lieh Tzu was studying archery.

Tao makes no difference between the sacred and the profane. All the organized religions make a distinction between the sacred and the profane. Archery is a profane art—as is swordsmanship, or cooking, or carpentry, or painting, or poetry. You cannot think of Buddha painting and you cannot think of Buddha as an archer. You cannot even think of Buddha composing poetry. These are mundane activities; Buddha is transcendental.

Can you imagine Buddha doing any ordinary day-to-day activity? No, he simply meditates. He remains in the purest sky. He walks on the earth but he does not belong to the earth. He walks on the earth but he never touches the earth. He is not an earthly being.

But Tao is something rare and extraordinary. Tao says that any activity can be turned into a sacred activity—any activity whatsoever, even archery, even swordsmanship. In China and Japan there are schools of archery and swordsmanship, but in the hall where the archer learns archery you will find a sign: *Meditation Hall*. People learn archery or sometimes wrestling—but the hall is known as the Meditation Hall. What type of meditation is this? People are fighting, wrestling, learning archery—all murderous arts. What type of meditation is this? Why do they call these places meditation halls?

Tao says that any activity done with full awareness becomes a meditation. Activity is not the real thing—how you do it, what consciousness you bring to it, is the real

thing. You can pray in an earthly way and it will become mundane—and you know it. If you go to the temple and listen to people's prayers, you will know it. Their prayers are not real prayers. Somebody is asking to win the lottery; somebody is asking that his wife who is ill should be made well again; somebody is saying that his son has failed, next time God should please take care that he passes his exams. Somebody is saying that her daughter has grown up and it is difficult to find a boy for her—please help. These are their prayers. They are mundane activities, very ordinary. Why do you call them prayers? What is sacred about them? Nothing seems to be sacred about them. You may be sitting in a temple but that doesn't make much difference.

If prayer can be profane, then surely ordinary activities can be sacred. That is a Taoist contribution to the world. The activity is not the real thing, but the consciousness you bring to it.

Take wrestling, for example. The Taoist wrestler first has to bow down to his opponent and meditate on the opponent as being divine, an expression of godliness—not as the enemy. If he cannot meditate on the enemy as being an expression of the divine, as being a friend, then he is not Taoist. Then it is ordinary wrestling. But if he can see the same godliness in his opponent as he feels in himself, then wrestling is wrestling only on the surface; deep down it has become prayer.

If you observe from the outside, you will be puzzled. Two swordsmen fighting with their swords first have to look into one another's

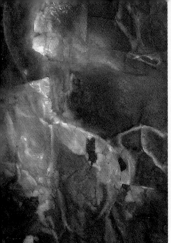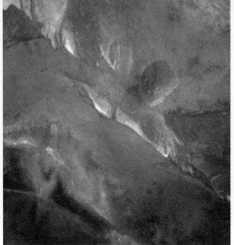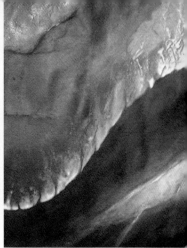

eyes, in through the window of each other's eyes, to get the feel of each other's being. It is exactly like his own being. Then when they fight, the fight is totally different. The fight is not aggressive or egoistic; the fight is a play. The wrestlers or the swordsmen are not interested in killing each other. They are not even interested in protecting themselves. They simply relax and let go. Then two energies are there, dancing. It is wrestling to you if you look from the outside, but from the inside it is just a dance of two energies. It is almost a love affair, this meeting of two energies.

And, you will be surprised to know that if somebody is defeated, that person is thought to be the one who is not yet in a let-go. He was still an egoist; that's why he was defeated.

Sometimes it happens that two Taoist wrestlers have been wrestling again and again for years and neither has been defeated—because both were non-egoists. How can you defeat a non-egoist? Both are non-aggressive. Both are in such tremendous love that neither can defeat the other. Two swordsmen may fight for hours and neither

gets hurt. This is the art. The whole art is to be so empty that the sword cannot cut anything.

Now, if somebody hits you, you shrink; if somebody hits you, you resist. The Taoist art is: when somebody hits you, you expand. You take the attack into yourself and absorb it.

If somebody is throwing energy at you, don't fight with that energy, absorb it. He is giving you energy and you are fighting with it? Absorb it instead!

Try it sometime. If somebody hits you or punches you one day, try to absorb it. Just go with it. Don't get hard, don't become stiff, let it be absorbed. You will be surprised. You will be surprised because it will be a totally new experience. If one fighter absorbs the other's energy—whatever he is throwing out—the one who is throwing out energy will be defeated. It is not that the other has defeated him—he has defeated himself. He will become weaker and weaker, and he will be defeated. The other fighter will come out of it radiant.

Every activity can be turned into meditation. Even the murderous arts of archery and fighting can be turned into nonviolent arts. This is a great revolution.

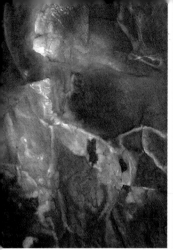 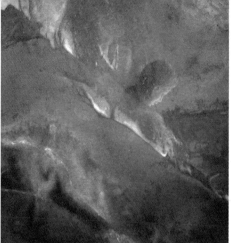 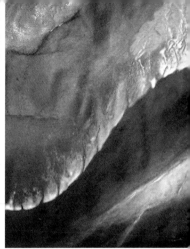

The ego is hard and masculine. Tao believes in the feminine. The ego is aggressive; the feminine is receptive. Tao believes in the receptive. Tao believes in becoming a womb. The ego, the masculine ego, is determined to penetrate rather than be penetrated. The masculine ego is always trying to penetrate the other—just as in sex.

In everything the male ego does, there is an effort at penetration, an effort to violate the other. And the feminine is absorbing —just as in sex. As in sex, so in everything.

Have you not watched it happening every day? You may not have thought about it in that way. Women are always the winners. Napoleon may be a great man outside his house, but when he comes back home he is nothing. The woman may be tiny, a wisp of a woman, but she dominates. Every husband is henpecked. If you can find a husband who is not henpecked, then know well that he is a Taoist. He is not masculine, that's why he is not henpecked. He is already feminine. Each husband has to be henpecked because the egoistic energy cannot win against the non-egoistic energy.

Have you not watched it? A woman crying is very powerful. You may have all the muscles in the world, you may be the great Mohammed Ali, but even Mohammed Ali, when his girlfriend is crying, just does not know what to do. The tears seem to be more powerful.

What is the power in the tears of a woman? She is so fragile, she is so vulnerable, she is so soft—from where comes the power of the woman? Why does she dominate, how does she manage? She manages without managing. She takes care of you; she serves you in a thousand and one ways. And that's how she becomes the conqueror. She never tries to penetrate you, she never tries to conquer you—that is her victory. She is defenseless. But still some great strength comes from some unknown source.

Taoists say that this is the strength of the water element. Man is like rock and woman is like water. When the water falls on the rocks, the rock disappears and becomes sand— sooner or later. It is only a question of time. On the first contact of the water with the rock, the rock is so strong and the water is so soft that you cannot logically imagine that one day the

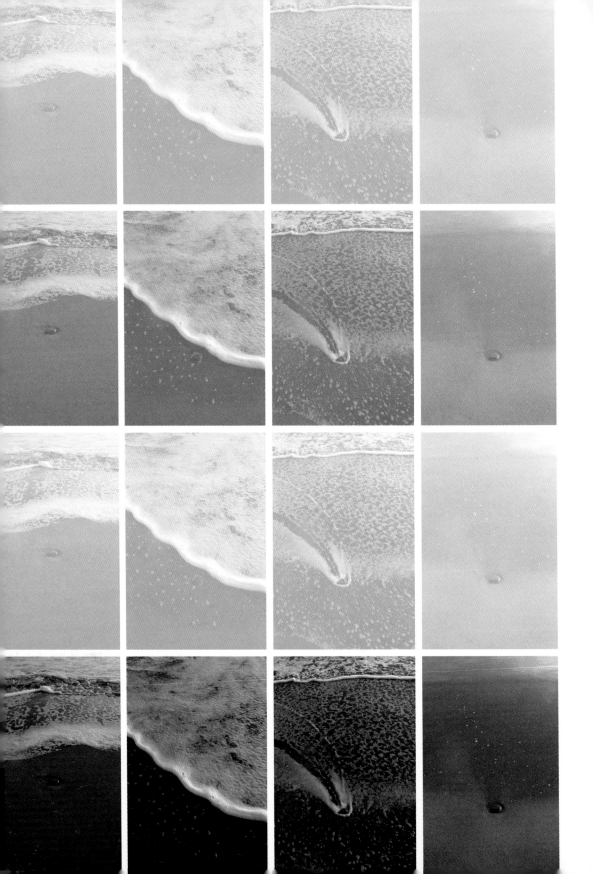

water will destroy the rock, that the rock will disappear as sand and the water will still be there.

This is what Lao Tzu calls "the watercourse way"—the strength of the feminine.

The energy of the masculine is that of the woodcutter. Have you watched a woodcutter chopping wood? That is the energy of the masculine—destructive, aggressive, violent. The feminine energy is that of the surfer. The male wrestles with life rather than swimming with it; the feminine goes with it, swims with it, does not wrestle with it. The feminine is pliant and supple, more like liquid.

If somebody is studying archery he can study it as a masculine energy. Then he will become technically expert but he will miss the deeper art of it.

Lieh Tzu was studying archery, and hit the target.

Now this is the male understanding. If you hit the target you have learned the art. What more is needed? If out of a hundred tries you can hit the target a hundred times, what more is needed?

In Japan, a German professor, Herrigel, was learning archery with a Zen master. He became perfect, one hundred percent perfect—not a single target was ever missed. Naturally he said to the master, "Now what more is there? Now what more have I to learn here? Can I go now?"

The master said, "You can go but you have not learned even the ABC of my art."

Herrigel said, "The ABC of your art? My target is one hundred percent perfect now."

The master said, "Who is talking about the

> *When the water falls on the rocks, the rock disappears and becomes sand—sooner or later. It is only a question of time.*

target? Any fool can do that just by practicing. That is nothing much. Now the real thing starts.

"When the archer takes his bow and arrow and aims at the target, there are three elements. One is the archer: the most fundamental and basic thing, the source, the innermost. Then there is the arrow that will pass from the archer to the target. And then there is the bullseye: the target, the farthest—away thing. If you hit the target you have touched the farthest, you have touched the periphery. You have to touch the source. You can become technically expert in hitting the target, but that is not much—not much if you are trying to get into deeper waters. You are an expert, you are a man of knowledge, but not a man of knowing.

"The arrow moves from you—but you don't know from with what energy the arrow moves. How does it move? Who is moving it? You don't know that. You don't know the archer. Archery you have studied, the target you have achieved, a hundred percent perfect was your aim, at a hundred percent perfection level you have become efficient—but this is about the target. What about you? What about the archer? Has anything happened in the archer? Has your consciousness changed a little bit? No, nothing has changed. You are a technician; you are not a real artist."

Taoists say that the real thing is to see the source of the aim from where this arrow takes the energy. Who is it that has succeeded? What is the energy? What being is hidden behind you? That is the real target. If that is the target and sometimes you miss the outer target, it's not a problem.

It is said about a great archer in Japan that he always used to miss his target. He was the greatest master, but he was never able to aim rightly. What was his mastery? His mastery was of a totally different kind. He had penetrated into the source; he had made the target his center.

The periphery is not the point. You may succeed or you may fail, but that is not the point at all. The real thing is: have you succeeded in becoming centered in your being? Has that target been achieved?

To succeed with the outer target is the masculine energy, to succeed with your inner source is the feminine energy. To succeed with the outer source you have to be aggressive, ambitious, concentrated, attentive, outgoing, extrovert—the arrow will be going out, will be going away from you. The arrow will be going into the world.

To move into your center you need to be feminine, passive, inactive, nondoing, noninterfering, wu-wei meditative. Meditation and relaxation, not concentration, are needed.

You have to relax yourself completely and utterly. When you are not doing anything, then you are at your center; when you are doing something, you have gone away. When you do too much you are far away. Coming closer means dropping your activities, learning how to be inactive, learning how to be a non-doer.

Herrigel's master said to him, "You have become a doer, a perfect doer, but that is not the point. That you could have learned in Germany, there was no need to come to Japan. Masculine arts are available in the West. But if you have come to the East, then please learn the real thing. Now you have to take your bow without being a doer; you have to pull your arrow without being a puller; you have to aim at the target without aiming. There should be no tension, no effort, no doing on your part. Just be passive. Let it happen rather than doing it. Then you will be centered."

Do you know the difference between doing a thing and letting it happen? If you know the difference, then you can understand this parable, otherwise, it will be difficult.

Let me remind you, because you may not have noted it. Sometimes, making love, you were a doer. Then you missed. Yes, there was a sexual release, but it was not a true orgasm. Sometimes it was not a doing, you allowed it to happen—then it was a release, certainly, but with a plus. It was an orgasm. You had a feeling of expansion, you became enormous and huge; you touched the very boundaries of existence. In that moment you disappeared as an ego; you were not. You pulsated from one core to another core, you pulsated in all your layers, but you

道

were not the doer. Bring the doer in, and the pulsation stops. Drop the doer and the pulsation starts again.

Sometimes, swimming in a river, you start floating. Swimming is beautiful, but nothing compared with floating. Sometimes, just lying in the river, not making any effort, you start floating with the river—then you know a totally different quality of experience. The river takes you in her arms, the river supports you, the river and you are no longer enemies—there is a sort of inner connectedness. You have fallen *en rapport* with the river energy; your energy and the energy of the river are making love. Then there is an orgasm.

Sometimes, sitting silently, doing nothing, you have become aware of letting go. And there is a benediction. Sometimes, looking at the stars or at the trees, suddenly it is there. You were not doing anything.

These moments come to everybody. They come when you are not expecting them, they come only when you are *not*; they steal in when your doors are open and you are relaxed. Sometimes out of nothingness and from nowhere a great benediction comes. These moments come to everybody, but you have not observed them, you have not noticed them. These are gifts from existence. They are reminders: "You are in a strange land—come back home." Existence knocks on your heart again and again—whenever an opportunity is there, whenever you allow it.

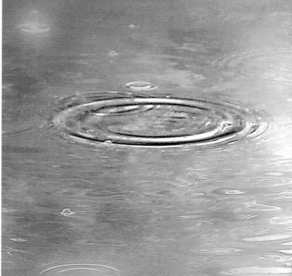

On a Sunday you can lie in bed, not in any hurry to go to the office, and the children are awake and rushing around the room and your

partner is preparing the tea and there is the sound of the kettle, and the traffic slowly moving outside, and you turn in your bed and you pull your blanket up again and there is nowhere to go—it is Sunday. Christianity has given one beautiful thing to the world—Sunday. Hinduism has no Sunday. Sunday is the greatest contribution of Christianity. You can dream a little more; you can float into sleep again. There are scents from the kitchen, breakfast is being made, and you are in a state of relaxation, not tense, —and suddenly you feel tremendously beautiful. Life has meaning. Something flowers in you. Something unknown enters you. These are the moments when you are feminine.

Rushing to the office you become male. You may walk on the street along which you go to the office every day—but when you are just going for a walk, you are a female. When you are going for a walk, you are not going anywhere in particular, you are just enjoying the birds in the trees and the wind and the morning and the sun and the children laughing and going to school. You are enjoying, not going anywhere in particular, and at any point you can turn back home; there is no target, there is no goal, you are simply enjoying a morning walk—and suddenly it is there, that moment of let-go.

Watch these moments of let-go, because they are messages from the beyond. Watch these moments of let-go: cherish them, taste them. Welcome them so that they become more and more available to you. Receive the guest gratefully so that it will come more and more often.

Tao says that the real happens only when you are in such a state of diffused relaxedness that you cannot say "I am." "I am" means you are tense.

Lieh Tzu was studying archery, and he hit the target. He sought advice from Kuan Yin who asked him, "Do you know why you hit the target?"

Kuan Yin is a Taoist master and an archer. Lieh Tzu said, "I have become an expert. Technically, I have attained my goal. I have hit the target."

The master asked, "Do you know why you hit the target?" From where? Who are you? Who is this one that has hit the target? Have you looked deep into the source of your energies? Forget the target and look at the archer. Archery you have learned, what about the archer? Now you have to learn the archer. And the processes are very different. You have learned archery, but if you want to learn the archer you will have to unlearn archery."

By learning, you know the world; by unlearning, you know yourself. By learning, you accumulate knowledge; by unlearning, you become a knower. By learning, you hoard; by unlearning, you become nude, empty.

The master asked, "Do you know why you hit the target?" Why did he ask? That's what Socrates means when he says to his disciples that an unexamined life is not worth living. You may succeed, but your life is not worth living if it has not been examined so deeply that you know the source of it, the very foundation of it.

You see the flowers of a tree, but that is not real knowledge unless you go deep enough to know the roots. The flowers depend on the roots. The flowers are nothing but the innermost core of the roots, come to be expressed. The roots are carrying the poetry, the source, the juice, which will become flowers, which will become fruits, which will become leaves. And if you continually count the leaves and the flowers and the fruits and never go deep into the darkness of the earth, you will never understand the tree because the tree is in the roots.

Where are the roots of the archer? You have succeeded in hitting the target—that is a flowering—but where are your roots? Do you know why you hit the target? Do you know why these flowers have bloomed? Do you know from what source? The flower is the last activity, the most peripheral. The roots are the seed, the primary activity, the most basic. The roots can exist without the flowers, but the flowers cannot exist without the roots. You can cut the flowers off and another flower will come; in fact, a far better flower will come. If you cut the flower, the roots will take up the challenge immediately and they will send a bigger flower. They will say, "Let us see who wins."

I once had a gardener, a very rare man, a master-gardener, who used to win all the competitions in the city. Nobody was ever able to produce such big flowers as he—all sorts of flowers. I asked him, "What is your secret?"

He said, "This is my secret: I challenge the roots."

I said, "What do you mean?"

He said, "I cut the flowers. I don't allow ordinary flowers to happen to the tree at all. If the tree can give a hundred flowers, I allow only one. Ninety-nine I drop; I cut them off immediately because they are a waste. And the roots get madder and madder and angrier and angrier. And then comes the biggest flower—as if all one hundred flowers were made into one. Finally, the roots win. That is my secret: I make them mad."

You can cut the flower and it will come again; cut another and it will be replaced. But cut the roots and the tree is gone.

The master asked, "Do you know why you hit the target?" The disciple said, without any hesitation, without waiting for a single moment, "No." This is honesty. The disciple is really a disciple. It is Lieh Tzu himself, the man we have been talking about all this time. He said, "No." This is honesty.

If I ask you, "Do you know who you are?" only the very honest will say, "No." The dishonest will start brooding; the dishonest will say, "Let me think about it." What are you going to think about? If you know, you know; if you don't know, you don't know. What are you going to think about? Thinking means you will try to manage an answer, you will try to manufacture an answer. It is difficult to find a person who can admit that they don't know. And that is the one who can become a real disciple; that is the one who one day can know.

You will not say, "No." Somebody will say, "Yes, God exists. I know," and somebody else will say "I know there is no God"—but both know. Few are able to say, "I don't know."

Lieh Tzu said "No"—he is a real disciple, a true disciple, authentic. The disciple has to open his heart before the master—the disciple has to be nude. He cannot hide anything, because if you hide from the master you will never grow.

Lieh Tzu said, "No."

Then the Master said, "It won't do yet. It is good, you have progressed, and your no is a good indication, but it won't do yet. You have to go further still.

He went away to practice and after three years again reported to Kuan Yin.

What did Lieh Tzu do for three years? He had attained his target, so what was he doing for three years? The parable does not say, because this is a parable to be meditated upon. A parable is such that it says only a few things and leaves many things unsaid, so that you have to meditate and fill in the gaps. You have to find where the intervals are. And in those intervals lies the real thing.

What did he do for three years? When you have hit the target, what more can you do? He was unlearning. Learning was finished; learning was complete—so he was unlearning, or he was turning his eyes inward.

Watch. When an archer takes the bow and the arrow in his hand his eyes are on the target, naturally. So what was Lieh Tzu doing for three years? When he took up his bow and arrow he would look at the target, but deep down he would look at himself. The target became secondary. The arrow of his consciousness became a double-arrow—that's what Gurdjieff calls self-remembering.

When you look at me, you are seeing me; your consciousness is one-arrowed, aimed toward me. If you change…. This you can do right now, and it will be right to do it in order to understand. You are looking at me; your eyes are on me. If you are focused on me you will forget

道

yourself. This is a kind of forgetfulness. Now make your consciousness a double-arrow: Look at me and at the same time, simultaneously, look at yourself. Look at the seen and look at the seer.

When you are listening to someone, listen—but always become aware of the listener, too. The talker has to be listened to and the listener also has to be listened to. Then your consciousness has double arrows. Right now it is one-way traffic: you look at me and you are not looking at yourself. This is a sort of self-forgetfulness. If you look at me and simultaneously become capable of looking at yourself, in that moment self-awareness happens.

What Lieh Tzu did for three years in the forest was a harder task. Learning was simple. He was male. Now he had to become female. First he was trying to penetrate the target outside; now he started moving inside, into the womb of his own being. He became feminine.

Knowledge is aggression; knowing is passivity.

There are two types of mind mentioned in Tao: one they call *mui* and the other they call *ui*. *Mui* means "natural, relaxed," and *ui* means "unnatural, tense." When you are fighting with life you exist as *ui*; when you are flowing with life you exist as *mui*. Swimming, you function as *ui*; floating, you function as *mui*.

When you are in a let-go, it is the natural mind in tune with the whole, in tune with Tao. Then the birds singing are not a distraction—on the contrary, they enrich the silence. Then everything is allowed. All the doors are open. You are not resisting, you are not struggling, you simply are. That is the state of *mui*.

First Lieh Tzu learned and created the state of *ui*: he became aggressive, extroverted, pointed toward the outside. It was ambition. He succeeded; he fulfilled his target. Then the master said this was nothing, he had to go further. Then what did he do for three years? He became *mui*: he relaxed. He would sit silently and feel the let-go. And by and by, he would take his arrow and bow and release the arrow in a state of let-go. He would not shoot it—he would allow it to be shot. That is difficult. He would not shoot it—he would wait for it to shoot itself.

Herrigel tried with his master but could not succeed. Then one day, desperate, he said, "I don't think I will ever be able to succeed. I cannot understand what you call this mui; it is all nonsense. How can the arrow shoot itself if I don't shoot it? If I don't pull the bow, how can things happen on their own? It is impossible."

We can understand Herrigel. That is the Western attitude: "It is impossible."

The master said, "Then you can go."

Herrigel asked, "Will you give me a certificate?"

The master said, "Impossible, because you have not learned anything. Whatsoever you have learned you could have learned anywhere else, so it is of no significance that you were here. You can go." So Herrigel booked a flight, made the arrangements to leave, forgot all about everything. He had been there for three years—it was too long.

He went to say goodbye to the master, but the master was teaching other disciples so he had to wait. He sat on a bench while the master was teaching and for the first time he was in a relaxed state because now he was no longer worried—he was leaving, it was finished—and he was no longer greedy. There was no effort. He just looked—and he could see that the master was not shooting. The master took the bow in his hand, and he pulled on the bow with his hand—but the arrow shot itself. He could see it—it was a vision. How he had missed it up to now, he could not believe!

For three years he had been watching his master again and again, but his own logical mind had been an interference. It would not allow him to see. He said, "How can it be? He may be more of an expert, but how can it be that the arrow goes by itself?" This morning he could see it. Now he was relaxed. Now he was not worried about attaining anything When you are no longer engaged in effort, greed, or desire, you are relaxed.

He rushed to the master, touched his feet, and without saying anything took the bow from his hand and shot the arrow. And the master put his hand on his head and said, "You have done it. You can have the certificate. And you can still go because now there is no need to wait. Finished. You have known it, you have tasted it."

Things can happen on their own. You were born—you did not manage it. You fell in love—you did not do it. Hunger comes, you eat and feel satisfied. Thirst arises, you drink and feel quenched. You are young; you will become old. One day you will die. Everything is happening. The doer is a false illusion. Be in the state of *mui*.

The society creates the state of *ui*. It makes you unnatural, tense, knowledgeable; it makes you cultivated, cultured—but it creates a hard crust around your heart and you lose your real nature, Tao.

He went away to practice and after three years again reported to Kuan Yin. "Do you know why you hit the target?"—again the same question—*"I know,"* said Lieh Tzu. Again it is simple—as simple as the first "No." It is not a pretension. When a person pretends, he thinks before he says, "I know." He tries to rehearse it in his mind—that's what you call thinking. The answer is without any thinking on Lieh Tzu's part. It is as it is. First he said simply, "No." Now, in exactly the same humble way— with no claim, remember—he says, "I know."

Many times you get too involved in words. The Upanishads say that one who says "I know" does not know. Right—but there can be a person who says, "I know," and does know. If you can say, "I know," in a simple, humble way, with no claim, then there is no problem. When the Upanishads say that if a person says, "I know" he does not know, the emphasis of the Upanishadic seer is on the *I*. When somebody says, "I know" the emphasis is on the *I*; it is underlined. When a person *really* knows and says, "I know," the *I* is not underlined. The "know" is just a fact. How can Lieh Tzu say something untrue? If he knows, he knows. He has to say it. But it is not a claim.

So don't get too burdened with words. People do get burdened with words. For example, if a Vedantin reads this he will say, "He says 'I know' so he cannot know because of what the Upanishads say." Words are words, and one has to feel the innermost core of the words, the heart of the words.

When Lieh Tzu says "I know," he knows. And his "I know" means exactly the same as when the Upanishads say, "I don't know." It means exactly the same as when Socrates says, "I don't know a thing." By saying, "I don't know a thing," Socrates is denying the *I*. But by saying, "I know," as a simple fact, as an ordinary fact, with no claim, Lieh Tzu is doing a far greater miracle because—listen to it— sometimes a pretender can pretend and say, "I don't know," in the hope that you will think that he knows. Because the Upanishads say so and Socrates says so, a pretender can say, "I don't know," in the hope that you will think that he is a knower, that he is another Socrates. Mind is very cunning. So remember one thing: if a mind is simple, humble, and simply states the fact, then that is the truth—whatsoever the fact.

"It will do," said the master.

Very easily he said, "It will do." It is not a question of what Lieh Tzu is saying, it is a question of what Lieh Tzu is—the simplicity, humbleness, meekness of the person, the innocence of the person. When you say, "I know," a subtle ego arises. Just say the words "I know" and you will feel a subtle ego strengthening in you.

The master must have been looking into Lieh Tzu. Masters don't look at you, they look into you. They don't watch your face, they watch your heart. He must have looked into the heart when Lieh Tzu said, "I know." Did something arise there? Did something integrate, become an ego? Nothing. The space remained untouched, virgin. He said, "I know" and nothing happened inside him. The master said:

"It will do. Hold on to this awareness and do not lose it."

It is difficult to gain a glimpse of this let-go and it is easy to lose it, because for centuries, for many lives, we have practiced doing. When those moments of nondoing come, our whole

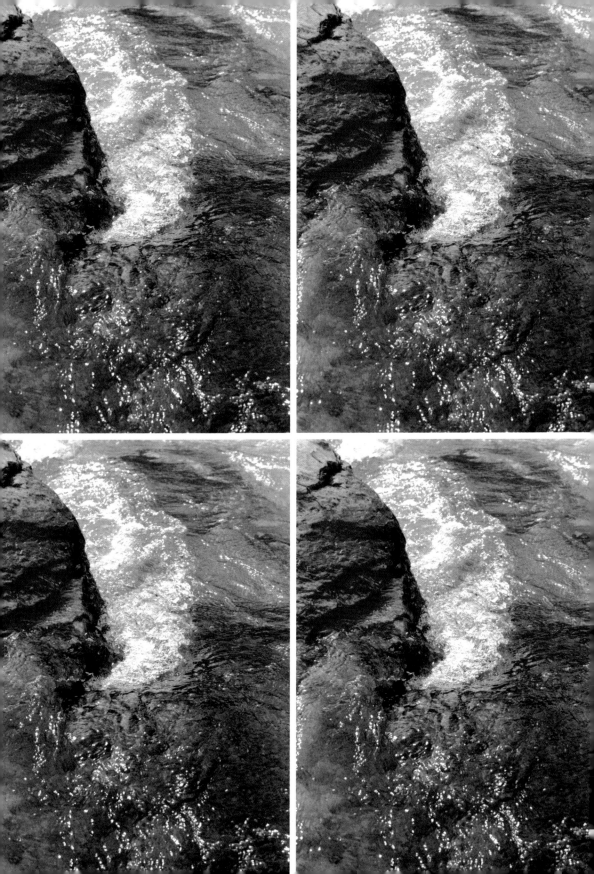

practice of many lives is against them; our habit is against them, our whole mechanism is against them. Their happening is a breakthrough and your past will struggle to close your doors again.

That's why the master says, "Hold on to this awareness and do not lose it." This is the treasure, the kingdom of God within you. This is the treasure—to be in a relaxed state and allow Tao to function. Now Lieh Tzu was not doing anything. Yes, he took the bow, he took the arrow, he aimed at the target, but he was not—it was Tao in him.

This applies not only to archery, but also to ruling oneself: therefore, the sage scrutinizes not the fact of survival or ruin, but its reasons.

"This applies not only to archery but to ruling oneself"—in fact, in Tao and Zen, archery is just a way to learn something about life. When somebody insults you, remember that the person who has insulted you is outside you, on the periphery, like the target. You are

deep within yourself, the source. And between you and the insulter stands the mind—like the arrow.

If your mind is arrowed on the person who has insulted you, you will miss. Let it be arrowed toward the source. Rather than thinking that he has insulted you, look into your own being: you must be carrying some wound, that's why you feel insulted. Otherwise, how can anybody insult you?

If somebody calls you a fool and you feel insulted that simply means you think that you are wise—nothing else. If you yourself think you are a fool, you will hug the person. You will say, "Right! Exactly right! That's how I feel!" Then where is the insult?

If somebody says you are a thief and you feel humiliated, that simply means that you have been thinking that you are a great moralist, virtuous, this and that—but deep down you know also that you are a thief. He has hit the sore spot in your being, a fragile

道

point. So now there are two possibilities: either you jump on him and prove that you are not a thief, or you look inside yourself.

Always go to the source. In yoga, going to the source is called *pratyahara*. Mahavira calls this going to the source *pratikramana*. Jesus calls it "repent." Christians have misunderstood this concept. *Repent* has nothing to do with repentance. Repent originally meant, "return, go back, go inside yourself." The Greeks have the right word for it: *metanoia*—turn into yourself, take a 180-degree turn. You must have seen in some old ancient mystery books the symbol of a snake eating its own tail—that is *metanoia*.

Go back to yourself. Rather than going to the other, turn back and go to yourself. Let your arrow move in a circle and come back to the source from where it started. Somebody has insulted you and turmoil arises—this is the beginning of the arrow. The arrow starts moving toward the other person. It wants to hit the other person, to insult the other person. Don't be deceived by it. Let it move in a circle. Let it come 180 degrees back to you—to where it started, to where you felt the turmoil. Let it come back; look there.

This can become the key for an inner transformation. A new being is possible. Archery is just a device. Taoists have created many devices. But in all devices the basic thing, the essential thing, is to turn to your own nature.

Meditate on this parable and start using it in your life. First, look for moments of letting go. Wait for them and receive them with great welcome and rejoicing. Invite them again and again. Become more feminine.

Second, if any opportunity arises when your arrow starts to move outward, remember immediately and turn it inward. Turn it in. Rather than turning on, turn in! If somebody insults and you are turned on, if a beautiful woman passes by and you are turned on and sex arises—turn in rather than turning on. A beautiful woman passing by is not the real target: you have some sexuality in you. Go to the source. Let it be a great opportunity for meditation. Transform each ordinary opportunity into meditation and great will be the payoff. Each moment will become luminous.

Remember that there is no mundane or profane activity. All activities can be turned into meditation—they have to be. This is my message, too. Meditation must not be something apart from life; it has to become the innermost core of it. Each activity, small and great, has to be luminous with meditative awareness. Then you will see that each activity brings you to your innermost core, each activity brings you home, each activity becomes a liberation.

Each activity has to fall back into the original source. The anger that arises from your being has to fall back into your being; the sex that arises from your being has to fall back to the source itself. There, where the alpha and the omega meet, where the beginning and the end meet, where the snake turns to its own tail and starts eating it, you become complete, a whole circle. That's the stage of the sage.

ko hsuan:

no doctrine, no teaching

Consciousness is experienced only when you are unconditioned and

not reconditioned again, when you are left alone to yourself, utterly

innocent. One can call it purity. That's the essence of Ko Hsuan's Tao.

The verses of Ko Hsuan are called The Classic of Purity. Tao has no

doctrines, no teachings. It believes in absolute emptiness of the mind,

in nothingness. When you are utterly empty you come in contact with

the beyond. The beyond is not far away, but you are so full of rubbish,

so full of junk, that there is no space for the beyond to enter in you. It

is like a room is full of furniture. Empty the room of all furniture: on the

one hand the room is emptied, all furniture is removed from the room;

on the other hand the room is becoming full of emptiness, the sky is

entering, the space is entering—the room is becoming more spacious.

That's what happens when your being is unconditioned and left alone.

道

the classic of purity

The Classic of Purity is one of the most profound insights into nature. I call it an insight—not a doctrine, not a philosophy, not a religion—because it is not intellectual at all; it is existential. The man who is speaking in it is not speaking from the mind. He is not speaking as himself, either; he is an empty passage for existence itself to say something through him.

THAT'S HOW THE great mystics have always lived and spoken. These are not their own words—they are no more, they have disappeared long before— it is the whole pouring through them. Their expressions may be different, but the source is the same. The words of Jesus, Zarathustra, Buddha, Lao Tzu, Krishna, and Mohammed are not ordinary words. They are not coming from the memory; they are coming from experience. They have touched the beyond, and the moment you touch the beyond you evaporate: you cannot exist any more. You have to die for God to be.

This is a Taoist insight. Tao is another name for God, far more beautiful than God, because the word *God* has been exploited too much by the priests. They have exploited in the name of God for so long that even the word has become contaminated. Anyone of intelligence is bound to avoid it because it reminds you of all the nonsense that has happened on the earth down the ages in the name of God, in the name of religion. More mischief has happened in the name of God than in any other name.

Tao in that sense is tremendously beautiful. You cannot worship Tao because Tao does not give you any idea of a person. It is a principle, not a person. You cannot worship a principle— you cannot pray to Tao. It would look ridiculous, it would be utterly absurd to pray to a principle. You don't pray to the law of gravity; you cannot pray to the theory of relativity.

Tao is the ultimate principle that binds the whole of existence together. Existence is not chaos; that much is certain. It is a cosmos. There is immense order in it, an intrinsic order in it, and the name of that order is Tao.

Tao simply means the harmony of the whole. No temples have been built for Tao: no statues, no prayers, no priests, no rituals— that's the beauty of it. Hence, you cannot call it a doctrine, nor can you call it a religion. It is a pure insight. You can call it Dharma; that is Buddha's word for Tao. The word in English that comes closest to Tao is *Nature*, with a capital N.

This profound insight of Ko Hsuan is also one of the smallest treatises ever written. It is condensed—as if millions of roses have been condensed into one drop of perfume. That's the ancient way of expressing truth: because books were not in existence, people had to remember it.

It is said that Ko Hsuan's *Classic of Purity* is the one of the first mystic treatises ever set down in book form. It is not much of a book; not more than a couple of pages, but it existed for hundreds of years before it was written. It existed through private and personal communion. That has been always the most significant way to transmit truth. To write it down makes it more difficult because then one never knows who will be reading it; it loses all the immediacy of personal contact and touch.

In Egypt, in India, in China, in all the ancient civilizations, for thousands of years, the mystic message was carried from one person to another, from the master to the disciple. And the master would say these things only when the disciple was ready, or he would say only as much as the disciple could digest.

For centuries all the mystics resisted writing down their insights. This was the first treatise ever written; that's its significance. It marks a certain change in human consciousness, a change that was going to prove of great importance later on, because even though it is beautiful to commune directly, person to person, the message cannot reach many people; many are bound to miss. True, if it is not written down it will not fall into the wrong hands, but many right hands will also remain empty. And one should think more of the right hands than of the wrong hands. The wrong people are going to be wrong whether some profound insight falls into their hands or not, but the right people will be missing something that can transform their being.

Ko Hsuan, who wrote this small treatise, marks a milestone in the consciousness of humanity. He understood the significance of the written word, knowing all its dangers. In the preface he writes: "Before writing down these words I contemplated ten thousand times whether to write or not, because I was taking a dangerous step." Nobody had gathered that much courage before. But he also says, "Ten thousand times I contemplated," because it is no ordinary matter.

Even a man like Buddha contemplated for seven days before uttering a single word. When he attained enlightenment, for seven days he remained utterly silent, wavering about

whether to say anything or not. His question was: "Those who cannot understand, what is the point of talking to them about such profound insights? They will misunderstand. They will misinterpret and do harm to the message. Rather than allowing the message to heal them, they will wound the message itself—they will manipulate the message according to their own minds and prejudices. Is it right to allow the message to be polluted by foolish people, by mediocre people, by ignorant people?"

Buddha was very hesitant. Yes, he also thought of the few people who would be able to understand it, but then he could see: "Those people who are able to understand my words will be able to find truth on their own, because they cannot be ordinary people. They would have to be the most intelligent people; otherwise, they would not be able to understand what I am saying to them. If they can understand my words they will be able to find their own way, they will be able to reach the truth on their own, so why bother about them? Maybe it will take a little longer for them. So what? Because there is eternity, time is not short. But the message, once it gets into the wrong hands, will be corrupted forever." Even to utter anything at all, Buddha was hesitant.

I can understand Ko Hsuan contemplating over the matter ten thousand times—whether to write it down or not—because when you *say* something to people, if they are stupid they are bound to forget it very soon. If they are mediocre people they will not bother even

> *Unless you have tasted something of no-mind, you cannot understand a paradox.*

道

to listen; they won't care. But once it is written down then they will read it, study it. Then it will become part of their schools, colleges, and universities, and scholars will ponder over it and they will write great scholarly treatises on it. People who know nothing will be talking about it for centuries and the truth will be lost in all that noise that scholars make. They will argue for and against it.

It is said that once a disciple of the devil ran to him and said, "What are you doing sitting here under this tree? Have you not heard?—one man has found the truth! We have to do something, and urgently, because if this man has found the truth our existence is in danger. Our profession is in danger—he can cut our very roots!"

The old devil laughed. He said, "Calm down, please. You are new, that's why you are so disturbed by it. Don't be worried. I have got my people, they have already started working."

The disciple said, "But I have not seen any of our people there."

The devil said, "I work in many ways. Scholars are there, pundits are there, philosophers are there, and theologians are there. Don't be worried. They will make so much noise for and against, they will create so much argumentation, that the still small voice of truth will be silenced by them. We need not worry. These scholars and pundits and these professors are my people: I work through them—they are in my service, they are my secret agents. Don't be worried. You may not have seen my disciples there, because I have to go in disguise. But I have arrived there and my people have started working—they have surrounded the person; he cannot do any harm. And soon he will be dead—he is old—and then my people will be his apostles, his priests, and they will manage the whole affair."

Priests are in the service of the devil, not in the service of God. The so-called great scholars who go on and on with logic-chopping, hair-splitting arguments are in the service of the devil, not in the service of God. Once you write down something you are giving a chance to these people; they won't miss the opportunity. They will mess the whole thing up; they will create great confusion around it. That is their expertise.

Hence, I can understand Ko Hsuan contemplating ten thousand times whether to write or not. But finally he decided to write and I think he did the right thing. One should never be afraid of darkness. Light, however small, is far more powerful than darkness, however big, however old.

In fact, darkness has no power. Light has power. These words are powerful words. The way the mystics speak the truth, it is almost beyond the scholars; they cannot destroy its beauty. In fact, they cannot even touch its truth; it is impossible for the simple reason that the mystics speak in a paradoxical language. They don't speak logically; thus, they are beyond the grasp of the scholars. The scholars can only see contradictions, because the scholar functions through logic and all the mystic expressions are paradoxical—illogical or supralogical. Taoist sayings in particular are superb in that way; nobody has been able to sort out their paradoxes. Even in this small treatise there are paradoxes almost in every sentence, in every utterance.

That, too, has to be understood. Why do mystics speak in paradox? To remain unavailable to the scholars. The paradox can be understood only by a meditator; it can never be understood by a person who lives in the head, in the mind. Unless you have tasted something of the no-mind, you cannot understand a paradox. That is a safeguard, an inbuilt safeguard. Speak paradoxically, speak as if you are almost mad.

Once a journalist went to see George Gurdjieff. Gurdjieff was drinking his morning tea. He always avoided journalists because they are the most mediocre people around, and his way of avoiding them was unique. He asked the woman who was pouring tea for him, as the journalist sat by his side, "What day is it today?"

The woman said, "Today is Saturday."

Gurdjieff went into a rage and threw the cup on the floor. The cup was shattered into thousands of pieces. The journalist became very much afraid...because it was Saturday, and Gurdjieff said, "You are always talking nonsense to me! Just the other day you were telling me that it was Friday and now today it is Saturday? How can it be? How can Saturday come after Friday?"

The journalist thought this man was mad. He escaped without even saying goodbye, and Gurdjieff had a good laugh. He said, "Now this man will never come back; I have put him off for his whole life. He will go and spread rumors about me to his professional colleagues, so not only has he been thrown out, many more who might have bothered me will never come here." He was thought to be a madman, utterly mad.

The paradoxical statements of the mystics have a purpose. The purpose is so that the scholars will avoid them. The moment the scholars come across a mystic, deep down they will believe that this person is mad and they won't waste their time.

Secondly, paradox is the only way to indicate something that is true. Logic is always half, it never takes in the whole, it cannot take in the whole. Life consists of polarities: just as electricity consists of positive and negative poles, the whole of life consists of polarities. And polarities are only *apparently* opposite to each other; deep down they are not. Deep down, for those who understand, for those who have the intelligence to see that deeply, they are not opposites, they are complementaries.

But for that you will need a deep experience of meditation; the mind alone won't help. The mind will say, "These are contradictory statements. This person is saying one thing at the beginning of the sentence but by the end of the sentence has uttered just the opposite." But the mystic knows what he is doing: he is trying to put the whole truth in what he is saying. The whole truth can be understood only by a person who has tasted something of the whole.

Mind always splits things; it divides, it separates, it functions like a prism. When a white sunray passes through the prism, it is divided into seven colors. That's how a rainbow is created: it is created by small drops of water hanging in the air. Those drops of water function like prisms and the sunrays passing through them are divided into seven colors. The mind is a prism; it divides one thing into many. The truth is one, but if you look through the mind, it appears to be many. The mystic's way of saying things is such that he wants to put all the colors of the rainbow back together again as they were in the beginning before they passed through the prism.

Because of this paradoxical way of expression, scholars avoid the mystics. People who live in the mind cannot comprehend them; it is a safeguard. That's how such beautiful treatises have survived for centuries.

Ko Hsuan is simply writing it, remember; he is not the creator of the treatise. He has also experienced the same truth, because the truth

> **" The mind is a prism; it divides one thing into many. The truth is one. "**

is always the same, whoever experiences it. Whenever one experiences it, it is always the same; it does not change; time makes no difference. But what he is saying has been transferred by word of mouth for hundreds, maybe thousands of years. That's why we don't exactly know whose words they are.

He begins like this:

The venerable master said:

The supreme Tao is formless, yet it produces and nurtures heaven and earth.

The supreme Tao has no desires, yet by its power the sun and moon revolve in their orbits.

The supreme Tao is nameless, yet it ever supports all things.

I do not know its name but for title call it Tao.

The venerable master said... Who is this master? Nothing is said about him. Perhaps the master simply represents all the masters of the past and all the masters of the present and all the masters of the future. Maybe it simply represents the essential wisdom—not any particular person, but simply the principle.

Nothing is known about Ko Hsuan, nothing at all. Hence, for a few centuries it had been thought that these words belonged to Lao Tzu.

But Lao Tzu has a different way of speaking, a totally different way; these words can't be coming from Lao Tzu. We have gone into the words of Lao Tzu; he is even more mad than Ko Hsuan, he is even more mystical. And it is a well-known fact that he never wrote anything other than the *Tao Te Ching*, and that he wrote under pressure, at the last moment, when he was leaving China to die in the Himalayas.

He had decided to die in the mountains, and you cannot find a more beautiful place to die than the Himalayas—the silence of the Himalayas, the virgin silence, the beauty, nature in its most profound splendor. So when he became very old he said to his disciples, "I am going to the Himalayas to find a place where I can disappear into nature, where nobody will know about me, where no monument will be made in honor of me, no temple, not even a grave. I simply want to disappear as if I had never existed."

When he was passing through the country he was stopped at the border because the king had alerted all the borders and ordered that, "If Lao Tzu passes out of the country through any gate he should be prevented unless he writes down what he has experienced." His whole life Lao Tzu had avoided this. In the end, it is said, because he was caught on the border and they wouldn't allow him to go to the Himalayas, he stayed in a guard's hut for three days and wrote down the small treatise, *Tao Te Ching*.

So it cannot be that *The Classic of Purity* belongs to Lao Tzu. But because nothing much is known about Ko Hsuan, people used to think that it must be the words of Lao Tzu, and that

Ko Hsuan must have been a disciple of Lao Tzu who simply wrote them down—the notes of a disciple. That's not so. Ko Hsuan himself is a master in his own right.

In the preface to his treatise, he says a few things that have to be remembered. First he says, "When I attained to union with Tao, I meditated upon this insight ten thousand times before writing it down." He says, "When I attained union with Tao…" He is not just a disciple; he is an enlightened man. He has attained union with Tao. He is not writing notes on what he heard from somebody else, he has experienced it himself. He has attained to the ultimate union with Tao; he has become one with nature.

He says in the preface, "It is only for the seekers of the beyond; the worldly cannot understand it." He makes it clear in the preface that if you are a worldly person, it is not meant for you, it will not be of any use to you. It may even confuse you and distract you from your worldly affairs. Don't waste your time. It is better not to get involved with things in which you are not really interested. It is better not to be accidental.

There are many people who are accidental, who are just "by the way." They will meet somebody and become interested. These people are like driftwood: they simply move with any wave; they are at the mercy of the winds, having no sense of direction.

Ko Hsuan says, "It is only for the seekers of the beyond." He makes it clear that if you are a seeker of the beyond, if you are ready to risk, then move forward, because the search for the

道

> *The first thing to decide is whether there is a deep longing in you to know the truth.*

beyond is risky. It is the greatest adventure, tremendously ecstatic, but not easy at all; it is arduous. It has its ecstasy and it has its agonies—it has its own cross. Of course, resurrection comes through it, but the resurrection cannot happen unless you are crucified. So he makes it clear that it is only for the seekers.

You have to be certain about yourself, whether you are a seeker or not. Are you interested in truth?—because every child is distracted from the very beginning. Few children seem to be interested in God, but so many parents force the idea of God on their children. If by chance you happen to be born into a family of atheists, then they impose the idea of atheism on you. If you are born in a communist country then, of course, communism will be imposed upon you. If not the Bible, then *Das Kapital*. If not the holy trinity, then the trinity of Marx, Engels, and Lenin, but something is bound to be imposed upon you.

No parent is loving enough to leave you alone to yourself to grow, to help you, to nourish you, and to give you total freedom to be yourself, authentically yourself. Hence, there are many people who think they are seekers of God—but they are not. Their seeking is an imposed phenomenon, a conditioning. If you are searching for God only because you have been told again and again to do it, then the word has become a reality in you but it is not part of you. It is not intrinsic; it has come from the outside and you are just like a parrot—or perhaps parrots are more intelligent than you are.

An overly enthusiastic Italian communist finds a parrot that can sing the popular communist song, "Bandiera Rosa." He buys it and takes it home, but after a few days the wife can no longer stand it. The parrot keeps singing the song all day long.

In a moment of rage she knocks the parrot over and then covers it with a cloth. When the husband comes back she tells him everything.

In despair the man lifts the cloth to see how the parrot is.

Opening one eye the parrot whispers, "Hey, comrade, are those dirty fascists gone?"

Even parrots are more intelligent than so-called human beings, who simply repeat clichés that have been handed over to them by their parents, priests, and teachers, schools, colleges, universities. This society conditions you in a certain way, and after twenty-five years of conditioning, if you forget what you really want to do, what you really want to be, it is only natural.

The first thing to decide is whether there is a deep longing in you to know the truth. Are you ready to risk everything for it, even your life if the need arises? If it is so, "Then," Ko Hsuan says, "...these words are for you." If you are only a worldly person—by "worldly" he means one who is interested in money, power, prestige—then it would be better if you don't bother about such great things. They are not for you—at least, not yet. First you have to become fed up with all your worldly desires. Go into those desires. Unless you become tremendously frustrated, unless you see that they are all futile—that whether you succeed or fail you always fail; that whether you have money or you are poor you are always poor; that whether you are a beggar or an emperor you are always a beggar...when that insight dawns on you, only then can you become a seeker of the beyond. Otherwise, if you pretend to be a seeker of the beyond, you will bring your whole world with you, you will bring all your desires with you.

That's why people think of God, of heaven. It is not that they are interested in God and heaven; they are only interested in power and prestige. Maybe they are afraid of death, and out of fear and greed they start praying to God. But a prayer that arises out of fear and greed is not prayer at all. A real prayer arises out of gratitude, never out of fear and greed. A real prayer arises out of love for truth, whatsoever it may be. Otherwise, your worldly desires will again be projected onto God, onto heaven.

If you compare the descriptions of paradise in different religions and different countries, you will be surprised: what they desire is projected. For example, the Tibetan paradise is described as warm—obviously, because

Tibetans suffer from the cold so much that they would like heaven to be full of sun and warmth so that they can at least take a bath every day. In Tibet the scriptures say that it is your duty to take a bath at least once a year!

The Indian paradise is cool, air-conditioned. They did not know about air-conditioning at that time so it is described as "air-cooled." It is bound to be so—India has suffered so much from the heat, all the Indian mind wants is a little shade and coolness. So the Indian paradise is always full of cool breezes and there are big trees, so big that a thousand bullock carts can rest under a single tree. The Indian idea is of heaven is shade and coolness.

The Tibetan hell is absolutely icy and the Indian hell is full of fire. Now, there cannot be so many hells and so many paradises: these are our projections. Whatever we desire we project onto heaven and whatsoever we are afraid of we project onto hell. Hell is for others, for those who don't believe in our ideology, and paradise is a reward for those who do believe in our ideology—it is the same worldly mind. These are not religious people.

In the Mohammedan heaven there are streams of wine. This is very strange. Here you condemn wine—it is a sin—and there you reward your saints with wine?

All the paradises of all the cultures are full of beautiful women because the ideas of paradise are created by men. I have never come across a description of beautiful men. If women someday write about paradise, they won't talk about beautiful women, they will talk about beautiful men, men always following the women like shadows, obedient, just like servants! That's how women have been painted by men in their heaven.

And the women are always young; they never grow old. This is strange! If you look at the idea of God, all the religions think of God as a very old man. Have you ever thought of God as a young man? No country has ever thought of God as a young man because you cannot trust young people: they are dangerous and a little foolish, too. A wise man has to be old, so God is very old. But the women he is surrounded with are all very young—in fact, stuck at the age of eighteen; they don't grow beyond that. Stagnant! They must be getting tired of remaining eighteen for millions of years. But this is a man's idea. Here the saints renounce women, they renounce sex; they condemn sex, they praise celibacy—and, of course, they are hoping they will be paid well: they will be rewarded with beautiful young women in heaven.

These are our worldly desires coming from the unconscious; you cannot push them away. Unless you have encountered them, unless you have watched them, you cannot just repress them.

Ko Hsuan is right. He says, "The worldly cannot understand it." They are bound to misunderstand.

The new patient comes into the analyst's office. He is a theologian, a great scholar, and a philosopher. He says, "Doctor, I came here because everybody says I think too much of myself."

"Let's get into this," says the doctor. "To analyze your problem it is necessary that you

tell me your story; it is necessary that you tell me your problem from the very beginning."

"Okay," says the professor, and sitting down, he continues. "In the beginning all was darkness…"

You see? He really begins from the very beginning! His understanding is bound to remain with him wherever he goes, whatever he does. Whatever he chooses is going to be out of his mind and mentality. How long can you repress? How long can you hide? It is going to come up, if not from the front door, then from the back door.

Two madmen in an asylum look at the clock: it is twelve o'clock.

One says, "It is midday."

The other says, "It's midnight."

The discussion becomes so heated that they decide to ask the director. "Is it midday or midnight, sir?" they ask him.

The director looks at his watch and says, "Well, I don't know—my watch has stopped."

In a madhouse, you can't expect the director to be less mad than the madmen. In fact, he may be the director because he is more mad! He may be the oldest inmate; hence, he has been chosen to be the director.

Ko Hsuan says in his preface: "I received these words from the divine ruler of the Golden Gate."

Truth is always a gift; it is not an achievement, because all achievements belong to the ego and truth cannot be part of your ego trip. Truth happens only when the ego is dropped, so you cannot say, "I have achieved it," you can only say, "It has been given. It is a

doing for centuries and what masters have been instructing their disciples to do. Empty yourself, become a nothingness, and the moment you are absolutely nothing, at that very moment, truth descends in you—you become full of it. First you have to be empty of yourself and then you become full of God, Tao, Dharma, or whatever name you choose to call it.

Ko Hsuan says, "I received it from the divine ruler of the Golden Gate." This is a mysterious saying, "the Golden Gate." That is the Taoist way of saying that God is not a person but a gate, an opening into existence. If you are empty, the door opens *within you*. It is your ego that is blocking the door; it is *you* who are blocking the door; except for you, there is no hindrance. Remove yourself, don't stand between, and suddenly the Golden Gate opens. It is called "golden" because the moment you pass through it, you are pure gold. The dust disappears, is transmuted, is transformed; it becomes divine.

This is the definition of alchemy: transforming dust into the divine, transforming base metal into gold. And it happens simply by becoming a receiver. You have to be utterly a nonentity.

gift." Ko Hsuan is right. He says, "I received it..."

Remember: you have to be at the receiving end. You are not to be aggressive about truth. The real seeker is not an achiever. The real seeker is not aggressive, is not masculine.

When you are a real seeker you become feminine. You are like a womb—you receive. You empty yourself completely, so that space is created to receive. That's the whole art of meditation, and that's what mystics have been

Ko Hsuan says, "It has been previously only transmitted by word of mouth. Those who will be able to comprehend the meaning will become ambassadors of the divine and enter the Golden Gate."

This small preface says, "Those who will be able to comprehend it, understand it, will become ambassadors of the divine...." Not that they *have to* become, they will become—

naturally, without any effort, effortlessly. They *will* start radiating godliness, they will start radiating light, and they will become luminous. Miracles will happen through them without any effort.

It is said that many miracles happened in Ko Hsuan's life. They are the same miracles that have been happening to many mystics. For example, it is said that he was able to walk on water. The same is said about Jesus. It is not a fact, remember—Jesus is not so foolish neither is Ko Hsuan so foolish; as to walk on water. There is no need to walk on water. Then what does it mean? It is a poetic expression; it is a metaphor. It means they were able to do the impossible. And what is the most impossible thing in the world? The most impossible thing in the world is to transcend the world. The most impossible thing in the world is to know oneself. The most impossible thing in the world is to become utterly empty.

This is a metaphor: "walking on water." Don't take it as fact. It is a poetic way of saying something.

The second thing said about Ko Hsuan is that he knew the secret of the elixir of life, the secret of alchemy. One who knows his consciousness—the consciousness that is a witness to his thoughts—one who comes to know his state of no-mind, knows absolutely that there is no death for him. No birth, no death—he knows that he has never been born and will never die; he has gone beyond both. This is the secret of life; this is the secret science of alchemy.

The third thing said about Ko Hsuan is that he ascended to the beyond in the full light of day. That is said about Mohammed also, and about many others. These are all beautiful ways of expressing the inexpressible. These people have ascended to the ultimate, but not by any back door; they have achieved to the ultimate in the full light of the day. Those who had eyes have seen them ascending. Those who had ears have heard the music when they were ascending. Those who had hearts to feel have felt their transformation. These people lived on the earth and yet they belonged not to the earth. They were not earthly people; they were utterly unearthly.

Don't be misguided by religious fanatics who insist that these metaphors are not metaphors but facts, that these poetic expressions are not poetic expressions, but part of history. Be a little more poetic if you really want to understand the mystic way of life.

The perfection of paradise was such that Peter got bored. One day, when everyone was sitting all together, he said to God, "I am so bored...I'd love to visit earth now and then, wouldn't you?"

"Not at my age," replies God.

Says Jesus, "Once has been enough for me."

Says the Holy Ghost, "Not until they stop shooting at doves!"

Jesus is called by his Father, who tells him that he has to sacrifice himself once more for the redemption of mankind.

Though rather unwillingly, Jesus agrees to go.

He goes around heaven saying goodbye to all his friends and promising to come back in thirty-three years. Then, followed by all the angels, he comes down to earth.

Thirty-three years go by, but there is no sign of Jesus. Finally, after eighty years, a lean old man comes to heaven saying that he is Jesus. He is taken to God, who recognizes him immediately and exclaims in astonishment, "What happened? Why did you take so long?"

"Well, you see, Father," replies Jesus, "... there is no more capital punishment on earth, so I was condemned to a life sentence!"

Jesus is walking among the people and performing miracles. Suddenly a man falls at his feet and says, "Lord, Lord, cure me, cure me!"

"Calm down, son. Have faith and you will be cured."

Jesus moves closer to the man and looks into his eyes, then backs away and signals to Peter to come over. As Peter draws near, Jesus whispers to him, "It's not going to work, Peter. Pretend we have to go—he's got cancer!"

Reality is reality!

Either these miracles are metaphors or some coincidence. For example, Lazarus coming back to life—he may have been in a coma. Or it may be just a beautiful metaphor, because every master calls his disciple to come back to life from his grave. Ordinarily, you are dead; you have not tasted of life at all. You are all Lazaruses! And Lazarus was dead for only four days; everybody has been dead for millions of lives. It would certainly be a miracle to call you forth! And if you listened and came back to life it would be just as much a miracle done by you as it would be a miracle done by the master. In fact, you will be doing a greater miracle than the master!

The same miracles are described in all the lives of the saints; there are not many differences for the simple reason that every mystic lives such a life that he is in the world and yet not in the world. How to express it? How to say something significant about him? It can be said only through miracles. The language of miracles is the only possible way to express something, at least to hint at something, that is indescribable.

But there are foolish people who cling to these things and then start creating an account of history. They are not helpful in spreading the divine message; they create obstacles and hindrances. In fact, many more intelligent people would be with Jesus if all these miracles and the nonsense attached to them were dropped. Yes, fools would desert him because they are only with him because of the miracles, but intelligent people would be with him.

Sometimes coincidences happen and sometimes a series of coincidences can make a person believe. When these things happen—and these things can happen, it is such a vast world—people are bound to believe. People are gullible. But there are no miracles. There is only one miracle—*the* miracle—and that is your being utterly empty. The death of the ego is the only miracle; if that happens you have passed through the Golden Gate. You have known what eternity is; you have gone beyond time.

Now these small verses of Ko Hsuan:

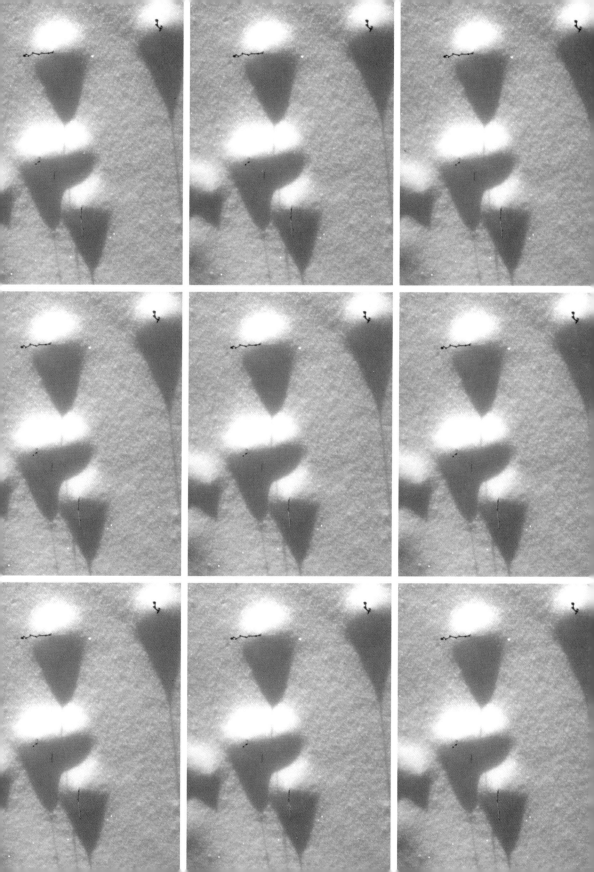

The venerable master said,

"The supreme Tao is formless..."

From the beginning, Ko Hsuan wants you to know that Tao has no form, so you cannot make a statue of Tao, you cannot create a temple around Tao, you cannot create rituals; no priesthood is possible.

The supreme Tao is formless; it is the universal law of existence. You cannot worship it and you cannot pray to it. All your worship is foolish and all your prayers are unheard and will remain unheard. There is nobody to hear your prayers or to fulfill your prayers. Your prayers are your desires in a new form. Watch your prayers—see what they are. The garb is religious, the jargon is religious, but nothing has changed; the desires are the same. People are asking for money, power, prestige. Whatever you are asking for, you are asking for something wrong, because there is nobody to give you anything. The very idea of receiving by asking is absurd. Be utterly silent.

Tao is not the path of prayer. It is the path of meditation.

"...Tao is formless, yet it produces and nurtures heaven and earth."

It does not mean that Tao is indifferent to you; it simply means you cannot worship it, you cannot pray to it. But it nourishes you, it nurtures you. The whole breathes it. It is the heartbeat of the cosmos, but not a person.

"The supreme Tao has no desires..."

If you want to have a communion with Tao, you will have to drop all desires. People change their desires, but they basically remain the same. People change their outer structures

of life: they call it "character." Somebody smokes, you may not smoke, you start chewing gum. It is the same stupidity. Or you may stop chewing gum and start doing something else. But because you are the same, nothing is going to change. If you go to the moon, you will do the same things that you are doing here. Everything will be different and nothing will be different.

A human couple has been captured by aliens from Mars and is taken to the living room of the flying saucer. They are greeted by a Martian couple, offered green drinks, and begin chatting. After several drinks, everyone relaxes. The man from Earth asks the Martians, "How do you procreate?"

"My wife and I will demonstrate for you," answers the Martian.

The Martians go over to a refrigerator-like closet and the female picks up a bottle containing brown liquid and the male picks up a bottle containing white liquid. They go over to a table where there is an empty jar. Each pours the liquid into the empty jar.

"Now we put the jar in this closet," explains the Martian, "and in nine months we will have another baby. How do you do it on Earth?"

So the Earth couple demonstrates for the Martians. They take off their clothes and lie down on the floor with the man on top of the woman. As they are coming and going, they notice the Martians are laughing at them.

"What are you laughing at?" they ask.

"Excuse us," they answer, "...but we find it very funny because that is the same way we make coffee!"

You can be here, you can be on the moon,

you can be on Mars, you can change outer things—it makes no difference. Either you will make love in a stupid way or you will make coffee in a stupid way, but you will do something stupid unless intelligence arises in you, unless your unconsciousness is transformed into consciousness, unless your darkness disappears and becomes light.

The supreme Tao has no desires yet by its power the sun and moon revolve in their orbits. The supreme Tao is nameless, yet it ever supports all things. I do not know its name...

These are immensely valuable words: "I do not know...." That's how the people who know speak. The people who claim that they know are utterly ignorant. The real knower functions out of a state of not knowing.

Ko Hsuan says, *I do not know its name... but for title call it Tao.*

We have to call it something. Note the non-fanatic attitude. You can call it anything—XYZ. Tao simply means XYZ. Because we have to call it something, we call it Tao. If you choose some other name, there is no problem.

When Buddhists reached China they were surprised because Taoist mystics agreed with them. They said, "Perfectly right! We call it Tao; you call it Dharma. It is the same thing, because we define Tao as nameless and you define Dharma as nameless. We say Tao is formless and you say Dharma is formless, so there is no problem. We are only speaking different languages, but we are indicating the same truth."

That is one of the most beautiful things that has ever happened in history. When Buddhism reached China there was no conflict, no

THE PRACTICAL WAY

Tao does not believe in miracles; it believes in scientific methods to transform your life.

Lao Tzu, Chuang Tzu, and Lieh Tzu were walking together along a forest path one day when they came upon a fast-flowing river that barred their way. Immediately Lieh Tzu sat down on the bank of the river and meditated upon the eternal Tao. Ten minutes later he stood up and proceeded to walk on the water to the other side.

Next, Chuang Tzu sat in the lotus posture for twenty minutes, whereupon he stood up and also walked across the river.

Lao Tzu, watching this in amazement, shrugged his shoulders, sat down on the riverbank like the others and meditated for over an hour. Finally, with complete trust in the Tao, he closed his eyes, took one step into the river, and fell in.

On the other shore, Chuang Tzu laughed, turned to Lieh Tzu and said, "Should we tell him where the rocks are?"

Tao does not believe in any nonsense. It is very pragmatic, practical, and down to earth.

argumentation, no conversion, yet Buddhists and Taoists met and mingled and became absolutely one. It has not happened in the history of Christianity or Judaism or in the history of Mohammedanism: their history is full of ugliness. It has happened only in the tradition of Buddha and Lao Tzu. A very rare phenomenon—no argumentation. They simply tried to understand each other and they laughed and hugged and they said, "Perfectly true!"

A Christian missionary went to see a Zen master, and he started reading the beatitudes from the Bible. He said, "Blessed are the meek for theirs is the kingdom of God."

The Master said, "Stop! That's enough. Whoever has said it is a buddha."

The missionary was utterly dumbstruck. He had come to argue; he had come to convert; he had come to convince the Zen master that Buddha was wrong and Jesus was right. And this man said, "Whosoever has said it—I don't know who has said it—but whosoever has said it is a buddha. There is no need to read more; that one sentence is enough. You can taste the ocean from anywhere, it tastes the same—it is salty. This one sentence will do!"

The same happened in China. Buddhists arrived and the whole of China became Buddhist without anybody converting anybody else. Because Taoism was so generous and Buddhism was so understanding; there was no question of converting anybody. The whole idea of converting anybody is ugly, violent. They never argued—yes, they communed, they nodded at each other's understanding, and they said, "Yes, that's true. That's what Lao Tzu also says. That's what Buddha has said in his own words." And out of this meeting—which is the rarest in the whole of humanity—Zen was born. Out of the meeting of Buddha and Lao Tzu, out of the meeting of Buddha's insight and Taoist insight, out of the meeting of Dharma and Tao, Zen was born. Hence, Zen is a rare flowering. Nowhere else has it happened that way—so silently, without bloodshed, without a single argument. There was no question of argument; the difference was only of language.

This is how a truly religious person is. He is not a fanatic—he cannot be.

Ko Hsuan says:

I do not know its name but for title call it Tao.

It is a nameless experience, but we have to call it something so we will call it Tao. That is arbitrary. If you have some other name— God, Logos, Dharma, Truth, Nirvana—you can choose from those names; they are all beautiful. Because it has no name of its own, any name will do.

This approach should be our approach. We should not be part of any dogma—Christian, Mohammedan, Hindu. We should not belong to any church; that is all childish, political. A religious person is absolutely free from all dogma. Only in freedom understanding grows.

Understand this approach toward life; this is fundamental. Once you are rooted in it you will start growing. Great foliage will happen to you and great flowering and fulfillment.

TANTRA
the way of acceptance

The most basic thing about Tantra is this—and it is radical,

revolutionary, rebellious—the basic principle of Tantra is that the

world is not divided into the lower and the higher, but that it is one

piece. The higher and the lower are holding hands. The higher

contains the lower, and the lower contains the higher. The higher

is hidden in the lower—so the lower has not to be denied, has not

to be condemned, has not to be destroyed or killed. The lower has

to be transformed. The lower has to be allowed to move upward

and in that way the lower becomes the higher.

Another way of saying it is that there is no unbridgeable gap between the Devil and God—the Devil is carrying God deep down in his heart. Once that heart starts functioning, the Devil becomes God. In fact, the word *devil* comes from the same root as the word *divine*; it is the divine not yet evolved, that's all. Not that the Devil is against the divine, not that the Devil is trying to destroy the divine—in fact, the Devil is trying to *find* the divine. The Devil is on the way to the divine; it is not the enemy, it is a seed. The divine is the tree fully in bloom, and the Devil is the seed—but the tree is hidden in the seed. The seed is not against the tree; in fact, the tree cannot exist if the seed is not there. And the tree is not against the seed—they are in deep friendship; they are together.

Poison and nectar are two phases of the same energy. So are life and death—and so is everything: day and night, love and hate, sex and superconsciousness. Tantra says, Never condemn anything; the attitude of condemnation is destructive. By condemning something, you deny yourself the possibilities that would have become available to you if you had encouraged the lower to evolve. Don't condemn the mud, because the lotus is hidden in the mud. Use the mud to produce the lotus. Of course, the mud is not the lotus yet, but it can be. A creative person will help the mud to release its lotus, so that the lotus can be freed.

The Tantra vision is of tremendous import, particularly for the present moment in human history, because a new type of human being is striving to be born; a new consciousness is knocking on the door. The future is going to be that of Tantra because dualistic attitudes will no longer hold power over the human mind. For centuries, these dualistic attitudes have crippled human beings and made them feel guilty. They have not made people free, they have made them prisoners. They have not made people happy, either; they have made them miserable. They have condemned everything from food to sex; they have condemned *everything*—from relationship to friendship. Love is condemned, the body is condemned, the mind is condemned. They have not left a single inch for you to stand on; they have taken away everything, and you are left hanging.

This state cannot be tolerated any more. Tantra can give you a new perspective.

tantra: the meeting of

earth and sky

Have you watched a tree growing—how it gropes and grows—what method does it follow? From the seed comes the sprout, and then slowly, slowly, it starts rising upward. It comes from deep down in the earth, and then it starts rising into the sky, from root to trunk and branch and leaf and flower and fruit.... This is what happens with your tree of life, too. There is no distinction between the sacred and the profane.

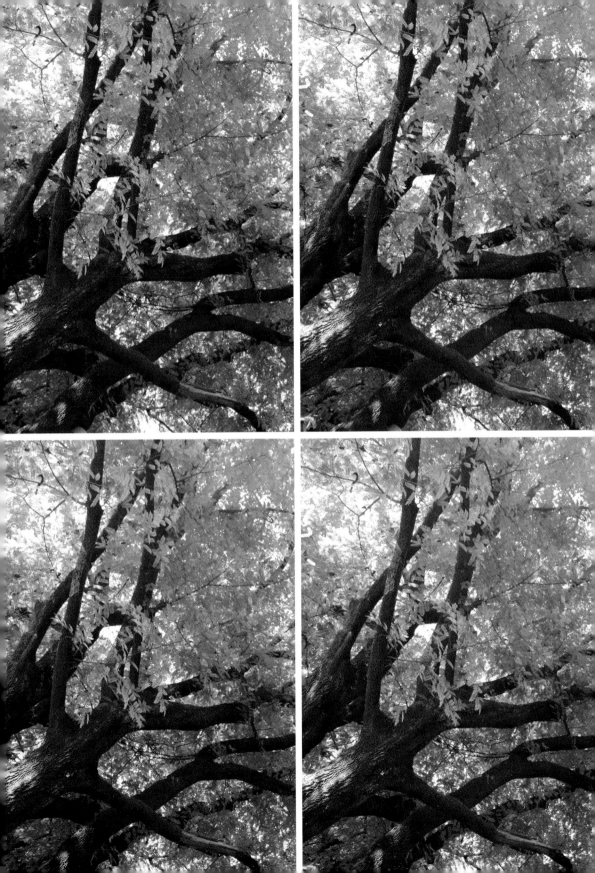

the serpent
is the savior

Sex is as sacred as Samadhi. The lowest and the highest are part of one continuum. The lowest rung is as much part of the ladder as the highest rung; they are nowhere divided. If you deny the lower, you will never be able to reach to the higher.

Sex is nothing to feel guilty about; it is your life. It is where you are—how can you avoid it? If you avoid it, you will be inauthentic, untrue. If you avoid it or repress it, you will not be able to move upward because your energy will be repressed through it.

When your sexuality starts moving, that's a good sign. It shows that you have been contacted, that something has stirred in you, that something has become a movement in you: you are no longer a stagnant pool—you have started flowing toward the ocean.

Certainly, the ocean is far away. It will come at the very end. But if you stop this small muddy pool from flowing, you will never reach the ocean. I know the mud of it, but it has to be accepted. You have to start flowing!

The serpent and the savior are not two—they are one. In fact, there is an ancient tradition that says that after God created Adam and Eve and told them they should not go to the Tree of Knowledge and they should not eat the fruit of it—then God became the serpent. He coiled himself around the tree and seduced Eve to eat the fruit of the tree. God himself became the serpent!

I love this story. Some Christians will be shocked. But only God can do such a thing—nobody else. From where can the serpent come? And without God's help, how can the serpent convince Eve? In fact, the whole thing was decided beforehand: God wanted man to go astray, because only by going astray does one become mature. God wanted man to commit sin, because only through sin does one someday arrive at sainthood. There is no other way.

That's why God said, "Don't eat the fruit of this tree!" This is simple psychology. What Christians say, if they are right, means that God is not even as much a psychologist as Sigmund Freud. It is simple psychology that if you prohibit somebody from something, that something becomes more attractive, more magnetic. If you say, "Don't do this!" you can be sure it will be done. Every parent knows this, and God is the ultimate parent. Will he not know it?

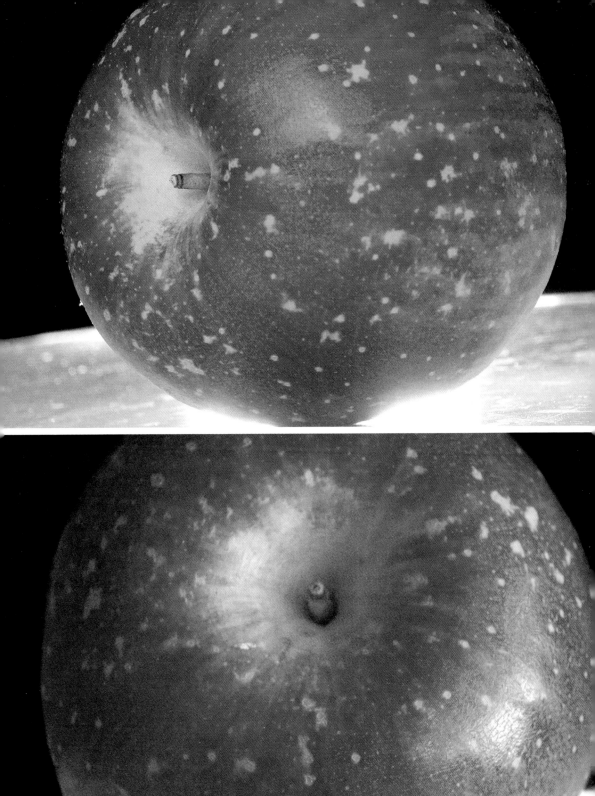

> *In the East, the serpent has never been in the service of the Devil; it has always been in the service of God.*

There is a story:

Freud had gone to a garden park with his wife and child, and they walked around in the beautiful spring evening. They were paying no mind to the child when suddenly it was time for closing. The bell began to ring and everybody was supposed to leave. Freud's wife said, "But where is our child? He has disappeared!" And it was a big park.

Freud said, "Tell me only one thing: did you prohibit him from going anywhere?"

And she said, "Yes, I told him not to go near the fountain."

Then he said, "Let's go. If my insight is true, he will be there at the fountain." And the child was found at the fountain.

The wife was puzzled; she said, "How did you know?"

Freud said, "This is simple psychology. Every parent should know."

No, I cannot trust the Christian interpretation that makes God look very foolish. He must have planned it, knowing perfectly well that if Adam was prohibited from eating the fruit—if he was told, commanded,

absolutely ordered to "Never touch the fruit of that tree!"—then it was absolutely certain that he would eat it.

But Adam was the first man, and was not aware of the ways of man yet. He was the first child and may have been an obedient child. There are obedient people, also. So God must have waited for a few days, and Adam did not go to the tree.

Now God must have decided to become a serpent and try through the woman, because when you cannot do anything to the man, the right way is always through the woman. He must have tried through the woman; he must have talked to Eve. And he succeeded!

That's why I say the serpent and the savior are one.

In the East, the serpent has never been in the service of the Devil; it has always been in the service of God. In the East, this is the symbology: the serpent is inside you, coiled at your sex center. It is called *kundalini*—the coiled serpent. It is there—asleep—at the lowest level, the roots. The tree of life is your spine—it holds your life; it is your trunk. It nourishes you, your energy runs through it, and the serpent is lying there at the base.

When anything stirs you it will stir the serpent, too, because that is where your energy is. So when it happens, don't be worried, don't feel guilty. Never feel guilty for anything! All that happens is good. The bad does not happen and cannot happen—the world is so full of godliness, how can the bad happen? The bad must be our interpretation.

Sex and superconsciousness are both the same energy. The serpent and the savior are not two. There is a link between the lowest and the highest. There is a sequence that leads from one to the other—a way of life, a way of love, natural and inevitable as the way of a growing tree.

Have you watched a tree growing, how it gropes and grows upward—what method does it follow? From the seed comes the sprout, and then slowly, slowly, it starts rising upward. It comes from deep down in the earth and then it starts rising into the sky, from root to trunk and branch and leaf and flower and fruit.... This is what happens with your tree of life, too.

There is no distinction between the sacred and the profane.

There is no separation between divine love and human, four-lettered love. It is one continuity. Your love and divine love are two ends of the same phenomenon, the same energy. Your love is too muddy, true—too full of many other things like hatred, anger, jealousy, and possessiveness—true. But still it is gold—mixed with mud—but still it is gold. You have to pass through fire, and all that is not gold will be gone and only gold will remain.

Accept yourself, because only through acceptance is transformation possible. If you start feeling guilty, you will become repressive.

At the temples of Khajuraho and Konarak in India, you will see what I am talking about. These are Tantra temples, the most sacred temples that still exist on the earth. All other temples are ordinary. Only Khajuraho and

Konarak, these two temples, have a message that is not ordinary, that is extraordinary— extraordinary because it is true.

What is their message?

If you have been to these temples, you will have seen illustrated on the outer sunlit walls all kinds of sexual postures—men and women making love in so many postures, conceivable and inconceivable, possible and impossible. The walls are full of sex. You are shocked. You start thinking, "What obscenity!" You want to condemn it; you want to lower your eyes. You want to escape. But that is not because of the temple; it is because of the priests and their poisons inside you.

Go inside. As you move inside the temple, the figures become fewer and fewer, and the quality of the love starts changing. On the outer walls is pure sexuality; as you enter inside, you will find that sex is disappearing. Couples are still there—deeply in love, looking into each other's eyes, holding hands, embracing each other—but the sexuality is no longer there. Go still deeper— the figures are even fewer. Couples are there, but they are not even holding hands, not even touching. Go still deeper and the couples have disappeared. Go still deeper....

At the innermost core of the temple— what in the East is called the *gharba*, the womb—there is not a single figure. The crowd is gone; the many are gone. There is not even a window to the outside. No light comes from the outside; it is utter darkness, silence, calm, and quiet. There is

> **When sex is accepted naturally, it starts growing higher.**

not even a figure of a god—it is emptiness, it is nothingness.

The innermost core is nothingness, and the outermost circumference is a carnival. The innermost core is meditation, *samadhi*, and the outermost circumference is sexuality. This is the whole life of humanity depicted. But remember: if you destroy the outer walls, you will destroy the inner shrine, too, because the innermost silence and darkness cannot exist without the outer walls. The center of the cyclone cannot exist without the cyclone. The center cannot exist without the circumference. They are together!

Your outermost life is full of sexuality— perfectly good and perfectly beautiful! Khajuraho simply depicts you. It is the human story in stone; it is the human dance in stone—from the lowest to the highest rung of the ladder, from the many to one, from love to meditation, from the other to one's own emptiness and aloneness.

Courageous were the people who created these temples. The still point is shown together with the turning world.

The way of Tantra is neither one of blind sensuality nor only of spirituality. It is of both/and. Tantra does not support the philosophy of either/or; it supports the philosophy of both/and. It does not reject anything—it transforms everything.

Only cowards reject. If you reject something you will be that much poorer, because something will have been left untransformed. A part of you will remain ungrown; a part of you will remain childish. Your maturity will never be complete. It will be as if one leg remains on the first rung of a ladder and your hand has reached the last rung: you will be stretched along this polarity and you will be in anguish, in agony; your life will not be of ecstasy.

That's why I preach Epicurus and Buddha together. Epicurus remains with the outer wall of the Khajuraho temple: he is right as far as he goes, but he does not go far enough. He simply takes a walk around the temple and goes home. He is not aware that he has missed the very point of the temple. Those outer walls are only outer walls; they exist to support the inner shrine.

Buddha goes into the inner shrine and sits there. In that silence he remains, but he forgets about the outer wall. And without the outer wall there is no inner shrine.

To me, both are lopsided. Something has been rejected and something has been chosen—they have not been choiceless. I say accept all—the outer and the inner, the without and the within—and you will be the richest people upon the earth.

Tantra is the way of wholeness—neither obsession with the world, nor withdrawal from it. It is being in the world lightly, with a little smile. It is playfulness. It doesn't take things seriously. It is light of heart; it laughs. It is unashamedly earthly and infinitely otherworldly. The earth and the sky meet in Tantra; it is the meeting of polar opposites.

If you go to Khajuraho, you will see it: on the face of every lover sculpted on the outer walls, there is great ecstasy. Many people go to Khajuraho and Konarak, but they only look at the lower half of these figures: they become focused on the genitalia. Few people have been able to see the whole figures. And rarely has anybody been able to see the faces of the figures, because people are so obsessed with sexuality—for or against—that they remain confined to the lower.

If you go to see Khajuraho, don't miss the faces of the lovers—they reveal the real message. Those faces are so blissful, so calm, so meditative, that you will not find such faces sculpted anywhere else. Such great ecstasy! Even the stone has bloomed in those faces; those faces have transformed the stone into rose flowers, into lotuses.

Seeing those faces you will be able to see that these lovers are no longer part of time and space; they have gone beyond.

The figures are sexually active, but they are not obsessed with sex—neither for nor against. Both are obsessions—being for or against simply mean that things are no longer natural. When things are natural, you are neither for nor against.

Are you for sleep or against sleep? If you are for, you have become unnatural; if you are against, you have become unnatural. You cannot be for or against sleep; it is a natural thing—so is sex. When sex is accepted naturally, it starts growing higher. Then one day, the bud spontaneously becomes a flower. Not that you have to *do* anything—just let the energy move, let the sap flow, and the bud will become the flower.

The Khajuraho faces are utterly at ease in a state of letting go. They are in the world, but not of it. They are not doing anything wrong; they are just like small children playing on the beach. They are playful. But sexually obsessed people have been very much against Khajuraho. Mahatma Gandhi wanted it to be covered with earth so that only once in a while, when some special guest came from another country, it could be uncovered for the guest. He thought it should be closed for ordinary people.

Now, if Mahatma Gandhi were to go to see Khajuraho, I don't think he would be able to see the faces of the figures; I don't think he would be able to go inside the temple—the outer would be enough to prevent him. I don't think he would be able to look at the outer: he would feel so angry, so guilty, so ashamed. If you talk to many of the so-called educated Indians about Khajuraho, you will find that they feel ashamed. They will say, "We are sorry, but these temples don't represent our mainstream. They are not representative of our culture. They are freak events in our culture—they don't represent us and we are sorry that they exist."

But these temples represent one of the most holistic attitudes toward life—all is accepted, because all is divine.

To me, the final stage of a human being is not the sage, not the Buddha, but Shiva Nataraj—Shiva the Dancer. Buddha has gone very deep, but the outer wall is missing, the outer wall is denied. Shiva contains all contradictions—contains the whole of existence, choicelessly. He lives in the innermost core of the shrine and he dances on the outer walls, too.

Unless the sage can dance, something is missing.

Life is a dance. You have to participate in it. The more silent you become, the deeper your participation. Never withdraw from life. Be true to life; be committed to life. Be utterly for life.

It happens when you have reached the innermost core of the temple. There is no reason for you to dance; you can remain there, silent. Just as Buddha says: When you have attained enlightenment, then two paths are open for you—either you can become an *arhat*—you can withdraw to the other shore; or you can become a *bodhisattva*—you can remain on this shore. In fact, there is no reason to be on this shore when you have become enlightened. But Buddha says, For the sake of others, for compassion's sake, create such compassion in yourself that you can linger a little longer and help people.

In the same way, when you become enlightened, two possibilities open—you can remain inside the temple, in the womb, where it is dark and windowless. Not going out at all,

not even a light penetrates; there is no sound from the outside, nothing of the marketplace. You can sit there in absolute silence, in timeless silence. There is no reason to come out and have a dance. Still, I hope that you would come back, although there is no reason. Although your journey will be complete, something will still be missing. You will have learned how to be silent—now you have to show whether you can be silent in the midst of sound. You have learned how to be alone—now you have to show whether you can be alone and love, too. You have to come back to the marketplace from the mountains. The ultimate test is there.

There is no reason for this—that I would like to repeat. There is no reason for this world, but there is a rhyme and a rhythm. No reason, but rhyme and rhythm. When you have become silent, create sound—and your silence will go deeper because of the contrasting sound. When you have known what aloneness is, be together with people—and the people and their presence will help you to know your aloneness far more deeply. When you have known how to remain still, dance—and the dance will give you the background in which the stillness will come loud and clear.

There is no reason for it, but there is a rhyme and a rhythm in it. Go to the opposite. That is the meaning of Shiva Nataraj—Shiva, the dancer of dancers. He is a buddha, but in his outer activities he is a worldly man.

This is the ultimate for Tantra, to become gods and yet be part of this world. When you can come back to the marketplace with a wine bottle in your hand, the ultimate is achieved.

HINDU AND BUDDHIST TANTRA

There are only two basic paths: the path of devotion, prayer, and love, and the path of meditation and awareness. These two different approaches persist.

Shiva's approach is that of devotion, prayer, love. Saraha's approach is that of meditation, awareness. The distinction is just a formality, because the lover and the meditator arrive at the same goal. Their arrows are released from different bows, but they reach the same target. The bow does not matter, finally. What type of bow you have chosen does not matter as long as the target is attained.

These are the two bows—the path of meditation and the path of devotion—because humans are divided into thinking and feeling. Either you can approach reality through thinking or you can approach reality through feeling.

The Buddhist approach—the approach of Buddha and Saraha—is through intelligence. It is basically through the mind that Saraha moves. Of course, the mind has to be left behind in the end, but it is the *mind* that has to be left behind. By and by, the mind has to disappear into meditation, but it is the mind that has to disappear, it is the thinking that has to be transformed and a state of no-thought has to be created. Just remember: it is a state of no-thought, and that can be created only by slowly dropping thoughts. So the whole work consists in the thinking part.

Shiva's approach is that of the feeling, of the heart. The feeling has to be transformed. Love has to be transformed so that it becomes prayerfulness. On Shiva's way, the devotee and the deity remain, but at the ultimate peak they disappear into each other. Listen to it carefully: when Shiva's Tantra reaches its ultimate orgasm, the *I* is dissolved into *Thou* and the *Thou* is dissolved into *I*— they are together, they become one unity.

When Saraha's Tantra reaches its ultimate peak, the recognition is that neither I nor Thou is right, neither I nor Thou is true, neither I nor Thou exists—both disappear. There are two zeros meeting—not *I* and *Thou* but neither *I* nor *Thou*.

Two zeros, two empty spaces, dissolve into each other because the whole effort on Saraha's path is in how to dissolve thought, and *I* and *Thou* are part of thought.

When thought is utterly dissolved, how can you call yourself I? And whom will you call your God? God is part of thought, God is a thought-creation, a thought-construct, a mind-construct. So all mind-constructs dissolve and *shunya*, emptiness, arises.

On Shiva's path you no longer love the form, you no longer love the person—you start loving the whole existence. The whole existence becomes your *Thou*—

you are addressed to the whole existence. Possessiveness is dropped, jealousy is dropped, hatred is dropped—all that is negative in feeling is dropped. The feeling becomes purer and purer until a moment comes when there is pure love. In that moment of pure love, you dissolve into "Thou" and "Thou" dissolves into you. You also disappear, but you disappear not like two zeros, you disappear as the beloved disappears into the lover and the lover disappears into the beloved.

Up to this point the paths are different, but that too is just a formal difference. Beyond this, what does it matter whether you disappear like a lover and a beloved or you disappear like two zeros? The basic point, the fundamental point, is that you disappear, nothing is left, no trace is left. That disappearance is enlightenment.

So you have to understand this: if love appeals to you, Shiva will appeal to you and *The Book of Secrets* will be your Tantra bible. If meditation appeals to you, then Saraha will appeal to you. Both are right, both are going on the same journey. With whom you would like to travel—that is your choice.

If you can be alone and blissful, then choose Saraha; if you cannot be blissful when you are alone, if your bliss comes only when you relate, then choose Shiva.

This is the difference between Hindu Tantra and Buddhist Tantra.

saraha, founder of buddhist tantra

You may not have heard the name of Saraha, but Saraha is the founder of Tantra. He is one of the great benefactors of humanity. Born about two centuries after Buddha, he was a branch of the great tree that started with Gautam Buddha. One branch moves from Buddha to Mahakashyap to Bodhidharma, where Zen was born—and it is still full of flowers, that branch. Another branch moves from Buddha to his son, Rahul Bhadra, from Rahul Bhadra to Sri Kirti, and from Sri Kirti to Saraha. From Saraha it moved to Nargarjuna and Tilopa—that is the Tantra branch of the tree planted by Buddha. It is still bearing fruit in Tibet. Tantra converted Tibet and Saraha is the founder of Tantra just as Bodhidharma is the founder of Zen. Bodhidharma conquered China, Korea, Japan. Saraha conquered Tibet.

A few things about Saraha's life: He was born in Vidarbha, which is part of Maharashtra state in India near Pune. When King Mahapala was the ruler of Maharashtra, Saraha was born to a very learned Brahmin who was in the king's court. The father was in the court, so the young man grew up there; he had four other brothers and they were all great scholars. Saraha was the youngest child and the most intelligent of them all. The four older brothers were nothing compared with Saraha. The four matured and got married. Saraha's fame was spreading all over the country and the king was enchanted by him. He was willing to give his own daughter in marriage to Saraha, but Saraha wanted to renounce everything to become a sannyasin, a wandering seeker.

The king was hurt; he tried to persuade Saraha to remain. This young man was so beautiful and so intelligent, it was because of him that Mahapala's court was becoming famous. The king was worried; he didn't want this young man to become a sannyasin. He wanted to protect him and give him all the comforts possible —he was ready to do anything for him. But Saraha persisted, and permission had to be given —he became a sannyasin and a disciple of Sri Kirti.

Sri Kirti is in the direct lineage of Buddha— first Gautam Buddha, then his son Rahul Bhadra, and then Sri Kirti. There were just two masters between Saraha and Buddha, so the tree must have been very green; the vibration must have been very much alive. Buddha had just recently left; the climate must have been full of his fragrance.

The king was shocked, because Saraha was a Brahmin—if he wanted to become a sannyasin he should have become a Hindu sannyasin, but instead he chose a Buddhist master, Sri Kirti. The first thing Sri Kirti told Saraha was, "Forget all your Vedas, all your learning, all that nonsense." It was difficult for Saraha, but he was ready to stake everything. Something about the presence of Sri Kirti had attracted him like a great magnet. He dropped all his learning; he became unlearned again.

This is one of the greatest renunciations— it is easy to renounce wealth, it is easy to renounce a great kingdom, but to renounce knowledge is the most difficult thing in the world. In the first place, how can you renounce it? It is there inside you. You can escape from your kingdom, you can go to the Himalayas, you can distribute your wealth—but how can you renounce your knowledge? It is so painful to become ignorant again. It is the greatest austerity there is, to become ignorant again, to become again innocent like a child. But Saraha was ready.

Years passed, and by and by he erased all that he had known. He became a great meditator. Just as he had started to become famous as a great scholar, now his fame as a great meditator started spreading. People started coming from far and away just to have

a glimpse of this young man who had become so innocent, like a fresh leaf, like dewdrops on the grass in the morning.

One day while Saraha was meditating, he saw a vision—a vision of a woman in the marketplace who was going to be his real teacher. Sri Kirti had just put him on the path, but the real teaching was to come from a woman.

Now, this has to be understood. Only Tantra has never been male chauvinistic. In fact, to go into Tantra you need the cooperation of a wise woman; without a wise woman, you will not be able to enter the complex world of Tantra.

Saraha had a vision that his teacher would be a woman in the marketplace. First, a woman and second, in the marketplace! Tantra thrives in the marketplace, in the thick of life. It is not an attitude of negation; it is utter positivity.

Saraha stood up to leave. Sri Kirti asked him, "Where are you going?"

Saraha said, "You have shown me the path—you took my learning away. You have done half the work—you have cleaned my slate. Now I am ready for the other half." With the blessings of Sri Kirti, who was laughing, Saraha went away. He went to the marketplace and he was surprised: he really found the woman that he had seen in the vision! The woman was making an arrow; she was an arrowsmith.

The third thing to be remembered about Tantra is that the more cultured, the more civilized a person, the less likely that person's Tantric transformation. The less civilized, the more primitive, the more alive a person is. The more you become civilized, the more you become plastic—you become artificial. If you become too cultivated, you lose your roots in the earth. You are afraid of the muddy world and you start posing as though you are not of the world. Tantra says that in order to find the real person, you will have to go to the roots. Those who are still uncivilized, uneducated, uncultured are more alive; they have more vitality. In the world of those who are still primitive, there is a possibility of starting to grow. You have grown in a wrong direction and they have not grown yet—they can still choose the right direction, therefore they have more potential. They don't have anything to undo; they can proceed directly.

An arrowsmith woman in India is a low-caste woman, and for Saraha—a learned Brahmin, a famous Brahmin, who had belonged to the court of a king—going to an arrowsmith woman was symbolic. The learned has to go to the vital. The plastic has to go to the real.

He saw this woman—a young woman, very alive, radiant with life—cutting an arrow shaft, looking neither to the right nor to the left, but wholly absorbed in making the arrow. He immediately felt something extraordinary in her presence, something that he had never come across. Even his master Sri Kirti paled before the presence of this woman. Something so fresh, something from the very source....

Sri Kirti was a great philosopher. Yes, he had told Saraha to drop all his learning, but still he was a learned man. He had told Saraha to drop all the Vedas and scriptures, but he had his own scriptures and his own Vedas. Even though he was anti-philosophical, his anti-philosophy was a sort of philosophy. Now, here was a woman who was neither philosophical nor anti-philosophical —who simply did not know what philosophy was, who was blissfully unaware of the world of philosophy, of the world of thought. She was a woman of action and she was utterly absorbed in her action.

Saraha watched carefully: The arrow ready, the woman closed one eye and opened the other, assumed the posture of aiming at an invisible target. Saraha came still closer. Now, there was no target; she was simply posing. She had closed one eye, her other eye was open, and she was aiming at some unknown, invisible target.

Saraha started sensing some message. This posture was symbolic, he felt, but the meaning of it was very dim and dark. He could feel something there, but he could not figure out what it was.

He asked the woman whether she was a professional arrowsmith, and the woman laughed, a wild laugh, and said, "You stupid Brahmin! You have left the Vedas, but now you are worshipping Buddha's sayings. So what is the point? You have changed your books, you have changed your philosophy, but you remain the same stupid man."

Saraha was shocked. Nobody had ever talked to him that way. Only an uncultured woman can talk that way. And the way she laughed was so uncivilized, so primitive—but still, very much alive. He was feeling pulled. She was a great magnet and he was a piece of iron. Then she said, "You think you are a Buddhist?" He must have been wearing the robe of the Buddhist monk, a yellow robe. She laughed again. She said, "Buddha's meaning can only be known through action, not through words and not through books. Are you not yet at the point where enough is enough? Are you not yet fed up with all this? Don't waste any more time in that futile search. Come and follow me!"

Then something happened, something like a communion. Saraha had never felt like that before. In that moment, the spiritual significance of what she was doing dawned on him. Neither looking to the left, nor looking to the right, he had seen her—just looking in the middle. For the first time he understood what Buddha meant by being in the middle, avoiding the extremes. First he had been a philosopher, then he had become an anti-philosopher—from one extreme to another. First he was worshipping one thing, now he was worshipping just the opposite, but the worship continued.

You can move from the left to the right, from the right to the left, but that is not going to help. You will be like a pendulum moving from left to right, from right to left... and have you observed? When the pendulum is going to the right, it is gaining momentum to go to the left; when it is going to the left it is again gaining momentum to go to the right. And the clock continues, the world continues.

To be in the middle means the pendulum just hangs there in the middle, moving neither to the right nor to the left. Then the clock stops. Then the world stops. Then there is no more time; then the state of no-time arises. Saraha had heard it said so many times by Sri

Kirti; he had read about it, he had pondered it, contemplated it. He had argued with others about it, that to be in the middle is the right thing. For the first time he had seen it in action. The woman was not looking to the right and not looking to the left... she was just looking in the middle, focused in the middle.

The middle is the point from which transcendence happens. Think about it, contemplate it, watch it in life. A person is running after money, mad, money-mad; money is the only god. One day or other, the god fails—it is bound to fail. Money cannot be your god; it is an illusion, you are projecting. One day you realize that there is no god in money—there is nothing in it and you have been wasting your life. Then you turn against it, you take the opposite attitude, you won't touch money. Both ways you are obsessed. Now you are *against* money, but the obsession remains. You have moved from the left to the right, but money is still at the center of your consciousness.

You can change from one desire to another. You were too worldly, now you become otherworldly—but *you* remain the same, the disease persists.

Buddha says, To be worldly is to be worldly, and to be otherworldly is also to be worldly; to worship money is to be mad, to be against money is to be mad; to seek power is foolish, to escape from it is also foolish.

Just to be in the middle is what wisdom is all about. For the first time Saraha actually saw it—he had not even seen it in Sri Kirti. And the woman was right. She said, "You can only learn

through action." She was so utterly absorbed that she was not even looking at Saraha, who was standing there watching her. She was utterly absorbed; she was totally in the action.

That is again a Buddhist message: To be total in action is to be free of action. Karma is created because you are not totally in your acts. If you are totally in an action, it leaves no trace.

Do anything totally and not only is it finished, but also you will not carry the psychological memory of it. Do anything incompletely and it stays with you, it goes on and becomes a hangover. The mind wants to continue and complete it. Mind has a great temptation to complete things. Complete anything, and the mind is gone. If you continue doing things totally, one day you suddenly find there is no mind. Mind is the accumulated past of all incomplete actions. You wanted to love a woman and you didn't love; now the woman is gone. You wanted to go to your father and to be forgiven for all that you had done in such a way that he was hurt; now he is dead.

The hangover will remain with you like a ghost. Now you are helpless—what to do? Whom to go to, and how to ask forgiveness? You wanted to be kind to a friend but you could not because you became closed.
Now the friend is no more, and it hurts. You start to feel guilty. You repent. Things go on like this.

Do any action totally and you are free of it; you don't look back because there is nothing to see. You have no hangovers. You simply go ahead. Your eyes are clear of the past; your vision is not clouded. In that clarity, you will come to know what reality is.

You are so worried... with all your incomplete actions you are like a junkyard. One thing is incomplete here, another thing is incomplete there—nothing is complete.

Have you observed it? Have you ever completed anything, or is everything incomplete? We push aside one thing and start something else, and before this is complete we start another. We become more and more burdened—this is what karma is. Karma means incomplete action.

Be total and you will be free.

The arrowsmith woman was totally absorbed. That's why she looked so luminous—she was so beautiful. She was an ordinary woman but her beauty was not of this earth. Her beauty was because of her total absorption in her action. The beauty was because she was not an extremist. The beauty was because she was in the middle, balanced. Out of balance comes grace.

For the first time, Saraha had encountered a woman who was not just physically beautiful, but who was spiritually beautiful—absorbed totally, absorbed in whatever she was doing. He understood for the first time: This is what meditation is! Not that you sit for a special period of time and repeat a mantra, not that you go to the church or to the temple or to the mosque—but to be in life, to go on doing trivial things, but with such absorption that the profundity is revealed in every action. He understood meditation for the first time. He had been meditating, he had been struggling hard, but for the first time meditation was there in front of him, alive. He could feel it; he could have touched it. It was almost tangible.

Closing one eye and opening the other is a Buddhist symbol. Buddha says—and psychologists agree with him now; after 2500

> *Do any action totally and you are free of it. You don't look back because there is nothing to see.*

years, psychology has come to the same understanding that Buddha had so long ago—Buddha says that half the brain reasons and half the brain intuits. The brain is divided in two parts, two hemispheres. The left side holds the faculty of reason, logic, discursive thought, analysis, philosophy, theology...

Suddenly Saraha realized that the woman had closed one eye as a symbol of closing the eye of reason, logic. And she had opened the other eye, symbolic of love, intuition, awareness.

Then he realized something about her posture. Aiming at the unknown, at the

words and words and words, and arguments and syllogisms and inferences. The left side of the brain is Aristotelian. The right side is intuitive, poetic—from there comes inspiration, vision, a priori consciousness, a priori awareness. Not that you argue—you simply come to *know*. Not that you infer—you simply *realize*. That is the meaning of a priori awareness; it is simply *there*. The truth is *known* by the right side of the brain; truth is *inferred* by the left side. Inference is just inference, it is not experience.

invisible, we are on the journey toward knowing the unknown—toward knowing that which cannot be known. That is real knowledge—to know that which cannot be known, to realize that which is unrealizable, to attain that which cannot be attained. This impossible passion is what makes a person a spiritual seeker.

Yes, it is impossible. By "impossible," I don't mean that it will not happen; I mean that it cannot happen unless you are utterly transformed. As you are, it cannot happen, but there are different ways of being, and you can be totally new. Then it happens. It is possible for a different kind of human being. That's why Jesus said that until you are reborn, you will not know it. A new human being will know it.

As you are, you will have to disappear. Then the new is born, a new consciousness comes in because there is something indestructible in you; nobody can destroy it. Only the destructible will be destroyed and the indestructible will be there. When you attain to that indestructible element in your being, to that eternal awareness in your being, you are a new consciousness. Through that consciousness the impossible is possible, the unattainable is attained.

So Saraha noted the woman's posture. Aiming at the unknown, the invisible, the unknowable, the one—that is the target. How to be one with existence? The nondual is the target, where subject and object are lost, where "I and Thou" are lost.

There is a great book by Martin Buber entitled *I And Thou*. Martin Buber says the experience of prayer is an *I–Thou* experience—he is right. God is the *Thou* and you remain an *I*. You have a dialogue, a communion with the *Thou*. But Buddhism has no prayer in it. Buddhism goes higher than prayer. It says: Even when there is an *I–Thou* relationship, you remain divided, you remain separate. You can shout at each other, but there will be no communion. The communion happens only when the *I–Thou* division is no more; when subject and object disappear; where there is no *I* and no *Thou*, no seeker and no sought... when there is unity, unison.

Saraha said to her, "You are not an ordinary arrowsmith woman. I am sorry to have even thought that you were an ordinary arrowsmith woman. Excuse me, I am tremendously sorry. You are a great master and I am reborn through you. Till yesterday I was not a real Brahmin; from today I am. You are my master and you are my mother and you have given me a new birth. I am no longer the same."

The arrowsmith woman accepted him. She had been waiting for Saraha to come. They moved to a cremation ground and started living together.

Why to a cremation ground? Because unless you understand death you will not be

able to understand life. Unless you die, you will not be reborn. After Saraha, many Tantra disciples have lived on the cremation ground because he was the founder, and he lived on a cremation ground. Dead bodies would be brought and burned, yet he lived there; that was his home. He lived with the arrowsmith woman; they lived together. There was great love between them—not the love of a woman and a man, but the love of a master and a disciple, which is certainly higher than any man-woman love can ever reach. Which is more intimate—certainly more intimate—because a man-woman love affair is between bodies; at the most, sometimes it encompasses the mind; otherwise, it remains in the body. But disciple and a master—it is a love affair of souls. Saraha had found his soulmate. They were in tremendous love, great love, which rarely happens on the earth. She taught him Tantra.

Only a woman can truly teach Tantra. Sometimes a man can become a Tantra teacher, but he will have to become very feminine. A woman is already feminine; she already has those loving, affectionate qualities; she naturally has that care, that love, that feeling for the soft. Saraha became a tantrika under the guidance of the arrowsmith woman. He was no longer meditating. One day he had left behind all the Vedas, scriptures, and knowledge; now he left behind even meditation. Rumors started spreading all over the country: "He no longer meditates. He sings, of course, and dances, too, but no meditation anymore." Now singing was his meditation. Now dancing was his meditation. Now celebration was his whole lifestyle.

Living in a cremation ground and celebrating? Living where only death happens and living joyously? This is the beauty of Tantra—it joins together the opposites, the contraries, the contradictories. If you go to the cremation ground you will feel sad; it will be difficult for you to be joyous. It will be difficult for you to sing and dance where people are being cremated and their friends and relatives are crying and weeping. Every day death and more death, all day and night, death. How can you rejoice?

But if you cannot rejoice there, then all that you think is your joy is just make-believe. If you can rejoice there, then joy has *really* happened to you. Now it is unconditional. Now it doesn't make any difference whether death happens or life, whether somebody is born or somebody is dying.

Saraha started singing and dancing. He was no longer serious—Tantra is not serious. Tantra is playfulness. Yes, it is sincere—but not serious. It is joyous. Play entered Saraha's being. Tantra is play, because Tantra is a highly evolved form of love. Love is play.

There are people who would not like even love to be playful. Many religions say you should make love only when you want to reproduce. Even love they change into work—"reproduction." This is just ugly! Make love only when you want to reproduce—is the woman a factory!? *Reproduction*—the very word is ugly. Love is fun! Make love when you are feeling happy, joyous, when you are at the top of the world. Share that energy. Love your partner when you have that quality of dance and song and joy—not for reproduction! The word *reproduction* is obscene! Make love out of joy, out of abundant joy. Give when you have it.

Play entered into Saraha's being. A lover always has a spirit of play. The moment the spirit of play dies, you become a husband or a wife. Then you are no longer lovers; then you reproduce. The moment you become a husband or a wife, something beautiful has gone dead. It is no longer alive, the juice flows no more. Now it is pretension, hypocrisy.

Play entered Saraha's being, and through play, true religion was born. His ecstasy was so infectious that people started coming to watch

RAHUL BECOMES SARAHA

Saraha's original name was Rahul, the name given by his father. The arrowsmith woman called him Saraha. Saraha is a beautiful word. It means "he who has shot the arrow." The moment he recognized the significance of the woman's actions, those symbolic gestures, the moment he could read and decode what the woman was trying to give him, what the woman was trying to show him, the woman was tremendously happy. She danced and said, "Now, from today, you will be called Saraha: you have shot the arrow. Understanding the significance of my actions, you have penetrated the truth."

> *Tantra is play, because Tantra is a highly evolved form of love. Love is play.*

him dancing and singing. When people came to watch, they would also start dancing and singing with him. The cremation ground became a place of great celebration. Yes, bodies were still being burned, but more and more people started gathering around Saraha and the arrowsmith woman, and great joy was created.

It became so infectious that people who had never heard anything about ecstasy would come, dance and sing, and fall into ecstasy. His very vibration, his very presence, became so potent that if you were ready to participate with him, it would happen… it was a contact high. He was so drunk that his inner drunkenness started overflowing to other people. He was so stoned that others started becoming more and more stoned.

Then the inevitable happened: the Brahmins and the priests and the scholars and the righteous people started vilifying and slandering him. I say inevitable because whenever there is a man like Saraha, the scholars are going to be against him, the priests are going to be against him, and the so-called moral people—puritans, self-righteous people—will be against him. They started spreading absolutely baseless rumors

about him. They started saying to people, "He has fallen from grace. He is a pervert. He is no longer a Brahmin. He has given up celibacy.

He is no longer even a Buddhist monk. He indulges in shameful practices with a low-caste woman and runs around like a mad dog in all directions." His ecstasy looked like a mad dog to them—it all depends on how you interpret things. He was dancing all over the cremation ground. He was mad, but he was not a mad dog—he was a mad god! It depends on how you see it.

The king was anxious to know exactly what was happening. More and more people had been coming to him. They knew that the king had always been deeply respectful toward Saraha and that he had wanted to appoint him as his counselor in the court, but that Saraha had renounced the world. The king was worried. He loved the young man and respected him, and he was concerned. So he sent a few people to persuade Saraha: "Come back to your old ways. You are a Brahmin, your father was a great scholar, and you yourself were a great scholar—what are you doing? You have gone astray. Come back home. The king wants you to go back to the palace and be part of his family. What you are doing is not good."

It is said that Saraha sang one hundred sixty verses to those people who had come to convert him. Upon hearing those one hundred sixty verses, the people started dancing and they never went home! Now the king was even more worried.

The queen had also always been interested in the young man. She wanted him to marry her daughter, so she went to see him. Saraha sang eighty verses to the queen and she never went home. Now the king was *really* puzzled: "What is going on?" Finally the king himself went to the cremation ground, and Saraha sang forty verses for him. And the king started dancing on the cremation ground like a mad dog.

So there are three scriptures in the name of Saraha: first, *The People's Song of Saraha*, one hundred sixty verses. Second, *The Queen's Song of Saraha*, eighty verses; and finally, *The Royal Song of Saraha*. There were one hundred sixty verses for the people because their understanding was not great; eighty for the queen—she was a little higher, her understanding was a deeper; and forty verses for the king because he was a man of intelligence, awareness, and understanding.

Because the king was converted, the whole country, by and by, was converted. And it is said in the old scriptures that a time came when the whole country became empty. Empty?!—it is a Buddhist word. It means people became nobodies, they lost their ego-trips. People started enjoying the moment. The hustle and bustle, the competitive violence, disappeared from the country. It became a silent country. It became empty... as if no one were there. The "people" as such disappeared; a great godliness descended on the country. These verses of Saraha were at the root of it, the very source of it.

saraha's royal song

Listen to this beautiful verse from Saraha:

Though the house lamps have been lit,
the blind live on in the dark.
Though spontaneity is all-encompassing and close,
To the deluded it remains always far away.

He says: Look! I have become enlightened. Though the house lamps have been lit... my innermost core is no longer dark. See! There is great light in me; my soul is awakened. I am no more the same Rahul you used to know. I am Saraha; my arrow has reached the target.

Though the house lamps have been lit,
the blind live on in the dark.

But what can I do? Saraha says. If somebody is blind, even when the house lamps are lit he goes on living in darkness. The lamps are not missing, but his eyes are closed. So don't listen to blind people—just open your eyes and look at me. See the person standing in front of you, whom you are confronting. The blind live on in the dark, though the house lamps have been lit.

Though spontaneity is all-encompassing
and close...

And I am so close to you... the spontaneity is so close to you, you can already touch it and eat it and drink it. You can dance with me and you can move into ecstasy with me. I am so close—you may not find spontaneity so close again!

... to the deluded it remains always
far away.

They talk about enlightenment and they read the Patanjali Sutras; they talk about great things, but whenever a great thing happens they are against it.

This is something strange about humans. Humans are strange animals. You can appreciate Buddha, but if Buddha comes and confronts you, you will not be able to appreciate him at all—you may go against him, you may become his enemy. Why?

When you read a book about Buddha, everything is okay—the book is in your hands. When a living buddha has to be confronted, he is not in your hands—you are falling into his hands. Hence the fear, resistance, and desire to escape. The best way to escape is to convince yourself that he has gone wrong, something is wrong with him. That is the only way to

escape—if you can prove to yourself that he is wrong. You can find a thousand and one things in a buddha that look wrong because you are squinting and you are blind and your mind is in turmoil. You can project anything.

Now this man has attained buddhahood, and everybody is talking about the low-caste woman. They have not looked into that woman's reality. They have only been thinking about the fact that she is an arrowsmith woman, low-caste, a sudra, untouchable. How can a Brahmin touch an untouchable woman? How can the Brahmin live there? They have heard that the woman cooks food for him—this is a great sin, this is a great fall, a Brahmin eating food cooked by a sudra, an untouchable, a low-caste woman!

And why should a Brahmin live on the cremation ground? Brahmins live in the temples and in the palaces as part of the court. Why on the cremation ground?—a dirty place, with skulls and dead bodies all around. This is perversion!

But they have not looked into the fact that unless you understand death you will never be able to understand life.

> 66 *Don't listen to blind people—*
> *just open your eyes and look.* 99

When you have looked deeply into death and found that life is never dead, when you have penetrated deeply into death and found that life continues even after death, that death makes no difference, that death is immaterial....

People don't know anything about life—life is eternal, timeless. Only the body dies, so only the dead dies; the alive continues. For this understanding, you have to go into a deep experimentation—but these people would not look at that. They heard that Saraha was participating in strange practices. They must have gossiped and exaggerated; things must have gotten out of hand, and everyone must have been multiplying the gossip.

And there are plenty of Tantra practices that can be gossiped about! In Tantra, the man sits in front of the naked woman and he has to watch her so deeply, to see her through and through, that all desire to look at a woman naked disappears.

Then the man is free from the form. This is a great secret technique; otherwise, you go on continuously seeing the woman naked in your mind. Each woman that passes by on the road, you want to undress her—that idea will be there.

Now suddenly you see Saraha sitting before a naked woman—how will you interpret it? You will interpret it according to yourself. You will say, "So okay, he is doing what we always wanted to do but didn't, so we are better than him. At least we are not doing it. Of course we fantasize sometimes, but it is only in thought, not in deed. He has fallen." You will not miss the opportunity to gossip about it.

But what is Saraha really doing? It is a secret science. By watching, for months together, the tantrika will meditate on the woman's body, her form, he will meditate on her beauty. He will look at everything, whatever he wants to look at. Do the breasts have some appeal? He will look and meditate on the breasts. He has to get rid of the form and the only way to get rid of the form is to know it so deeply that it has no attraction anymore.

Now something just the opposite is happening from what the gossipers are saying. Saraha is going beyond.

Never again will he want to undress a woman, not even in his mind, not even in a dream. That obsession will not be there. But the crowd, the mob, has its own ideas. Ignorant, unaware, they go on talking about things they don't understand.

Though spontaneity is all-encompassing and close,
To the deluded it remains always far away.
Though there may be many rivers, they are one in the sea,
Though there may be many lies, one truth will conquer all.
When one sun appears, the dark,
However deep, will vanish.

Saraha says: Just look at me—the sun has risen. So I know, howsoever deep your darkness, it is going to vanish also. Look at me—the truth is born in me! You may have heard thousands of lies about me, but one truth will conquer them all.

Though there may be many rivers, they are one in the sea.

Just come close to me. Let your river drop into my ocean, and you will have my taste.

Though there may be many lies, one truth
will conquer all.

Truth is one, only lies are many. Only lies
can be many. Truth cannot be many. Health is
one; diseases are many. One health conquers
all diseases and one truth conquers all lies.

When one sun appears, the dark,
However deep, will vanish.

In these four verses, Saraha has invited
the king to enter into his inner being; he has
opened his heart. And he says: I am not here
to convince you logically, I am here to convince
you existentially. I will not give any proof and I
will not say anything in defense of myself. The
heart is open—you come in and see what has
happened. So close is spontaneity, so close is
God, so close is truth. The sun has risen—open
your eyes!

Remember, a mystic has no proof.

He cannot have any proof by the very
nature of things. He is the only proof... so all he
can do is to bare his heart to you.

These verses, these songs of Saraha,
have to be meditated on deeply. Each song
can become the opening of a flower in your
heart. The king was liberated—so can you be.
Saraha has penetrated the target. You can also

> **You are focused on the cloud**
>
> **but you have forgotten the sky.**

penetrate the target. You can also become a
Saraha—one whose arrow has been shot.

As a cloud that rises from the sea
Absorbing rain, the earth embraces,
So, like the sky, the sea remains
Without increasing or decreasing.

He is saying to the king: Look at the
sky. There are two phenomena, the sky
and the cloud. The cloud comes and goes.
The sky never comes and never goes. The
cloud is there sometimes, and sometimes
it is not there; it is a time phenomenon, it
is momentary. The sky is always there; it is
a timeless phenomenon, it is eternity. The
clouds cannot corrupt it, not even the black
clouds can corrupt it. There is no possibility
of corrupting it; its purity is absolute, its purity
is untouchable. Its purity is always virgin; you
cannot violate it. Clouds can come and go,
and they have been coming and going, but
the sky is as pure as ever; not even a trace is
left behind.

So there are two things in existence: one
is like the sky, and one is like the cloud. Your
actions are like the cloud—they come and go.
You? You are like the sky: you never come and
you never go. Your birth and your death are
like the clouds, they *happen*. You? You never
happen; you are *always* there. Things happen
in you, *you* never happen.

Things happen just like clouds happen
in the sky. You are the silent watcher of the
play of clouds. Sometimes they are white and
beautiful and sometimes they are dark and
dismal and ugly. Sometimes they are full of rain
and sometimes they are empty. Sometimes

they greatly benefit the earth and sometimes they cause great harm. Sometimes they bring floods and destruction and sometimes they bring life, greenery, crops. But the sky remains always the same: good or bad, divine or devilish, the clouds don't corrupt the sky.

Actions are clouds. Doings are clouds.

Being is like the sky.

Saraha is saying: Look at my sky! Don't look at my actions. It needs a shift of awareness, nothing else—just a shift of awareness. It needs a change of gestalt. You are looking at the cloud, you are focused on the cloud, but you have forgotten the sky. Then suddenly you remember the sky—you drop your focus on the cloud and you focus on the sky. Then the cloud becomes irrelevant; then you are in a totally different dimension.

Just a shift of focus... and the world is different. When you watch a person's behavior, you are focusing on the cloud. When you watch the innermost purity of the person's being, you are watching the sky. If you watch the innermost purity, then you will never see anyone evil, then the whole of existence is holy. If you see the actions, then you cannot see anyone holy. Even the holiest person is prone to commit many errors as far as actions are concerned. If you watch the actions, you can find wrong actions in Jesus, in Buddha, in Mahavira, in Krishna, in Rama. Then even the greatest saint will look like a sinner.

There are many books written about Jesus; he is the object of thousands of studies. Many are written to prove he is the only begotten son of God—and of course they can prove it.

Then many are written to prove that he is just a neurotic and nothing else—they can also prove it. And all are talking about the same person! What is happening? How do they manage? One party chooses the white clouds, another party chooses the black clouds—and both are there, because no action can be just white or just black. To be, it has to be both.

Whatever you do will bring some good into the world and will bring some bad into the world—whatever you do. Just in making the choice to do something, many things will be good and many things will be wrong after that choice is made. Think of any action: you give some money to a beggar—you are doing good. But the beggar then purchases some poison and commits suicide. Your intention was good, but the total result is bad. You help a man who is ill by taking him to the hospital. Then when he is healthy, he commits murder. Now, without your help there would have been one murder less in the world. Your intention was good, but the total result is bad.

So do we judge by the intention or do we judge by the result? And who knows about your intention? Intention is internal... maybe deep down you were hoping that when this man got healthy he would commit a murder.

Sometimes it happens that your intention is bad and the result is good. You threw a rock at a person who had been suffering from migraine for many years, and the rock hit his head. Since then, his migraine has disappeared. Now what to do? What to say about your act? Was it moral? Immoral? You wanted to kill the man, but you could only kill the migraine.

That's how acupuncture was born. A great science, one of the most beneficial boons to humanity, was born in this way. A man had been suffering from headaches for many years. And another man, his enemy, wanted to kill him. Hiding behind a tree, the enemy shot an arrow; the arrow hit the man's leg and he fell down... but his headache disappeared. The people who were looking after him and the doctors of the town were puzzled as to how it happened. By chance, by coincidence, the arrow had hit an acupuncture point on the leg and the inner electrical flow of the man's body energy changed. Because the inner flow of the electricity changed, his headache disappeared.

That's why when you go to the acupuncturist and say, "I have a headache," she may not touch your head at all. She may start pressing your feet or your hand, or she may needle your hand or your back. And you will be surprised: "What are you doing? My head is the trouble, not my back!" But she knows better. The whole body is an interconnected electrical phenomenon; there are hundreds of points, and she knows where to stimulate the energy to change the flow. Everything is interconnected.

But this is how acupuncture was born. The man who shot the arrow at his enemy—was he a great saint or was he a sinner? Difficult to say. If you look at actions, it is up to you. You can choose the good ones or you can choose the bad ones. In the overall reality, each act brings something good and something bad.

In fact, this is my understanding—meditate on it—whatever you do, the goodness of it

and the badness of it are always in the same proportion. Let me repeat: good and bad are always in the same proportion, because they are two aspects of the same coin. You may do good—but something bad is bound to happen, because where will the other aspect go? You may do bad—but some good is bound to happen, because where will the other aspect go? The coin exists with both aspects together; a single aspect cannot exist alone.

Sinners are sometimes beneficial and saints are sometimes harmful. Saints and sinners are both in the same boat! Once you understand this, a change is possible. Then you won't look at the actions. If the proportion is the same whether you do good or bad, then what is the point of judging a man by his actions? Change the whole emphasis and move to another gestalt—the sky.

That's what Saraha is saying to the king. He is saying: Right you are! People have told you these things and they are not wrong. I run around like a mad dog! Yes, if you just watch the action you will be misguided; you will not be able to understand me. Watch my inner sky. Watch my inner priority. Watch my inner core. That's the only way to see the truth. Yes, I live with this woman, and ordinarily living with a woman means what it means. But this is no ordinary living together. There is no man-woman relationship at all; it has nothing to do with sexuality. We live together as two spaces, we live together as two freedoms; we live together as two empty boats. But you have to look into the sky, not into the clouds.

As a cloud that rises from the sea

absorbing rain, the earth embraces.

So, like the sky, the sea remains

without increasing or decreasing.

And another thing Saraha reminds him of: Watch the sea. Millions of clouds rise out of the sea, so much water evaporates, but the sea does not decrease because of that. The clouds will rain on the earth, rivulets will become great rivers, many rivers will be flooded, and the water will rush back to the ocean, to the sea. All the rivers of the earth will pour their water into the sea, but that does not make the sea increase— the sea remains the same. Whether something is taken out of it or something is poured into it makes no difference; its perfection is such that you cannot take anything out of it and you cannot add anything to it.

Saraha is saying: Look! The inner being is so perfect that your actions may be those of a sinner, but nothing is taken away. Your actions may be those of a saint, but nothing is added to you. You remain the same.

It is a tremendously revolutionary saying. It is a great statement. Saraha says: Nothing can be added to you and nothing can be deleted from you, your inner perfection is such. You cannot become more beautiful and you cannot become ugly. You cannot become rich and you cannot become poor. You are like the sea.

One of the Buddhist sutras, Vaipulya Sutra, describes two very costly jewels in the ocean: one jewel prevents the ocean from becoming less when water is drawn from it, and the other keeps it from becoming too large when water

flows into it. Those two great jewels prevent these things from happening: the ocean never becomes less and it never becomes more. It is so vast, it does not matter how many clouds arise out of it and how much water evaporates. It is so vast, it does not matter how many rivers fall into it and bring great amounts of water. It remains the same.

Such is the inner core of your being. Such is the inner core of existence. Increase and decrease are on the periphery, not at the center. You can accumulate great knowledge or you can remain ignorant; that is only on the periphery. No knowledge can make you more knowing than you already are. Nothing can be added to you. Your purity is infinite; there is no way to improve upon it.

This is the Tantra vision. This is the core of the Tantra attitude: you are as you are; there is no hankering for improvement. Not that you have to become good, not that you have to change this and that—you have to accept all, and remember your sky, remember your sea. By and by, an understanding arises, when you know what is a cloud and what is the sky, what is a river and what is the sea. Once you are in tune with your sea, all anxiety disappears, all guilt disappears. You become innocent like a child.

The king had known Saraha as a great man of knowledge, and now he was behaving like an ignorant man. He had stopped reciting his Vedas, he no longer did the rituals that his religion prescribed, he no longer even meditated. He was doing nothing that was ordinarily thought to be religious. What was

he doing here, living on a cremation ground, dancing and singing like a madman, and doing so many untraditional things? Where had his knowledge gone?

Saraha says: You can take all my knowledge away and it will not make any difference because I am not lessened by it. Or you can bring all the scriptures of the world and pour them into me and that won't make any difference. I won't become more because of that.

He had been a respectable man, the whole kingdom had respected him; and suddenly he had become one of the most disreputable men. Yet Saraha says: You can give me all the honors that are possible, and nothing is added to me. Or you can take all the honors away and insult me. You can do whatever you want to destroy my respectability, but nothing is happening to me. No matter what, I remain the same. I am that which never increases and never decreases. Now I know that I am not the cloud,

I am the sky. I am not much worried whether people think the cloud is black or white, because I am not the cloud. I am not the small river, the tiny river, or a tiny pool of water...I am not a cup of tea.

Storms arise in a cup of tea very easily, it is so tiny. Take just one spoonful out of it and something is lost; pour in one more spoonful and it is too much and spills out. Saraha says: I am the vast sea. Take whatever you want to take, or give whatever you want to give— either way it does not matter.

Look at the beauty of it! The moment nothing matters, you have come home. If something still matters, you are far away from home. If you are still watching and being cunning and clever about your actions—you have to do this and you have not to do that, and there are still shoulds and should-nots— then you are far away from home. You still think of yourself in terms of the momentary and not in terms of the eternal.

BEING AND ACTION

Tantra believes in being, not in action and character, because once being is transformed, actions are transformed. That is the only way to change your actions. Who has ever been able to change his actions directly? You can only pretend.

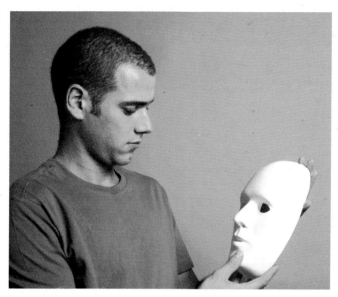

If you have anger in you and you want to change your action, what will you do? You will suppress the anger and you will show a false face; you will have to wear a mask. If you have sexuality in you, what will you do to change it? You can take a vow of celibacy and you can pretend, but deep down the volcano continues. You are sitting on a volcano that can erupt any moment. You will be constantly trembling, constantly afraid, in fear.

Have you not watched the so-called religious people? They are always afraid—afraid of hell—and always trying to get into heaven. But they don't know what heaven is; they have not tasted it at all. If you change your consciousness, heaven comes to you, not that you go to heaven. Nobody has ever gone to heaven, and nobody has ever gone to hell. Let it be decided once and for all: heaven comes to you, hell comes to you—it depends on you. Whatsoever you call, it comes.

If your being changes, you suddenly become available to heaven—heaven descends on you. If your being does not change, you are in a conflict; you are forcing something that is not there. You become false and more false, until you become two persons, you become schizophrenic, split. You show one thing, but you are something else. You say something but you never do it; instead, you do something else. You are continuously playing hide-and-seek with yourself. Anxiety and anguish are natural in such a state—that's what hell is.

understanding the

science of tantra

Tantra is science, not philosophy. To understand philosophy

is easy because only your intellect is required. If you can

understand language, if you can understand concept,

you can understand philosophy. You need not change;

no transformation is required of you. As you are, you can

understand philosophy—but not Tantra. To understand Tantra you

will need a change... rather, a mutation. Unless you are willing to

undergo a mutation you will not understand, because Tantra is not

an intellectual proposition, it is an experience. Only when you are

receptive, ready, and vulnerable to the experience, is it going to

come to you.

the language
of silence

We have lost contact with existence; we have lost our roots in it. We are like an uprooted tree—the sap flows no more, the juice has dried up. No more flowers will bloom, no more fruits will ripen. Not even birds come to take shelter in us. This happens because we are not yet born. We have taken the physical birth to be our birth—it is not our birth. We exist only as potentialities; we have not become actual—hence our misery. The actual is blissful, the potential is miserable. Why is it so? Because the potential cannot be at rest. The potential is continuously restless—it has to be restless! Something is going to happen and it hangs in the air. We are in limbo.

t is like a seed—how can a seed rest and relax? Rest and relaxation is known only by the flowers. The seed has to be deep in anguish; the seed has to continuously tremble. The trembling is because it does not know whether it will be able to become actual, whether it will find the right soil, whether it will find the right climate, whether it will find the right sky. Is it going to happen, or will it simply die without ever being born? The seed trembles inside. The seed has anxiety, anguish. The seed cannot sleep; the seed suffers from insomnia.

The potential is ambitious. The potential longs for the future. Have you not watched this in your own being? You are continuously longing for something to happen and it is not happening; you are continuously hankering, hoping, desiring, dreaming… and it is not

happening! Life goes on flowing by. Life goes on slipping out of your hands. Death comes closer, and you are not yet actual. Who knows? Which will come first? Actualization, realization, blossoming, or maybe death? Who knows? Hence the fear, the anguish, the trembling.

Soren Kierkegaard has said man is a trembling. Yes, man is a trembling because man is a seed. Friedrich Nietzsche has said man is a bridge. Exactly right! Man is not a place to rest; he is a bridge to pass over. Man is a door to go through. You cannot rest at being human. Man is not yet a *being*; man is an arrow on the way, a rope stretched between two eternities. Man is a tension. Only humans suffer from anxiety—we are the only animals on the earth that suffer from anxiety. What can be the cause of it?

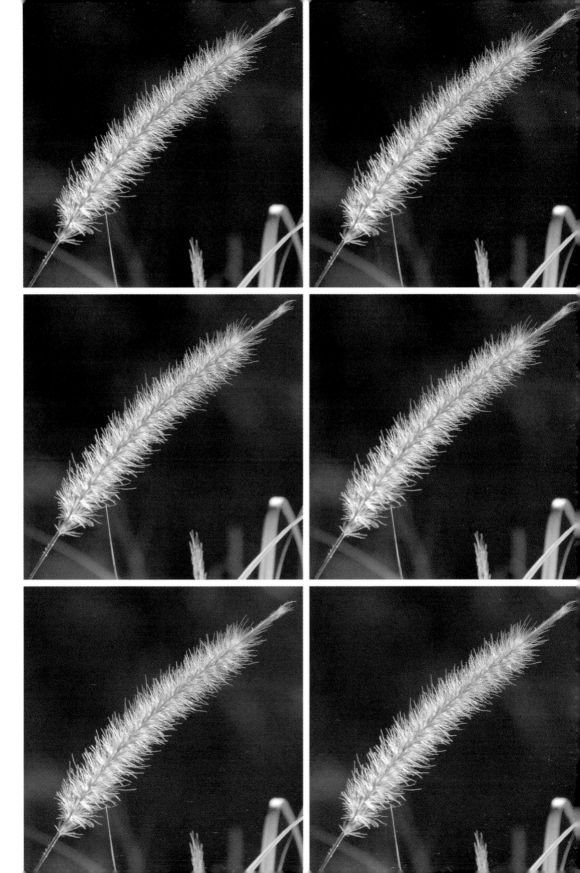

It is only humans who exist as potentiality. A dog is actual; there is nothing else waiting to happen. A buffalo is actual; there is nothing more, it has already happened. Whatever could happen, has happened. You cannot say to a buffalo, "You are not yet a buffalo." That would be foolish. But you can say to a man, "You are not yet a man." You can say to a woman, "You are incomplete." You cannot say to a dog, "You are incomplete." That would be stupid. All dogs are fully complete.

The human being has a possibility, a future. The human being is an opening. So there is a constant fear: Are we going to make it or not? How many times have we missed before? Are we going to miss again? That's why we are not happy. Existence goes on celebrating, there is great singing, there is great joy, there is great rejoicing! The whole of existence is always in an orgy; it is a carnival. The whole of existence at each moment is in orgasm! But somehow the human being has become a stranger.

Humans have forgotten the language of innocence. Humans have forgotten how to relate with existence. Humans have forgotten how to relate with themselves!

To relate with yourself is meditation and to relate with existence is prayer. People have forgotten the very language. That's why we appear like strangers in our own home, strangers to ourselves. We don't know who we are and we don't know why we are, and we don't know for what we go on existing. It seems to be an endless waiting… waiting for Godot.

Nobody knows whether Godot is ever going to come or not. In fact, who is this Godot? Nobody knows even that, but you have to wait for something, so you create some idea and wait for it. God is that idea. Heaven is that idea. Nirvana is that idea. You have to wait because you have to fill your being, otherwise you feel so empty. Waiting gives a sense of purpose and a direction. You can feel better because at least you are waiting. It has not happened yet but it is going to happen some day.

What is it that is going to happen? We have not even asked the right question—and remember, once the right question is asked, the right answer is not far away. It is just around the corner. In fact, it is hidden within the right question itself. If you ask the right question, you will find the right answer through that questioning itself.

The first thing that I would like to say is that we are continually missing, because we have used the mind as the language to relate with existence and the mind is a way to cut yourself off from existence. It is the way to set yourself apart; it is not the way to turn yourself on. *Thinking is the barrier*. Thoughts are like the Great Wall of China around you, and when you are groping through the thoughts you cannot touch reality. Not that reality is far away—it is always close by, just a prayer away at the most. But if you are thinking, brooding, analyzing, interpreting, or philosophizing, then you start falling farther and farther away from reality. The more thoughts you have, the more difficult it is to see through them. They create a great fog; they create blindness.

This is another fundamental of Tantra: a thinking mind is a mind that misses; thinking is not the language to relate with reality. Then what is the language to relate with reality? Non-thinking. Words are meaningless with reality. Silence is meaningful. Silence is pregnant; words are dead. You have to learn the language of silence.

You were in your mother's womb—you have forgotten it completely, but for nine months you had not yet spoken a single word—you were together, in deep silence. You were one with your mother; there was no barrier between you and your mother. You didn't exist as a separate self. In that deep silence, your mother and you were one. There was tremendous unity—not union—unity. You were not two, so it was not union—it was simple unity.

The day you become silent again, the same thing happens: again you fall into the womb of existence; again you relate. You relate in a totally new way. Not quite *totally* new, because you knew it in your mother's womb, but you have forgotten it. That's what I mean when I say humans have forgotten the language to relate. That is the way—as you related with your mother in her womb. Your every vibe was conveyed to your mother; every vibe of your mother was conveyed to you. There was a simple understanding; no misunderstanding existed between you and your mother. Misunderstanding comes only when thinking comes in.

How can you misunderstand somebody without thinking? Can you? Can you misunderstand me if you don't think about me? How can you misunderstand? And how can you understand me if you think? Impossible—the moment you think, you have started interpreting. The moment you think, you are not looking at me; you are avoiding me. You are hiding behind your thoughts. Your thoughts come from your past. I am here, present. I am a statement here and now, and you bring your past.

You must know about the squid. When it wants to hide, it releases a cloud of black ink around itself. Then nobody can see it. It is simply lost in its cloud of black ink; the cloud is its safety measure. Exactly the same thing is happening when you release a cloud of thoughts around you—you become lost in it. Then you cannot relate and nobody can relate to you.

It is impossible to relate to a mind; you can relate only to a consciousness. A consciousness has no past. A mind is just past and nothing else.

So Tantra says you have to learn the language of orgasm. Again, when you are making love to a woman or to a man, what happens? For a few seconds—it is very rare and becoming even rarer as humans become more and more civilized—for a few seconds, you are no longer in the mind. With a shock, you are cut off from the mind. In a leap, you are outside the mind. For those few seconds of orgasm when you are out of the mind, you can relate. Again you are back in the womb... in the womb of your woman or in the womb of your man. You are no longer separate. Again there is unity, not union. When you start making love, there is the beginning of a union. But when orgasm comes, there is no union—there is unity. The duality is lost.

What happens in that deep, peak experience? Tantra reminds you again and again that whatever happens in that peak moment is the language to relate with existence. It is the language of the guts; it is the language of your very being. So either think in terms of when you were in the womb of your mother, or think in terms of when you are lost in the womb of your beloved and, for a few seconds, the mind simply does not work! Those moments of no-mind are your glimpses into eternity, glimpses of awakening, glimpses of the beyond. We have forgotten that language and that language has to be learned again.

Love is the language. The language of love is silent. When two lovers are in deep harmony, or what Carl Jung used to call synchronicity—when their vibes are synchronizing with each other and they are both vibrating on the same wavelength—then there is silence. Then the lovers don't need to talk. It is only husbands and wives who talk. Lovers fall silent.

In fact, the husband and wife cannot keep silent because language is a way to avoid each other. If you are not avoiding the other, if you are not talking, the presence of the other becomes embarrassing. So the husband and wife immediately release their cloud of black ink! Any excuse will do, but they release ink around themselves; they get lost in the cloud, then there is no problem.

Language is not a way to relate more or less, it is a way to avoid. When you are deeply in love you may hold the hand of your beloved but you will be in silence... utter silence, not a ripple. In that rippleless lake of your consciousness, something is conveyed, the message is given. It is a wordless message.

Tantra says you have to learn the language of love, the language of silence, the language of each other's presence, the language of the heart, the language of the guts. We have learned a language that is not existential. We have learned an alien language—utilitarian, of course; it fulfills a certain purpose. But as far as the higher exploration of consciousness is concerned, it is a barrier.

On the lower level it is okay—in the marketplace you need a certain language; silence won't do. But as you move deeper and higher, language won't do.

tantra and yoga

Tantra and yoga are basically different. They reach the same goal; however, their paths are not only different, but contrary. This has to be understood clearly.

The yoga process is also methodology; yoga is also technique. Yoga is not philosophy; just like Tantra, yoga depends on action, method, technique. Doing leads to being in yoga also, but the process is different. In yoga one has to fight; it is the path of the warrior. On the path of Tantra one does not have to fight at all. On the contrary, one has to indulge, but with awareness.

Yoga is suppression with awareness; Tantra is indulgence with awareness. Tantra says that whatsoever you are, the ultimate is not opposite to it. It is a process of growth; you can grow to be the ultimate. There is no opposition between you and reality. You are part of it, so no struggle, no conflict, no opposition to nature is needed. You have to use nature; you have to use whatsoever you are to go beyond.

In yoga you have to fight with yourself to go beyond. In yoga, the world and *moksha*, liberation—you as you are, and you are as you can be—are two opposite things. Suppress, fight, dissolve that which you are so you can attain that which you can be. Going beyond is a death in yoga. You must die for your real being to be born. In the eyes of Tantra, yoga is suicide. You must kill your natural self—your body, your instincts, your desires, everything. Tantra says accept yourself as you are. It is a deep acceptance. Do not create a gap between you and the real, between the world and Nirvana. Do not create any gap. There is no gap for Tantra; no death is needed. For your rebirth, no death is needed—rather, a transcendence is required. For this transcendence, use yourself.

For example, sex is there: the basic energy you are born through, born with. The basic cells of your being and of your body are sexual, so the human mind revolves around sex. For yoga you must fight with this energy. Through fighting you create a different center in yourself. The more you fight, the more you become integrated in a different center. Then sex is not your center. Fighting with sex—of course, consciously—will create in you a new center of being, a new emphasis, and a new crystallization. Then sex will not be your energy. You will create your energy fighting with sex. A different energy will come into being and a different center of existence.

For Tantra you have to use the energy of sex. Do not fight with it, transform it. Do not think in terms of enmity, be friendly to it. It is your energy.

It is not evil; it is not bad. Every energy is natural. It can be used for you or it can be used against you. You can make a block or a barrier of it, or you can make it a step. Rightly used, it becomes friendly; wrongly used, it becomes your enemy. But it is neither. Energy is just natural. As ordinary people are using sex, it becomes an enemy. It destroys; they dissipate in it.

Yoga takes the opposite view—opposite to the ordinary mind. The ordinary mind is being destroyed by its own desires, so yoga says stop desiring, be desireless. Fight desire and create an integration in you that is desireless.

Tantra teaches you to be aware of the desire; do not create any fight. Move in desire with full consciousness, and when you move into desire with full consciousness, you will transcend it. You are into it and still you are not in it. You pass through it, but you remain an outsider.

Yoga has much appeal because yoga is the opposite of the ordinary mind, so the ordinary mind can understand the language of yoga. You know how sex is destroying you—how it has destroyed you, how you revolve around it like a slave, like a puppet. You know this by your experience. So when yoga says fight it, you immediately understand the language. That is the appeal, the easy appeal of yoga.

Tantra cannot be so easily appealing. It seems difficult: How to move into desire without being overwhelmed by it? How to be in the sex act consciously, with full awareness? The ordinary mind becomes afraid. It seems dangerous. Not that it is dangerous; whatsoever you know about sex creates this danger for you. You know yourself, you know how you can deceive yourself. You know very well that your mind is cunning. You can move in desire, in sex, in everything, and you can deceive yourself that you are moving with full awareness. That is why you feel the danger.

The danger is not in Tantra; it is in you. The appeal of yoga is because of you, because of your ordinary mind—your sex-suppressed, sex-starved, sex-indulging mind. Because the ordinary mind is not healthy about sex, yoga has an appeal. With a better humanity, with a healthy sex—natural, normal—the case would be different. We are not normal and natural. We are absolutely abnormal, unhealthy, insane. But because everyone is like us, we never feel it.

Madness is so normal that not to be mad may look abnormal. A Buddha seems abnormal. A Jesus is abnormal amidst us. They do not belong to us. Our "normalcy" is a disease. This "normal" mind has created the appeal of yoga. If you take sex naturally—with no philosophy around it, either for or against— if you take sex as you take your hands or your eyes, as accepted and natural, then Tantra will have an appeal. Only then can Tantra be useful for many.

But the days of Tantra are coming. Sooner or later Tantra will explode for the first time in the masses, because for the first time the time is ripe—ripe to take sex naturally. It is possible that the explosion may come from the West, because Freud, Jung, and Reich have prepared the background. They did not know anything about Tantra, but they have prepared the basic ground for Tantra to evolve. Western psychology has come to the conclusion that the basic human disease is related to sex, the basic insanity of man is sex-oriented.

Unless this sex orientation is dissolved, people cannot be natural and normal. Humans have gone wrong only because of the prevailing attitudes about sex. No attitude is needed. Only then are you natural. What attitude have you about your eyes? Are they evil or are they divine? Are you for your eyes or against them? There is no attitude! That is why your eyes are normal.

Take an attitude—think that eyes are evil. Then seeing will become difficult. Seeing will take the same problematic shape that sex has taken. Then you will want to see, you will desire and you will hanker to see. But when you see, you will feel guilty. Whenever you see, you will feel that you have done something wrong, that you have sinned. You would like to kill your very instrument of seeing; you would like to destroy your eyes. And the more you want to destroy them, the more you will become eye-centered. Then you will begin an absurd activity. You will want to see more and more, and simultaneously you will feel more and more guilty. The same phenomenon has happened with the sex center.

Tantra says, Accept whatsoever you are. This is the basic note—total acceptance. Only through total acceptance can you grow. Then use every energy you have. How can you use them? Accept them, then find out what these energies are—what is sex, what is this phenomenon? We are not acquainted with it. We know many things about sex, taught by others. We may have passed through the sex act, but with a guilty mind, a suppressive attitude, in haste, in a hurry. Something has to be done in order to become unburdened. The sex act is not a loving act. You are not happy in it, but you cannot leave it. The more you try to leave it, the more attractive it becomes. The more you want to negate it, the more you feel invited.

You cannot negate it, but this tendency to negate and destroy destroys the mind, the awareness, the sensitivity that can understand it. So sex goes on with no sensitivity in it. Then you cannot understand it. Only a deep sensitivity can understand anything; only a deep feeling, a deep moving into it, can understand anything. You can understand sex only if you move in it as a poet moves amidst flowers—only then! If you feel guilty about flowers, you may pass through the garden, but you will pass with closed eyes. And you will be in a hurry, in a deep, mad haste. Somehow you have to go out of the garden. Then how can you be aware?

So Tantra says, accept whatsoever you are. You are a great mystery of many multi-dimensional energies. Accept it, and move with every energy with deep sensitivity, with awareness, with love, with understanding. Move with it! Then every desire becomes a vehicle to go beyond it. Then every energy becomes a help. Then this world becomes Nirvana, this body becomes a temple—a holy temple, a holy place.

Yoga is negation; Tantra is affirmation. Yoga is defined in terms of duality—that is the reason for the word *yoga*. It means to put two things together, to "yoke" two things together. But two things are there; the duality is there. Tantra says there is no duality. If there is duality, then you cannot put them together. Howsoever you try, they will remain two and the fight will continue, the dualism will remain.

If the world and the divine are two, then they cannot be put together. If they are not two, if they only *appear* as two, only then can they be one. If your body and your soul are two, then they cannot be put together. If you and God are two, then there is no possibility of putting you together. You will remain two.

Tantra says there is no duality; it is only an appearance. So why help this appearance of duality to grow stronger? Dissolve it this very moment! Be one! Through acceptance you become one, not through fight. Accept the world, accept the body, accept everything that is inherent in it. Do not create a different center in yourself, because for Tantra that different center is nothing but the ego. Do not create an ego. Just be aware of what you are. If you fight, then the ego will be there.

It is difficult to find a yogi who is not an egoist. And yogis may go on talking about egolessness, but they cannot be egoless. The very process they go through creates the ego. The fight is the process. If you fight, you are bound to create an ego. And the more you fight, the more strengthened the ego will be. If you win your fight, then you will achieve the supreme ego.

Tantra says, no fight! Then there is no possibility of ego. If we understand Tantra, there will be many problems because, for us, if there is no fight there is only indulgence. No fight means indulgence for us. Then we become afraid. We have indulged for lives together and we have reached nowhere. But in Tantra, indulgence is not "our" indulgence. Tantra says, Indulge, but be aware.

You are angry... Tantra will not say, Do not be angry. Tantra will say, Be angry wholeheartedly, but be aware. Tantra is not against anger. Tantra is only against spiritual sleepiness, spiritual unconsciousness. Be aware *and* be angry. And this is the secret of the method: if you are aware, anger is transformed; it becomes compassion. So according to Tantra, anger is not your enemy; it is compassion in seed form. The same anger, the same energy, will become compassion.

If you fight with your anger, then there will be no possibility of compassion. If you succeed in fighting, in suppression, you will be dead. There will be no anger because you have suppressed it, but there will be no compassion either, because only anger can be transformed into compassion.

If you succeed in your suppression— which is impossible—then there will be no sex, but no love either, because with sex dead there is no energy to grow into love. So you will be without sex, and you will also be without love. And then the whole point is missed, because without love there is no divineness, without love there is no liberation, and without love there is no freedom.

Tantra says that these same energies are to be transformed. It can be said in this way: if you are against the world, then there is no Nirvana, because this world itself is to be transformed into Nirvana. Then you are against the basic energies that are the source.

So Tantric alchemy says, Do not fight, be friendly with all the energies that are given to you. Welcome them. Feel grateful that you have anger, that you have sex, that you have greed. Feel grateful because these are the hidden sources and they can be transformed, they can be opened. When sex is transformed it becomes love. The poison is lost and the ugliness is lost.

The seed is ugly, but when it becomes alive it sprouts and flowers. Then there is beauty. Do not throw away the seed, because then you are also throwing away the flowers in it. They are not yet manifest so that you can see them. They are unmanifest, but they are there. Use this seed so that you can attain flowers. So first let there be acceptance, a sensitive understanding and awareness. Then indulgence is allowed.

One thing more which, although strange, is one of the deepest discoveries of Tantra, and that is: Whatsoever you take as your enemies—greed, anger, hate, sex—your attitude that they are enemies makes them your enemies. Take them as divine gifts and approach them with a grateful heart.

For Tantra, everything is holy. Remember this: for Tantra, *everything* is holy, nothing is unholy. For an irreligious person, everything is unholy and for so-called religious persons something is holy and something else is unholy. Tantra says everything is holy, that is why we cannot understand it. It is the deepest non-dual standpoint—if we can call it a standpoint. Because any standpoint is bound to be dual and Tantra is not against anything, it is not any standpoint. It is a felt unity, a lived unity.

These are two paths, yoga and Tantra. Tantra could not be as appealing because of our crippled minds. But for someone who is healthy inside, not in chaos, Tantra has a beauty. Only such a person can understand what Tantra is. Yoga has an easy appeal because of our disturbed minds. Remember, it is ultimately your mind that makes anything attractive or unattractive. You are the deciding factor.

the inner map of the chakras

Tantra has a certain map of the inner man. It will be good if you understand that map, as it will help you. Both Tantra and yoga suppose that there are seven centers in human physiology—the subtle physiology, not the material physiology of the body. In fact, these centers are metaphors, but they are helpful in understanding something of the inner being. These are the seven chakras.

First and most basic is *muladhar*, which means the most fundamental or basic. *Mul* means "of the roots." The muladhar chakra is the center where sex energy is, but society has badly damaged that chakra.

This muladhar chakra has three aspects to it: one is oral; the second is anal, and the third is genital. These are the three aspects of the muladhar. The child begins his life in the oral, and because of wrong upbringing many people remain at the oral stage; they never grow beyond it. That's why there is so much smoking, chewing gum, constantly eating. This is an oral fixation: these people remain centered in the mouth.

There are many primitive societies in which partners don't kiss. In fact, if the child has grown well, kissing will disappear. Kissing shows the person has remained oral. Otherwise, what does sex have to do with lips? When for the first time primitive societies came to know about civilized man's kissing, they laughed. They simply thought it ridiculous. Two persons kissing each other? It seems unhygienic too: transferring all sorts of illnesses and infections to each other. What are they doing and why? But most of humanity has remained oral.

If the child is not satisfied orally—the mother does not give her breast as much as the child needs—the lips remain unsatisfied. So the child will grow up to smoke cigarettes, become a great kisser, chew gum, or become a great eater, continually eating this or that. If mothers give their breasts as much as the children need, then the muladhar is not damaged.

If you are a smoker, try a pacifier—and you will be suddenly surprised. It has helped many people. I suggest it to many people. If somebody asks me how to stop smoking, I say, "Just get a pacifier and keep it in your mouth. Let it hang around your neck and whenever you feel like smoking, just put the pacifier in your mouth and enjoy it. Within

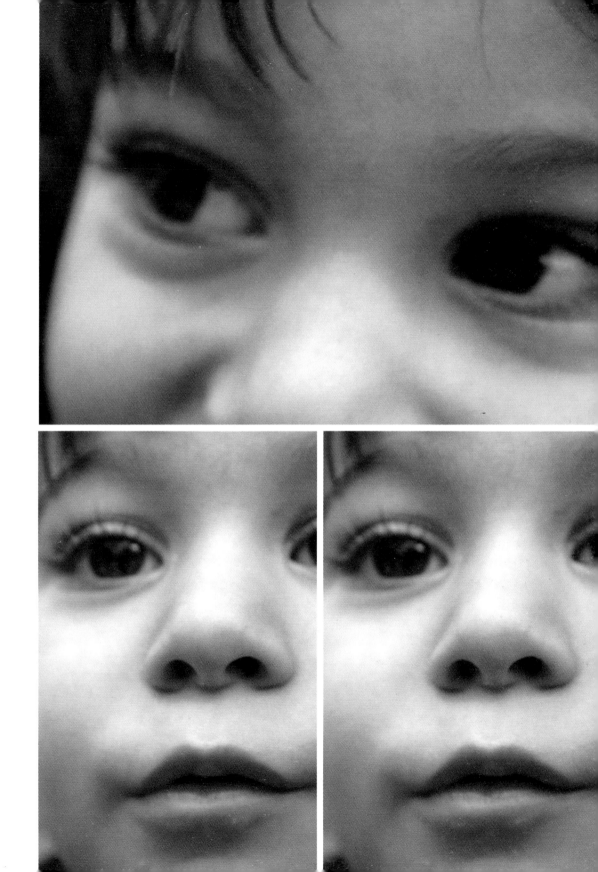

three weeks you will be surprised: the urge to smoke has disappeared."

Somewhere in the psyche the breast is still appealing. That's why men are so focused on breasts. There seems to be no reason why. Why are men so interested in breasts? Painting, sculpture, film, pornography—everything seems to be breast-oriented! And women are always trying to hide and yet show their breasts; otherwise, the bra is just foolish. It is a trick to hide and to exhibit together; it is a contradictory trick. And now they are stuffing breasts with silicon so they become bigger and can take on the shape that un-grown-up humanity wants to see. Such a childish idea! But humanity remains oral.

This is the lowest state of the muladhar.

A few people change from oral and become stuck at anal, because the second great damage happens with toilet training. Children are forced to go to the toilet at a certain time. Young children cannot control their bowel movements; it takes time, it takes years for them to develop control. So what do they do? They force themselves, they close their anal mechanism, and because of this they become anally fixated.

That's why so much constipation exists in the world. Only humans suffer from constipation. In the wild state, no animal suffers from constipation. Constipation is more psychological; it is the result of damage to the muladhar. Because of constipation many other things develop in the human mind. A person becomes a hoarder—a hoarder of knowledge, of money, of virtue—and becomes miserly. He

cannot let go of anything! Whatever he grabs, he holds on to it. With this anal emphasis, great damage happens to the muladhar. When things develop naturally, the man or the woman will move on to the genital. If people get fixated at the oral or at the anal, they never move on to the genital—that is the trick that society has used until now not to allow you to become fully sexual. The anal fixation becomes so important that the genitals become less important.

Finally, some people become genital—if somehow they are not fixated at the oral and the anal—and then guilt is created in humanity about sex. Sex is equivalent to sin. Christianity has considered sex so much a sin that they go on trying to prove the foolish idea that Christ was born out of a miracle, that he was not born out of a man-woman relationship, but that Mary was a virgin. Sex is such a sin... how could Jesus' mother have sex? It is okay for ordinary people, but for Jesus' mother to have sex... how could Jesus, such a pure man, be born out of sex?

Sex has been condemned so much that you cannot enjoy it. That's why energy remains fixated somewhere else, whether oral, anal, or genital. It cannot go upward.

Tantra says that the first great work has to happen in the muladhar. For oral freedom, screaming, laughing, shouting, crying, and weeping are all helpful. That's why I emphasize cathartic methods of meditation—they help to relieve the oral fixation. To relieve you of the anal fixation, fast, chaotic breathing is helpful because it hits directly on the anal center and enables you to relax the anal mechanism. Here the Dynamic Meditation is of tremendous value.

Then the sex center has to be relieved of the burden of guilt and condemnation. You have to

DYNAMIC MEDITATION

OSHO DYNAMIC MEDITATION is an hour-long process consisting of five stages: (1) vigorous, chaotic breathing; (2) catharsis; (3) grounding and centering; (4) silent watchfulness; and (5) celebration through dance. Osho developed the meditation specifically for modern men and women, and guided the composition of music to support each stage in the process. For more detailed instructions and information about where to find the music, see *www.osho.com/dynamic*

learn about it all over again; only then can the damaged sex center function in a healthy way. You have to relearn it to enjoy it without any guilt.

There are a thousand and one types of guilt. In the Hindu mind, there is a fear that semen represents a great energy—if even a single drop is lost, you are lost. This is a constipated attitude —hoard the semen so nothing is lost! But you are such a dynamic force that, in fact, you create that energy every day. Nothing is lost.

The Hindu mind is too obsessed with veerya, with semen energy. Since not a single drop should be lost, they are continuously afraid. Whenever they make love—if they make love—then they feel frustrated and depressed, because they start thinking so much energy has been lost.

Nothing is lost. You don't have a fixed quota of energy. You are a dynamo. You create energy; you create it each day. In fact, the more you use it, the more you have it. It functions like the rest of the body. If you use your muscles, they will grow. If you walk, your legs will be strong. If you run, you will have more energy to run. Don't think that a person who has never run and suddenly runs will have energy—he will not have energy. He will not have even the musculature to run. Use all that has been given to you by nature and you will have more of it.

The Hindu madness, to hoard, is on the lines of constipation. There is an American madness that is like diarrhea: just throw everything out, meaningfully or meaninglessly, go on squandering your energy and indulging. Even a man of eighty years still thinks in childish ways.

Sex is good, sex is beautiful, but it is not the end. It is the alpha but not the omega. You have to go beyond it. But to say that you have to go beyond it is not a condemnation! You have to go *through* it to go beyond it.

Tantra is the healthiest attitude about sex. It says sex is good, sex is healthy, sex is natural, and sex has more possibilities than just reproduction. Sex has more possibilities than just fun. Sex carries something of the ultimate in it, something of *samadhi*, of transcendence.

The muladhar chakra has to be relaxed—relaxed from constipation, relaxed from diarrhea. The muladhar chakra has to function at the optimum, one hundred percent, then energy starts moving.

The second chakra is *svadhisthan*—that is, the hara, the death center. These first two centers are both damaged because man has been afraid of sex and man has been afraid of death. Death has been avoided: don't talk about death, just forget about it! It does not exist. Even if sometimes it happens, don't take any note of it. Go on thinking that you will live forever—avoid death.

Tantra says: Don't avoid sex and don't avoid death. That's why Saraha went to the cremation ground to meditate—not to avoid death. And he went with the arrowsmith woman to live a life of healthy, full sex, of optimum sex. On the cremation ground, living with a woman, these two centers had to be relaxed: the center of death and the center of sex. Once you accept death and are not afraid of it, once you accept sex and are not afraid of it, your two lower centers are relaxed.

Those are the two lower centers that have been damaged by society, badly damaged. Once they are relieved, the other five centers are accessible. They are not damaged. There has been no need to damage them because people don't live in those other five centers.

These two centers are naturally available— birth has happened, the sex center, muladhar. And death is going to happen—the second center, svadhisthan. These two things are in everyone's life, so society has destroyed both centers and tried to manipulate people, to dominate them through these two centers.

Tantra says: Meditate while you make love. Meditate while somebody dies—go, watch, see. Sit by the side of a dying man. Feel, participate in his death. Go in deep meditation with the dying man. When a man is dying, there is the possibility of having a taste of death—because when a man is dying, he releases so much energy from the svadhisthan chakra. The whole repressed energy of the svadhisthan chakra will be released as he is dying. Without releasing it, he will not be able to die.

So when a man dies or a woman dies, don't miss the opportunity. If you are close to a dying person, sit silently, meditate silently. When the person dies, in a sudden burst the energy will be all around and you can taste death. It will give you a great sense of relaxation: you will experience that, yes, death happens, but nobody dies. Yes, death happens, but in fact death *never* happens.

While making love, meditate so that you can know that something of samadhi penetrates into sexuality. While meditating on death, go deep into it so that you can see that something of the deathless enters into death. These two experiences will help you to go upward very easily.

The other five centers, fortunately, are not destroyed; they are perfectly in tune—only the energy has to be freed to move through them. If the first two centers are helped to relax, energy starts moving. So let death and love be your two objects of meditation.

Muladhar means the base, the root. It is the sex center, or you can call it the life center, the birth center. It is from muladhar that you are born. It is from your mother's muladhar and your father's muladhar that you have come into your body. The death chakra is *svadhisthan*: it means "the abode of the self."

This is a very strange name to give to the death chakra—"abode of the self," svadhisthan, where you really exist. In death? Yes. When you die, you come to your pure existence—because the only part of you that dies is that which you are not. The body dies—the body is born out of the muladhar. When you die the body disappears, but do you? No. Whatever has been given by the muladhar is taken away by svadhisthan. Your mother and father have given you a certain mechanism of the body—that is taken away in death. But you? You existed even before your father and mother knew each other; you have existed always.

Somebody asks Jesus about Abraham, what he thinks about the prophet Abraham, and he says: "Abraham? I am before Abraham ever was." Abraham lived almost two thousand, three thousand years before Jesus, and he says, "I am before Abraham was." What is he talking about? As far as bodies are concerned, how can he exist before Abraham? He is not talking about the body—he is talking about "I-am-ness," his pure being. That pure being is eternal.

So this name, svadhisthan, is beautiful. It is exactly the center that in Japan is known as the hara. That's why in Japan suicide is called *harakiri*—to kill yourself through the hara center. The svadhisthan takes only that which has been given by the muladhar. But that which has come from eternity, your consciousness, is not taken away.

Hindus have been great explorers of consciousness. They called this center svadhisthan because when you die, then you know who you are. Die in love and you will know who you are. Die in meditation and you will know who you are. Die to the past and you will know who you are. Die to the mind and you will know who you are. Death is the way to know.

These two centers have been poisoned by society because these are the centers easily available to society. Beyond these two are five more centers.

The third center, *manipura*, is the center of all your sentiments, emotions. It means the diamond—life is valuable because of sentiments, emotions, laughter, crying, tears, and smiles. Life is valuable because of all these

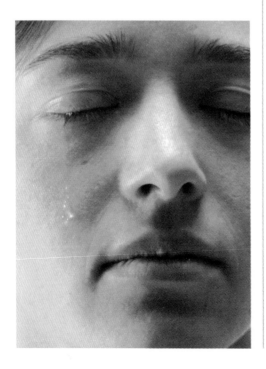

things. These are the glory of life—hence the chakra is called manipura, the diamond chakra.

Only humans are capable of having this precious diamond. Animals cannot laugh; naturally, they cannot cry either. Tears are a certain dimension that is available only to humans. The beauty of tears, the beauty of laughter; the poetry of tears, and the poetry of laughter are available to humans only. All other animals exist with only two chakras: muladhar and svadhisthan. They are born and they die. If you are also born and you die, and nothing else happens, you are like an animal—you are not human yet. Yet many millions of people exist only with these two chakras; they never go beyond them.

We repress our emotions in the manipura. We have been taught to repress sentiments. We have been taught that sentimentality does not pay—be practical, be hard; don't be soft, don't be vulnerable; otherwise, you will be exploited. Be hard! At least *show* that you are hard, at least pretend that you are dangerous, that you are not a soft being. Create fear around you. Don't laugh—if you laugh you cannot create fear around you. Don't weep—if you weep you show that you are afraid. Don't show your human limitations; pretend that you are perfect.

Much work is done in Tantra to relax this third center. Emotions have to be relieved, relaxed. When you feel like crying you must cry; when you feel like laughing you must laugh. You must drop this nonsense of repression, you have to learn expression, because only through your sentiments, your

emotions, and your sensitivity, do you come to that vibration through which communication is possible.

Have you not seen it? You can say as much as you want, and nothing is said; but a tear rolls down your cheek and everything is said. A tear can say much more. You can talk for hours and it won't do, yet a tear can say all. You can say, "I am happy," but a little laughter—real, authentic laughter—and you need not say anything; the laughter says it all. When you see your friend, your face beams, flashes with joy.

The third center has to be made more and more available. It is against thinking, so if you allow the third center, you will relax in your tense mind more easily. Be authentic, sensitive: touch more, feel more, laugh more, cry more. Remember, you cannot do more than

is needed; you cannot exaggerate. You cannot even bring a single tear more than is needed, and you cannot laugh more than is needed. So don't be afraid and don't be miserly.

Tantra allows life all its emotions.

These are the three lower centers—lower but not in any sense of valuation—these are the three lower rungs of the ladder.

Then comes the fourth center, the heart center, called *anahata*. The word is beautiful. *Anahata* means "unstruck sound." It is exactly what Zen people mean when they say, "Do you hear the sound of one hand clapping?" Unstruck sound.

The heart is in the middle—three centers below it, three centers above it. The heart is the door from the lower to the higher, or from the higher to the lower. The heart is like a crossroad.

The heart has been completely bypassed. You have not been taught to be heartful. You have not even been allowed to go into the realm of the heart, because it is very dangerous. It is the center of the soundless sound, the unstruck sound, the non-linguistic center. Language is struck sound: we have to create it with our vocal chords.

> " You cannot laugh more than is needed. So don't be afraid and don't be miserly. "

Language is two hands clapping. The heart is one hand clapping. In the heart there is no word; it is wordless.

We have avoided the heart completely; we have bypassed it. We move in such a way in our being as if the heart does not exist—or, at the most, as if it is only a pumping mechanism for breathing. It is not. The lungs are not the heart. The heart is hidden deep behind the lungs. And it is not physical either. It is the place from which love arises.

That's why love is not a sentiment. Sentimental love belongs to the third center, not to the fourth. Love is not just sentimental. Love has more depth than sentiment; love has more validity than sentiment. Sentiments are momentary.

More or less, the sentiment of love is misunderstood as the experience of love. One day you fall in love with a man or a woman, and the next day it is gone—and you call it love. It is not love, it is a sentiment. You liked the man—*liked*, remember, not *loved*—it was a "liking" just as you like ice cream. Likings come and go. Likings are momentary; they cannot stay long; they don't have any capacity to stay long. You liked a man, you made love with him, and finished! The liking is finished. Just as you liked ice cream—you have eaten it and now you don't look at the ice cream at all. And if somebody gives you more ice cream, you will say, "Now it is making me sick—stop! I cannot take any more."

Liking is not love. Never misunderstand liking for love, otherwise your whole life you will be only driftwood... you will be drifting from one person to another and intimacy will never grow.

The fourth center, the anahata, is significant because it is through the heart that you were first related to your mother. It was through the heart that you were related to your mother, not through the head. In deep love, in deep orgasm, again you are related through the heart, not through the head. In meditation, in prayer, the same thing happens: you are related with existence through the heart— heart-to-heart. Yes, it is a dialogue heart-to-heart, not head-to-head. It is non-linguistic.

The heart center is the center from which the soundless sound arises. If you relax into the heart center, you will hear it. That is a great discovery. Those who have entered the heart hear a continuous chanting inside their being which sounds like *aum*. Have you ever heard anything like a chanting that goes on by itself, not that you are *doing* it?

That's why I am not in favor of mantras. You can continuously chant *aum*, *aum*, *aum*, and create a mental substitute for the heart. It is not going to help you. It is a deception. You can chant for years and create a false sound within yourself as if your heart is speaking—it is not.

To know the heart you are not to chant *aum* —you have only to be silent. One day, suddenly, the mantra is there. One day, when you have fallen silent, you will hear the sound coming from nowhere. It is arising out of you from the innermost core. It is the sound of your inner silence. Just as in a silent night there is a certain sound, the sound of silence, exactly like that but on a much deeper level, a sound arises in you.

It arises—let me remind you again and again—it is not that you bring it in; it is not that you repeat *aum*, *aum*. No, you don't say a single word. You are simply quiet. You are silent. It bursts forth like a spring... suddenly it starts flowing... it is there. You hear it—you don't say it—you hear it.

When Mohammedans say that Mohammed *heard* the Koran, that is their meaning. That is exactly what happens at the innermost core of your heart. Not that you say it, but that you *hear* it. Mohammed heard the Koran—he heard it happening inside. He was puzzled; he had never heard anything like this. It was

so unknown, so unfamiliar. The story says that he became ill. If one day, while sitting in your room, you suddenly start hearing inside *aum*, *aum* (or anything else) you will start to wonder, "Am I going mad?" You are not saying it, nobody else is saying it... are you going mad?

Mohammed was sitting on a hilltop when he heard it. He came home trembling and perspiring with a high fever. He became disturbed. He told his wife, "Bring all the blankets and cover me! I have never had such a trembling. A great fever has come to me," But his wife could see that his face was illuminated.

"What type of fever is this? His eyes are burning, afire with something tremendously beautiful. A grace has entered with him into the house. A great silence has fallen over the house." Then his wife started hearing something. She said to Mohammed, "I don't think it is a fever—I think God has blessed you. Don't be afraid! What has happened? Tell me!"

His wife was the first Mohammedan—Khadija was her name. She was the first convert. She said, "I can see—God has happened to you, something is flowing from your heart all over the place. You have become luminous! You have never been like this—something extraordinary has happened. Tell me why you are so worried and trembling. Maybe it feels strange, but tell me."

So Mohammed told her, afraid of what she would think, but she became converted—she was the first Mohammedan.

It has happened so always. Hindus say that the Vedas were recited by God himself. It simply means that they were *heard*. In India, we have a word for the holy scriptures: the word is *shruti* and it means "that which has been heard."

At the center of the heart, in the anahata chakra, you hear. But if you have not heard anything inside you—no sound, no aum, no mantra—that simply means you have avoided the heart. The waterfall is there, and the sound of running water is there, but you have avoided it, you have bypassed it. You have taken some other route; you have taken a shortcut avoiding the fourth center.

> *The waterfall is there, and the sound of running water is there, but you have avoided it, you have bypassed it.*

The fourth is the most dangerous center because it is the center out of which trust and faith are born, and the mind wants to avoid it. If the mind does not avoid it, then there will be no possibility for doubt. Mind lives through doubt.

This is the fourth center. And Tantra says, Through love you will come to know this fourth center.

The fifth center is called *visuddhi*, which means "purity." Certainly, after love has happened, there is purity and innocence—never before it. Only love purifies—*only love*—nothing else purifies. Even the homeliest person in love becomes beautiful. Love is nectar. It cleanses all poisons. So the fifth chakra is purity, absolute purity. It is the throat center.

Tantra says: Only speak when you have come to the fifth center via the fourth—only speak through love; otherwise, don't speak. Speak through compassion; otherwise, don't speak! What is point of speaking? If you have come through the heart and if you have heard existence speaking there, or existence running there like a waterfall, or if you have heard the sound of existence in the sound of one hand clapping, then you are allowed to speak. Then your throat center can convey the message, then something can be poured into words. When you *have* it, it can be poured even into words.

Few people come to the fifth center, because they don't come even to the fourth, so how can they come to the fifth? It is very rare. Sometimes a Christ, a Buddha, or a Saraha, comes to the fifth. The beauty of even their words is tremendous—what to say about their silence? Even their words carry silence. They speak and yet they speak not. They say and they say the unsayable, the ineffable, the inexpressible.

You also use the throat, but that is not visuddhi. When that chakra truly starts functioning, your words have honey in them. Then your words have a fragrance, a music to them, a dance. Then whatever you say is poetry, whatever you utter is sheer joy.

The sixth chakra is *ajna*, which means "order." With the sixth chakra, never before it, you are in order. With the sixth chakra, never before it, you become the master. Before it you were a slave. With the sixth chakra, whatsoever you say will happen and whatsoever you desire will happen. With the sixth chakra, never before it, you have will. Before it, will does not exist.

But there is a paradox in it. With the fourth chakra, ego disappears. With the fifth chakra, all impurities disappear and then you have will—so you cannot do harm through your will. In fact, it is no longer your will: it is the will of

existence, because the ego disappears at the fourth and all impurities disappear at the fifth. Now you are the purest being, just a vehicle, an instrument, a messenger. Now you have will because you are not—now the will of existence is your will.

Very rarely does a person come to this sixth chakra because this is the last, in a way. In the world, this is the last. Beyond this is the seventh, but then you enter a totally different world, a separate reality. The sixth is the last boundary line, the last outpost.

The seventh is *sahasrar*, which means "one-thousand-petaled lotus." When your energy moves to the seventh, sahasrar, you become a lotus. Now you need not go to any other flower for honey—now the bees start coming to you. Now you attract bees from the whole earth. Your sahasrar has opened and your lotus is in full bloom. This lotus is Nirvana.

The lowest is muladhar. From the lowest, life is born—the life of the body and the senses. With the seventh, again life is born—life eternal, not of the body, not of the senses.

This is the Tantra physiology. It is not the physiology of the medical books. Please don't look for it in the medical books—it is not there. It is a metaphor, it is a way of speaking. It is a map to make things understandable. If you move in this way, you will never come to that cloudiness of thoughts. If you avoid the fourth chakra, then you go into the head. To be in the head means not to be in love; to be in thoughts means not to be in trust; to be thinking means not to be looking.

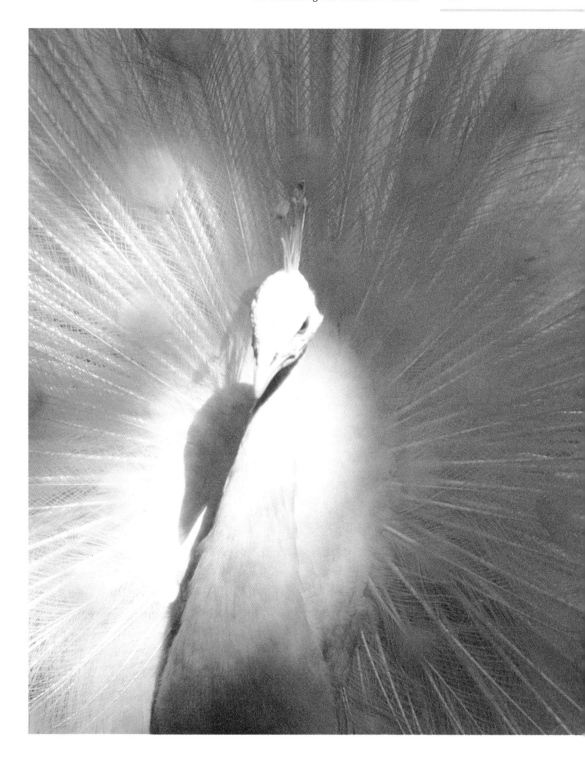

tantra is transcendence

Tantra is transcendence. It is neither indulgence nor repression. It is walking on a tightrope in one of the greatest of balances. It is not as easy as it appears—it needs delicate awareness. It is a great harmony.

It is easy for the mind to indulge. The opposite is also easy, to renounce. To move to the extreme is easy for the mind. To remain in the middle, exactly in the middle, is the most difficult thing for the mind because it is a suicide for the mind. The mind dies in the middle and the no-mind arises. That's why Buddha has called his path *majjhim nikaya*—the middle path.

Saraha is a disciple of Buddha—in the same lineage, with the same understanding, with the same awareness. This fundamental point has to be understood; otherwise, you will misunderstand Tantra. What is this razor's edge? What is this being exactly in the middle?

To indulge in the world, no awareness is needed. To repress worldly desires, no awareness is needed. Your so-called worldly people and your otherworldly people are not very different. They may be standing back-to-back, but they are of exactly the same type of mind. Somebody is hankering for money, and somebody is so against money that he is afraid even to look at currency. These people are not different—for both of them, money is of great importance. One is in greed and one is in fear, but the importance of the money is the same—both are obsessed with money.

One is continuously thinking of women, dreaming, fantasizing, while another has become so afraid that he has escaped to the Himalayas to avoid women—but both are the same. For both, the woman is important, or the man; the other is important. One seeks the other, one avoids the other, but the other remains their focus.

Tantra says: The other has not to be the focus, neither this way nor that way. This can happen only through great understanding. The lust for another has to be understood—neither indulged in nor avoided, but understood.

Tantra is scientific. The word *science* means understanding. The word *science* means knowing. Tantra says: Knowing liberates. If you know exactly what greed is, you are free of greed and there is no need to renounce it. The need to renounce arises only because you have not understood what greed is. The need to take a vow against sex is needed only because you have not understood what sex is.

And society does not allow you to understand it. Society helps you *not* to understand. Society has been avoiding the subjects of sex and death down through the centuries. These subjects are not to be thought about, not to be contemplated, not to be discussed, written about, or researched; they are to be avoided. Through that avoidance, a great ignorance has existed about them and that ignorance is the root cause. There are two types of people who act out of that ignorance: one who indulges madly and one who becomes tired and escapes.

Tantra says: The one who is indulging madly will never understand, because he will simply be repeating a habit. He will never look into the habit or the root cause of it, and the more he indulges the more mechanical he becomes.

Have you not observed it? Your first love had something superb, the second was not so superb, the third was even more ordinary, and the fourth, mundane. What happened?

Why has the first love been so praised? Why have people always said that love happens only once? Because the first time it was not mechanical, so you were a little more alert about it. The next time, you were expecting it: you were not so alert. The third time, you thought you knew about it, so there was no exploration in it. The fourth time it was mundane; you settled into a mechanical habit.

Through indulgence, sex becomes a habit. Yes, it gives a little release, just like a sneeze— but not more than that. It is a physical release of energy. You become too burdened with energy and you have to throw out that energy just to gather it again through food, through exercise, through sunlight. Again gather it and again throw it out. That's what the person who indulges goes on doing: he creates great energy and then throws it out for no purpose, with no significance. Having it, he suffers the tension of it. Throwing it out, he suffers the weakness of it. He simply suffers.

Never think that the one who indulges is happy. Never! He is the most miserable person in the world. How can he be happy? He hopes, he desires happiness, but he never achieves it.

Remember that in saying these things, Tantra does not propose that you move to the other extreme.

Tantra is not saying that you should escape from this world of indulgence. Escaping will again become a mechanical habit. While the man is sitting in a cave, the woman will not be available, but that doesn't make much difference. If at any time the woman does become available, the man who has renounced will be more prone to fall than the man who was indulging in the world. Whatever you repress becomes powerful within you. Whatever you repress will become your attraction and will have a magnetic pull on you. The repressed becomes powerful; it gains power out of all proportion.

Listen to this anecdote:

Deep in a beautiful woodland park stood two lovely bronze statues: a boy and a girl, posed in attitudes of love and longing. They had stood thus for three hundred years, their arms held out yearningly to each other, yet never touching. One day a magician passed by and with compassion said, "I have enough power to give them life for one hour, so I am going to do this. For one hour they will be able to kiss, to touch, to embrace, to make love to each other." So the magician waved his magic wand. Immediately the statues leaped off their pedestals, and hand in hand ran into the shrubbery.

There was a great commotion, loud thumps, shouts, squawkings and flutterings. With irresistible curiosity, the magician tiptoed over and peered into the leaves.

The boy was holding down a bird, over which the girl squatted. Suddenly he jumped up. "Now it is your turn to hold him down while I shit on him!" he exclaimed.

Three hundred years of birds shitting on them... then who bothers about lovemaking? That was their repression.

You can sit in a cave and become a statue, but that which you have repressed will hover around you. It will be the only thing that you will ever think about. Tantra says: Beware. Beware of indulgence and beware of renunciation. Beware of both—both are traps. Either way, you are trapped in the mind.

Then where is the way?

Tantra says: Awareness is the way. Indulgence is mechanical, repression is mechanical; both are mechanical things. The only way out of mechanical things is to become aware, alert. Don't go to the Himalayas, bring about a Himalayan silence within you. Don't escape, become more awake. Look into things deeply with no fear... without fear, look into things deeply. Don't listen to what your so-called religious people are teaching. They make you afraid; they don't allow you to look into sex, they don't allow you to look into death. They have exploited your fears tremendously.

The only way for someone to exploit you is to first make you afraid. Once you are afraid, you are ready to be exploited. Fear is the basis and has to be created first. You have been made afraid. Sex is sin, so is fear. Even while making love to your woman or man, you never look directly into it. Even while making love, you are avoiding it. You are making love and avoiding sex. You don't want to see into the reality of it—what it is exactly, why it infatuates you, why it has a magnetic pull over you. Why? What is it exactly, how does it arise, how does it take possession of you, what does it give you, and where does it lead? What happens in it and what happens out of it? Where do you arrive again and again making love? Do you arrive anywhere? These things have to be encountered.

Tantra is an encounter with the reality of life. Sex is fundamental. So is death. They are the two most basic, fundamental chakras—muladhar and svadisthan. When you understand them, the third chakra opens. When you understand the third, the fourth opens, and so on and so forth. When you have understood the six chakras, that understanding hits the seventh chakra and it blooms into a one-thousand-petaled lotus. That day is of superb glory. That day is the meeting day, the day of cosmic orgasm. That day you embrace the divine and the divine embraces you. That day the river disappears into the ocean forever and ever. Then there is no coming back.

From each state of your mind, understanding has to be gained. Wherever you are, don't be afraid. That is the Tantra message: Wherever you are, don't be afraid. Drop only one thing—fear. Only one thing has to

be feared, and that is fear. Unafraid, with great courage, look into the reality, whatever the reality is. If you are a thief, then look into that. If you are an angry person, look into that. If you are greedy, look into that. Wherever you are, look into it. Don't escape. Looking into it, go through it. Watching, go through it. If you can walk the path into greed, into sex, into anger, into jealousy, with eyes open, you will be freed of it.

This is the Tantra promise: Truth liberates. Knowing frees. Knowing is freedom. Otherwise, whether you repress or you indulge, the end is the same.

It happened:

There was a man who had a most attractive wife. But he began to be suspicious of her. At last he could stand it no longer. Being on the night shift, he asked the foreman for a pass out, and went home at two in the morning to find his best friend's car outside, just as he had feared. He let himself in, crept up the stairs and rushed into his wife's bedroom. There she lay on top of the bed, stark naked, but smoking a cigarette and reading a book.

He went wild and searched under the bed and in the closet but he could not find any man. He went berserk and wrecked the bedroom. Then he started on the living room—he threw the TV out of the window, slashed the armchairs, overturned the table and sideboard. Then he turned his attention to the kitchen, where he smashed all the dishes and then he threw the fridge out of the window. Then he shot himself.

When he got up to heaven's gates, who should he see waiting for admission but his

late best friend, who asked him, "What are you doing up here?"

The wronged husband explained all about how he had lost his temper, and added, "But how does it come about that you are up here, too?"

"Ah, me? I was in the fridge."

Both end the same way—whether you are in the Himalayan cave or in the world does not make much difference. The life of indulgence and the life of repression both end in the same way because their mechanism is no different. Their appearance is different, but their inner quality is the same.

Awareness brings a different quality to your life. With awareness, things start changing, changing tremendously—not that you change them, no, not at all. A person of awareness does not change anything, and a person of unawareness continuously tries to change everything. But the person of unawareness never succeeds in changing anything and the person of awareness simply finds change happening, tremendous change happening.

> *You are your world, so if you change, the world changes.*

It is awareness that brings change, not your effort. Why does it happen through awareness? Because the awareness changes *you*, and when you are different the whole world is different. It is not a question of creating a different world, it is only a question of creating a different *you*. You are your world, so if you change, the world changes. If you don't change, you can go on changing the whole world but nothing changes; you will create the same world again and again.

You create your world. It is out of you that your world is projected. Tantra says: Awareness is the key, the master key that opens all the doors of life.

Remember, it is delicate. If I talk about the foolishness of repression, you start thinking about indulging. If I talk about the foolishness of indulgence, you start thinking about repression. It happens every day: you move to the opposite immediately. But the whole point is not to be tempted by the opposite.

To be tempted by the opposite is to be tempted by the Devil. That is the Devil in the Tantra system: to be tempted by the opposite. There is no other devil. The only Devil is that the mind can play a trick on you:

it can propose the opposite. You are against indulgence? The mind says, "So simple… now repress. Don't indulge, escape. Drop this whole world. Forget all about it." But how can you forget all about it? Is it so simple to forget all about it? Then why are you escaping far away and why are you afraid? If you can forget all about it so simply, then be here and forget all about it. But you can't be here. You know the world will tempt you. This momentary understanding, this false understanding that you think you have, will not be of much use. When the temptation comes from desires, you will be a victim. You know it. Before it happens you want to escape, you want to escape fast. You want to escape from the opportunity. Why? Why do you want to escape from the opportunity?

In India, the so-called saints won't stay with householders. Why? What is the fear? In India, the so-called saints won't touch a woman, won't even look. Why? What is the fear? From where does this fear come? They are just avoiding the opportunity. But to avoid the opportunity is not a great achievement.

Just avoiding the opportunity is not of much use. It is a false facade. You can believe in it, but you cannot deceive existence. In fact, you cannot even deceive yourself. In your dreams, that which you have left behind in a repressive way will pop up again and again. It will drive you crazy. Your so-called saints are not even able to sleep well; they are afraid of sleep. Why? Because in sleep, the world that they have repressed asserts itself in dreams;

the unconscious starts relating its desires. The unconscious says, "What are you doing here? You are a fool." The unconscious spreads its net again.

While you are awake you can repress, but when you are asleep, how can you repress? You lose all control. The conscious mind represses, but the conscious mind goes to sleep. That's why in all the old traditions saints have always been afraid of sleep. They cut down their sleep from eight hours to seven, from seven to six, from six to five... four, three, two. And foolish people think it a great achievement. They think, "This saint is a great saint. He sleeps only two hours." In fact, he is simply showing one thing: that he is afraid of his unconscious. He does not allow the unconscious time to surface.

When you sleep for two hours, the unconscious cannot surface, because those two hours are needed for the body's rest. You dream better dreams—good dreams, beautiful dreams—during the time after your sleep is complete. That's why you dream better in the morning, in the early morning. First the need of the body has to be taken care of; the body needs rest. Once the body has rested, then the mind needs rest—that is a secondary thing.

And when the mind takes its rest, then the unconscious, in a restful mood, releases its desires and dreams arise.

The second thing is that if you only rest for two hours in the night there may be dreams, but you will not be able to remember them. That's why you remember only the late

dreams, those that you dream early in the morning. You forget the other dreams of the night because you are so deeply asleep that you cannot remember them. So the saint thinks he has not dreamed about sex, he has not dreamed about money, he has not dreamed about power, prestige, respectability. If he sleeps for two hours, the sleep is so deep and it is such a necessity for the body that it is almost like a coma, so he cannot remember.

You remember dreams only when you are half awake and half asleep. Then the dream can be remembered, because it is close to the conscious. Half asleep, half awake, something of the dream filters into your consciousness, moves into the conscious mind. In the morning you can remember a little bit of it.

That's why you will be surprised that if you ask a laborer who works hard the whole day, "Do you dream?" he will say, "No." Everybody dreams, but not everybody can remember. Working hard the whole day, eight hours, chopping wood or digging a ditch or breaking stones is such hard work that when you fall asleep you are almost in a coma. Dreams come, but you cannot remember them, you cannot recapture them.

So listen to your body, your bodily needs. Listen to your mind, listen to your mind's needs. Don't avoid them. Go into those needs, explore them with loving care. Befriend your body, befriend your mind, if you want to get beyond them one day. Befriending is essential.

That is the Tantra vision of life: Befriend your life energies. Don't become antagonistic.

the four mudras

Tantra describes four seals, or mudras. *To attain the ultimate, a person passes through four doors and has to open four locks. Those four locks are called the four seals, or four* mudras. *These are very important.*

The first mudra is called Karma Mudra. It is the outermost door, the very periphery of your being. It is the outermost area—just like action, that's why it is called Karma Mudra. *Karma* means "action." Action is the outermost core of your being; it is your periphery. What you *do* is your periphery. You love somebody, you hate somebody, you kill somebody, you protect somebody— what you do is your periphery. Action is the outermost part of your being.

The first seal is opened by becoming total in your action... *total* in your action. Whatever you do, do totally, and there will arise great joy. If you are angry, be totally angry; you will learn much from total anger. If you are totally angry and fully aware of your anger, anger will disappear one day. There will be no point in being angry anymore. Once you have understood it, it can be dropped.

Anything that is understood can be dropped easily. Only things not understood continue hanging around you. Try to be total and alert—this is the first lock to be opened.

Remember always, Tantra is scientific. It does not tell you to repeat a mantra. It says, Become aware in your action.

The second seal is called Gyana Mudra—a little deeper than the first, a little more inward than the first—like knowledge. *Gyana* means "knowledge." Action is the outermost thing and knowledge is a little deeper. You can watch what I am doing, but you cannot watch what I am knowing. Knowing is internal. Actions can be watched; knowings cannot be watched. The second seal is that of knowing, Gyana Mudra.

Now, start knowing what you really know, and stop believing things that you really don't know. Somebody asks you, "Is there a God?" and you say, "Yes, God exists"—remember, do you really know? If you don't, please don't say you do. Say, "I don't know." If you are honest and only say what you know, and only believe what you know, the second seal will be broken. If you go on believing things that you don't really know, the second seal will never be broken. False knowledge is the enemy of true knowledge. All beliefs are false knowledge; you simply believe them. Your so-called saints keep telling you, "First believe, then you will know."

Tantra says, First *know*, then belief is there. But that is a totally different kind of belief—it is

and you are only in the now; only the purest of time remains.

Meditate over it. In the *now*, there is no knowledge. Knowledge is always about the past. In the now-moment there is no knowledge; it is completely free from knowledge. Just this moment, what do you know? Nothing is known. If you start thinking that you know this and that, it will come from the past. It will not come from *this* moment, not from *now*. Knowledge is either from the past or it is a projection into the future. The *now* is pure of knowledge.

So the third is Samaya Mudra—to be in this moment. Why does Tantra call it *samaya*, time? Ordinarily you think that past, present, and future are three divisions of time, but that is not the Tantra understanding. Tantra says: Only the present is time. The past is not, it has already gone. The future is not, it has not yet come. Only the present is.

To be in the present is to be truly in time. Otherwise, you are either in memory or you are in dreams, which are both false, delusions. So the third seal is broken by being in the now.

First, be total in your action and the first seal is broken. Second, be honest in your knowing and the second seal is broken. Now, be just here and now and the third seal is broken.

The fourth seal is called *mahamudra*, "the great gesture." It is the innermost layer, like space. Now, only purest space remains. Action, knowing, time, space—these are the four seals. Space is your innermost core, the hub of the wheel, or the center of the cyclone.

In your innermost emptiness is space, sky.

trust. You "believe in" God; you *know* the sun. The sun rises; you need not believe in it—it is simply there and you *know* it. God you "believe in." That God is bogus.

There is another God—the godliness that comes through knowing. But the first thing is to drop all that you don't know but only *believe* that you know. You have always believed and you have always carried the load—drop that load. Out of a hundred things you will be unburdened of almost ninety-eight—unburdened.

Only a few things will remain that you truly *know*. You will feel great freedom. Your head will not be so heavy. With that freedom and weightlessness, you enter the second mudra. The second seal is broken.

The third mudra is called Samaya Mudra. *Samaya* means "time." The first outermost layer is action, the second layer is knowing, the third layer is time. Knowledge has disappeared

PLEASURE, JOY, BLISS

The first pleasure is when your energy is flowing out—bodily pleasure. Joy is when your energy is flowing in—subjective, psychological joy. And when does bliss happen? When your energy is not flowing anywhere—when it is simply there. You are not going anywhere, you are simply there: you are just a being. Now you don't have any goals and you don't have any desires to fulfill. You don't have a future; you are just here now. When the energy has become just a pool—not going anywhere, not flowing anywhere, no goal to be attained, nothing to be sought, you are just here, tremendously here, totally here; this *now* is all the time that is left for you, and this *here* is all the space—then suddenly this gathering of energy that is not moving anywhere and is not distracted by body or mind, becomes a great rush in you. And the one-thousand-petaled lotus opens. So, joy and pleasure are the buds, grace and gratitude and glory are the leaves, and this ultimate flowering of bliss is the fulfillment, the fruition. You have come home.

essentials of the

tantra vision

Real Tantra is not technique but love. It is not technique but prayerfulness. It is not head-oriented but a relaxation into the heart. Please remember it. Many books have been written on Tantra, and they all talk about technique. But the real Tantra has nothing to do with technique. The real Tantra cannot be written about; the real Tantra has to be imbibed.

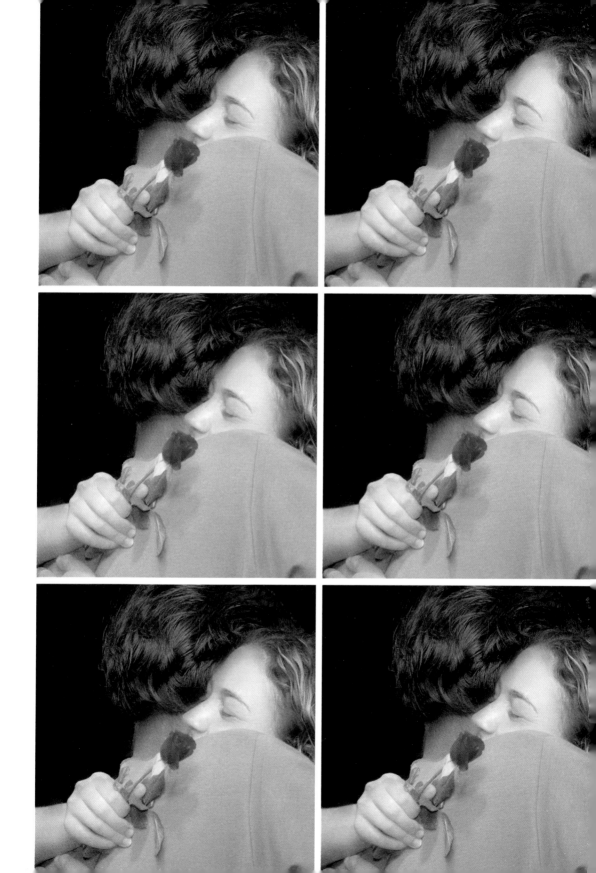

the way of intelligence

There are two ways to approach reality: the way of the intellect and the way of intelligence. The way of the intellect is to theorize, to think about, to speculate. All speculation is meaningless, because how can you speculate about that which you don't know? How can you even think about that which you don't know?

The unknown cannot be thought—there is no way to think about the unknown. All that you think is the known that goes on repeating in your mind. Yes, you can create new combinations of old thoughts, but just by making new combinations, you are not going to discover the real. You will be deceiving yourself.

Intellect is the greatest deceiver in the world. Through intellect man has deceived himself down the ages. Through intellect you *explain away* the reality, you don't explain it. Through intellect you create such a dust around yourself that you cannot see the reality at all, and you are cut off from the existential. You are lost in your scriptures—no one has ever been lost anywhere else. It is in the jungle of the scriptures where you get lost.

Tantra is the way of intelligence, not of intellect. It does not answer any questions, it does not explain anything at all; it is non-explanatory. It is not a questioning, it is a quest. It is not inquiry *about* the truth, it is an inquiry *into* the truth. It penetrates reality. It tries to destroy all the clouds that surround you so that you can see the reality as it is.

Tantra is to go beyond thinking. That's why love has been so much praised by the tantrikas. That's why the orgasm has become a symbol for the ultimate reality. The reason is that it is only in orgasm that you lose your mind for a few moments. That is the only state of no-mind that is available to the ordinary person. That is the only possibility for you to have a glimpse of reality.

Hence, sexual orgasm has become tremendously important on the path of Tantra. Not because it gives you ultimate reality, but because at least it gives you a chance to peek beyond the mind. It gives you a small window—momentary—it does not stay long, but still it is the only possibility for you to have some contact with reality. Otherwise, you are always surrounded by your thoughts and your thoughts explain nothing. All explanations are simply nonsense.

> " *To know the truth, you are moving into the greatest adventure there is. You may be lost, who knows?* "

The reality of a human being is a mystery. There is no answer that can answer it, because it is not a question in the first place. It is a mystery to be lived, not a problem to be solved. Remember the distinction between a problem and a mystery: a mystery is existential, a problem is intellectual. The mystery is not created by the mind, so the mind cannot solve it. The problem is created by the mind in the first place so the mind can solve it. But the mystery of life—this existential mystery that surrounds you, these trees, these stars, these birds, people, you yourself—how can you explain them through the mind?

The mind is a recent arrival. Existence has lived without the mind for a long time. The mind is a recent addition that has just happened. Scientists say that if we divide human history into twenty-four hours, into one day, then the mind came just a few seconds ago... just seconds ago! How can it solve anything? What can it solve? It has not known the beginning, it has not known the end; it has come just now in the middle. It has no perspective.

If you want to know what this unknown is, you have to drop out of the mind, you have to disappear into existence. That is the Tantra way.

Tantra is not a philosophy. Tantra is absolutely existential. And remember, when I say that Tantra is existential, I don't mean the existentialism of Sartre, Camus, Marcel, and others. That existentialism is a philosophy, a philosophy of existence, but not the Tantra way. And the difference is vast.

The existential philosophers in the West have only stumbled upon the negative: anguish, angst, depression, sadness, anxiety, hopelessness, meaninglessness, purposelessness—all the negatives. Tantra has stumbled upon all that is beautiful, joyful, blissful. Tantra says: Existence is an orgasm, an eternal orgasm going on and on and on. It is forever and ever an orgasm, an ecstasy.

They must be moving in different directions. Sartre thinks about existence. Tantra says, Thinking is not the door; it leads nowhere. It is a blind alley. It brings you only to a cul-de-sac. Philosophy is great if you are just fooling around. Then philosophy is great: you can make mountains out of molehills and you can enjoy the trip.

Philosophy is creating mountains out of molehills. You can go on and on—there is no end to it. For at least five thousand years, people have been philosophizing about each and every thing: about the beginning, about the end, about the middle. Yet not a single question has been solved. Not a single—not the smallest—question has been solved or dissolved. Philosophy has proved to be the most futile of efforts. But still we continue,

knowing perfectly well that it never delivers anything. Why? It promises, but it never delivers. Then why do we continue with this effort?

Philosophy is cheap. It does not require any involvement; it is not a commitment. You can sit in your chair and think. It is a dream. It does not require you to change in order to see reality. That's where courage is needed; adventurous courage is needed.

To know the truth, you are moving into the greatest adventure there is. You may be lost, who knows? You may never come back, who knows? Or you may come back utterly changed, and who knows whether it will be for the good or not?

The journey is unknown, so unknown that you cannot even plan it. You have to take a jump into it. Blindfolded, you have to jump into it, in the dark night, with no map, not knowing where you are going, not knowing what you are going for. Only a few daredevils enter into this existential quest. Tantra has only appealed to a few people, but those were the salt of the earth.

beyond indulgence

Tantra is not a way of indulgence. It is the only way to get out of indulgence. It is the only way to get out of sexuality. No other way has ever been helpful for humanity; all other ways have made people more and more sexual.

Sex has not disappeared—the moralists have only poisoned it more and more. It is still there in a poisoned form. Yes, guilt has arisen in human beings, but sex has not disappeared. It cannot disappear because it is a biological reality. It is existential; it cannot simply be made to disappear by repressing it. It can disappear only when you become so aligned that you can release the energy encapsulated in sexuality—the energy is released not by repression but by understanding. Once the energy is released, out of the mud comes the lotus. The lotus has to come up out of the mud; it has to go higher. Repression takes it deeper into the mud.

The whole of humanity has repressed sex in the mud of the unconscious. People go on repressing it, sitting on top of it; not allowing it to move. They kill it by fasting, by discipline, by going to a cave in the Himalayas, by moving to a monastery where women are not allowed. There are monasteries where no woman has ever entered for hundreds of years; there are convents where only nuns have lived and a man has never entered. These are ways of repressing and they create more and more sexuality and more and more dreams of indulgence.

No, Tantra is not a way of indulgence. It is the only way of freedom. Tantra says: Whatever exists has to be understood, and through understanding, changes occur of their own accord.

Indulgence is suicidal—as suicidal as repression. These are the two extremes that Buddha says to avoid. One extreme is repression, the other is indulgence. Be in the middle: neither be repressive nor indulgent. Just be in the middle, watchful, alert, aware. It is your life! Neither does it have to be repressed, nor does it have to be wasted—it has to be understood.

It is your life—take care of it, love it, befriend it! If you can befriend your life, it will reveal many mysteries to you, it will take you to the very door of the beyond.

Tantra is not indulgence at all. Repressive people have always thought that Tantra is indulgence because their minds are so much obsessed. For example, how can a man who lives in a monastery without ever seeing a woman believe that Saraha is not indulging

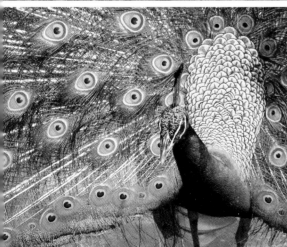

when he lives with a woman? Not only lives with a woman but practices strange things: sitting with the woman naked while he just watches her; or even while making love to the woman, he watches himself and his lovemaking.

Now, you cannot see his watching; you can see only that he is making love to a woman. And if you are repressive, your whole repressed sexuality will bubble up. You will start going mad! You will project all that you have repressed in yourself onto Saraha—and Saraha is not doing anything like that; he is moving in a totally different dimension. He is not really interested in the body. He wants to see what this sexuality is; he wants to see what this appeal of sex is; he wants to see what exactly orgasm is; he wants to be meditative in

that peak moment so that he can find the clue and the key... maybe there is the key to open the door of the beyond. In fact, it is there.

Nature has hidden the key in your sexuality. On the one hand, through your sexuality, life survives but that is only a partial use of your sex energy. On the other hand, if you move with full awareness into your sex energy, you will find a key that can help you enter the eternal. One small aspect of sex is that your children will be born. The other aspect, a higher aspect, is that you can live in eternity.

Sex energy is life energy. Ordinarily we don't move further than the porch. We never go into the palace. Saraha is trying to go into the palace. The people who came to the king must have been suppressed people—as all people are suppressed.

The politician and the priest have to teach suppression because it is only through suppression that people can be driven insane. You can rule insane people more easily than sane people. And when people are insane in their sex energy, they start moving in other directions—they start moving toward money or power or prestige. They have to express their sex energy somewhere or other; it is boiling and they have to release it. So money-madness or power-addiction becomes their release.

This whole society is sex-obsessed. If sex-obsession disappears from the world, people will not be money-mad. Who will bother about money? And people will not be bothered by power. Nobody will want to become a president or a prime minister—for what? Life is so tremendously beautiful in its ordinariness, it is so superb in its ordinariness, why should anyone want to become "somebody"? Being nobody is so delicious—nothing is missing. But if you destroy people's sexuality and repress them, so much is missing that they are always hankering, thinking that somewhere there must be joy, because here it is missing.

Sex is one of the activities given by nature in which you are thrown again and again to the present moment. Ordinarily you are never in the present, except when you are making love, and then too for only a few seconds.

Tantra says you have to understand sex, to decode sex. If sex is so vital that life comes out of it, then there must be something more to it. That something more is the key to transcendence.

beyond the taboo

Why has sex been a taboo in all societies down the ages? It is a complicated question, but important too—worth going into.

Sex is the most powerful human instinct. The politician and the priest have understood from the very beginning that sex is the most driving human energy. It has to be curtailed; it has to be cut. If people are allowed total freedom in sex, then there will be no possibility of dominating them; making slaves out of them will be impossible.

Have you not seen it being done? When you want a bull to be yoked to a cart, what do you do? You castrate him—you destroy his sex energy. And have you seen the difference between a bull and an ox? What a difference! An ox is a poor phenomenon, a slave. A bull is a beauty; a bull is a glorious phenomenon, a great splendor. See a bull walking, how he walks like an emperor! Then see an ox pulling a cart.

The same has been done to human beings: the sex instinct has been curtailed, cut, crippled. A man does not exist as a bull now, he exists like the ox, and each man is pulling a thousand and one carts. Look, and you will find behind you a thousand and one carts, and you are yoked to them all.

Why can't you yoke a bull? The bull is too powerful. If he sees a cow passing by, he will throw aside both you and the cart and he will

go to the cow. He will not bother a bit about who you are and he will not listen to you. It will be impossible to control the bull.

Sex energy is life energy; it is uncontrollable. The politician and the priest are not interested in you, they are interested in channeling your energy in other directions. So there is a certain mechanism behind it that has to be understood.

Sex repression, tabooing sex, is the very foundation of human slavery. People cannot be free unless sex is free. People cannot be truly free unless their sex energy is allowed natural growth.

These are the five tricks through which the human being has been turned into a slave, an ugly phenomenon, a cripple.

The first: Keep people as weak as possible if you want to dominate them. If the priest wants to dominate you or the politician wants to dominate you, you must be kept as weak as possible. Yes, in certain cases, exceptions are allowed—that is, when the service of fighting the enemy is needed. The army is allowed many things that other people are not allowed. The army is in the service of death; it is allowed to be powerful. It is allowed to remain as powerful as possible because it is needed to kill the enemy.

Other people are destroyed. They are forced to remain weak in a thousand and one ways, and the best way to keep a person weak is not to give love total freedom. Love is nourishment. Psychologists have discovered that if a child is not given love, he shrivels up into himself and becomes weak. You can give him milk, you can give him medicine, you can give him everything else, just don't give love. Don't hug him, don't kiss him, don't hold him close to the warmth of your body and the child will become weaker and weaker. There are more chances of his dying than surviving. What happens? Why? Just hugging, kissing, giving warmth, somehow the child feels nourished, accepted, loved, needed. The child starts feeling worthy; the child starts feeling a certain meaning in his life. From childhood we starve children: we don't give love as much as is needed. Then we force the young men and young women not to fall in love unless they get married. By the age of fourteen, they become sexually mature. But their education may take more time—ten years more, twenty-four, twenty-five years—then they will be getting their MAs, or PhDs, or MDs, so we have to force them not to fall in love.

Sexual energy comes to its climax near the age of eighteen. Never again will a man be so potent and never again will a woman be able to have a greater orgasm than she can experience near the age of eighteen. But we try to force them not to make love. We force boys and girls

to have separate dormitories. Girls and boys are kept separate, and between the two stands the whole mechanism of police, magistrates, chancellors, principals, headmasters. They are all holding the boys back from going to the girls, holding the girls back from going to the boys. Why is so much care taken? They are trying to kill the bull and create an ox.

By the time you are eighteen you are at the peak of your sexual energy, your love energy. By the time you get married you are twenty-five, twenty-six, twenty-seven... and the age has been going up and up. The more cultured a country, the longer you wait, because there is more to be learned, a job has to be found, this and that. By the time you get married you are almost declining in your powers.

Then you make love, but the lovemaking never becomes really hot—it never comes to the point where people evaporate—it remains lukewarm. And when you have not been able to love totally, you cannot love your children because you don't know how. When you have not known the peaks of love, how can you teach your children? How can you help your children to know the peaks of it?

Down the ages we have been denied love so that we should remain weak.

Second: Keep people as ignorant and deluded as possible so that they can easily be deceived. If you want to create a sort of idiocy—which is a must for the priest and the politician and their conspiracy—then the best thing is to prevent people from moving into love freely. Without love, a person's intelligence falls low. Have you not seen it? When you fall in love, suddenly all your capacities are at their peak, at their crescendo. Just a moment ago you were looking dull, and then you met your woman... and suddenly a great joy erupted in your being; you are aflame. When people are in love, they perform at their maximum. When love disappears or when love is not there, they perform at their minimum.

The greatest, most intelligent people are the most sexual people. This has to be understood, because love energy is basically intelligence. If you cannot love, you are closed and cold; you cannot flow. While in love you flow. While in love, you feel so confident that you can touch the stars. That's why a woman becomes a great inspiration or a man becomes a great inspiration. When a woman is loved, she becomes more beautiful *immediately*, instantly! Just a moment ago she was an ordinary woman and now love has showered upon her—she is bathed in a totally new energy and a new aura arises around her. She walks more gracefully—a dance has entered her step. Her eyes have tremendous beauty now, her face glows, she is luminous. And the same things happen to the man.

When people are in love they perform at the optimum. Don't allow love and they will remain at the minimum. When they remain at the minimum, they are stupid, they are ignorant, they don't bother to know. When people are ignorant and stupid and deluded, they can be easily deceived. When people are sexually repressed, when their love is repressed, they start hankering for the "other life." They think about heaven or paradise, but they don't think to create the paradise here and now.

When you are in love, paradise is here and now. Then you don't bother to go to the priest. Then who worries about a paradise? You are already there! You are no longer interested. But when your love energy is repressed, you start thinking, "Here there is nothing. Now is empty. There must be somewhere, some goal...." You go to the priest and ask about

heaven and he paints beautiful pictures of heaven.

Sex has been repressed so that you can become interested in the other life. And when people are interested in the other life, naturally they are not interested in this life.

Tantra says: This life is the only life. The other life is hidden in this life. It is not against it, it is not away from it; it is *in* it. Go into it. *This is it!* Go into it and you will find the other, too. God is hidden in the world—that is the Tantra message. A great message, superb, incomparable: God is hidden in the world, God is hidden here now. If you love, you will be able to feel it.

The third secret: Keep people as frightened as possible. The sure way is to not allow them love, because love destroys fear... "Love casteth out fear." When you are in love, you are not afraid. When you are in love, you can fight against the whole world. When you are in love, you feel infinitely capable of anything. But when you are not in love, you are afraid of small things. When you are not in love, you become more interested in security, in safety. When you are in love, you are more interested in adventure, in exploration.

People have not been allowed to love because that is the only way to make them afraid. And when they are afraid and trembling, they are always on their knees, kneeling to the priest and bowing to the politician.

It is a great conspiracy against humanity. It is a great conspiracy against you! Your politician and your priest are your enemies, but they pretend that they are public servants. They say, "We are here to serve you, to help you attain a better life. We are here to create a good life for you." Yet they are the destroyers of life itself.

The fourth: Keep people as miserable as possible—because miserable people are confused, miserable people have no self-worth, miserable people are self-condemnatory. A miserable man feels that he must have done something wrong. A miserable woman has no grounding: you can push her from here to there—she can be turned into driftwood easily. A miserable man is always ready to be commanded, to be ordered, to be disciplined, because he knows: "On my own I am simply miserable. Maybe somebody else can discipline my life." He is a ready victim.

And the fifth: Keep people as alienated from each other as possible, so that they cannot band together for any purpose of which the priest and the politician may not approve. Keep people separate from each other. Don't allow them too much intimacy. When people are separate, lonely, and alienated from one another, they cannot band together. And there are a thousand and one tricks to keep them apart.

For example, if you are holding the hand of a man—you are a man and you are holding the hand of another man and walking down the road singing—you will feel guilty because people will start looking at you: Are you gay, homosexual or something? Two men are not allowed to be happy together. They are not allowed to hold hands, they are not allowed to hug each other. They are condemned as homosexuals. Fear arises.

If your friend comes and takes your hand in his hand, you look around: "Is somebody looking or not?" And you are in a hurry to drop his hand. You shake hands in such a hurry. Have you watched it? You just touch each other's hand and shake and you are finished. You don't hold hands; you don't hug each other. You are afraid.

Do you remember your father ever hugging you? Do you remember your mother hugging you after you became sexually mature? Why not? Fear has been created. A young man and his mother hugging? Maybe some sex will arise between them, some idea, some fantasy. Fear has been created: the father and the son, the father and the daughter, no. The brother and the sister, no; the brother and the brother—no! People are kept in separate boxes with great walls around them. Everybody is classified, and there are a thousand and one barriers.

Yes, one day, after twenty-five years of all this training, you are allowed to make love to your wife. But now the training has gone too deep into you, and suddenly you don't know what to do. How to love? You have not learned the language. It is as if a person has not been allowed to speak for twenty-five years. For twenty-five years he has not been allowed to speak a single word and then suddenly you put him on a stage and tell him, "Give us a great lecture." What will happen? He will fall down then and there! He may faint, he may die... twenty-five years of silence, and now suddenly he is expected to deliver a great lecture? It is not possible.

This is what is happening. Twenty-five years of anti-love training, of fear, and then suddenly you are legally allowed—a license is issued—

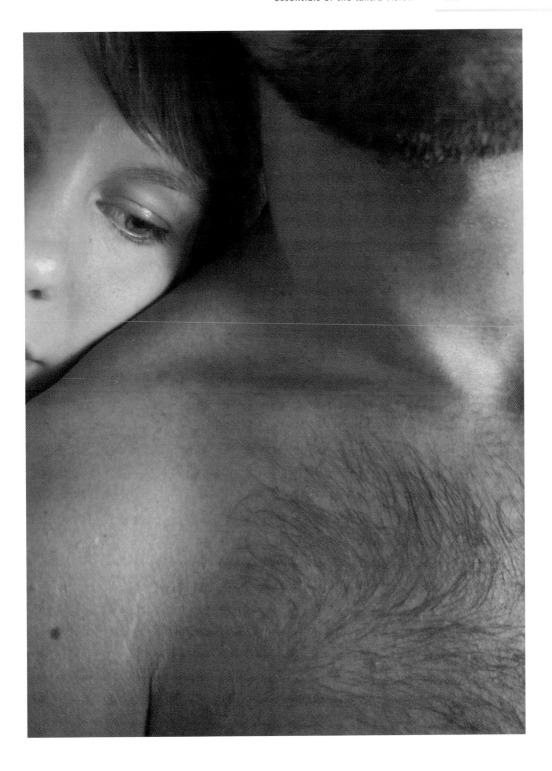

and now you can love this woman. This is your wife, you are her husband, and you are allowed to love. But what happens to those twenty-five years of wrong training? They will still be there.

Yes, you will "love"... you will make a gesture. It is not going to be explosive, it is not going to be orgasmic—it will be very tiny. That's why you are frustrated after making love. Ninety-nine percent of people are frustrated after making love, more frustrated than they have ever been before. And they think, "What is this? There is nothing in it, it is not real!" First the priest and the politician have managed things so that you have not be able to make love, and then they come and they preach that there is nothing meaningful in sex. And certainly their preaching looks right, exactly in tune with your experience. First they create the experience of futility and frustration, then they deliver their teaching. And they look logical together—of one piece.

This is a great trick, the greatest that has ever been played upon humanity. These five things can be managed through one single thing, and that is the taboo against love. It is possible to accomplish all these objectives by preventing people from loving each other. And the taboo has been managed in such a scientific way. This taboo is a great work of art—great skill and great cunningness have gone into it. It is really a masterpiece. This taboo has to be understood.

First—it is indirect. It is hidden. It is not apparent, because whenever a taboo is too obvious, it will not work. The taboo has to be hidden, so that you don't know how it works.

The taboo has to be so hidden that you cannot even imagine that being against it is possible. The taboo has to go into the unconscious, not into the conscious. How to make it so subtle and so indirect?

The trick is: first go on teaching that love is great, so people never think that the priests and the politicians are against love. Go on teaching that love is great, that love is the right thing, and then don't allow any situation where love can happen. Don't allow the opportunity. Go on teaching that food is great, that eating is a great joy: "Eat as well as you can." But don't supply anything to eat. Keep people hungry and go on talking about love.

All the priests go on talking about love. Love is praised as just next to God, and every possibility of its happening is denied. Directly, they encourage it; indirectly, they cut its roots. This is the masterpiece.

No priests talk about how they have done the harm. It is as if you say to a tree, "Be green, bloom, enjoy," and then you cut the roots so that the tree cannot grow. And when the tree does not become green, you can jump upon the tree and say, "Listen! You don't listen. You don't follow us. We are saying 'Be green, bloom, enjoy, dance'"... and meanwhile you go on cutting the roots.

Love is denied so much. It is the rarest thing in the world and it should not be denied. If you can love five people, you should love five. If you can love fifty, you should love fifty. If you can love five hundred, you should love five hundred.

Love is so rare that the more you can spread it the better.

But you are forced into a narrow corner: you can love only your wife, you can love only your husband, you can love only this, you can love only that. It is as if there were a law that you can breathe only when you are with your wife, you can breathe only when you are with your husband. Soon breathing will become impossible. Then you will die! And you will not even be able to breathe while you are with your wife or with your husband. You have to breathe twenty-four hours a day.

Be loving.

Then there is another trick: they talk about "higher love" while they destroy the lower. They say that the lower has to be denied: bodily love is bad, spiritual love is good. Have you ever seen any spirit without a body? Have you ever seen a house without a foundation? The lower is the foundation of the higher. The body is your abode, the spirit lives in the body, with the body. You are an embodied spirit and an ensouled body. You are together. The lower and the higher are not separate, they are one—both rungs of the same ladder.

This is what Tantra wants to make clear: the lower is not to be denied, the lower has to be transformed into the higher. The lower is good. If you are stuck with the lower, the fault is with you, not with the lower. Nothing is wrong with the lower rung of a ladder. If you are stuck with it, *you* are stuck. It is something in you.

The lower is not to be denied; the lower has to be transformed into the higher.

Move.

Sex is not wrong. *You* are wrong if you are stuck there. Move higher. The higher is not against the lower; the lower makes it possible for the higher to exist.

These tricks have created many other problems. Each time you are in love, somehow you feel guilty; guilt has arisen. When there is guilt, you cannot move totally into love—the guilt prevents you, it holds you back. Even while making love to your wife or your husband, there is guilt. You know this is sin, you know you are doing something wrong. "Saints don't do it." You are a sinner. So you cannot move totally even when you are allowed—superficially—to love your spouse. The priest is hidden behind you in your guilt feelings; he is pulling you from there, pulling your strings.

When guilt arises, you start believing that you are wrong; you lose self-worth, you lose self-respect.

And another problem: When there is guilt you start pretending. Mothers and fathers don't allow their children to know that they make love: they pretend. They pretend that love does not exist. Their pretense will come to be known by the children sooner or later and when the children come to know about the pretense, they lose all trust. They feel betrayed, they feel cheated. Then fathers and mothers say that their children don't respect them. You are the cause of it—how can they respect you? You have been deceiving them in every way. You have been dishonest; you have been mean. You were telling them not to fall in love—"Beware"—and you were making love all the time. And the day will come, sooner or later, when they will realize that even their father, even their mother, was not true with them—so how can they respect you?

First guilt creates pretense, then pretense creates alienation from others. Even your own child will not feel in tune with you; there is a barrier—your pretense. And you know that everybody is pretending....

One day, you will come to know that you are just pretending and so are others. When everybody is pretending, how can you relate? When everybody is false, how can you relate? How can you be friendly when everywhere there is deception and deceit? You become disillusioned about reality, you become bitter, and you see it only as a devil's workshop. Everybody has a false face; nobody is authentic. Everybody is wearing a mask; nobody shows his original face.

You feel guilty, you feel that you are pretending, and you know that everybody is pretending, everybody is feeling guilty, and everybody has become like an ugly wound. Now it is easy to make these people slaves—to turn them into clerks, stationmasters, schoolmasters, collectors, ministers, governors, presidents. Now it is easy to distract them. You have distracted them from their roots. Sex is the root.

A curate and a bishop were in opposite corners of a railway car on a long journey. As the bishop entered, the curate put away his copy of Playboy and started reading the Church Times. The bishop ignored him and began doing the Times crossword. Silence prevailed. After a while the curate tried to make conversation. When the bishop began to do a lot of head scratching and "tut-tut-tutting," he tried again: "Can I help you, sir?"

"Perhaps. I am only beaten by one word. What is it that has four letters, the last three are u-n-t, and the clue is, 'essentially feminine?'"

"Why, sir," said the curate, after a slight pause. "That would be 'aunt.'"

"Of course, of course!" said the bishop. "I say, young man, can you lend me an eraser?"

When you repress things on the surface, they go deep inside, into the unconscious. It is there. Sex has not been destroyed—fortunately. It has only been poisoned. It cannot be destroyed; it is life energy. It has become polluted, and it can be purified.

Tantra can purify your sex energy. Listen to the Tantra message. Try to understand it. It is a great revolutionary message. It is against all priests and politicians. It is against all those poisoners who have killed all joy on the earth just so that people can be reduced to slaves.

Reclaim your freedom. Reclaim your freedom to love. Reclaim your freedom to be and then life will no longer be a problem. It is a mystery, it is an ecstasy, and it is a benediction.

EXPANSION

Tantra means expansion. This is the state when you have expanded to the utmost. Your boundaries and the boundaries of existence are no longer separate—they are the same. Less than that will not satisfy. When you become universal, you come home. When you become all, when you become one with all, when you are as huge as this universe, when you contain all—when stars start moving within you and earths are born in you and disappear—when you experience this cosmic expansion, then the work is finished. You have come home. This is the goal of Tantra.

without character

Be without character—that's what Tantra says. It is difficult even to understand, because down the centuries we have been taught to have character. Character means to have a rigid structure; character means the past; character means a certain enforced discipline. Character means you are no longer free—you only follow certain rules and you never go beyond those rules. You have solidity. A man of character is a solid man.

Tantra says: Drop character, be fluid, be flowing, live moment-to-moment. It does not mean irresponsibility. It means greater responsibility because it means greater awareness. When you can live through character, you need not be aware—character takes care. When you live through character, you can fall asleep easily; there is no need to be awake since the character will continue in a mechanical way. But when you don't have any character, when you don't have a hard structure around you, you have to be alert each moment. Each moment you have to see what you are doing. Each moment you have to respond to the new situation before you.

A man of character is a dead man. He has a past but no future. A man who has no character... and I am not using the word in the same sense as when you say that somebody is characterless. When you use the word "characterless" you are not using it rightly, because whomsoever you call characterless has a *character*. Maybe it is against society, but he has a character; you can depend on him, too.

The saint has a character and so does the sinner—they both have characters. You call the sinner characterless because you want to condemn his character; otherwise, he has as much character as the saint. You can depend on him: give him the opportunity and he will steal—he has character. Give him the opportunity and he is bound to steal; give him the opportunity and he will do something wrong—he has character. The moment he comes out of the jail, he starts thinking, "What to do now?" Again he is thrown in jail, again he comes out... no jail has ever cured anybody. In fact, jailing a person, imprisoning a person, makes him even cleverer, that's all. Maybe you won't be able to catch him so easily next time. But nothing else is achieved by throwing him in jail; you just give him more cleverness. He has character.

Can't you see?—a drunkard has character—a very stubborn character. A thousand and one times he vows not to drink anymore, and always his character wins over his vow and he is defeated.

The sinner has character, so has the saint.

What Tantra means by characterlessness is freedom from character. The character of the saint and the character of the sinner both make you solid like rocks, like ice. You don't have any freedom, you can't move easily. If a new situation arises you cannot respond in a new way—you have character, how can you respond in a new way? You have to respond in the old way. The old, the known, the well practiced—you are skilled in it.

A character becomes an alibi: you need not live.

Tantra says: Be characterless, be without character. Characterlessness is freedom.

A characterless person does not follow any rules—he follows his awareness. He doesn't have any discipline—he has only his consciousness. His only shelter is his consciousness. He doesn't have any conscience—his consciousness is his only shelter.

Conscience is character and it is a trick of society. Society creates a conscience in you so that you need not have any consciousness.

It makes you follow certain rules for a long time; it rewards you if you follow and it punishes you if you don't follow. It makes you a robot. Once it has created the mechanism of conscience in you, then society can be free of you—then you can be trusted, you will be a slave your whole life. It has put a conscience in you just as if Delgado had put an electrode in you; it is a subtle electrode. But it has killed you. You are no longer a flow, no longer a dynamism.

Tantra says: Walking, walk; sitting, sit; being, be! Exist without thinking. Let life flow through you without any blocks of thoughts. Let life flow through you without any fear. There is nothing to fear—you have nothing to lose. There is nothing to fear because death will take only that which birth has given to you. And it is going to take it anyway, so there is nothing to fear.

Let life flow through you.

s p o n t a n e i t y

In Tantra, spontaneity is the greatest value—to be natural, to allow nature to happen. Not to obstruct it, not to hinder it; not to distract it, not to take it in some direction where it was not going on its own. To surrender to nature, flow with it. Not pushing the river, but going with it all the way, wherever it leads. This trust is Tantra. Spontaneity is its mantra, its foundation.

S pontaneity means you don't interfere, you are in a let-go. Whatever happens, you watch, you are a witness to it. You know it is happening, but you don't jump into it and you don't try to change its course. Spontaneity means you don't have any direction, you don't have any goal to attain. If you have some goal to attain, you cannot be spontaneous. How can you be spontaneous if your nature is going one way, and your goal is in a different direction? How can you be spontaneous? You will drag yourself toward your goal.

That's what millions of people are doing—dragging themselves toward some imaginary goal. And because they are dragging themselves toward this goal, they are missing their natural destiny—which is the only goal! That's why there is so much frustration, so much misery, and so much hell. When you are chasing a goal, whatever you do will never satisfy your nature. That's why people seem so dull and dead. They live and yet they live not. They are moving like prisoners, chained. Their movement is not free, their movement is not a dance—it cannot be—because they are fighting constantly with themselves. There is a conflict each moment. You want to eat *this* and your religion does not approve of it; you want to go with *this* woman but that will not be respectable. You want to live *this* way, but society prohibits it. You want to be in one way, you feel that that is how you can flower, but everybody else is against it.

So do you listen to your being, or do you listen to everybody else's advice? If you listen to everybody's advice, your life will be an empty life of nothing but frustration. You will finish without ever being alive; you will die without ever knowing what life is.

But society has created such conditioning in you that it is not only outside—it is inside you. That's what conscience is all about. Whatever you want to do, your conscience says, "Don't do it!" The conscience is your parental voice; the priest and the politician speak through it. It is a great trick! They have created a conscience in you from childhood, when you were not aware at all of what was being done to you. They have put a conscience

in you so that whenever you go against the conscience, you feel guilt.

Guilt means you have done something that others don't want you to do. So whenever you are natural, you feel guilty, and whenever you are not guilty, you are unnatural. This is the dilemma, this is the dichotomy, this is the problem. If you listen to your own naturalness, you feel guilty—then there is misery. You start thinking you have done something wrong. You start hiding, you start defending yourself; you start pretending that you have not done this thing. And you are afraid—somebody is bound to catch you sooner or later. You are afraid you will be caught and that brings anxiety, and guilt, and fear. You lose all love for life.

Whenever you do something against what others have taught you, you feel guilty. But whenever you do something just because others say you should, you never feel happy doing it, because it has never been your own thing to do. You are caught between these two polarities.

I was just reading an anecdote:

"What's this double jeopardy that the Constitution is supposed to guarantee against?" Roland asked his lawyer friend, Milt.

Said Milt, "It is like this, Rollie. If you are out driving your car and both your wife and her mother are sitting in the back seat telling you how to drive, well... that's double jeopardy. And you have a constitutional right to turn around and say,

the mahatma, the saint. They are all sitting in the back seat and they all are trying to advise you: "Do this! Don't do that! Go this way! Don't go that way!" They are driving you mad, yet you have been taught to follow them. If you don't follow them, that creates a fear in you that something is wrong—how can you be right when so many people are advising you differently? And they are always advising for your own good! How can you alone be right when the whole world is saying, "Do this!" Of course, they are in the majority and they must be right.

But remember: it is not a question of being right or wrong. It is a question of being spontaneous or not. Spontaneity is right! Otherwise, you will become an imitator, and imitators are never fulfilled human beings. You wanted to be a painter, but your parents said, "No, because painting is not going to give you enough money, and being an artist is not going to give you any respect in society. You will become a hobo, and you will be a beggar. So don't bother about painting. Become a lawyer!" So you have become a lawyer; now you don't feel any happiness. It is a plastic thing, this being a lawyer, and deep down you still want to paint.

While sitting in the court, you are still painting deep down. Maybe you are listening to the criminal, but you are thinking about his face, what a beautiful face he has and what a beautiful portrait would have been possible. You are looking at his eyes and the blueness of his eyes, and you are thinking of colors... and here you are, a prosecuting attorney! So you are constantly at unease and tension follows

'Now, who the hell's driving this car, dear, you or your mother?'"

You may be at the wheel, but you are not driving the car. There are many people sitting in the back seat—your parents, your parents' parents, your priest, your politician, the leader, you. By and by, you might start to feel that you are a respectable man—but you are just an imitation, you are artificial.

Tantra makes spontaneity the first virtue, the most fundamental virtue.

Now, one thing must be understood very deeply. Spontaneity can be of two types. One type is only impulsiveness, but then it is not very valuable. If it is of awareness, then it has a quality of being unique—the quality of a buddha. Many times you think you are becoming spontaneous when in fact you are becoming impulsive.

What is the difference between being impulsive and being spontaneous? There are two aspects to you: the body and the mind. The mind is controlled by society and the body is controlled by biology. The mind is controlled by your society because society can put thoughts into your mind; and your body is controlled by millions of years of biological evolution. The body is unconscious and so is the mind. You are a watcher, beyond both. If you stop listening to the mind and to society, there is every possibility you will start listening to your biology. Sometimes you might feel like murdering somebody, and you say, "It is good to be spontaneous, so I will do it. I have to be spontaneous." You have misunderstood. That is not going to make your life beautiful, blissful. You will be continually in conflict again—now with people outside.

By spontaneity Tantra means a spontaneity full of awareness. The first step in order to be spontaneous is to be fully aware. The moment you are aware, you are neither in the trap of the mind nor in the trap of the body. Then

real spontaneity flows from your soul—from the sky, from the sea, your spontaneity flows. Otherwise, you can change your masters: from the body you can change to the mind, or from the mind you can change to the body.

The body is fast asleep, so following the body will be like following a blind man and the spontaneity will just take you into a ditch. It is not going to help you. Impulsiveness is not spontaneity. Yes, impulse does have a certain spontaneity, more spontaneity than the mind, but it has not the quality that Tantra would like you to imbibe.

As we are now, we live unconsciously. Whether we live in the mind or in the body does not make much difference—we live unconsciously.

A drunk staggered from a tavern and started walking with one foot in the street and one on the sidewalk. After a block or two, a policeman spotted him. "Hey," said the cop. "You're drunk!"

The drunk sighed with relief. "Gosh!" he said. "Is that what's wrong? I thought I was lame."

When you are under the influence of the body, you are under the influence of chemistry. You are out of one trap, the trap of the mind, but you are in another trap, the trap of biology, chemistry. You are out of one ditch, but you have fallen into another one.

When you really want to be out of all ditches and living in freedom, you will have to become a witness of both body and mind. When you are witnessing, and your spontaneity arises out of your witnessing, that is the spontaneity Tantra is talking about.

intensity

Except for human beings, everything is fresh, because it is only we who carry the load, the luggage of memory. That's why people become dirty, unclean, loaded, burdened—otherwise, all of existence is new and fresh. It carries no past and it imagines no future. It is simply here, totally here! When you are carrying the past, much of your being is involved in the past—a past that is not. When you are imagining the future, much of your being is involved in the future, which is not, not yet. You are spread very thin; that's why your life has no intensity.

Tantra says that to know truth you need only one thing: intensity—total intensity. How to create this total intensity?

Drop the past and drop the future, then your whole life energy is focused on the small here and now. In that focusing you are afire, you are a living fire. You are the same fire that Moses saw on the mountain—and God was standing in the fire, and the fire was not burning him. The fire was not burning even the green bush; the bush was alive and fresh and young.

The whole of life is fire. To know it, you need intensity—otherwise, you live in a lukewarm way. Tantra has only one commandment: Don't live lukewarm. That is not a way to live; that is a slow suicide.

When you are eating, be intensely there. The ascetics have condemned tantrikas because they say they are just "eat, drink, and be merry" people. In a way they are right, but in another way they are wrong, because there is a great difference between the ordinary "eat, drink, and be merry" person and a tantrika. A tantrika says this is the way to know truth—but while you are eating, then let there be *only* eating and nothing else. Then let the past disappear and the future too; then let your whole energy be poured into your food. Let there be love and affection and gratitude for the food. Chew each bite with tremendous energy and you will have not only the taste of the food but the taste of existence—because the food is part of existence! It brings life; it brings vitality. It makes you tick, it helps you stay alive. It is not just food. Food may be the container, but *life* is contained in it. If you taste only food and you don't taste existence in it, you are living a lukewarm life; then you don't know how a tantrika lives.

When you are drinking water, become thirsty! Let there be an intensity to it so that each drop of cool water gives you tremendous joy. In the very experience of those drops of water entering your throat and giving you great contentment, you will taste God—you will taste reality.

Tantra is not ordinary indulgence, it is *extraordinary* indulgence. It is not ordinary indulgence because it indulges in God himself. But, Tantra says, it is through the small things of life that you have the taste.

There are no big things in life; everything is small. The small thing becomes big and great if you enter into it utterly, totally, wholly. Making love to a woman or a man, *be* the love. Forget everything else! In that moment let there be nothing else. Let the whole existence converge on your lovemaking. Let that love be wild, innocent—innocent in the sense that there is no mind to corrupt it. Don't think about it, don't fantasize about it, because all that imagination and thinking spreads you thin. Let all thinking disappear. Let the act be total! Be in the act—lost, absorbed, gone—and then, through love, you will know what godliness is.

Tantra says it can be known through drinking, it can be known through eating, it can be known through love. It can be known from every space, from every corner, from every angle—because all angles are God's. It is all truth.

Don't think that you are unfortunate because you were not around in the beginning when God created the world—God is creating the world right now! You are fortunate to be here. You can see the creation of this moment. And don't think you will miss when the world disappears with a bang—it is disappearing right now. Each moment the world is created; each moment it disappears. Each moment it is born;

each moment it dies. So Tantra says let that be your life also—each moment dying to the past; each moment being born anew.

Don't carry any load; remain empty.

the unity of opposites

Those who are too analytical, interpretative, continuously thinking in categories of the mind, are always divided. They are split. There is always a problem for them. The problem is not in existence; that problem comes from their own divided minds. That person's own mind is not a single unity.

Now, you can ask the scientist, also; he says the brain is divided into two parts, the left and the right, and they function differently—not only differently, they function diametrically opposite to each other. The left side of the brain is analytical, and the right side of the brain is intuitive. The left-side mind is mathematical, logical, syllogistic. The right-side mind is poetic, artistic, esthetic, mystic. They exist according to different categories, and there is only a small bridge between the two, just a small link.

It has now and then happened that in some accident that link was broken, and the person became two. In the Second World War there were many cases where the link was broken and the man became two. Sometimes he would say one thing in the morning and by the evening he would completely forget about it and he would start saying something else. In the morning one hemisphere was working and in the evening another hemisphere was working.

Modern science has to look deeply into it. Yoga has looked deeply into it. Yoga says that your breathing changes… for about forty minutes you breathe primarily through one nostril, and then for the next forty minutes you breathe primarily through the other nostril. Modern science has not researched why the breathing changes and what the implications of this change are. But Yoga has thought deeply about it.

When your left nostril is working, your right brain will function more; when your right nostril is working, your left brain will function more. This arrangement is so that one side of the brain can function for forty minutes and then it can rest.

Somehow, we have felt it even without knowing exactly what it is, that after each forty minutes we have to change our work. That's why in schools, colleges, and universities, they usually change the class after forty minutes. One part of the brain becomes tired. Forty minutes seems to be the ultimate limit, then it needs rest. So if you have been studying

mathematics, it is good after forty minutes to study poetry; later you can come back to mathematics again.

You can watch your own life and you will find a rhythm. Just a moment ago, you were so loving toward your wife, then suddenly something clicked and you no longer feeling loving. And you are worried—what happened? Suddenly the flow is not there; you are frozen. Maybe you were holding your wife's hand and the mind changed and another mind has come in, and suddenly energy is no longer flowing. Now you want to let go of the hand and escape from this woman. Just a moment ago you were promising, "I will love you forever," and now you are worried: "This is not right. Just a moment ago I promised, and I am already breaking the promise."

> « *This togetherness is the real meeting of man and woman.* »

You are angry and you want to hurt somebody—and just a few minutes later that anger is gone, you are no longer angry. You even start feeling compassion for the other person. Watch your mind and you will find this continual shift; this gear is always changing.

Tantra says there is a state of unity when the bridge between the two hemispheres of the brain is no longer a small link, but both sides are completely together. This togetherness is the real meeting of the man

and the woman—because one part of the brain, the right hemisphere, is feminine while the left hemisphere is masculine. When you are making love to a woman or a man, when orgasm happens, both hemispheres come very close. That's why the orgasm happens. It has nothing to do with the woman or the man; it has nothing to do with anything outside. It is just inside you. Watch....

Tantrikas have been watching the phenomenon of lovemaking closely, because they think, and they are right, that the greatest phenomenon on earth is love, and the greatest experience of humanity is orgasm. So if there is

> ❝ When you feel orgasmic and happy, it has nothing to do with the other person—the whole thing is happening within you. ❞

some truth, we must be closer to realizing that truth in the moment of orgasm than anywhere else. This is simple logic. One need not even be logical about it; it is such an obvious thing—this is our greatest joy, so this joy must somehow be a door to the infinite. It may be slight, it may be just a part of it, but something of the infinite enters in those moments of joy. For a moment the man and woman are lost, they are no longer in their egos; their separateness disappears.

What happens exactly? You can ask physiologists, too. Tantra has discovered many things. One, when you are making love to a woman or a man and you feel orgasmic and happy, it has nothing to do with the other person—the whole thing is happening within you. It has nothing to do with the other person's orgasm; they are not related to it at all.

When the woman is having an orgasm, she is having her orgasm—it has nothing to do with the man. Maybe the man functioned as a trigger point, but the woman's orgasm is her private orgasm, and the man's orgasm is his private orgasm. You are together with the other, but your orgasm is yours; and when you are having an orgasm your partner cannot share your joy, no. It is absolutely yours. It is private. Although the other can see that something is happening —on your face, in your body—that is just an observation from the outside. They cannot participate in it.

Even if you both have orgasms together, your orgasmic joy will not be more or less; it will not be affected by the orgasm of the other, and neither will the other's orgasm be

affected by you. You are completely private, totally in yourself—that's the first thing. This means that all orgasm, deep down, is masturbatory. The woman is a help, an excuse; the man is a help, an excuse—but not a must.

The second thing that tantrikas have observed is that when the orgasm is happening, it has nothing to with your sex centers—nothing. Because if the connection from the sex center to the brain is blocked, you will have an orgasm but you will not have any joy. So, deep down, the joy of orgasm is not happening at the sex center; it is happening in the brain. Something from the sex center triggers something in the brain— it is happening in the brain. Modern research perfectly agrees with this finding of the tantrikas.

You must have heard the name of the famous psychologist, Delgado. He put electrodes in the brain and those electrodes were operated by remote control. It's possible that you could have a small remote control box, keep the box in your pocket, and any time you want to have an orgasm, you could just push a button! It would have nothing to do with your sex center; that button would just trigger something in your head—inside the head it would stimulate those centers that are stimulated by sexual energy when it is released. It would stimulate them directly and you could have a great orgasm. Or, you could push another button and you would become immediately angry. Or you could push another button and you would fall into a deep depression. You could have all the buttons in the remote control box, and you could change your mood as you like.

When Delgado experimented with his animals for the first time, he was surprised. He fixed an electrode in his favorite mouse, which was well trained and intelligent. After Delgado fixed the electrode in the mouse's head, he gave a box to the mouse and trained him to push the button. Once the mouse knew that when the button was pushed he would have a sexual orgasm, he went mad. In one day, he pressed the button hundreds and hundreds of times. He died because he would not do anything else. He would not eat or sleep, he forgot everything else. He just went crazy pushing the button again and again.

This modern research into the human brain says exactly what Tantra has been saying. First, the orgasm has nothing to do with the person outside—your woman or your man.

Second, it has nothing to do with your sex energy. The other person triggers your sex energy, your sex energy triggers your brain energy, a brain center is triggered—but orgasm happens exactly there in the brain, in the head.

That's why pornography has so much appeal, because pornography can directly stimulate your brain. Whether a woman is beautiful or ugly has nothing to do with your orgasm. An ugly woman can give you as beautiful an orgasm as a beautiful woman, but why don't you like the ugly woman? She does not appeal to your brain, that's all. Otherwise, as far as orgasm is concerned, both are equally capable. The ugliest woman or the most beautiful woman is immaterial—your head, your brain, is more interested in the form, in the beauty.

Tantra says once we understand this whole mechanism of orgasm, a greater understanding can arise.

One step more:

Modern research agrees up to this point—that orgasm happens in the brain. The woman's orgasm happens in the right side of the brain—about that, modern research is not yet capable of saying anything, but Tantra is. Tantra says the woman's orgasm happens in the right-side brain, because that is the feminine center. And the male orgasm happens in the left—that is the male side of the brain. Tantra goes further into this work and says that when these two sides of the brain come together great joy arises, total orgasm happens.

These two sides of the brain can come together easily—the less analytical you are, the closer they are. That's why an interpretative mind is never a happy mind. A non-interpretative mind is happier. Primitive people are more joyous than so-called civilized, educated, cultured people. Animals are happier than human beings; they don't have the analytical mind. The analytical mind makes the gap between the two sides of the brain bigger.

The more you think logically, the bigger is the gap between the two hemispheres of the brain. The less you think logically, the closer they come. The more poetic, the more esthetic your approach is, the more they will come close and the more possibility of joy, delight, and celebration there will be.

Finally, the last point, which I think will take many centuries for science to reach. The last point is that the joy is not happening exactly in the brain either—it happens in the witness who is standing behind both sides of the brain. If the witness is too attached to the male mind, then the joy will not be so great. Or, if the witness is attached too much to the female mind, then joy will be a little more, but still not so great.

Can't you see? Women are happier creatures than men. That's why they look more beautiful, more innocent, younger. They live longer and they live more peacefully, more contentedly. They are not worried as much; they don't commit suicide as often, they don't go mad as often. Men go mad twice as often as women. In suicide also, men outdo the women. And all the wars—if you include them as suicidal and murderous activities, then men have been doing nothing else! Down the centuries men have been preoccupied with preparing for war and killing people.

The feminine mind is more joyous because it is more poetic, more esthetic, more intuitive. But if you are not attached to any part and instead are just a witness, then your joy is utter, ultimate. This joy we have called in the East anand—bliss. To know this witness is to become one, absolutely one; then the woman and the man in you disappear completely, then they are lost into oneness.

Then to be orgasmic is your moment-to-moment existence. In that state, sex disappears automatically—because there is no need. When a person lives orgasmically twenty-four hours a day, what is the need for sex?

In your witnessing you become orgasmic. Orgasm then is not a momentary thing—then it is simply your nature. This is what ecstasy is.

the tantra vision

in practice

The Tantra vision is one of the greatest visions ever dreamt by humanity: a religion without a priest, a religion without a temple, a religion without an organization, a religion that does not destroy the individual but respects individuality tremendously, a religion that trusts in the ordinary man and woman. This trust goes very deep.

tantra trust

Tantra trusts in your body. No other religion trusts in your body. And when religions don't trust in your body, they create a split between you and your body. They make you an enemy of your body and they start destroying the wisdom of the body.

Tantra trusts in your body. Tantra trusts in your senses. Tantra trusts in your energy. Tantra trusts in you—*in toto*. Tantra does not deny anything, but transforms everything.

How to attain this Tantra vision?

This is the map to turn you on, and to turn you in, and to turn you beyond.

The first thing is the body. The body is your base, it is your ground, it is where you are grounded. To make you antagonistic toward the body is to destroy you, is to make you schizophrenic, is to make you miserable, is to create hell. You are the body. Of course, you are more than the body, but that "more" will follow later on. First you are the body. The body is your basic truth, so never be against your body. Whenever you are against the body, you are going against God. Whenever you are disrespectful to your body, you are losing contact with reality, because your body is your contact. Your body is your bridge. Your body is your temple. Tantra teaches reverence for the body, love, respect for the body, gratitude for the body. The body is marvelous. It is the greatest of mysteries.

But you have been taught to be against the body. So sometimes you are overwhelmed by the green tree, sometimes mystified by the moon and the sun, sometimes mystified by a flower. But you are never mystified by your own body. Your body is the most complex phenomenon in existence. No flower, no tree has such a beautiful body as you have. No moon, no sun, no star has such an evolved mechanism as you have.

But you have been taught to appreciate the flower, which is a simple thing. You have been taught to appreciate a tree, which is a simple thing. You have even been taught to appreciate stones, rocks, mountains, and rivers, but you have never been taught to respect your own body, to be mystified by it. Yes, it is very close, so it is easy to forget about it. It is obvious, so it is easy to neglect it. But it is the most beautiful phenomenon.

If you look at a flower, people will say "How esthetic!" And if you look at a woman's beautiful face or a man's beautiful face, people will say, "This is lust." If you go to a tree, and stand there, or look in a dazed state at the flower—your eyes wide open, your senses

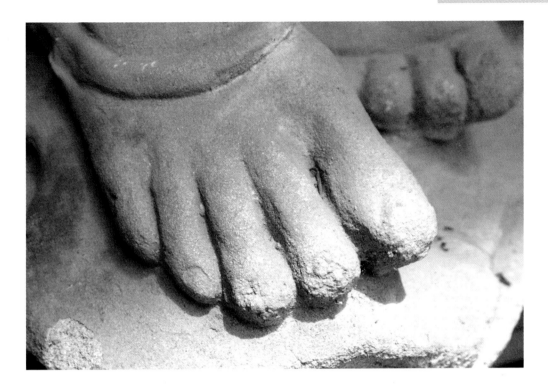

wide open to allow the beauty of the flower to enter you—people will think you are a poet or a painter or a mystic. But if you gaze on a woman or a man, just standing there with great reverence and respect, looking at the person with your eyes wide open and your senses drinking in the beauty, the police will catch hold of you! Nobody will say that you are a mystic or a poet, nobody will appreciate what you are doing. Something has gone wrong.

If you approach a stranger on the street and say, "What beautiful eyes you have!" you will feel embarrassed, he will feel embarrassed. He will not be able to say thank you to you. In fact, he will feel offended. He will feel offended, because who are you to interfere in his private life? Who are you to dare?

If you touch a tree, the tree feels happy. But if you touch a man, he will feel offended. What has gone wrong? Something has been damaged tremendously and deeply.

Tantra teaches you to reclaim respect for the body, love for the body. Tantra teaches you to look at the body as the greatest creation of existence. Tantra is the religion of the body. Of course it goes higher, but it never leaves the body; it is grounded there. It is the only religion that is really grounded in the earth: it has roots. Other religions are uprooted trees—dead, dull, dying; the juice does not flow in them.

Tantra is really juicy, very alive.

The first thing is to learn respect for the body, to unlearn all the nonsense that has been taught to you about the body. Otherwise, you

> " *The body has to become weightless, so that you almost start walking above the earth—that is the Tantra way to walk.* "

will never turn on, and you will never turn in, and you will never turn beyond. Start from the beginning. The body is your beginning.

The body has to be purified of many repressions. A great catharsis is needed for the body, a great purification. The body has become poisoned because you have been against it; you have repressed it in many ways. Your body is existing at the minimum, that's why you are miserable.

Tantra says: Bliss is possible only when you exist at the optimum—never before it. Bliss is possible only when you live intensely. How can you live intensely if you are against the body?

You are always lukewarm. The fire has cooled down. Down the centuries, the fire has been destroyed. The fire has to be rekindled. Tantra says: First purify the body—purify it of all repressions. Allow the body energy to flow, remove the blocks.

It is unusual to come across a person who has no blocks; it is unusual to come across a person whose body is not tight. Loosen this tightness—this tension is blocking your

energy; the flow cannot be possible with this tension. Why is everybody so uptight? Why can't they relax? Have you seen a cat sleeping, dozing in the afternoon? How simply and how beautifully the cat relaxes. Can't you relax the same way? You toss and turn, even in your bed you can't relax. The beauty of the cat's relaxation is that it relaxes utterly and yet is perfectly alert. A slight movement in the room and it will open its eyes, it will be ready to jump. It is not that it is just asleep—the cat's sleep is something to be learned—but people have forgotten how.

Tantra says: Learn from the cats—how they sleep, how they relax, how they live in a non-tense way. The whole animal world lives in that non-tense way. People have to learn this, because we have been conditioned wrongly. People have been programmed wrongly.

From childhood you have been programmed to be tight. You don't breathe... out of fear. Out of fear of sexuality, people don't breathe, because when you breathe deeply, your breath goes exactly to the sex center and hits it, massages it from the inside, excites it. Because you have been taught that sex is dangerous, each child starts breathing in a shallow way—hung up in the chest. They never go beyond that because if they go beyond it, suddenly, there is excitement: sexuality is aroused and fear arises. The moment you breathe deeply, sex energy is released.

Sex energy has to be released. It has to flow all over your being. Then your body will become orgasmic. But people are afraid to

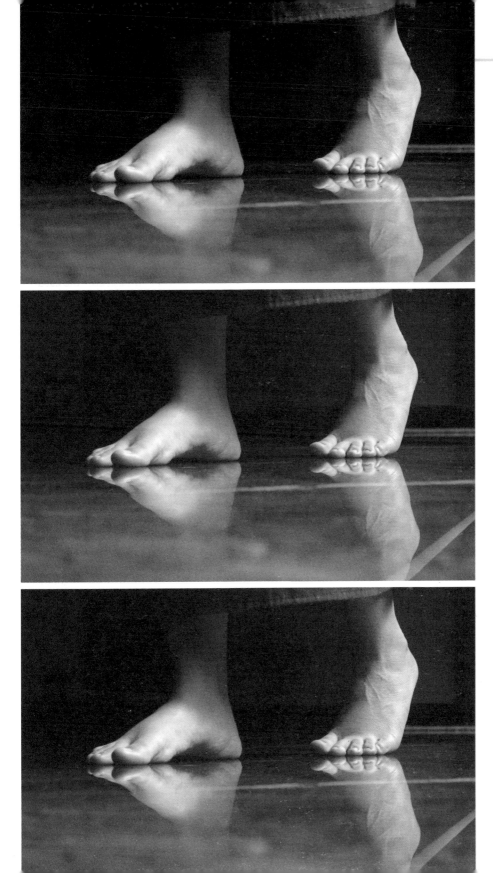

breathe, so afraid that almost half the lungs are full of carbon dioxide. That's why people are dull, that's why they don't look alert, that's why awareness is difficult.

It is not accidental that yoga and Tantra both teach deep breathing to unload the carbon dioxide from the lungs. The carbon dioxide is not for you—it has to be thrown out continuously, you have to breathe in new, fresh air, you have to breathe more oxygen. Oxygen will create your inner fire, oxygen will set you aflame. But oxygen will also inflame your sexuality. So only Tantra can allow truly deep breathing—even yoga cannot allow such deep breathing. Yoga also allows you to breathe in down to the navel—but not beyond that, not to cross the hara center, not to cross svadhisthan, because once you cross svadhisthan you jump into the muladhar.

Only Tantra allows you total being and total flow. Tantra gives you unconditional freedom, whatsoever you are and whatsoever you can be. Tantra puts no boundaries on you; it does not define you, it simply gives you total freedom. The understanding is that when you are totally free, then much is possible.

This has been my observation: people who are sexually repressed become unintelligent. Only very sexually alive people are intelligent people. Now, the idea that sex is sin must have damaged intelligence—must have damaged it badly. When you are really flowing and your sexuality has neither fight nor conflict with you, when you cooperate with it, your mind will function at its optimum. You will be intelligent, alert, alive.

The body has to be befriended, says Tantra.

Do you touch your own body sometimes? Do you ever feel your own body, or do you remain as if you were encased in a dead thing? That's what is happening. People are almost frozen; they are carrying the body like a casket. It is heavy, it obstructs, it does not help you to communicate with reality. If you allow the electricity of the body flow to move from the toe to the head, if you allow total freedom for its energy—the bioenergy—you will become a river and you will not feel the body at all. You will feel almost bodiless. Not fighting with the body, you become bodiless. Fighting with the body, the body becomes a burden. And carrying your body as a burden you can never fly into the sky.

The body has to become weightless, so that you almost start walking above the earth—that is the Tantra way to walk. You are so weightless that there is no gravitation—you can simply fly. But that comes out of great acceptance. It is going to be difficult to accept your body. You condemn it, you always find fault with it. You never appreciate it, you never love it, and then you want a miracle: that somebody will come along and love your body. If you yourself cannot love it, then how are you going to find somebody else to love your body? If you yourself cannot love it, nobody else is going to love your body, because your vibe will repel people.

You fall in love with a person who loves himself, never otherwise. The first love has to be toward oneself—only from that center can other kinds of love arise. You don't love your body. You hide it in a thousand and one ways. You hide your body's smell, you hide your body's shape in clothes, you hide yourself in ornamentation. You try to create some beauty that you continuously feel you are missing, and in that very effort you become artificial.

Do you ever come across a bird that is ugly? Do you ever come across a deer that is ugly? It never happens. They don't go to any beauty parlors, and they don't consult any experts. They simply accept themselves and they are beautiful in their acceptance. In that very acceptance they shower beauty upon themselves.

The moment you accept yourself you become beautiful. When you are delighted with your own body, you will delight others also. Many people will fall in love with you, because you yourself are in love with yourself. When you are angry with yourself, you know that you are ugly, you know that you are repulsive, horrible. This idea will repel people; this idea will not help them to fall in love with you, it will keep them away. Even if they were coming closer to you, the moment they feel your vibration, they will move away.

> *The beauty of tears, the beauty of laughter; the poetry of tears, and the poetry of laughter are available to humans only.*

There is no need to chase anybody. The chasing game arises only because we have not been in love with ourselves. Otherwise, people come to you. It becomes almost impossible for them not to fall in love with you if you are in love with yourself.

Why did so many people come to Buddha and why did so many people come to Saraha and why did so many people come to Jesus? These people were in love with themselves. They were in such great love and they were so delighted with their being that it was natural for whosoever would pass to be pulled by them; like magnets they pulled people. They were so enchanted with their own being, how could you avoid that enchantment? Just being there was a great bliss.

Tantra teaches the first thing: Be loving toward your body, befriend your body, revere your body, respect your body, take care of your body—it is nature's gift. Treat it well and it will reveal great mysteries to you. All growth depends on how you are related to your body.

The second thing Tantra speaks about is the senses. The senses are your doors of perception, the senses are your windows into reality. What is your eyesight? What are your ears? What is your nose? Windows into reality, windows into existence. If you see rightly, you will see God everywhere. The eyes are not to be closed, the eyes have to be opened rightly. The eyes are not to be destroyed. The ears are not to be destroyed because all these sounds are divine.

The birds are chanting mantras and the trees are giving sermons in silence. All sounds are divine, and all forms are divine. If you don't have sensitivity in you, how will you know the divine? You go to a church or to a temple to find God... yet godliness is all over the place! In a man-made temple, in a man-made church, you go to find God? Why? God is everywhere, alive and kicking everywhere. But for that you need clean senses, purified senses.

Tantra teaches that the senses are the doors of perception. The doors have been dulled. You have to drop that dullness and your senses have to be cleansed. Your senses are like a mirror that has become dull because so much dust has gathered upon it. The dust has to be cleaned away.

Look at the Tantra approach to everything. Taste God in every taste. Flow totally into your touch, because whatsoever you touch is divine. It is a total reversal of the ascetic, so-called religions. It is a radical revolution—from the very roots.

Touch, smell, taste, see, and hear as totally as possible. You will have to learn the language because society has deceived you; it has made you forget.

Every child is born with beautiful senses. Watch a child. When he looks at something, he is completely absorbed. When he is playing with his toys, he is utterly absorbed. When he looks, he becomes just the eyes. Look at the eyes of a child. When he hears, he becomes just the ears. When he eats something, he is just there on the tongue. He becomes just the taste. See a child eating an apple. With what gusto! With what great energy! With what delight! See a child running after a butterfly in the garden... so absorbed that even if God were available, he would not run that way. Such a tremendous, meditative state—and without any effort. See a child collecting seashells on the beach as if he were collecting diamonds. Everything is precious when the senses are alive. Everything is clear when the senses are alive.

Later on in life, the same child will look at reality as if hidden behind a darkened glass. Much smoke and dust have gathered on the glass, and you are hidden behind it and you are looking. Because of this, everything looks dull and dead. You look at the tree and the tree looks dull because your eyes are dull. You hear a song, but there is no appeal in it because your ears are dull. You can hear a Saraha and you will not be able to appreciate him, because your intelligence is dull.

Reclaim your forgotten language. Whenever you have time, be more in your senses. Eating—don't just eat, try to learn the forgotten language of taste again. Touch the bread, feel the texture of it. Feel with open eyes, feel with closed eyes. While chewing, chew it—you are chewing God. Remember it! It will be disrespectful not to chew well, not to taste well. Let it be a prayer, and you will start the rising of a new consciousness in you. You will learn the way of Tantra alchemy.

Touch people more. We have become very touchy about touch. If somebody is talking to you and comes too close, you start moving

Go to the river and let the river flow through your hands. Feel it! Swim and feel the water again as the fish feels it. Don't miss an opportunity to revive your senses.

on you. Lie down on the ground, naked, feel the earth. Lie down on the beach, feel the sand. Listen to the sounds of the sand, listen to the sounds of the sea. Use every opportunity—only then will you be able to learn the language of the senses again. Tantra can be understood only when your body is alive and your senses feel.

Free your senses from habits. Habits are one of the root causes of dullness. Find out new ways of doing things. Invent new ways of loving.

I have heard:

The doctor told the working chap that he could not complete his examination without a sample of urine. The small boy who was sent with the specimen spilled most of it while messing around. Fearing a good beating, he topped it off with a bit more urine from a cow in the field.

The doctor hastily sent for the man, who returned home to his wife in a furious temper and said, "That's you and your fancy positions! You would be on top, wouldn't you? And now I am going to have a baby!"

People have fixed habits. Even while making love they often make it in the same position, "the missionary posture."

Find new ways of feeling. Each experience has to be created with great sensitivity. When you make love, make it a great celebration. Each time, bring some new creativity into it. Sometimes dance before you make love. Sometimes pray before you make love. Sometimes go running into the forest, and then make love. Sometimes go swimming and then make love. Then each love experience will

backward. We protect our territory. We don't touch and we don't allow others to touch; we don't hold hands, we don't hug. We don't enjoy each other's being.

Go to the tree and touch the tree. Touch the rock. Go to the river and let the river flow through your hands. Feel it! Swim, and feel the water again as the fish feels it. Don't miss any opportunity to revive your senses. There are a thousand and one opportunities the whole day. There is no need to make separate time for it. The whole day is a training in sensitivity. Use all the opportunities.

Standing under your shower, use the opportunity—feel the touch of the water falling create more and more sensitivity in you and it will never become dull and boring.

Find out new ways to explore the other. Don't get fixed in routines. All routines are anti-life: routines are in the service of death. You can always invent—there is no limit to inventions. Sometimes a small change will tremendously benefit you. If you always eat at the table, sometimes go out to the lawn—sit on the lawn and eat there. You will be surprised: it is a totally different experience. The smell of the freshly-cut grass, the birds hopping around and singing, the fresh air, the sunrays, and the feel of the grass underneath. It cannot be the same experience as when you sit on a chair and eat at your table; it is a totally different experience—all the ingredients are different.

Some time try just eating naked and you will be surprised. Just a small change—nothing much, you are sitting naked—but you will have a totally different experience because something new has been added to it. If you eat with a spoon and fork, eat sometimes with bare hands and you will have a different experience; your touch will bring new warmth to the food. A spoon is a dead thing: when you eat with a spoon or a fork, you are far away. It is that same fear of touching anything—even food cannot be touched. You will miss the texture, the touch, the feel of it. The food has as much feel as it has taste.

Many experiments have been done in the West on the fact that when we are enjoying anything, there are many things we are not aware of that contribute to the experience. For example, close your eyes and hold your nose and then eat an onion. Tell somebody to give it to you when you don't know what he is giving—whether he is giving you an onion or an apple. It will be difficult for you to make out the difference if your nose is completely closed and your eyes are closed. It will be impossible for you to decide whether it is an onion or an apple, because the taste is not only taste; fifty percent of it comes from the nose, and much comes from the eyes. It is not just taste; all the senses contribute. When you eat with your hands, your touch is contributing. It will be more tasty. It will be more human, more natural.

Find new ways in everything. Let that be one of your disciplines.Tantra says: If you can continue finding new ways every day, your life will remain a thrill, an adventure. You will never be bored. You will always be curious to know, you will always be on the verge of seeking the unknown and the unfamiliar. Your eyes will remain clear and your senses will remain clear, because when you are always on the verge of seeking, exploring, finding, searching, you cannot become dull, you cannot become stupid.

Psychologists say that by the age of seven, stupidity starts. It initially starts about the age of four, but by the seventh year it is very apparent. Children start becoming dull by the age of seven.

In fact, the child learns fifty percent of all the learnings of his whole life by the time he is seven. If he lives to seventy, in the remaining sixty-three years, he will learn only fifty percent—fifty percent he has already

> *Look at the Tantra approach to everything. Flow totally into your touch, because whatsoever you touch is divine... Touch, smell, taste, see, and hear as totally as possible.*

learned. What happens? He becomes dull; he stops learning. If you think in terms of intelligence, by the age of seven a child starts becoming old. Physically he will become old later on—from the age of thirty-five he will start declining—but mentally he is already on the decline.

You will be surprised that the average mental age is twelve. People don't often grow beyond that; they are stuck there. That's why you see so much childishness in the world. Insult a person who is sixty years of age, and within seconds he is just a twelve-year-old child. He will behave in such a way that you will not believe that a grownup could be so childish.

People are always ready to fall back. Their mental age is just skin-deep, hidden behind. Just scratch a little, and their mental age comes out. Their physical age is not of much importance.

Most people die childish; they never grow.

Tantra says: Learn new ways of doing things and free yourself of habits as much as possible. Tantra says: Don't be imitative; otherwise, your senses will become dull.
Find out ways of doing things in your own way. Have your signature on everything that you do.

Just the other night a woman was telling me that the love between her and her husband has disappeared. Now they are staying together just for the children. I told her to meditate, to be friendly to the husband. If love has disappeared, all has not disappeared; friendship is still possible. Be friendly. And she said, "It is difficult. When a cup is broken, it is broken."

I told her that it seemed she had not heard that Zen people in Japan will first purchase a cup from the supermarket, bring it home, break it, then glue it together again to make it individual and special. Otherwise, it is just a marketplace thing. And if a friend comes to visit and you give him tea in an ordinary cup and saucer, that is not good; that is ugly, that is not respectful. So they will bring a fresh new cup and break it. Of course, then there is no other cup in the world exactly like it—there cannot be. Glued together, now it has some individuality, a signature. And when Zen people go to each other's house or each other's monastery, they will not just sip the tea. First they will appreciate the cup, they will look at it. The way it has been joined together is a work of art—the way the pieces have been broken and put together again. The woman understood and she started laughing. She said, "Then it is possible."

The Pillars
of
Consciousness

B U D D H A
Z E N
T A O
T A N T R A

Design © Alexian Ltd

This 2013 edition published by Shelter Harbor Press by arrangement with
Alexian Limited

The text material in this book is selected from various discourses by Osho given to a live audience
over a period of more than thirty years. All of Osho discourses have been published in full as
books, and are also available as original audio recordings. Audio recordings and the complete
text archive can be found via the online OSHO Library at www.osho.com

OSHO is a registered trademark of Osho International Foundation, used with permission/licence.

Picture acknowledgments
The publishers would like to thank the following for permission to reproduce their images:
Corbis p.25 (Leonard de Selva), p.233TL (Michael S. Yamashita), p.302 (Joe Cornish), p.487
(Jose Luis Pelaez, Inc.), p.489 (Larry Williams); Ma Deva Padma (www.embraceart.com) for the
illustration on p.173; Tenri University, Fuzoku Tenri Library, Japan, for the illustrations on pp.198-201.

Special thanks to Siddhena Ian Murray-Clark for the images on pages 291, 295, 301, 314, 325, 349,
367, 382, 383, 384, 401, 417, and for the drawings of Taoist masters on pages 307, 309, 311, 323, 333,
335, 341, 345, 357, 363, 365, 399, 419.

Special thanks also to Atmo Sharna for the images on pages 450, 511, 513, 515, 516, 517.

The publishers would like to thank Osho International Foundation for permission to reproduce all
the other images.

Cataloging-in-Publication Data has been applied for and may be obtained from the Library of
Congress.

Shelter Harbor Press
603 W. 115th Street
Suite 163
New York, NY 10025

ISBN: 978-1-62795-009-1

Printed and bound in India

10 9 8 7 6 5 4 3 2 1